# My Dark

James Ellroy was born in Los Angeles in 1948. He is the author of the acclaimed 'LA Quartet': *The Black Dahlia*, *The Big Nowhere*, *LA Confidential* and *White Jazz*. His most recent novel, *Blood's a Rover*, completes the magisterial 'Underworld USA Trilogy' – the first two volumes of which (*American Tabloid* and *The Cold Six Thousand*) were both *Sunday Times* bestsellers.

# ALSO BY JAMES ELLROY

THE UNDERWORLD U.S.A. TRILOGY
*American Tabloid*
*The Cold Six Thousand*
*Blood's a Rover*

THE L.A. QUARTET
*The Black Dahlia*
*The Big Nowhere*
*L.A. Confidential*
*White Jazz*

MEMOIR
*My Dark Places*
*The Hilliker Curse*

SHORT STORIES
*Hollywood Nocturnes*

JOURNALISM/SHORT FICTION
*Crime Wave*
*Destination: Morgue!*

EARLY NOVELS
*Brown's Requiem*
*Clandestine*
*Blood on the Moon*
*Because the Night*
*Suicide Hill*
*Killer on the Road*

Praise for James Ellroy

'A master of private languages, he isn't in any way a conventional historical novelist . . . he gives you the sense of being plugged directly into an entire culture's unsavoury dream life'

*Guardian*

'His style is unique and compelling, and his theories of what lies behind the great unresolved events of America's noir history are utterly believable . . . He is certainly one of the most original and daring writers alive. He's a sort of godfather – in the mafia sense – of American letters. He sits there perched on a rooftop like a dark, brooding and knowing angel.'

*Independent on Sunday*

'The man who calls himself "the demon dog" of American crime fiction is still the classiest act around'

*Daily Mail*

'James Ellroy is the best crime writer in the world.'

Stuart Neville, *Irish Times*

'Without him and his crime fiction, there's no David Peace or *The Sopranos* or Ian Rankin or *The Wire* or the work of countless writers and film makers who saw a different way of doing things when they first cracked the spine on an Ellroy.'

*GQ*

# My Dark Places

## An L.A. Crime Memoir

JAMES ELLROY

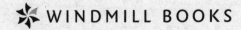

**✳ WINDMILL BOOKS**

Published by Windmill Books 2010

2 4 6 8 10 9 7 5 3 1

First published in Great Britain in 1996 by Century
First published in paperback in 1997 by Arrow Books

Windmill Books
The Random House Group Limited
20 Vauxhall Bridge Road, London SW1V 2SA

Addresses for companies within The Random House Group Limited can be found at:
www.randomhouse.co.uk/offices.htm

The Random House Group Limited Reg. No. 954009

www.rbooks.co.uk

A CIP catalogue record for this book
is available from the British Library

ISBN 9780099537847

The Random House Group Limited supports The Forest Stewardship
Council (FSC), the leading international forest certification organisation. All our titles
that are printed on Greenpeace approved FSC certified paper carry the FSC logo.
Our paper procurement policy can be found at:
www.rbooks.co.uk/environment

**Mixed Sources**
Product group from well-managed
forests and other controlled sources
www.fsc.org   Cert no. TT-COC-2139
© 1996 Forest Stewardship Council

Typeset by SX Composing DTP, Rayleigh, Essex
Printed and bound in Great Britain by
CPI Cox & Wyman, Reading, RG1 8EX

TO
Helen Knode

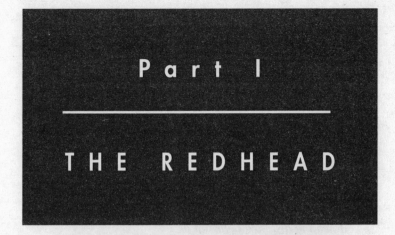

# Part I

# THE REDHEAD

*A cheap Saturday night took you down. You died stupidly and harshly and without the means to hold your own life dear.*

*Your run to safety was a brief reprieve. You brought me into hiding as your good-luck charm. I failed you as a talisman—so I stand now as your witness.*

*Your death defines my life. I want to find the love we never had and explicate it in your name.*

*I want to take your secrets public. I want to burn down the distance between us.*

*I want to give you breath.*

Some kids found her.

They were Babe Ruth League players, out to hit a few shag balls. Three adult coaches were walking behind them.

The boys saw a shape in the ivy strip just off the curb. The men saw loose pearls on the pavement. A little telepathic jolt went around.

Clyde Warner and Dick Ginnold shooed the kids back a ways—to keep them from looking too close. Kendall Nungesser ran across Tyler and spotted a pay phone by the dairy stand.

He called the Temple City Sheriff's Office and told the desk sergeant he'd discovered a body. It was right there on that road beside the playing field at Arroyo High School. The sergeant said stay there and don't touch anything.

The radio call went out: 10:10 a.m., Sunday, 6/22/58. Dead body at King's Row and Tyler Avenue, El Monte.

A Sheriff's prowl car made it in under five minutes. An El Monte PD unit arrived a few seconds later.

Deputy Vic Cavallero huddled up the coaches and the kids. Officer Dave Wire checked out the body.

It was a female Caucasian. She was fair-skinned and redheaded. She was approximately 40 years of age. She was lying flat on her back—in an ivy patch a few inches from the King's Row curb line.

Her right arm was bent upward. Her right hand was resting a few inches above her head. Her left arm was bent at the elbow and draped across her midriff. Her left hand was clenched. Her legs were outstretched.

She was wearing a scoop-front, sleeveless, light and dark blue dress. A dark blue overcoat with a matching lining was spread over her lower body.

Her feet and ankles were visible. Her right foot was bare. A nylon stocking was bunched up around her left ankle.

Her dress was disheveled. Insect bites covered her arms. Her face was bruised and her tongue was protruding. Her brassiere was unfastened and hiked above her breasts. A nylon stocking and a cotton cord were lashed around her neck. Both ligatures were tightly knotted.

Dave Wire radioed the El Monte PD dispatcher. Vic Cavallero called the Temple office. The body-dump alert went out:

Get the L.A. County Coroner. Get the Sheriff's Crime Lab and the photo car. Call the Sheriff's Homicide Bureau and tell them to send a team out.

Cavallero stood by the body. Dave Wire ran over to the dairy and commandeered a length of rope. Cavallero helped him string up a crime scene perimeter.

They discussed the odd position of the body. It looked haphazard *and* fastidious.

Spectators drifted by. Cavallero pushed them back to the Tyler Avenue sidewalk. Wire noticed some pearls on the road and circled each and every one in chalk.

Official cars pulled up to the cordon. Uniformed cops and plain-clothesmen ducked under the rope.

From El Monte PD: Chief Orval Davis, Captain Jim Bruton, Sergeant Virg Ervin. Captain Dick Brooks, Lieutenant Don Mead and Sergeant Don Clapp from Temple Sheriff's. Temple deputies called out to contain the civilians and plain curious on- and off-duty cops.

Dave Wire measured the exact position of the body: 63 feet west of the first locked gate on the school grounds/2 feet south of the King's Row curb. The photo deputy arrived and snapped perspective shots of King's Row and the Arroyo High playing field.

It was noon—and closing in on 90 degrees.

The photo deputy shot the body from straight-down and sideways angles. Vic Cavallero assured him that the guys who found it did not touch it. Sergeants Ward Hallinen and Jack Lawton arrived and went straight to Chief Davis.

Davis told them to take charge—per the contract mandating all El Monte city murders to the L.A. Sheriff's Homicide Bureau.

Hallinen walked over to the body. Lawton diagrammed the area in his notebook.

Tyler Avenue ran north–south. King's Row intersected it at the southern edge of the school property. King's Row ran east about 175 yards. It terminated at Cedar Avenue—the eastern edge of the school property. It was nothing more than a paved access road.

A gate closed off the Cedar Avenue end. An inner gate sealed some bungalows near the main Arroyo High buildings. The only way to enter King's Row was via Tyler Avenue.

King's Row was 15 feet wide. The sports field ran along the northern edge. A shrub-covered chain-link fence ran behind the southern curb line and a 3-foot-wide ivy thicket. The body was positioned 75 yards east of the Tyler–King's Row intersection.

The victim's left foot was two inches from the curb. Her weight had pressed down the ivy all around her.

Lawton and Hallinen stared at the body. Rigor mortis was setting in—the victim's clenched hand had gone rigid.

Hallinen noted a fake-pearl ring on the third finger. Lawton said it might help them ID her.

Her face had gone slightly purple. She looked like a classic late-night body dump.

Vic Cavallero told the coaches and baseball kids to go home. Dave Wire and Virg Ervin mingled with the civilians. Sergeant Harry Andre showed up—an off-duty Sheriff's Homicide man hot to lend a hand.

The press showed up. Some Temple deputies cruised by to check out the scene. Half the 26-man El Monte PD cruised by— dead white women were some kind of draw.

The coroner's deputy showed up. The photo deputy told him he could examine the victim.

Hallinen and Lawton pushed forward to watch. The coroner's deputy lifted the coat off the victim's lower body.

She was not wearing a slip, a girdle or panties. Her dress was pushed up above her hips. No panties and no shoes. That one stocking down around her left ankle. Bruises and small lacerations on the insides of her thighs. An asphalt drag mark on her left hip.

The coroner's deputy turned the body over. The photo deputy snapped some shots of the victim's posterior. The victim's back was dew-wet and showed signs of postmortem lividity.

The coroner's deputy said she was probably dead eight to twelve hours. She was dumped before sunrise—the dew on her back was a plain indicator.

The photo deputy took some more pictures. The coroner's deputy and his assistant picked up the body. It was limp—still shy of full rigor mortis. They carried the victim to their van and placed her on a gurney.

Hallinen and Lawton searched the ivy thicket and the adjoining curbside.

They found a broken car antenna on the road. They found a broken string of pearls in the flattened ivy near the dump position. They picked up the pearls circled in chalk and strung them on the necklace. They saw that they had a complete set.

The clasp was intact. The string was broken in the middle. They evidence-bagged both pieces of the necklace.

They did not find the victim's panties, shoes or purse. They did not spot tire marks in the gravel near the curb. There were no drag marks on any surface along King's Row. The ivy surrounding the dump position did not look trampled.

It was 1:20 p.m. The temperature was up in the mid-90s.

The coroner's deputy cut off samples of the victim's head and pubic hair. He trimmed the victim's fingernails and placed the cuttings in a small envelope.

He had the body stripped and positioned face-up on his gurney.

There was a small amount of dried blood on the victim's right palm. There was a small laceration near the center of the victim's forehead.

The victim's right nipple was missing. The surrounding areola was creased with white scar tissue. It appeared to be an old surgical amputation.

Hallinen removed the victim's ring. The coroner's deputy measured the body at 66 inches and guessed the weight at 135 pounds. Lawton left to call the stats in to Headquarters Dispatch and the Sheriff's Missing Persons Squad.

The coroner's deputy took a scalpel and made a deep 6-inch-long incision in the victim's abdomen. He parted the flaps with his fingers, jabbed a meat thermometer into the liver and got a reading of 90 degrees. He called the time of death as 3:00 to 5:00 a.m.

Hallinen examined the ligatures. The stocking and cotton cord were separately lashed around the victim's neck. The cord resembled a clothesline or Venetian blind sash-pull.

The cord knot was tied at the back of the victim's neck. The killer tied it so tight that one of the ends broke off—fraying and the odd lengths of the knot ends proved that fact conclusively.

The stocking around the victim's neck was identical to the stocking bunched around her left ankle.

The coroner's deputy locked up his van and drove the body to the L.A. County Morgue. Jack Lawton put out a police band broadcast:

All San Gabriel Valley units be alert for suspicious males with fresh cuts and scratches.

Ward Hallinen rounded up some radio reporters. He told them to put it on the local air:

Dead white woman found. Forty/red hair/hazel eyes/ 5'6"/135. Direct potential informants to the El Monte PD and Temple City Sheriff's Office—

Chief Davis and Captain Bruton drove to El Monte PD Headquarters. Three ranking Sheriff's Homicide men joined them: Inspector R. J. Parsonson, Captain Al Etzel, Lieutenant Charles McGowan.

They settled in for a skull session. Bruton called the Baldwin Park PD, Pasadena PD, San Dimas Sheriff's Office,

Covina and West Covina PDs. He ran their victim's stats by them and got identical responses: she doesn't match any of our short-term missing females.

Uniformed deputies and El Monte cops grid-searched the Arroyo High grounds. Hallinen, Lawton and Andre canvassed the immediate neighborhood.

They talked to people out walking and people sunning in their yards. They talked to a long string of customers at the dairy stand. They described their victim and got down-the-line responses: I don't know who you're talking about.

The area was residential and semi-rural—small houses interspersed with vacant lots and blocks of undeveloped ranchland. Hallinen, Lawton and Andre wrote it off as futile canvassing turf.

They drove south to the main El Monte throughways: Ramona, Garvey, Valley Boulevard. They swept a string of cafes and a few cocktail bars. They talked up the redhead and got a run of negative responses.

The initial canvass was tapped out.

The grid search was tapped out.

No patrol units were reporting suspicious males with cuts and scratches.

A call came in to the El Monte PD. The caller said she just heard a radio bulletin. That lady they found at the school sounded just like her tenant.

The switchboard operator radioed Virg Ervin: See the woman at 700 Bryant Road.

The address was El Monte—about a mile southeast of Arroyo High School. Ervin drove there and knocked on the door.

A woman opened up. She identified herself as Anna May Krycki and stated that the dead woman sounded like her tenant, Jean Ellroy. Jean left her little house on the Krycki property last night around 8:00. She stayed out all night—and still hadn't returned.

Ervin described the victim's overcoat and dress. Anna May Krycki said they sounded just like Jean's favorite outfit. Ervin described the scarring on the victim's right nipple. Anna May Krycki said Jean showed her that scar.

Ervin went back to his car and radioed the information to the El Monte switchboard. The dispatcher sent a patrol car out to find Jack Lawton and Ward Hallinen.

The car found them inside of ten minutes. They drove straight to the Krycki house.

Hallinen pulled out the victim's ring straight off. Anna May Krycki ID'd it as Jean Ellroy's.

Lawton and Hallinen sat her down and questioned her. Anna May Krycki said she was *Mrs.* Krycki. Her husband's name was George, and she had a 12-year-old son from a previous marriage named Gaylord. Jean Ellroy was technically *Mrs.* Jean Ellroy, but she'd been divorced from her husband for several years. Jean's full first name was Geneva. Her middle name was Odelia and her maiden name was Hilliker. Jean was a registered nurse. She worked at an aircraft-parts plant in downtown L.A. She and her 10-year-old son lived in the little stone bungalow in the Kryckis' backyard. Jean drove a red-and-white '57 Buick. Her son was spending the weekend with his father in L.A. and should be home in a few hours.

Mrs. Krycki showed them a photograph of Jean Ellroy. The face matched their victim's.

Mrs. Krycki said she saw Jean leave her bungalow last night around 8:00. She was alone. She drove off in her car and did not return. Her car was not in her driveway or her garage.

Mrs. Krycki stated that the victim and her son moved into the bungalow four months ago. She stated that the boy spent weekdays with his mother and weekends with his father. Jean was originally from a little town in Wisconsin. She was a hard-working, quiet woman who kept to herself. She was 37 years old.

The boy's father picked him up in a taxicab yesterday morning. She saw Jean doing yard work yesterday afternoon. They talked briefly—but Jean did not discuss her Saturday-night plans.

Virg Ervin brought up the victim's car. Where did she get it serviced?

Mrs. Krycki told him to try the local Union 76 station. Ervin got the number from Information, called the station and talked to the proprietor. The man checked his records and came back on the line with a plate number: California/KFE 778.

Ervin called the number in to the El Monte PD switchboard. The switchboard shot it out to all Sheriff's and local PD units.

The interview continued. Hallinen and Lawton pressed one topic: the victim and her relationships with men.

Mrs. Krycki said that Jean had a limited social life. She seemed to have no boyfriends. She went out by herself sometimes—and usually came home early. She was not much of a drinker. She often said she wanted to set a good example for her son.

George Krycki walked in. Hallinen and Lawton asked him about his Saturday-night activities.

He told them Anna May went to a movie around 9:00. He stayed home and watched a fight card on TV. He saw the victim drive off between 8:00 and 8:30 p.m. and did not see or hear her return home.

Ervin asked the Kryckis to accompany him to the L.A. County Morgue. They had to log a positive ID on the body.

Hallinen called the Sheriff's Crime Lab and told them to roll a print deputy out to 700 Bryant, El Monte—the small house behind the larger house.

Virg Ervin drove the Kryckis to the L.A. Hall of Justice—a twelve-mile shot up the San Bernardino Freeway. The Coroner's Office and the morgue were in the basement below the Sheriff's Homicide Bureau.

The victim was stored on a slab in a refrigerated vault. The Kryckis viewed her separately. They both identified her as Jean Ellroy.

Ervin took a formal statement and drove the Kryckis back to El Monte.

The print deputy met Hallinen and Lawton outside the Ellroy bungalow. It was 4:30 p.m. and still hot and humid.

The bungalow was small and built of maroon-colored wood and river rock. It stood behind the Krycki house, at the far end of a shared backyard. The yard featured shade palms and tall banana plants, with a rock-and-mortar pond as a centerpiece. The two houses were situated at the southeast corner of Maple and Bryant. The Ellroy place had a Maple Avenue address.

The front door faced the pond and the Kryckis' back door. It was constructed of louvered glass affixed to wood framing. A pane near the keyhole was missing. The door could not be locked from the inside or outside.

Hallinen, Lawton and the print deputy entered the house. The interior was cramped: two tiny bedrooms off a narrow living room; a stand-up kitchen, breakfast nook and bathroom.

The place was neat and orderly. Nothing looked disturbed. The victim's bed and her son's bed had not been slept in.

They found a glass in the kitchen, partially filled with wine. They checked the drawers in the victim's bedroom and found some personal papers. They learned that the victim worked at Airtek Dynamics—2222 South Figueroa, L.A.

They learned that the victim's ex-husband was named Armand Ellroy. He lived at 4980 Beverly Boulevard, L.A. His phone number was HOllywood 3-8700.

They saw that the victim did not have a telephone herself.

The print deputy dusted the wineglass and several other print-sustaining surfaces. He came up with no viable latent fingerprints.

Hallinen walked over to the Kryckis' house and called the ex-husband's number. He let it ring a good long time and got no answer.

Virg Ervin walked in. He said, Dave Wire found the victim's car—parked behind a bar on Valley Boulevard.

The bar was called the Desert Inn. It was located at 11721 Valley—two miles from the dump site and a mile from the victim's house. It was a flat one-story building with a red clay-shingle roof and front window awnings.

The rear lot extended back to a line of cheap stucco bungalows. A grass strip covered with sycamore trees divided four parking space rows. Low chain-links closed the lot in sideways.

A red-and-white Buick was parked by the west-side fence. Dave Wire was standing beside it. Jim Bruton and Harry Andre were standing by a Sheriff's prowl unit.

Al Etzel was there. Blackie McGowan was there.

Hallinen and Lawton pulled into the lot. Virg Ervin and the print deputy pulled up in separate cars.

Dave Wire walked over and laid it all out.

He caught the license plate call and started checking side streets and parking lots. He found the victim's car at 3:35 p.m. It was unlocked and appeared to be unransacked. He checked the front and back seats and did not find car keys or the victim's purse, undergarments and shoes. He *did* find a half-dozen empty beer cans. They were wrapped in brown paper and tied up with string.

Hallinen and Lawton examined the car. It looked pristine inside and out. The print deputy photographed the interior and exterior and dusted the doors and dashboard. He came up with no viable latent fingerprints.

A Temple deputy arrived. He impounded the Buick and drove it to a nearby Ford dealership for safekeeping.

Some civilians were lounging on the grass strip. Wire pointed out Roy Dunn and Al Manganiello—two Desert Inn bartenders.

Andre and Hallinen talked to them. Dunn said he worked last night; Manganiello said he only worked days. Hallinen showed them Mrs. Krycki's snapshot of the victim. Both men said they'd never seen the woman before.

They never saw the red-and-white Buick before. Dunn was on duty last night—but he was buried behind the service bar and didn't see any customers come and go. They both figured the Buick had been parked in the lot all day—maybe even overnight.

Andre asked them who else was working last night. Dunn said, Talk to Ellis Outlaw, the manager.

Hallinen and Andre walked inside. Captain Etzel and Lieutenant McGowan tagged along.

The Desert Inn was narrow and L-shaped. Leatherette booths lined the walls. A sit-down bar faced three rows of tables and the front door; the service bar and kitchen stood directly behind it. A dance floor and raised bandstand formed the short part of the L.

Andre and Hallinen braced Ellis Outlaw and showed him their photo of the victim. Outlaw said he'd never seen her—or that '57 Buick out back. He wasn't working last night, but he knew who was.

He gave them some names:

His wife, Alberta "Bert" Outlaw. His sister, Myrtle Mawby. They were both at his place now. Try the Royal Palms Apartments—321 West Mildred Avenue, West Covina. And try Margie Trawick— Gilbert 8-1136. She waitressed at the Desert Inn on and off—and he heard she was in last night.

Hallinen wrote down the information and followed the other cops outside. The parking lot was full of El Monte PD guys keeping up with the action. A second bunch of guys were staked out at Bryant and Maple—waiting for the victim's ex-husband and kid to show up.

It was 6:30 p.m. and cooling off a little. It was a long early summer day and nowhere near dark.

A string of car radios crackled all at once.

The kid and the ex were back. Separate units were transporting them to the El Monte Station.


The victim's ex-husband was a week shy of 60 years old. He was tall and athletically built. He seemed to be in control of his emotions.

The victim's son was pudgy, and tall for 10 years old. He was nervous—but did not appear in any way distraught.

The boy arrived home in a cab, alone. He was informed of his mother's death and took the news calmly. He told a deputy that his dad was at the El Monte bus depot—waiting for a Freeway Flyer to take him back to L.A.

A patrol car was dispatched to pick up Armand Ellroy. Father and son had not been in contact since their goodbyes at the depot. They were now being held in separate rooms.

Hallinen and Lawton interviewed the ex-husband first. Ellroy stated that he had been divorced from the victim since 1954 and that he was exercising his child visitation rights this weekend. He picked the boy up in a cab at 10:00 a.m. Saturday and did not see his ex-wife. He and his son took a bus to his apartment in Los Angeles. They ate lunch and went to a movie called *The Vikings* at the Fox-Wilshire Theatre. The show ended at 4:30. They did some grocery shopping and returned home. They ate dinner, watched TV and went to bed between 10:00 and 11:00 p.m.

They slept late this morning. They took a bus downtown and ate lunch at Clifton's Cafeteria. They spent several hours window-shopping and caught a bus back to El Monte. He put his son in a cab at the depot and sat down to wait for an L.A.-bound bus. A cop approached him and told him the news.

Hallinen and Lawton asked Ellroy how he got on with his ex. He told them they met in '39 and got married in '40. They got divorced in '54—things went bad and they came to hate each other. The divorce proceedings were acrimonious and adversarial.

Hallinen and Lawton quizzed Ellroy on his ex-wife's social life. He told them Jean was a secretive woman who kept things to herself. She lied when it suited her—and she was really 43, not the 37 she claimed. She was promiscuous and an alcoholic. His son found her in bed with strange men on several occasions. Her recent move to El Monte could only be explained as a run from or run to some lowlife she was seeing. Jean was secretive about her private life because she knew he wanted to prove her an unfit mother—and thus gain full-time custody of his son.

Hallinen and Lawton asked Ellroy to name his ex-wife's specific boyfriends. He told them he only knew one name: Hank Hart, a fat blue-collar type missing one thumb.

Hallinen and Lawton thanked Ellroy for his cooperation and walked to an interview room down the hall. Some off-duty cops were keeping the victim's kid company.

The boy was bucking up nicely. He was hanging in tough all the way.

Hallinen and Lawton handled him gently. The boy confirmed his father's account of the weekend down to the smallest detail. He said he only knew the names of two men his mom went out with: Hank Hart and a teacher at his school named Peter Tubiolo.

It was 9:00 p.m. Ward Hallinen gave the boy a candy bar and walked him down the hall to see his father.

Armand Ellroy hugged his son. The kid hugged him back. They both looked relieved and strangely happy.

The boy was released to Armand Ellroy's custody. A cop drove them to the El Monte bus station. They caught a 9:30 Freeway Flyer back to L.A.

Virg Ervin drove Hallinen and Lawton to the Royal Palms Apartments. They showed their snapshot and ran their standard line of questions by Bert Outlaw and Myrtle Mawby.

Both women recognized the picture. Both women stated that the victim was not a Desert Inn regular—although she was in the place last night. She was sitting with a small-built man with straight black hair and a thin face. They were the last two patrons to leave—at closing time, 2:00 a.m.

Both women stated that they'd never seen the small-built man before.

Myrtle Mawby said they should call Margie Trawick. She was sitting by the bar earlier in the evening and might have something to add. Jack Lawton dialed the number Ellis Outlaw gave them. Margie Trawick picked up.

Lawton ran some preliminary questions by her. Margie Trawick came on strong—she *did* see an attractive redhead sitting with a group of people last night. Lawton told her to meet him at the El Monte Police Station in half an hour.

Ervin drove Lawton and Hallinen back to the station. Margie Trawick was waiting for them. She came off as high-strung and anxious to help.

Hallinen showed her the Jean Ellroy snapshot. She ID'd it flat out.

Ervin split for the Desert Inn—to show that snapshot around. Hallinen and Lawton got Margie Trawick comfortable and let her talk without interruption.

She said she wasn't employed by the Desert Inn—but she'd waitressed there sporadically for the past nine years. She recently underwent major surgery and enjoyed going to the place strictly for fun.

She arrived around 10:10 last night. She sat down at a table near the bar and had a few drinks. The redhead walked in the door about 10:45 or 11:00. She was accompanied by a heavyset dishwater blonde with a ponytail. The blonde was about 40—the same age as the redhead.

The redhead and the blonde sat down at a table. A Mexican-looking man walked over immediately and helped the redhead off with her coat. They headed to the dance floor and began dancing.

The man was 35 to 40, 5'8" to 6'. He had a slender build and dark hair slicked back from a widow's peak. He had a swarthy complexion. He was wearing a dark suit and a white shirt open at the throat.

The man seemed to *know* the two women.

Another man asked Margie to dance. He was 25-ish, light-haired, medium height and build. He was wearing sloppy clothes and tennis shoes. He was drunk.

Margie declined his invitation. The drunk got snotty and walked off. A short while later she saw him dancing with the dishwater blonde.

Other things distracted her. She ran into a friend and decided to take a drive with him. They left at 11:30. The drunk was sitting with the redhead, the blonde and the Mexican then.

She'd never seen the redhead or the blonde before. She'd never seen the Mexican. She might have seen the drunk—he looked sort of familiar.

Lawton and Hallinen thanked Margie Trawick and drove her home. She agreed to come in for a backup interview sometime in the next few days. It was pushing midnight—a good time to brace bar people.

They circled back to the Desert Inn. Jim Bruton was there—hitting patrons up with questions. Lawton and Hallinen grabbed him and ran down Margie Trawick's story.

They had more workable information now. They table-hopped and laid it out all over the room. They got a bite straight off.

Somebody thought the drunk sounded like a clown named Mike Whittaker. He did construction work and had a flop in South San Gabriel.

Bruton went out to his car and radio-patched a query to the California State Department of Motor Vehicles. He got a quick positive:

Michael John Whittaker, white male, DOB 1/1/34. 5'10", 185 pounds, brown hair, blue eyes. 2759 South Gladys Street, South San Gabriel.

The address was a run-down rooming house. The owner was a Mexican woman named Inez Rodriguez.

Hallinen, Lawton and Bruton badged her at the door. They said they were looking for Mike Whittaker—as a possible homicide suspect.

The woman said Mike didn't come home last night. He might have come and gone during the day—she didn't know. He was quite a big drinker. Most of the time he hung out at the Melody, over on Garvey Boulevard.

Their "murder suspect" line spooked Inez Rodriguez.

Hallinen, Lawton and Bruton drove to the Melody Room. A man matching Mike Whittaker's description was sitting at the bar.

They surrounded him and badged him. The man said he *was* Michael Whittaker.

Hallinen said they had some questions—pertaining to his whereabouts last night. Lawton and Bruton frisked him and manhandled him out to the car.

Whittaker played the roust submissive.

They drove him to the El Monte Station. They hustled him to an interview room and got up in his face.

Whittaker smelled. He was jittery and half-drunk.

He copped to being at the Desert Inn last night. He said he was looking for cooze. He was pretty blitzed last night, so he might not remember things too good.

Tell us what you *do* remember, Michael.

He remembered going to the bar. He remembered asking a girl to dance and getting brushed off. He remembered crashing a table party. The party consisted of a redhead, another girl and an Italian-type guy. He didn't know their names and he'd never seen them before.

Lawton told him the redhead got murdered. Whittaker seemed genuinely shocked.

He said he danced with the redhead and the other girl. He hit the redhead up for a Sunday-night date. She nixed it and said something about her kid coming back from a weekend with his father. The Italian-type guy was dancing with the redhead, too. He was a good dancer. He *might* have said his name was Tommy—but I don't remember too good.

Tell us what you *do* remember, Michael.

Michael remembered that he fell off his chair. Michael remembered that he outstayed his welcome at the table. Michael remembered the three people bugging out of the joint together to be rid of him.

He stayed at the bar and got more blitzed. He walked to Stan's Drive-In for a late-night snack. A Sheriff's prowl team rousted him a few blocks up Valley Boulevard. They popped him for plain drunk and drove him to the Temple City Station.

The drunk tank there was packed. The cops drove him to the Hall of Justice Jail and booked him in. Some beaners stole his shoes and socks while he was sleeping.

The tank deputy kicked him loose in the morning. He walked back to South San Gabriel barefoot—maybe 12 miles. The day was a scorcher. The pavement chewed up his feet and gave him big red blisters. He went by his room and grabbed some money and a pair of shoes and socks. He walked to the Melody and hunkered down to drink.

Bruton left the room and called the Temple City Sheriff's Office. A deputy confirmed Whittaker's story: the man was in custody from 12:30 a.m. on. He was alibied up for the victim's probable time of death.

Bruton walked back to the interview room and laid out the news. Whittaker was thrilled. He said, Can I go home now?

Bruton told him he'd have to submit a formal statement within 48 hours. Whittaker agreed. Jack Lawton apologized for the heavy treatment and offered him a lift to his rooming house.

Whittaker accepted. Lawton drove him to his place and dropped him off at the curb.

His landlady had dumped his belongings out on the front lawn. The front door was latched and bolted.

She didn't want no fucking murder suspects under her roof.

It was 2:30 a.m., Monday, June 23, 1958. The Jean Ellroy job—Sheriff's Homicide File #Z-483-362—was now 16 hours old.

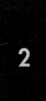

**2**

The San Gabriel Valley was the rat's ass of Los Angeles County—a 30-mile stretch of contiguous hick towns due east of L.A. proper.

The San Gabriel Mountains formed the northern border. The Puente-Montebello Hills closed the valley in on the south. Muddy riverbeds and railroad tracks cut through the middle.

The eastern edge was ambiguously defined. When the view improved, you knew you were out of the valley.

The San Gabriel Valley was flat and box-shaped. The mountain flank trapped in smog. The individual towns—Alhambra, Industry, Bassett, La Puente, Covina, West Covina, Baldwin Park, El Monte, Temple City, Rosemead, San Gabriel, South San Gabriel, Irwindale, Duarte—bled together with nothing but Kiwanis Club signs to distinguish them.

The San Gabriel Valley was hot and humid. Wicked winds kicked dust off the northern foothills. Packed-dirt sidewalks and gravel-pit debris made your eyes sting.

Valley land was cheap. The flat topography was ideal for grid housing and potential freeway construction. The more remote the area, the more land your money got you. You could hunt coons a few blocks off the local main drag and nobody would give you any grief. You could fence in your yard and raise chickens and goats for slaughter. You could let your toddlers run down the block in their shit-stained diapers.

The San Gabriel Valley was White Trash Heaven.

\*

Spanish explorers discovered the valley in 1769. They wiped out the indigenous Indian population and established a mission near the Pomona Freeway—Rosemead Boulevard juncture. La Misión del Santo Arcángel San Gabriel de los Temblores predated the first L.A. settlement by ten years.

Mexican marauders took over the valley in 1822. They kicked out the Spaniards and appropriated their mission land. The United States and Mexico fought a brief war in '46. The Mexicans lost and had to fork over California, Nevada, Arizona, Utah and New Mexico.

The White Man got business going. The San Gabriel Valley enjoyed a long agriculture boom. Confederate sympathizers moved west after the Civil War and bought a lot of valley land.

The railroad shot through in 1872 and sparked a real-estate boom. The valley's population increased by 1,000%. L.A. was becoming a good-sized burg. The valley cashed in on it.

Real-estate profiteers annexed the valley into small cities. A development boom followed and continued straight through the 1920s. City populations grew exponentially.

Housing bans were enforced valley-wide. Mexicans were restricted to slum districts and tin-roof shantytowns. Negroes were not allowed on the streets after dark.

Walnut crops were big. Citrus crops were big. Dairies were a real moneymaker.

The Depression put the skids to San Gabriel Valley growth. World War II resurrected it. Returning GIs got hip to westward migration. Real-estate developers got hip to their hipness.

Tracts and subdivisions went up. Walnut groves and orchards were blitzed to make room for more and more of them. City boundaries expanded.

The population skyrocketed through the '50s. The agriculture biz declined. Manufacturing and light industry flourished. The San Bernardino Freeway stretched from downtown L.A. to south of El Monte. Automobiles became a necessity.

Smog arrived. More housing developments went up. The boom economy brought a new look to the valley—but did not in any way alter its Wild West character.

You had Dust Bowl refugees and their teenage kids. You had pachucos with duck's-ass haircuts, Sir Guy shirts and slit-bottomed khakis. Okies hated spics the way the old cowboys hated Indians.

You had a big influx of men fucked up by World War II and Korea. You had packed suburbs interspersed with large rural patches. You could walk down the Rio Hondo Wash and catch fish with your hands. You could jump into the Rosemead cattle pens and shoot yourself a cow. You could carve yourself a nice fresh steak right there.

You could go drinking. You could hit the Aces, the Torch, the Ship's Inn, the Wee Nipee, the Playroom, Suzanne's, the Kit Kat, the Hat, the Bonnie Rae or the Jolly Jug. You could see what was shaking at the Horseshoe, the Coconino, the Tradewinds, the Desert Inn, the Time-Out, the Jet Room, the Lucky X or the Alibi. The Hollywood East was good. The Big Time, the Off-Beat, the Manger, the Blue Room and the French Basque were okay. Ditto the Cobra Room, Lalo's, the Pine-Away, the Melody Room, the Cave, the Sportsman, the Pioneer, the 49'er, the Palms and the Twister.

You could belt a few. You might meet somebody. The '50s divorce boom was peaking. You could draw from a big pool of at-the-ready women.

El Monte was the '58 hub of the valley. Early settlers called it "the End of the Santa Fe Trail." It was a shitkicker town and a good place to have fun. Recent settlers called it "the City of Divorced Women." It was a honky-tonk place with a more-than-distinct western atmosphere.

The population hovered around 10,000. It was 90% white and 10% Mexican. The city was five miles square. Unincorporated county land bordered it.

The population expanded on Saturday nights. Out-of-towners drove in to prowl the cocktail joints on Valley and Garvey. The El Monte Legion Stadium featured Cliffie Stone and Hometown Jamboree—broadcast live on KTLA-TV.

The audience wore cowboy garb: Stetsons and pipestem pants for the men; starched hoop skirts for the women. The Stadium ran doo-wop dances on Cliffie's off-Saturdays. Pachucos and white punks slugged it out in the parking lot regularly.

The San Berdoo Freeway cut through El Monte. Motorists exited and took Valley Boulevard eastbound. They stopped to eat at Stan's Drive-in and the Hula-Hut. They stopped to drink at the Desert Inn, the Playroom and the Horseshoe. Valley was *the* Saturday night thoroughfare. Eastbound motorists ended up dawdling there whether they planned to or not.

The action strip ended at Five Points—the juncture of Valley and Garvey. Stan's and the Playroom stood at the prime northeast corner. Crawford's Giant Country Market was just across the street. A dozen restaurants and juke joints were jammed together off the intersection.

Residential El Monte ran north, south and west of there. Houses were small and came in two styles: faux-ranch and stucco cube. Mexicans were isolated in a strip called Medina Court and a shack town named Hicks Camp.

Medina Court was three blocks long. The houses there were made of cinderblock and scavenged wood. Hicks Camp was just across the Pacific-Electric tracks. The houses there had dirt floors and were built from lumber ripped off of old boxcars.

The movie *Carmen Jones* was shot at Hicks Camp in '54. A Mexican slum was recast as a Negro sharecropper slum. The set designers did not have to change a single detail.

Medina Court and Hicks Camp were full of winos and hopheads. A favored Hicks Camp form of murder was to get your victim drunk and lay him on the railroad tracks for an oncoming freight to decapitate.

The El Monte PD handled patrol calls and investigated all crimes short of murder. The roster listed twenty-six cops, a matron and a parking meter man. The department had a relatively clean reputation. Local merchants kept the boys well lubed with foodstuffs and liquor. El Monte cops always shopped in their uniforms.

The guys patrolled in one-man cars. The work vibe was friendly—captains and lieutenants drank with plain old harness bulls. The PD was a choice job—you could help people or beat up wetbacks or promote lots of pussy, according to your inclination.

The boys wore all-khaki uniforms and drove '56 Ford

Interceptors. They repossessed cars for local dealers and beefed with the Sheriff's over various chickenshit matters. Half the men signed on under a patronage system. Half came in via civil service.

The PD ceded their murder jobs to Sheriff's Homicide. For a rough-and-tumble town, they got very few snuffs.

Two dykey-looking women killed an El Monte house painter on March 30, 1953. The man's name was Lincoln F. Eddy.

Eddy and Dorothea Johnson spent that day boozing in several El Monte bars. They stopped at Eddy's house in the late afternoon. Eddy coerced Miss Johnson into a blow job. Miss Johnson went home and discussed the matter with her roommate, Miss Viola Gale. The women got ahold of a rifle and walked back to the Eddy house.

They shot Lincoln Eddy. Two boys playing catch outside saw them enter and leave. They were arrested the next morning. They were tried, convicted and sentenced to lengthy prison terms.

On March 17, 1956, Mr. Walter H. Depew drove his car through the front wall of Ray's Inn on Valley Boulevard.

Two men were struck and killed. Mr. Depew's broadside ripped out a 16-foot chunk of the front wall and a 19-foot chunk at the rear. Several other bar patrons were seriously injured.

Mr. Depew was drinking at Ray's Inn earlier in the day. His wife was a barmaid there. Mr. Depew got into an argument with the owner. The owner ejected Mr. Depew a few hours before the incident.

Mr. Depew was arrested immediately. He was tried, convicted and sentenced to a short prison term.

Sheriff's Homicide handled both cases. Their last three El Monte murders got cleared in fucking record time.

The Jean Ellroy job was running longer already.

**3**

The *Times, Express* and *Mirror* gave it page-two play. It made the local TV news for five seconds.

The redhead rated zero. The Johnny Stompanato snuff was the real goods. Lana Turner's daughter shanked Johnny back in April. The story was still hot news.

The *Mirror* ran a shot of the redhead smiling. The *Times* ran a picture of the kid just after the cops gave him the word. Jean Ellroy was the twelfth county murder victim of 1958.

Armand Ellroy went down to the Coroner's Office early Monday morning. He identified the body and signed a Health and Safety Code form to release it to the Utter-McKinley Mortuary. Dr. Gerald K. Ridge performed the autopsy: Coroner's Case File #35339-6/23/58.

He ascribed cause of death to "asphyxia due to strangulation by ligature." His anatomic summary noted the "totally occlusive double ligature" around the victim's neck. He noted that the victim was in her menstrual phase. His smear for spermatozoa turned up positive. He found a tampon at the rear of the vaginal vault.

He noted the "surgical absence" of the victim's right nipple. He diagrammed the scrapes on her hips and knees and the bruises on the insides of her thighs. He described the body as being "that of a well-developed, well-nourished, unembalmed white female." His external examination notes cut straight to the two garrotes:

There is a double tightly occlusive ligature about the neck, producing deep grooving of the soft tissues. This ligature is comprised of both a length of apparent clothesline cord, which has apparently been placed first about the neck and knotted tightly in the left posterior region. The ends of the cord are free, one extremely short and apparently having been broken loose at the knot, while the other one is of moderate length and extends inferiorly. Apparently applied over the first ligature is a tightly knotted nylon stocking, the knot likewise located in the left posterior lateral surface. The nylon ligature overlies the long limb of the clothesline ligature at that point. The nylon stocking appears to have been tightly affixed by the usual overhand knot first and in the formation of the second knot, one limb of the free end has been looped under a partial slip knot, which is quite tightly drawn up.

Dr. Ridge removed the ligatures and noted the "deep pallid groove" around the neck. He shaved the victim bald and described her head tissues as "Intensely cyanotic and suffused with dark bluish-purple discoloration." He cut the scalp down to the skull and pulled the flaps back. He diagrammed eleven wounds and labeled them "intense red deep scalp ecchymoses."

The doctor sawed off the top of the head and examined the victim's brain tissue. He weighed it and found "no evidences of injury or other intrinsic abnormalities." He cut open the victim's stomach and found whole kidney beans, meat shards, orange-yellow masses resembling carrots or squash and yellowish masses resembling cheese.

He examined the rest of the body and found no other evidence of trauma. He took a blood sample to be held for chemical analysis and removed portions of the vital organs for potential microscopic study.

He extracted food particles from the stomach to be held and analyzed. He froze the spermatozoa smear—to be held and blood-typed.

A toxicologist took a blood sample and screened it for alcohol content. His reading was low: .08%.

A forensic chemist checked the body. He found small white carpetlike fibers under the victim's right middle fingernail and bagged them as evidence. He took the two garrotes, the victim's dress, right stocking and brassiere to the Sheriff's Crime Lab. He noted that the unraveled strangling cord was 17 inches long—yet had tightened to 3 inches around the victim's neck.

Dr. Ridge called Ward Hallinen and summarized his findings. He confirmed asphyxia as the cause of death and said that the victim had been struck in the head at least six times. She may have been unconscious when she was strangled. She'd engaged in recent sexual intercourse. She had probably eaten a full meal one to two hours before her death. It was most likely Mexican-type food—she had partially digested beans, meat and cheese in her stomach.

Hallinen wrote the information down and called Sheriff's Metro. He laid out his case to the squad lieutenant and requested two men to canvass bars and restaurants in the El Monte/Rosemead/Temple City area. The lieutenant said he'd send out Bill Vickers and Frank Godfrey. Hallinen said they should stress three things:

The victim ate Mexican-style food Saturday night or very early Sunday morning. She might have been out with a Mexican or a Latin-type Caucasian—possibly named Tommy. The victim was redheaded—the two probably stood out.

The lieutenant promised priority service. Hallinen said he'd be out canvassing himself.


Lawton and Hallinen connected at the El Monte Station. They split up and started working separate canvassing beats.

Jim Bruton teamed up with Captain Al Etzel. They drove to 700 Bryant and reinterviewed George and Anna May Krycki. Mrs. Krycki stuck to her Jean-didn't-drink/Jean-didn't-go-out-with-men story. She said that Jean answered a newspaper ad and rented the little back house impulsively. Jean liked the fenced-in yard and thick foliage. She said the place felt safe to her. The Kryckis had a hunch that Jean was hiding out in El Monte.

Jean did not have a telephone. She used the Kryckis' phone for local calls and made her other calls at work. The Kryckis received a few calls *to* her. They were strictly calls related to her job.

Bruton asked Mrs. Krycki if she had any more photos of Jean. She gave him six Kodachrome snapshots. Etzel asked her to go through the bungalow with them. They needed to inventory Jean's things and determine the shoes and purse she had with her Saturday night.

Mrs. Krycki walked Bruton and Etzel through the house and examined the victim's belongings. She drew a blank on the purse and said Jean's clear plastic high heels were missing.

Bruton and Etzel drove to the El Monte Station and dropped the snapshots off for reprinting.

Hallinen met up with Lawton.

Their canvassing runs were unsuccessful. They hit numerous bars and nightclubs—but nobody recalled a redhead and a dark man out Saturday night.

They drove to the Airtek Dynamics plant. It was just south of downtown L.A.—a big six-story structure. The personnel director was named Ruth Schienle.

She'd heard about the killing. She said the news was buzzing all over Airtek. She said she was friendly with Jean. Jean was a well-liked Airtek employee.

Airtek was a division of the Packmeyr Gun Company. They manufactured window casings for military planes. Jean was the plant nurse. She hired on in September '56.

Mrs. Schienle said she knew very little about Jean's private life. Hallinen and Lawton pressed her.

She said Jean had very few close friends. She was not much of a socializer and only an occasional drinker. Her friends were mostly older couples, dating back to the time of her marriage.

Hallinen and Lawton described the blonde and the dark man. Mrs. Schienle said they didn't sound like Airtek people— or any of the friends Jean told her about. The name Tommy did not ring a bell.

Hallinen and Lawton left her a card and said they'd be in

touch. They told her to call if she picked up on anything suspicious.

Mrs. Schienle assured them she'd cooperate. Hallinen and Lawton headed back to El Monte.

The Metropolitan Detail was a loan-out unit. It had one function: to assist the Headquarters Detective Bureau in major investigations. The assigned deputies wore plainclothes and were skilled at canvassing.

Frank Godfrey locked in to the Ellroy case on Monday afternoon. Bill Vickers was set to start soon.

Godfrey canvassed with a photo of the victim. He queried waitresses, carhops, bartenders, restaurant and cocktail lounge managers. He stressed the redhead, the blonde and a dark man who might be named Tommy. He said the redhead ordered Mexican food or a chili size with cheese.

He hit Staat's Cafe at Meeker and Valley. A waitress said the redhead looked familiar. She said a party of four came in Saturday night and ordered chili sizes. Pearl Pendleton waited on them.

Pearl was off today. Godfrey got her number from the manager and called her. Pearl listened to his questions and said that none of her Saturday-night customers resembled the people he described.

Godfrey hit Dick's Drive-In at Rosemead and Las Tunas. Nobody there was working Saturday night into Sunday morning. The manager was not on the premises.

A carhop gave him some names: Marlene, Kathy, Kitty Johnson, Sue the counter girl. They were all working Saturday-Sunday graveyard and would be rotating back on duty Wednesday.

Godfrey walked across the street and checked out the Clock Drive-In. The manager said none of his on-duty crew was working late Saturday night or early Sunday. He checked his 6/21 roster and kicked loose some names and numbers: two dining-room girls, one hostess, one counter girl and four carhops.

Godfrey circled over to Five Points and hit Stan's Drive-In.

The manager said his Saturday-Sunday girls were all off now. Godfrey wrote down their names and home numbers:

Eve McKinley/ED3-6733; Ellen "Nicky" Nichols/ED3-6442; Lavonne "Pinky" Chambers/ED7-6686.

It was 4:00 p.m. Godfrey swung south on Garvey and stopped at the Melody Room.

The owner introduced himself as Clyde. He heard out Godfrey's questions and told him to contact Bernie Snyder, the night barman. Bernie closed the place at 2:00 a.m. Sunday. Call Bernie and talk to him.

A customer butted in. He said *he* was here Sunday morning—and *he* saw a ponytailed blonde huddled up with a dark-haired guy. The guy was thirty to thirty-five. The ponytail and him were acting real nervous.

Clyde said the ponytail sounded like a regular named Jo. She worked for Dun & Bradstreet in L.A. He called the woman a "bar lizard." The dark-haired guy didn't come off familiar at all.

Godfrey took down the customer's name and phone number. Clyde urged him to call Bernie Snyder—Bernie knew all the faces.

Godfrey called from the bar. Bernie's wife answered. She said Bernie wouldn't be back until 5:30—try him then.

It was 4:30 p.m. Most of your local night spots didn't open until 6:00 or 7:00. Godfrey was running up a long phone call list.


The Desert Inn was a hillbilly joint. It used to be called the Jungle Room and Chet's Rendezvous. Myrtle Mawby bought the place for her kid brother, Ellis Outlaw. Ellis renamed it Outlaw's Hideout.

Ellis was always in trouble with the cops and the fucking Internal Revenue Service. The Feds shut him down for skimming withholding money from his employees—then let him reopen so he could pay off his debt. Ellis brained Al Manganiello with a bottle back in '55 and narrowly avoided a jail stretch. He just couldn't make the Hideout turn a steady profit.

He sold it back to Chet Williamson. Chet renamed it the Desert Inn and let Ellis run it. Ellis came from a barkeeping family. His sister Myrtle shot her husband in the ear once and got two cocktail bars in the ensuing divorce settlement.

Ellis owned the bungalows behind the Desert Inn parking lot. His pal Al Manganiello rented a flop from him. Ellis ran a small handbook out of the bar. He took action on all the races at Hollywood Park and Santa Anita.

Ellis got popped for drunk driving in May of '57. Two El Monte cops said he tried to bribe them—nice coin if they shitcanned the arrest report. A couple of Ellis's buddies offered them backup bribes.

The bribe offers were relative chump change. The thing escalated into a hick-town cause célèbre.

Ellis was convicted for drunk driving. Appeals kept him out of jail for over a year. Ellis and his pals beat the bribery rap.

The drunk driving appeals ran out on June 19th. A judge confirmed the conviction. Ellis was ordered to appear for sentencing on June 27th.

The Desert Inn was venerably shitkicker—and high-class by El Monte standards.

Spade Cooley played there on his way down from local TV. The quasi-Ink Spots played there on their post-Vegas slide.

Negro customers got the bum's rush. Spics got a wary welcome— if they didn't show up en masse.

The Desert Inn was a good place to drink and scout nookie. The Desert Inn was safe and civilized—by 1958 El Monte standards.


Jim Bruton met Hallinen and Lawton at the bar. It was 6:30 p.m.

They hit Al Manganiello up for the Desert Inn guest book. Al showed them a ledger filled with names and addresses. They skimmed it and found two men named Tom.

Tom Downey: 4817 Azusa Canyon Road, Baldwin Park. Tom Baker: 5013 North Larry Street, Baldwin Park.

Al said he didn't know Tom Baker. Tom Downey was more their speed—sort of a slick dark-haired guy like the one they said was dancing with the redhead.

Hallinen, Lawton and Bruton drove to Downey's address. A woman answered the door and ID'd herself as Mrs. Downey.

She said Tom was still at work—he sold Fords at El Monte Motors. He should be home in a few minutes.

They told her they'd be back later and staked out the house in Bruton's car. "A few minutes" stretched to nine and a half hours.

They called it quits at 5:00 a.m. Bruton radioed the station and told them to dispatch a patrol unit to relieve the stakeout.

A black & white arrived five minutes later. Bruton drove Hallinen and Lawton back to the Desert Inn to get their cars. Everybody dispersed and went home.

The patrol guys watched the Downey house. Tom Downey showed up twenty minutes into their stakeout.

The patrol guys grabbed him. They radioed the El Monte switchboard and told the operator to rouse Captain Bruton.

Tom Downey was pissed off and bewildered. The patrol guys drove him to the El Monte Station and placed him in an interview room.

Jim Bruton walked in. His first impression of Tom Downey: This guy is too stocky to be our suspect.

Bruton questioned him. Downey said he was out chasing cunt—and boy was he tired. Bruton told him to run down his Saturday-night activities.

Downey said he was at the Desert Inn on two different occasions. The first time was between 8:00 and 9:00. He sat at a table with Ben Grissman and another guy while they ate their dinner.

Ben and the other guy left. He stayed another ten minutes or so. He hit a few more spots, returned to the Desert Inn and had two drinks. He cashed a 20-dollar check with the bartender and split just prior to midnight. He went to another bar and met up with a friend. They drove to a steak house in Covina and had a late supper. He got home real late.

Bruton described the victim, the blonde and the dark man, and placed them at the Desert Inn roughly concurrent with Downey's visits. Downey said he didn't notice anybody resembling them.

Bruton wrote down "Ben Grissman" and got the name of Downey's other buddy. He told Downey that some Sheriff's men might want to talk to him.

Downey pledged his cooperation. Bruton sent him home in a patrol car.

A letter arrived at the El Monte Station Tuesday morning. It was scrawled on the back of a bank deposit slip and an employee's time clock sheet.

El Monte Chief of Police                                    6/23/58

Dear Sir,

I would suggest, in relation to your latest rape murder (that I read about in today's paper) you should question E. Ponce, a TV repair man, works for Dorn's, lives in Monterey Park. This is rather near El Monte and my wife charges that he raped her in April of last year, in my home. He also threatened her at that time and the rest of the family. Our matter is in the courts at this time. He is a tall slim Mexican, very pronounced accent. Make him account for his actions and or any others of a similar nature, as he is so inclined.

Ask Ponce if he was acquainted with the nurse that was raped & murdered. Find out if she ever bought a TV or had other dealings with Dorn's, and if Ponce had ever repaired sets or any other appliance for her. Look at Dorn's books and hours. Make him account for his time on the night of the crime. Substantiated. Ask me to identify him, just as if I had seen her with him. Let me get a close look.

The letter was signed "Lester A. Eby, 17152 Cires Avenue, Fontana, Calif." The Chief's secretary called Information and got the accompanying phone number: VA2-7814. She wrote it at the bottom of the time clock sheet and called Information back.

She asked for a listing on "E. Ponce" in Monterey Park. The operator gave her the only one she had: Emil Ponce, 320 East Fernfield Drive, PA1-3047. She wrote the information down below the informant's name and placed the letter in Captain Bruton's box.

*

Ruth Schienle called Sheriff's Homicide Tuesday morning. She left a detailed message for Ward Hallinen and Jack Lawton. The phone man wrote it down on the back of a teletype slip.

> Miss Schienle rptd that Henry Kurtz, 4144 Irving Pl.
> Culver City, NE8-5888, did not rpt for work last night
> and had phoned in that he would not be in tonight
> (6/24/58). Henry F. Kurtz/MW/39-42/5′-8″— 220/brown
> hair

The phone man placed the slip in Jack Lawton's box.

Jim Bruton called Frank Godfrey Tuesday morning. He told him to hustle down to Brea and talk to a Mexican girl named Carmen Contreras. They got a tip that she knew a Desert Inn habitué named Tommy. The girl's address was 248 South Poplar.

Godfrey drove to Orange County and found the address. The girl's mother sent him over to the Beckman Instrument Company—Carmen's place of employment.

Godfrey talked to Carmen. Carmen said she knew a man named Tommy—but she didn't know his last name. He was a Caucasian, 30 to 40, 5′6″ to 5′7″. He was dark complected and had brown eyes and dark curly hair.

Carmen thought he lived in Baldwin Park. He was married —but was trying to obtain a divorce. He drove a '57 Mercury coupe, pink over white. He told her he used to own a '52 Olds. He worked for a floor-installation company in Temple City. He hung out at the Ivanhoe in Temple City and the Desert Inn in El Monte. He liked to sit at the bar or table-hop. He took her to an Italian place on Valley a couple of times. She hadn't seen Tommy in a while.

Godfrey gave her a card. He told her to call him if she dredged up Tommy's last name. Carmen said she would.

Godfrey called Jim Bruton and ran the interview by him. Bruton said he'd check out the Ivanhoe.

*

An anonymous tipster called the Temple City Sheriff's Tuesday morning. He said this "Johnny" guy might be the one who choked that nurse.

The tipster said Johnny frequented the Desert Inn. He drove a pink-and-white Olds Holiday and considered himself a "lover boy." He was white, 30 to 35, 5'8" with a medium build. He had black hair and a dark complexion. He had an ex-girlfriend named Patricia Fields.

The desk sergeant relayed the information to Bill Vickers. Vickers found a phone listing for Patricia Fields and called her.

Miss Fields told him that Johnny had been working overseas since December. She'd been corresponding with him since that time. Vickers asked her if she could verify it. Miss Fields told him to call Peggy Narucore. Her number was GI3-2638.

Vickers called the number. Peggy Narucore confirmed Miss Fields' story.

It was mid-afternoon.

Frank Godfrey and Bill Vickers were canvassing bars and restaurants. Ward Hallinen and Jack Lawton were reinterviewing the victim's ex-husband and son.

Their apartment was small and hot. They sat around a small kitchen table.

Armand Ellroy mentioned the funeral next week. He'd arranged for a minister and burial at Inglewood Cemetery. Jean's sister and her husband were flying in from Madison, Wisconsin. He'd be taking his boy back to El Monte next Monday to pick up his things.

Hallinen and Lawton asked the boy some questions.

Did your mother know a blond woman with a ponytail? Did you ever see her with a Mexican man or a dark white man? Who were her friends at work? Did she make any friends since you moved to El Monte? *Why did she move to El Monte?*

The boy said his mother lied about the move to El Monte. She said she wanted him to live in a house, not an apartment. He knew she was lying.

He liked Santa Monica. El Monte scared him. He didn't understand why they moved so far away.

He didn't know any blond woman. He didn't know any Mexican guy or dark white guy. He didn't know his mother's work friends. He already told them about Hank Hart and Peter Tubiolo. Mrs. Krycki was his mother's friend—he knew that.

Lawton asked him if his mother drank liquor.

The boy said she drank a lot of Early Times bourbon.


Jim Bruton got a call Tuesday evening. The Temple Sheriff's forwarded a tip: Tommy just showed up at the Ivanhoe.

Bruton arranged for a Sheriff's unit to transport him to the El Monte Station. He set up an interview room with a one-way glass mirror and called Myrtle Mawby. She agreed to come in and view the suspect.

Two deputies brought Tommy in. It was Tom Baker from the Desert Inn guest book. Bruton had him run down his Saturday night.

Baker said he went to the races at Hollywood Park. He stayed through the seventh race and drove to a restaurant on Florence and Rosemead. He had a burger and drove to his place in Baldwin Park. He spent the rest of the evening watching TV with his landlord and the landlord's son. He was not at the Desert Inn Saturday night.

Myrtle Mawby observed Tom Baker. She told Bruton that he was not the man she saw with the redhead.

Tom Baker was released. A patrol car drove him back to the Ivanhoe.


It was 8:00 p.m.

Vickers and Godfrey were over at Temple—calling bartenders and carhops at home. Hallinen and Lawton were calling out from the El Monte Station.

They were trying to locate Margie Trawick and Mike Whittaker. They needed them to submit formal statements tonight.

They found Margie at her parents' house. They found Mike at the Melody Room and told him they'd send a car for him. They arranged for a Sheriff's stenographer to come out to the station.

The desk sergeant interrupted them. He said a tip just came in—a carhop at Stan's might have seen something Saturday night.


Lavonne Chambers was wearing a red-and-gold uniform. Hallinen and Lawton interviewed her in the manager's cubbyhole.

Stan's was circular and space-age modern. A neon spire poked out of the roof. The lot behind it was huge—cars could stack up three rows deep and flash their lights for service.

Lavonne said she heard a radio broadcast. She hemmed-and-hawed for a day or so and told her shift boss what she knew. He called the Sheriff's for her.

Hallinen and Lawton coaxed her a little. Lavonne relaxed and told them her story.

She recognized the description on the radio. She remembered the redhead—from her dress down to her pearl ring. She was certain that she served the redhead and her date *twice*—Saturday night and Sunday morning.

They came in shortly after 10:00. The woman ordered a grilled cheese sandwich; the man ordered coffee. The man was driving. The car was a '55 or '56 Olds sedan. It was two-tone green—with the lighter green probably on top. The man was very thin, 35 to 40, with black hair combed straight back. He looked like he might be of Greek or Italian extraction.

The woman acted lighthearted. She might have been intoxicated. The man acted bored and reserved.

They ate and drove off. They returned between 2:00 and 2:45 a.m. They parked in one of her stalls again.

The redhead ordered chili and beans. The man ordered coffee. She was still lighthearted. He was still bored and reserved. They ate, paid up and drove off.

Hallinen and Lawton displayed the victim's coat—covered with forensic tags now. Lavonne Chambers ID'd the lining immediately. She ID'd a photo of the victim just as fast. She agreed to submit a formal statement tomorrow—but only at her house. She couldn't leave her children alone.

Hallinen and Lawton set up a 3:30 appointment. Lavonne

went on and on about the redhead—she was so pretty and seemed so nice.

Mike Whittaker's formal statement was a mess.

He kept pleading drunkenness. He pegged the 43-year-old redheaded victim as a brunette in her 20s. He called the ponytailed blonde a Mexican girl.

His story was vague and filled with memory gaps. He kept contradicting his Sunday-night statement. His one chronological frame of reference was the moment he fell off his chair.

The interview concluded at 9:35 p.m.

Mike Whittaker walked out. Margie Trawick walked in.

STATEMENT OF MARGIE TRAWICK. TAKEN AT THE EL MONTE POLICE DEPARTMENT, 505 EAST VALLEY BOULEVARD, EL MONTE. PRESENT: SERGEANT W. E. HALLINEN, SERGEANT J. G. LAWTON. 9:41 P.M., JUNE 24, 1958. FOR FILE #Z-483-362. REPORTED BY: DORA A. BRITTON, STENOGRAPHIC REPORTER.

BY SGT. HALLINEN:

Q What is your full name?

A Margie Trawick.

Q Do you have a middle name?

A Yes, the middle name is Lucille.

Q Are you sometimes known by another last name?

A My maiden name was Phillips.

Q Where do you live?

A 413 Court Adair Street, El Monte.

Q Do you have a telephone?

A Gilbert 8-1136.

Q May I ask your age?

A I was thirty-six a week ago last Saturday the 14th of June.

Q Who do you live at that address with?

A My parents, Mr. and Mrs. F. W. Phillips.

Q Are you working at the present time?

A Right now, no. I do have an employer. I'm off on sick leave at present.

Q Who is your employer?

A Tubesales, 2211 Tubeway Avenue, Los Angeles 22.

Q Did you have previous employment as a waitress?

A Yes. Waitress. Mostly hostess at the Desert Inn, 11721 East Valley Boulevard, El Monte, right.

Q How long were you employed there?

A Approximately nine years. Not steady at any time, whenever they needed me. When business was real good.

Q When was your last date of employment?

A Let's see, I went to the hospital May 6th and it was the Saturday night before that Tuesday.

Q Referring to Saturday night, June 21st in the evening, do you recall this date?

A Yes, I do.

Q Would you tell us your movements starting with approximately 10:00 p.m. of that date?

A I left my home at about, between five and ten minutes after 10:00, went directly to the Desert Inn.

Q Pardon me, what type of place is the Desert Inn?

A It's a night club, strictly. Dancing and dinner house.

Q What time did you arrive at the Desert Inn?

A I would say about 10:15, to 10:20. Just what time it would take me to drive from here straight there.

Q Where did you sit?

A The table directly in front of the bar next to the service station.

Q By service station you mean there where the girls obtain their drinks for service to the customers?

A That's right.

Q While sitting at that table did you view the room and it's customers?

A Yes, as it's habit with me.

Q Could you tell us about the condition as to movement of customers and anyone in particular that you noticed?

A There were six people at two tables pulled together directly on the front row next to the dance floor.

Q Did you recognize any of these people?

A As regular customers of the Desert Inn, yes.

Q Can you name them?

A I can not.

Q Did you notice anyone at the bar?

A Yes, there was the colored singer sitting on the stool next to the service station. There was two other men at the bar.

Q Would you know their names?

A Only one that I know as Cliff. He's the man that left with me at 11:30.

Q You are referring to when you left the Desert Inn at 11:30 p.m.?

A Yes, that's right.

Q Any others you recognized or can name, sitting at any of the tables within your view?

A There was a dancer that used to dance at the Pioneer, a stripper, I mean, and I don't know whether it's her husband or agent, but he is always with her, sitting directly next to me. There was another regular sitting at the center table under the mirror on the side wall. They were regulars. There were four people at the third table next to the dance floor. I don't know them, but they have been in there a number of times. There was a young couple directly behind them. The young fellow I've seen. The girl I had not.

Q As you recall these people within your view at the tables, approximately what time was it?

A This was at the time that I went in.

Q Did anyone else seat themselves or come into the place that you took particular notice of?

A Two girls. One a redhead and one is, I call a dish-water blonde, came in and sat down at the center table, center row.

Q Would you describe these two ladies?

A The redhead was very attractive. I call it a Titian red. I don't know what you might call it. Not a dark red, not a light red. Very nicely dressed and a navy blue duster dress. Dress of print, the duster lined with the same material as the dress. The outside of the duster navy blue. At the time that they sat down, the waitress, which is a very dear friend of mine, was talking to a customer at the bar.

Q What is the waitress's name?

A Myrtle Mawby.

Q With reference to the redheaded girl, can you describe her as to approximate age, height and weight?

A I would say she was forty years old. I would judge her to be 5'5", her weight I'd say is hard for me to judge. I don't believe I stated her exact weight, possibly between 125 to 130 pounds.

Q Did you notice any jewelry on this girl?

A I did not.

Q Did you notice anything else that might be distinguishing?

A The reason I noticed the girl in particular was when she pulled her coat off to dance with a fellow that walked up to the table.

Q Can you describe the other girl sitting at the table?

A She was a dishwater blonde, had a short three-quarter length, beige or tan coat on across her shoulders. She had on flat heel shoes and until I saw her dance, that's as much of a description. Dancing, about her weight, I judged her to be heavier than the redhead by five or ten pounds. She was hippy or broad across the hips.

Q Her age?

A About the same as the other lady, about forty years old.

Q Height?

A About the same as the redhead. She had on flat heels. The redhead had high heels.

BY SGT. LAWTON:

Q Did you notice the shoes of the redhead?

A No, I did not.

Q Did the redhead appear to be intoxicated?

A Neither one of them appeared that way.

BY SGT. HALLINEN:

Q After the two girls you have just described sat at the table, what happened next?

A I called Mrs. Mawby's attention that she had two customers and she finished her conversation with the gentleman at the bar. In the meantime a tall thin Mexican fellow walked to the back of the chair of the redhead. I did not hear him ask her to dance. She immediately arose from her chair.

Q Before you go on, can you describe this person a little more fully?

A I would say he was between 5'9" and 6' tall, very thin body stature, thin in face. Dark hair, slicked back. Quite slicked down.

Q Was there any wave to this hair?

A No.

Q Was there any part?

A No, it was a receding forehead on both sides here.

Q What type clothes, if you recall?

A Dark suit. Dark sport shirt, worn open at the throat with the collar out of the suit coat.

Q Did you notice anything white or light on this man?

A I did not.

Q The age?

A I would say that he wasn't, he was around the same age as the women there.

Q Approximately forty years of age?

A Yes, sir. Between that and forty-five.

Q Did you hear any of the conversation when he came to the table?

A No, I did not.

Q Did you have any impression as to whether this man knew either one of the girls?

A It seemed to me that he was a member of the party. It looked that way.

Q And you obtained that impression from what?

A From the way he approached the redhead. She arose from her chair, she took her coat off, he helped her fold it, lining out, put it across the back of the chair and went to the dance floor.

Q At this time it left the other girl with the pony tail sitting alone at the table?

A Miss Mawby started then to take their order and came back and stood by my table because she had to wait to see whether they were all old enough before she could serve any drinks to that table. What happened next, she took their order; one beer, two highballs. I heard her call, "Tall," then I knew one of them had a tall drink.

Q At this time there were three at the table?

A Yes.

Q What is your next recollection as to the proceedings?

A The next recollection was of Mike coming off the dance floor with the blonde.

Q You don't know his name?

A No, I didn't at the time.

Q You have since learned his name is Mike?

A Yes.

Q I wish to go back just a small ways in this statement and ask you if you can recall the approximate time that the two girls arrived at and sat at the table you described?

A I would say I had been there at least a half-hour, which would make it about quarter to 11:00.

Q Would you describe the person you now know as Mike?

A Well, he has light brown hair. I would call him blonde because of his facial features. He strikes me as a blonde. Young fellow, 23, 24 years old. Had a dark shirt with navy blue or black. The thing most noticeable to me was that it was sloppy. It was unbuttoned all the way down the front. Dark trousers and fabric shoes on, kind of light tennis shoes.

Q This is the same description you related to us prior to knowing that this person's name was Mike?

A That's right.

Q What did Mike do?

A In reference to asking me to dance he walked in the front door, walked to the bar and ordered a beer, then came up to my table and asked me if I would like to dance, and I told him the number was too fast. Then he asked me would I dance a slow one and I told him, "No, thank you." He became very belligerent and asked me did I even know how to dance at all. He went back to the bar, picked up his beer and walked to the corner table that separates the cocktail lounge from the food side of the place. The waitress—I made the remark to the waitress that he was belligerent and looked rather young to me. She went and came back, gave him a clean ashtray and clean napkin, came back to my table and said, "No, he's plenty old enough." A short while later I noticed that he was dancing with the pony-tail blonde that was sitting at the center table, center row with the redhead.

Q Did you notice Mike go to the table prior to dancing with the girl with the pony tail?

A No, when I saw him sitting at the table with the party at that time that made four of them; the Mexican, the young fellow, and the two girls.

Q Do you recall in relation to the location of the bar what the position of the four people were?

A The two girls had their backs to me.

Q Which would make their backs to which side of the room?

A Their backs were at the north. They were facing the dance floor. Mike's chair was pulled in close at an angle where he could watch the dance floor, closer to the pony tail blonde.

Q Which would be the west side?

A Yes, west. The Mexican fellow was still facing me. That would make him face north.

Q And the bar and the girls?

A That's right.

Q And on the east side of Mike?

A Yes.

Q Did you see any more drinks ordered for the table?

A I only saw the waitress serve two rounds of drinks.

Q Do you recall who ordered those rounds?

A No, I don't.

Q Did you notice the condition as to intoxication of the four people sitting at this table?

A The young fellow now known as Mike was quite intoxicated. The other three people, no.

Q Did both men dance with the two girls?

A After that I didn't pay particular attention because I left at 11:30.

Q They were all four sitting at the table when you left?

A Yes, sir.

Q Did you go out of the Desert Inn with someone?

A Yes, I did.

Q And it was approximately 11:30 when you left?

A That's right.

Q Did you return at any time that evening?

A Ten minutes to one. I brought the same fellow back. Took him to collect money that was owed to him.

Q What time did you arrive back?

A Ten to one.

Q Did you notice the condition as to the occupancy of the table and the bar of the Desert Inn?

A It was practically empty on the cocktail lounge side.

Q Did you notice the table you have previously described as having the four people there?

A It was empty.

Q Did you see any of those people previously described in the restaurant?

A No, I did not.

Q How long did you stay there?

A Just a few very few minutes.

Q And then you left?

A Then I went home, yes.

BY SERGEANT LAWTON:

Q This tall or thin Mexican man that you have
   described, if you saw him again, would you be able to
   identify him?

A I believe I could. He was so thin in here, you might
   think he had no teeth until you saw him smile.

Q You are indicating the jaw area?

A Yes.

Q He's the one that asked the redhead to dance?

A Yes. I didn't hear him ask her.

Q But they danced?

A Yes.

Q He's the one you got the impression that they knew
   each other?

A That's right.

Q Thank you very much.

STATEMENT CONCLUDED AT 10:10 P.M.


Two letters arrived at the El Monte Station Wednesday
morning. Both were addressed to the Chief of Police.

The first letter was typed and postmarked Fullerton,
California.

We have been trailing Mr. C.S.I, from Santa Ana and
saw him throw that body, red-hair girl from his or a
1954 Plymouth two tone salmon pink, chocolate
brown car that evening. You see he has a police
record at various Southern California's Police Dept.
and has threatened several lives. We consider him
TRASH and he is the one you are looking for. KI-28114
will tell you some more.

The letter was signed "Eye Witness, Peggy Jane, Mr. and
Mrs. Virgil Galbraith, Fullerton."

The second letter was postmarked Los Angeles. It was
handwritten. "Consider Her Ways" was printed on the front of
the envelope.

So shall thy poverty come as one that travalleth and
thy want as an armed man.

Olga was raised in a house of ill fame, from other
pros she learned all about burglary, robbery, theft,
and the thief is like a murderer. Her trail leads past
hold ups of banks—the 9th and Spring cashier within
recent months as well as a "Job" of a bank in San
Francisco known locally as Grandma. She disguises—
having been around the movie studios and an elevator
operator at the Ambassador, from the latter and maid
work she developed the theft and murder technique
she worked out in Hollywood to kill a woman in a
hotel, Mrs. Greenwald, Miss Epperson and a woman in
an L.A. hotel. Numerous other murders—a
Stepanovich in MacArthur Park in recent months and
others not revealed to the public. She hangs about the
Santa Fe Trailways bus depot & museums and Forest
Lawn, as well as changeable areas and districts where
she may find a man to pick-pocket, a woman for
sodomy, a drunk to roll, a travellar to fleece or pick
pocket, Olivera Street where she sells her body &
picks travellar pockets, and young men—usually
two—to sleep with it in her gut.

She has to sleep so she finds a hotel over the bridge
to West 7th Str. in L.A. En route is the market run by
Anthony Jr. & the Senior Thomas. There Anthony
seduced her and frequently A pays her, now A lives in
El Monte, to prevent a new crime in El Monte, drive
Anthony (by quenching him with fire) out of El Monte
or she will slay you, your children and your love
because she wants to get money from Anthony.
Therefore drive him out of your City. If you do not
want—yes—if nothing else—a social disease. If your
town is wide open for pros like Olga we will continue to
stamp out that evil. Rulers are a terror for evil. Now the
writer is looking for two eunuchs to pitch Olga out of
the window. Therefore you must send her where
eunuchs are and are at a place where women plunge.
Send her to the state hospital on the pretext of fixing

her feet. She never wears pants—violates the law against indescent exposure—and so rolls her socks which cause varicose veins. She can get a cramp and fall in traffic & in the flurry of excitement the sheriff the superior court judge & the state hosp med director could be bumped into & perish. Where would you be? She is blond, 40 to 45, is your suspect.

If the crimes of theft and murder stop then Olga is the guilty party. The longer she stays in the institution the longer is the time needed for her habitual way to carry crime into there. It will be found out and then it will be realized that although there are other crimes unsolved in her area attributed to males you sheriff's have been looking for the wrong suspect in the book of the science of criminology of which you are paid to eat, sleep, talk and go on a journey about. Science—the thief is as a murderer, and the low pay person covets, Olga only gets a few replies for her ads & her feet force her to sleep. There are more females than males and disturbances of the area of birth by simulated actions and objects are part of a pro's show stag "Job." Therefore he or she that doeth violence to the body of any person shall flee to the pit. Let no man stay him, unless this female beast is gassed we will send you in.

The letter was unsigned. It was accompanied by a page torn from an Italian-language magazine. One side of the page featured scientific text. The other side featured a large photograph of a bumblebee.

The Chief's secretary dropped both letters in Captain Bruton's box.

An APB went out Wednesday morning.

```
ALL POINTS BULLETIN
SPECIAL ATTENTION . . . SAN GABRIEL VALLEY
POLICE
AGENCIES AND CHP
```

ON JUNE 22, 1958 THE STRANGLED BODY OF A
WOMAN WAS FOUND IN THE EL MONTE AREA. SHE
HAS BEEN IDENTIFIED AS JEAN ELLROY AKA JEAN
HILLIKER AKA GENEVA O. ELLROY. IT IS BELIEVED
THAT THE SUSPECT EITHER STILL HAS IN HIS
POSSESSION OR HAS THROWN AWAY ARTICLES OF
VICTIM'S CLOTHING AND PERSONAL EFFECTS
INCLUDING A PURSE, DESCRIPTION UNKNOWN, KEYS
TO VICTIM'S 1957 BUICK, A PAIR OF WOMAN'S
SHOES, POSSIBLY CLEAR PLASTIC WITH HIGH HEELS,
A WOMAN'S UNDERPANTS, GIRDLE AND SLIP.
ANY INFORMATION RE ABOVE FOR J. G. LAWTON &
W. E. HALLINEN, HOMICIDE DETAIL, SHERIFF'S
DEPARTMENT. (REFER LAWTON HQ DB HOMICIDE
DETAIL FILE Z-483-362).

E.W.BISCAILUZ, SHERIFF

It was Wednesday afternoon. Bill Vickers was hitting the El
Monte spots again.

He checked Suzanne's Cafe—with negative results. He
checked the Dublin Inn—with negative results.

He got a tip at the 49'er. A bartender said the victim might
have been in the place the previous Saturday night—June
14th.

She was with a guy. He was 5'8", with a stocky build and
slightly wavy blond hair. They were both drunk. They stayed
a short while and got into an argument—something about the
redhead refusing a drink. The bartender said he'd seen the
blond guy before—but he wasn't a regular and he didn't know
his name.

Vickers checked the Mama Mia Restaurant. The owner told
him to call his waitress Catherine Cathey—she was working
last Saturday night.

Vickers called her. Catherine Cathey said a redhaired
woman came in the place about 8:00 p.m., alone. Vickers said
he'd call her back and arrange to show her a photo of the
victim.

Vickers checked the Off-Beat. Nobody recognized his snapshot of the victim. The owner's wife told him a story that she thought might connect to his case.

A regular named Ann Mae Schidt was in the Off-Beat last night. She said she was drinking at the Manger Bar with her husband and another couple Friday night and got into an argument with them. She left the bar—alone—and got accosted by a Mexican outside.

The Mexican pulled her into a car and attempted to rape her. He couldn't accomplish the act. Ann Mae escaped.

She didn't report the assault. She was afraid she'd be arrested for plain drunk.

Ann Mae was 40-ish and redhaired. The owner's wife gave Vickers her phone number: GI8-0696.

Vickers left her a card and worked his way over to the Manger. He got negative results at Kay's Cafe and the El Monte taxi stand.

A guy named Jack Groves was working the bar at the Manger. He recognized the victim's photo and said she was in the place Saturday night between 8:00 and 9:00. He thought she was alone.

Groves did not know the name Ann Mae Schidt. He said the owners—Carl Manger and his wife—might know her. They were working Saturday night. They might have more information pertaining to the redhead.


Lavonne Chambers was divorced. She lived in a small house with her three small kids. Hallinen and Lawton took her formal statement there.

STATEMENT OF LAVONNE CHAMBERS. TAKEN AT 823 FOXDALE AVENUE, WEST COVINA. PRESENT: SERGEANT W. E. HALLINEN, SERGEANT J. G. LAWTON. 3:55 P.M., JUNE 25, 1958. FOR FILE #Z-483-362. REPORTED BY: DELLA ANDREW, STENOGRAPHIC REPORTER.

BY SGT LAWTON:

Q What is your name?

A Lavonne Chambers.

Q Do you have a middle name?

A Marie.

Q How old are you, Mrs. Chambers?

A Twenty-nine.

Q And your home address?

A 823 Foxdale, West Covina.

Q And your phone number?

A Edgewood 7-6686.

Q What is your business or occupation?

A Car hop at Stan's Drive-In.

Q Is that Stan's Drive-In, at Five Points, El Monte?

A Yes.

Q On Saturday night, June the 21st, in the early morning hours of June 22nd, were you working at Stan's, in that capacity as a car hop?

A Yes.

Q And during the course of the evening, when you were serving different cars, was there any particular car that came in—and occupants—that attracted your attention?

A Well, it was after I came back from eating. I usually eat at 9:00 o'clock. It's usually 10:00, when I come back. After that, I saw this woman—she's the one that attracted me, more than the man.

Q The woman attracted you, more than the man. And it was after ten?

A It was after ten.

Q Could it have been closer to eleven?

A It could have been, but it seems it was closer to ten, because it wasn't too long after I came back from eating.

Q What kind of car were this man and woman in?

A It was a dark green Oldsmobile, it was a '55 or '56, and more than likely, a '55, by the paint. It was a real dull finish, and the paint was like it had never been waxed.

Q What type of body?

A Sedan.

Q Do you know the difference in the Oldsmobile series, between the regular line and the Holiday series?

A Yeah. I know the Holiday is a longer car.

Q Is it your impression this was, or was not a Holiday?

A This was not.

Q It was not?

A Uh huh.

Q You recall we talked to you last night, over at Stan's, and it seems like you said something—it was a possibility it might have been two-toned?

A It is possible. If it was two-toned, it was all green—a lighter shade of green and a darker green.

Q What is your best recollection, at this particular time? You have probably thought about it since we talked to you last night, along those lines, as to whether it was or was not a two-tone.

A I still feel it was a two-tone.

Q The bottom part being the darkest of the two colors?

A Uhhuh.

Q You said that this woman is the one that attracted your attention the most? Why was that?

A Well, usually you walk up to a car and you ask them if they want a menu, and they say yes, or they say no. But she didn't know what she wanted. But she said, "I want a sandwich, the smallest sandwich you got." And I started to say, "A hot dog?" and she says, "Thinnest sandwich you have." I said, "That will be a grilled cheese." She said, "Okay". He didn't say anything, and I waited for him to order, and he said, "Just coffee." And I took the order. And when I went to pick up the tray, I noticed the ring—the way she was sitting. She was smiling and laughing all the time, real gay.

Q Excuse me. You said you noticed the ring, the way she was sitting?

A When I was at his window, the ring was on this finger, so I could see that. (Indicating.)

Q Indicating by that, you mean your wedding ring finger?

A Uh huh.

Q On her left hand?

A Uh huh.

Q Can you describe that ring?

A It was an enormous pearl, it was so big.

Q Anything else, in particular, about it?

A It looked really bigger, I guess, because the way her hand was. It looked like it went all the way around, because I could see the big part of the pearl.

Q Anything in addition to the pearl?

A No, just the pearl, and the dress she had on. The blue dress—I noticed that.

Q Again, if you recall, we showed you a coat that has two different types of material, the outside being linen, kind of dark blue, and the inside lining a silk material, like varied-colored blue.

A That's what it was, a blue print dress.

Q The cloth that you saw, that lined this coat that we showed you last night, was the same material?

A As the dress.

Q Was it your impression that this woman had been drinking?

A Yes, she was—oh, I'd say, pretty drunk.

Q You'd say she was pretty drunk?

A Uh huh.

Q How about the man?

A No, he wasn't. If he was drunk, he didn't show it. He seemed very sober.

Q Can you describe this woman to us?

A She was thin, with short dark red hair and very pleasant—real nice personality, or seemed to have. The kind you look twice at her.

Q How old a woman do you think she was?

A I don't know. I am not a very good judge of ages.

Q Well, as I recall, you are 29.

A I'd say she was older than I am.

Q How much older than you?

A Gee, I don't know.

Q Well, could she have been 40 years old, in your opinion?

A She could have been.

Q I don't want to put ideas in your mind, I want your best recollection, just trying to help you recollect, a little bit. How about the man, what did he look like?

A Dark, very thin. Thin face, had dark hair, hair combed straight back.

Q You say dark hair. Could it have been dark brown, or black?

A It was either black, or awfully dark brown.

Q Did it appear that he used some kind of preparation on it, that made it lay down?

A Oh, to make it lay down, maybe. I didn't notice much. He had quite a thick head of hair. It wasn't thick—it was receded back, a little bit. But he still had quite a bit of hair on top.

Q Lay down flat on top?

A Uh huh.

Q How old do you think he was?

A In his thirties—middle thirties, past.

Q Between thirty-five and forty, possibly?

A Uh huh.

Q What nationality would you think he might be?

A She, of course, I didn't think about her being anything but just American—but for him, I'd take him for a Greek or Italian.

Q Greek or Italian. Is it possible he might have been Mexican or Spanish-type, Latin-type?

A He could have been. (Pause.) His tan was, seemed like he wasn't dark enough to be a Mexican. 'Course, I know there's lots of light ones, but—

Q Was there anything particular about the condition of her clothing, at this time?

A No, I didn't notice. I noticed the dress she had on, when I first waited on them. I know it was low-necked, because the light was shining.

Q About this car. Since we have talked to you last

night, have you thought of anything, at all, that might be distinguishing about the car, that could help us?

A No, I thought about the car, last night. I thought, too, it must have had a California license on it. If it had been an out-of-state license, I would have noticed it. We work for tips, and about 99% of the out-of-state cars, you never make anything out of, so you notice them. And I didn't notice that the car didn't have the California license on it, so chances are that it did.

Q How about dented fenders, or broken grillwork, or anything like that? Do you recall anything—

A (Interrupting) I just noticed that the paint, the finish, was so dull.

Q Did you hear them—after they finished their order and paid you and left—did you hear or see them leave?

A No.

Q Did you, at any time, hear the car running?

A Huh uh. The car wasn't running when I went to pick up the tray.

Q And you didn't hear them drive away?

A No.

Q In other words, you wouldn't know whether it had loud pipes or anything like that on it?

A No.

Q Then, I understand that you saw this car again, later on. When was that?

A Sunday morning, after the bar was closed. It must have been around 2:15 or a little after, because we don't usually get a crowd in there until about 2:15. But usually the lot's full by 2:15, and they parked in back, almost to the back, right where we have the light shining over on the side, on her. And I went back to the car, and of course, asked them if they wanted a menu. She spoke up and said she wanted a bowl of chili and a cup of coffee. And I stood there, waiting for him to order, and I guess I wouldn't have noticed him—I waited for him to order, and finally he said, "Just coffee."

Q You said she ordered a bowl of chili?

A Uh huh.

Q Just chili, or chili and beans?

A Just chili and coffee.

Q Would there be some beans in the chili, though?

A Yes, always. That's always served as chili and beans. We don't serve straight chili.

Q What was her condition, at this time?

A She was a little drunker than she was the first time, but she was still very pleasant. She wasn't nasty. Real pleasant to wait on, gay and laughing, and when I picked up the tray, she said something—I tried to remember what she said to me, or to him, but I can't remember what she said, and who she was talking to, but she said something and laughed, and I smiled at her, and I couldn't remember what she said.

Q What was the condition of her clothing, at this time?

A Her clothes were all right, except for the front of her dress. 'Course, the way the dress was made, I could see practically the whole breast, one side.

Q It wasn't covered by a brassiere?

A No, I couldn't see no brassiere. I could see something white, that I took for a slip, with a little white lace on it.

Q Could that have been her brassiere, pushed down?

A It could have been, but they don't usually have lace on them.

Q Could you see her feet, at all?

A No, I couldn't see her feet. I could have, if I had looked, but I didn't. I have to reach quite a ways inside the car, to get the trays out, and put the inside trays in.

Q What impression did you get, at this time, regarding her appearance, as to what her activity had been, just prior to coming in, on this occasion?

A Oh, I don't know. She didn't look much different than she did the first time I saw her. I got a better look at her because I was on her side of the car.

Q Could it have been possible that, because of the appearance that you have just described her as being in, the clothing, that they could have just come from a petting party somewhere?

A They could have. It is possible.

Q She gave no indication, at this time, that she was upset or mad, or anything?

A No, she was very pleasant, very gay. She was laughing. The picture of her smiling, I remembered so well, because she laughed all the time.

Q He didn't smile any?

A No, he seemed very bored with it. Except, I had to wait for a minute for him to pay me. The last time I waited on him, I waited again, so I went up and told him how much the bill was. I had to wait a few minutes, 'fore he had the money in his hand, and gave me a dollar bill. I gave him change, walked around to the other side of the car. The tip he left was on the tray.

Q How did he pay you, each time? Both times with a dollar bill?

A I don't remember the first time, but I remember the last time.

Q Do you recall whether he took it out of his pocket, or out of a wallet?

A He had it in his hand, but it was a few minutes before he gave it to me, when I told him what the amount was.

Q Have you ever seen these persons before, either one of them?

A Not that I remember. I don't remember ever seeing them, before.

Q Is there any doubt in your mind, since we have talked to you the first time, and showed you the article of clothing and the pictures that we have of this woman, that they belong to and are the same person that you waited on that night?

A There is no doubt of it.

Q If you saw this man again, would you be able to identify him?

A I am quite sure I would. I remember him, in my mind. There is nothing so outstanding about him that I could describe him, no features that would point him out in a crowd. But I know, in my mind, what he looks like.

Q Well, you said he had a thin face. Was it an extremely thin face?

A It was like Italian or Greek—a nose like that. And thin, real thin face.

Q Did you get any impression that he might have had false teeth, or not?

A No.

Q You know, sometimes, people that have false teeth—either in or out—their jaws kind of sag, around here. Did you get that impression?

A No, I didn't.

Q Nothing other than the thinness?

A No.


BY SGT. HALLINEN:

Q You have probably given this considerable thought, since we talked to you yesterday. Would you describe, if you can, the man's clothing?

A It was light, that's all I can remember. It was a jacket, or something with long sleeves, and it was light.

Q You are fairly certain it was light?

A Uh huh.

Q On the sport side, or would it be of the regular suit type?

A No, it wasn't a suit. It was some kind of a jacket. I'd say it was a sport jacket.

Q You don't know the color of his trousers?

A No.

Q Do you recall whether he had a shirt on, light or dark?

A He had a shirt on, but I don't recall that—I don't remember if it was light or dark.

Q Would you be able to recognize a car similar to this one?

A Oh, yeah.

Q In other words, you'd be able to tell a car, whether it was similar, or not similar?

A I could tell, I'd know. I probably couldn't pick the car out, that particular car, but if I saw a car like it, I could tell.

Q You feel, at that time you'd know, when you saw it, whether the car you have in mind for this car would be two-toned or one-toned?

A Uh huh.

Q Did you notice whether either one of them smoked, while they were in there?

A I never noticed.

Q Going back to this man's features, was his skin swarthy, or regular, smooth, in your opinion?

A It was smooth, it was dark.

Q Would he be a light-complected man?

A No, he was a dark-complexioned man.

Q But light skin?

A No, his skin wasn't light, but it wasn't dark. Not like you see a real dark Mexican, like that. It was a dark skin, like an Italian.

Q You mentioned the hair as being black, and straight back?

A Uh huh.

Q And also, that it receded at the forehead?

A Slight—receded slightly. Not very much.

Q And a thick head of hair, though?

A Yes, his hair was quite thick on top.

Q Was there anything distinguishable about his ears?

A I don't remember.

Q Outstanding, or—

A (Shook head from left to right.)

SGT. LAWTON: One other thing. Did you notice whether
   he wore any kind of jewelry, such as rings?
A No, I didn't notice.

SGT. LAWTON: Thank you very much.

STATEMENT CONCLUDED AT 4:15 P.M.

A region-wide teletype went out Wednesday night. It
summarized the Ellroy case seventy-two hours in.

It mentioned the victim's missing purse and undergarments, the male suspect, the blond woman and the '55–'56
Olds. All police agencies with information were directed to
contact Sheriff's Homicide or the El Monte PD.

A California Highway Patrol man called in a tip at 10:10 p.m.
The El Monte PD desk man logged it.

The CHP man knew a "dark Latin type" with a two-tone
Olds. The guy hung out around Five Points. His vehicle had
press photographer plates and a whip antenna. The dark Latin
type had a surly disposition and liked to monitor police radio
calls. The CHP man said he'd get his plate number and call
it in.

The teletype drew heat fast. Dead white women always
stirred things up.

Thursday morning.

Vickers and Godfrey concluded their canvassing and
reached the last of their callback people. The victim's
Saturday-night whereabouts were now halfway sketched in.

Hallinen and Lawton sent a RUSH query to the California
DMV. They requested stats on all '55 and '56 Oldsmobiles
registered to San Gabriel Valley owners. They sent a second
RUSH order, to the Sheriff's Records Bureau.

They requested mug shots and file data on registered sex
offenders resembling the dark man. Their suspect was most
likely Caucasian—but he could be a racial Latin. They added
notes on the suspect's vehicle and the crime itself: beating,

strangulation, probable rape. Their victim was a 43-year-old white woman known to frequent cocktail bars.

Lavonne Chambers and Margie Trawick were transported to the Hall of Justice. A deputy helped them construct Identi-Kit portraits of the suspect.

The Identi-Kit was a new device. Witnesses picked out individual features printed on cardboard strips and built mix-and-match faces from memory. There were dozens of chins, noses, hairlines and mouths to build from. Skilled technicians helped the witnesses put them together.

The deputy worked with Lavonne and Margie separately. The result was two similar—but distinctly differentiated—faces.

Lavonne's man looked like a lean-faced average guy. Margie's man looked vicious.

A sketch artist was brought in. He sat down with both witnesses and elicited separate portraits of the suspect. His third run-through melded features from the two previous versions. Lavonne and Margie agreed: He's the guy we saw.

The sketch man mimeographed copies of the picture and gave them to Hallinen and Lawton. They routed them to the Information Bureau—to be included in a press release on the Ellroy homicide.

A deputy drove Lavonne and Margie home. Hallinen and Lawton arranged to interview the victim's co-workers and search her house again.

The case was four days old.


Thursday afternoon.

Jim Bruton called a contact at the El Monte Unified School District. The man gave him Peter Tubiolo's home number.

Bruton called Tubiolo and asked him to come to the station—for the purpose of answering a few questions. The matter to be discussed was the Jean Ellroy murder.

Tubiolo agreed to come in that afternoon. He stressed that he hardly knew the woman. Bruton told him it was just routine and assured him that the interview would remain confidential.

A time was set. Bruton called Hallinen and Lawton and told

them to drive out. They said they'd bring Margie Trawick and let her take a look at the man.

Peter Tubiolo was prompt. Bruton, Hallinen and Lawton talked to him in a mirrored interview room. Tubiolo was heavyset and round-faced. He did not resemble the dark man in any way, shape, manner or form.

He was the vice-principal of Anne LeGore Elementary School. The victim's son just completed the fifth grade there. He was a frightened and rather volatile child.

Tubiolo said he met Jean Ellroy on only one occasion. She came to his school to discuss her son's poor scholastic progress and inability to get along with other children. He did not "date" or "socialize" with the late Mrs. Ellroy. Such actions were against school district policy.

The cops told him the kid said otherwise. Tubiolo stuck to his story. All he knew about the Ellroys' private life was that the parents were divorced and the boy wasn't allowed to see his father during the week. Mrs. Ellroy was a fine woman—but there was nothing personal between them.

Margie Trawick observed Tubiolo. She got a good close look through the mirror.

She told the cops he wasn't the guy. They cut Tubiolo loose with apologies.


Ward Hallinen got a tip Thursday night. The West Covina PD had a suspect: a local foul ball named Steve Anthony Carbone.

Hallinen had Frank Godfrey check it out. Godfrey ran a make on Carbone and came back enthusiastic.

Carbone was a white male American of Italian descent. His DOB was 2/19/15. He was 5′ 10″ and 140 pounds, with hazel eyes, straight black hair and a high forehead. He owned a '55 Olds two-door sedan, polar white over green, license MMT 879.

He hailed from Detroit, Michigan. He was popped three times for indecent exposure: 10/41, 11/41, 8/53. He moved to West Covina in '57. He ran up a string of three drunk drivings and two assault-with-a-deadly-weapon beefs. His last ADW was notable. He pulled a 30.30 carbine on a cop.

Carbone was foul-tempered and belligerent. Carbone was a well-known cop hater and a sex offender.

Hallinen and Lawton jumped on him.

They had the West Covina PD haul him in. They had his Oldsmobile impounded and photographed in the PD parking lot. A Sheriff's lab man dusted it, checked it for bloodstains and vacuumed it for fibers resembling the white ones found on the victim.

The lab man came up empty.

Hallinen and Lawton leaned on Carbone. He gave them a vague account of his actions Saturday night. Jim Bruton brought Margie Trawick and Lavonne Chambers in for a show-up.

They both said he wasn't the guy they saw with the redhead.


Hallinen and Lawton worked straight through the weekend.

They talked to the victim's co-workers and failed to turn up any leads. They walked through the victim's house again. They spent hours at the Desert Inn and talked to dozens of patrons. Nobody could put a handle on the blonde or the dark man.

Metro got a tip on a guy named Robert John Mellon—a former mental patient from North Dakota. A deputy checked Mellon out and wrote the tip off as worthless.

A man named Archie G. Rogers called in a tip to the El Monte PD.

He said a guy named Bill Owen had a girlfriend named Dorothy. They sort of matched the description of those people in the paper—the folks seen with the dead nurse.

Owen was a painter and a mechanic. He used to live with Mr. Rogers' sister. Dorothy frequented the Manger and the Wee Nipee bar. She slept in Mr. Rogers' car Saturday night, June 21st.

Dorothy's phone number was ED4-6881. Dorothy said she had a new friend named Jean. Dorothy planned to bring Jean by Mr. Rogers' sister's house that Saturday night.

Mr. Rogers found the whole thing suspicious.

The El Monte PD forwarded the tip to Sheriff's Metro. Deputy Howie Haussner—Jack Lawton's brother-in-law—handled it.

He got Rogers' sister's address and matched Dorothy's phone number to a Harold T. Hotchkiss in Azusa. He attached the two addresses to the names William Owen and Dorothy Hotchkiss and teletyped them to the Criminal Records Bureau in Sacramento.

The kickback was inconclusive.

The name Dorothy Hotchkiss came back blank: no record, no wants, no warrants, no listing at the Azusa address. "William Owen" came back six times over—various Owens with criminal records dating back to '39. None of the Owens lived in the San Gabriel Valley.

The Owen-Hotchkiss paperwork was stuffed in an accordion file. The file was marked Z-483-362.


Jean Ellroy was buried on Tuesday, July 1st, 1958.

A rent-a-preacher performed a Protestant service. She was placed in the ground at Inglewood Cemetery—out in southwest L.A.

Jean's sister and brother-in-law were there. Some Airtek people showed up. Armand Ellroy and a few of Jean's old friends attended.

Jack Lawton and Ward Hallinen were there.

Jean's son copped a plea and stayed away. He spent the day watching TV with some friends of his dad's.

The headstone was marked "Geneva Hilliker Ellroy. 1915–1958."

The plot was on the west edge of the cemetery. It was inches from a busy street and a stretch of chain-link fence.

# 4

The L.A. Sheriff's Office hailed from the Wild West days. It was a modern police agency suffused with 19th-century nostalgia. The LASO embraced Wild West motifs wholesale. It made for brilliant PR.

The Sheriff's manned county lockups and patrolled county turf out of twelve substations. Said turf ran through the city of Los Angeles and out into the north-, south- and eastbound boonies. Deputies worked the desert, the mountains and a swanky stretch of beach. Their jurisdiction took in hundreds of square miles.

Malibu was plum duty. West Hollywood was good—the Sunset Strip was always percolating. East L.A. was full of rowdy Mexicans. Firestone was wall-to-wall colored. Temple City and San Dimas were out in the San Gabriel Valley. Deputies could drive up into the foothills and shoot coyotes for kicks.

The Sheriff's Detective Bureau investigated criminal actions county-wide. Sheriff's Homicide handled murders for numerous Mickey Mouse police departments. The Sheriff's Aero Bureau flew county skies and supplanted rescue operations.

The Sheriff's Office was expanding full-tilt. 1958 L.A. was a boomtown.

Los Angeles was always rough-and-ready. The place was built from land grabs and racial grief. The L.A. Sheriff's Office was chartered in 1850. It was meant to bring rule to an unruly slice of land.

The first string of County Sheriffs were elected to one-year terms. They dealt with marauding Indians, Mexican bandits and Chinese tong wars. Vigilantes were a significant threat. Drunken white men loved to lynch redskins and dusky bandidos.

L.A. County grew. Elected Sheriffs came and went. The sworn deputy force grew, concurrent with county expansion. Civilian help was often required. The Sheriff would deputize men and form them into mounted posses.

The L.A. Sheriff's Office modernized. Cars replaced horses. Larger jails and more substations were built. The L.A. Sheriff's Office grew to be the largest of its kind in the continental U.S. of A.

Sheriff John C. Cline resigned in 1920. Big Bill Traeger served the remainder of his term. Traeger was elected to three four-year terms of his own. He ran for Congress in 1932—and won. The County Board of Supervisors appointed Eugene W. Biscailuz Sheriff.

Biscailuz joined the Sheriff's Office in 1907. He was half Anglo and half Spanish-Basque. His people came from money. His California roots went back to the Spanish land-grant days.

Biscailuz was a brilliant administrator. He was politically deft and likable. He was a public relations genius with a huge love of Wild West lore.

Biscailuz was a half-assed progressive. Some of his views were near-Bolshevik. He expressed those views in an avuncular manner. He was rarely accused of spouting heresy.

Biscailuz mobilized forces to fight fires and floods and developed the county's "Major Disaster Plan." Biscailuz built the Wayside Honor Rancho and shaped its rehabilitative policy. Biscailuz launched a juvenile crime deterrence program.

Biscailuz intended to hold his post for a good long time. Wild West rituals helped assure his re-elections.

He reinstated the Sheriff's Mounted Posse. The Posse rode in parades and searched for occasional lost kids out in the boondocks. Biscailuz was often photographed with the Posse. He always rode a palomino stallion.

Biscailuz sponsored the annual Sheriff's Rodeo. Uniformed

deputies sold tickets all over the county. The rodeo usually sold out the L.A. Coliseum. Biscailuz appeared in western garb, replete with twin six-shooters.

The rodeo was a moneymaker and a goodwill extravaganza. Ditto the annual Sheriff's Bar-B-Q that fed at a rate of 60,000 a year.

Biscailuz took the Sheriff's Office out to the people. He seduced them with his very own myth. Mythic show-and-tell perpetuated his power. It was blue-ribbon disingenuousness.

Biscailuz knew that a lot of his boys called Negroes "niggers." Biscailuz knew that phone book beatings assured rapid confessions. Biscailuz rounded up Japs and locked them down at Wayside after Pearl Harbor. Biscailuz knew that one shot with a beaver-tail sap could knock a suspect's eyes clean out of his head. Biscailuz knew that police work was an isolating profession.

So he gave his constituents the Wild West as Utopian Idyll. It got him re-elected six times. He backed his ritualistic bullshit up to an ambiguous degree. His boys were less suppression-minded than their cross-town rivals in blue.

William Parker took over the LAPD in 1950. He was an organizational genius. His personal style was inimical to Gene Biscailuz's. Parker abhorred monetary corruption and embraced violence as an essential part of police work. He was an alcoholic martinet on a mission to reinstate pre-20th-century morality.

Biscailuz and Parker ruled parallel kingdoms. Biscailuz's myth implicitly stressed inclusion. Parker co-opted a TV honcho named Jack Webb. They cooked up a weekly saga called *Dragnet*—a crime-and-severe-punishment myth that ordained the LAPD with a chaste image and godlike powers. The LAPD took their myth to heart. They stuck their heads up their asses and isolated themselves from the public that Gene Biscailuz embraced. Bill Parker hated Negroes and sent goons down to Darktown to lean on club owners who admitted white women. Gene Biscailuz liked to schmooze with his Mexican constituents. He was sort of a taco-bender himself.

Gene Biscailuz's myth was strictly local stuff. Bill Parker's myth was marketed nationally. The Sheriff's resented the

LAPD's celebrity. The LAPD considered the Sheriff's a bush-league outfit and hogged the credit for their joint operations.

Ideology divided the two agencies. Topography divided them more. The LAPD pointed to their densely packed juris-diction and racial demographics as proof of their superiority and the justification for their state-of-siege mentality. The Sheriff's pointed to the county spreading out at a boom rate.

They had new turf to learn. New cities were signing up for contract services. They simply couldn't afford to kick indiscriminate ass.

Bill Parker turned 56 in 1958. His sensibility was on the rise. Gene Biscailuz turned 75 and planned to retire at the end of the year.

Biscailuz joined the Sheriff's Office 50 years before. He saw horses replaced by flivvers and "Grey Ghost" sedans and Ford black & whites. He saw his Wild West Los Angeles grow and reinvent itself—way outside the borders of his myth.

He probably knew that white settlers raped Indian squaws. He probably knew that Wild West lawmen were psychopaths and drunks. He might have conceded that his myth was mostly wishful thinking and moonshine.

He might call nostalgia an indulgence. He probably knew that the Wild West played hell on women—then and now.

He probably knew that Wild West Saturday Nights comprised a myth of their own. He might have written that redhaired nurse off as a mythic casualty.

**5**

The investigation continued.

Hallinen and Lawton worked it full-time. Jim Bruton stayed on board. Godfrey and Vickers moved on to fresh assignments.

The L.A. papers ran the sketch of the suspect and dropped the story cold. The redhead never clicked as a victim. The Lana Turner/Cheryl Crane/Johnny Stompanato case hogged all the headlines.

Hallinen and Lawton habituated the Desert Inn. They talked to regular patrons and people passing through. They got no solid leads. They hit the other bars around Five Points repeatedly. They tapped out everywhere.

The El Monte PD kept the pressure on. Patrol units rode with the sketch and a snapshot of the victim. Local awareness ran high.

The PD logged a tip on Thursday, July 3rd. A man said he saw four guys dumping beer cans in the Rio Hondo Wash a few weeks ago. They drove up in an Olds 88, license HHP 815. One of the guys said he had a date with a nurse named Jean coming up that evening.

The tip was checked out. The car was identified as a '53 Oldsmobile coupe. It was registered to Bruce S. Baker, 12060 Hallwood, El Monte. Baker and his friends were interviewed and crossed off as suspects.

Hallinen and Lawton reinterviewed the victim's co-workers and located her friends. Everybody stuck to the chaste Jean

Ellroy line. Nobody conjured up a ponytailed blonde or a dark man. Jean's ex-boyfriend Hank Hart was picked up and cut loose fast. He was short and fat and had one thumb. He was alibied up for the night of June 21st.

Hallinen and Lawton checked out recent choke jobs and tried to identify a pattern. One Sheriff's case and two city cases caught their attention.

Helene Kelly, DOD 10/30/53, Rosemead. Beaten and manually strangled inside her house. The victim was old. She wasn't raped. It looked like a botched burglary.

Ruth Goldsmith, DOD 4/5/57, the Wilshire District in L.A. The victim was 50 years old. She was found on her bathroom floor, partially clad. She was raped. Her wrists were bound behind her back with a nylon stocking. A washcloth was stuffed into her mouth and cinched by another nylon. The victim died of suffocation. Her apartment was not ransacked. LAPD detectives ruled out burglary.

Marjorie Hipperson, DOD 6/10/57, the Los Feliz District in L.A. The victim was 24 years old. She was found on her bed, with her nightgown up over her hips. She was raped. A nylon stocking was tied to her right wrist. A second nylon was cinched around her neck. Her lips were bruised. A white washcloth gag was found under her head.

All three cases were stalled dead. The MOs diverged from the Ellroy job more than they connected.

The Sheriff's Records Bureau kicked loose mug shots and rap sheets: forty-odd sex offenders resembling the dark man.

Most of the men were white. A dozen were classified "Male Mexicans." Their sex offenses ran the gamut. Most of the men were on county parole.

Some had left L.A. Some were back in jail. Hallinen and Lawton ran all the mugs by Lavonne Chambers and Margie Trawick. They struck out uniformly.

They leaned on the most dark-man-like guys just to be sure. They found them at home and had their parole officers roust them. They struck out all the way.

Other agencies sent in mug shots. Hallinen and Lawton ran them by Lavonne and Margie.

Lavonne and Margie kept saying no. They were decisive witnesses. They knew what they knew.

Lavonne had three kids out of one failed marriage. She was making good tax-free coin at Stan's Drive-In. Her boyfriend was a deputy at the Temple City Station. The carhops at Stan's fed the Temple boys for free—so they'd chase down check dashers and pry money out of them. Station trustees washed and waxed Lavonne's car. Lavonne knew her way around cops.

Margie had a 14-year-old daughter. Her bookie husband died of a heart attack back in '48. Margie blew the money he left her and moved in with her parents. She looked sort of like a brunette Jean Ellroy. She knew the El Monte bar scene intimately. She was in poor health and strung out on doctor-prescribed dope.

Lavonne and Margie dug the whole witness scene. Hallinen and Lawton liked them. They dawdled over coffee when they brought mug shots by.

They got a tip that the victim's hairdresser resembled the dark man. They took Lavonne by his salon and treated her to a rinse-and-style. Lavonne said he wasn't the guy. He was a flamboyant swish moreover.

More tips came in.

7/11/58:

A man named Padilla called the El Monte PD. He said he got released from the Hall of Justice Jail on June 30th. He saw a man resembling the suspect walk out of a bar on South Main Street.

7/13/58:

A man named Don Kessler called the Temple City Sheriff's Office. He stated that he worked at the El Monte Bowl and saw a man resembling the suspect in his establishment. Mr. Kessler's mother followed the man to the Bonnie Rae bar. The man ditched her. The man was dirty and appeared to be a Mexican.

7/14/58:

The Temple Sheriff's relayed a tip to the El Monte PD. It involved another dirty man at the El Monte Bowl.

The man resembled the suspect. The man was wearing

dirty tan trousers. An El Monte PD officer found a similar pair of trousers on the street a short time later. The officer picked them up, brought them to the station and placed them on Captain Bruton's desk.

The El Monte PD had Dead White Woman Fever.

A Coroner's Inquest was held on Tuesday, July 15th. Dr. Charles Langhauser presided. Jack Lawton represented the Los Angeles County Sheriff's Office.

Six jurors heard evidence. The inquest was held in Room 150 at the Hall of Justice.

Armand Ellroy testified first. He stated that he had no recent relationship with his ex-wife and hadn't seen her alive in over two years. He stated that he viewed her body on Monday, June 23rd, and acknowledged that her full name was Geneva Hilliker Ellroy, 43 years of age and a native of Wisconsin.

George Krycki testified. He described a brief conversation he had with the victim on Saturday, June 21st. Jean did not appear to be inebriated. He said it was funny—"Her face seemed to be always made up."

Jack Lawton asked Krycki several questions. He emphasized the victim's friends.

Krycki said he didn't know her friends. His wife might—she knew Mrs. Ellroy better than he did.

Anna May Krycki testified. Langhauser ran her through her activities on the night of June 21st and cut back to the issue of Jean Ellroy's friends. Mrs. Krycki said she only knew one couple—older people currently visiting Europe.

Lawton took over. He asked Mrs. Krycki if Jean ever asked her to recommend a place to have a drink.

Mrs. Krycki said, "Yes"—but she told Jean there was *no* place she could go unescorted. She *did* mention the Desert Inn and Suzanne's. They were popular El Monte nightclubs.

Lawton asked her if she ever recommended any restaurants. Mrs. Krycki said she recommended Valdez's and Morrow's. The conversation occurred a month before the murder. Jean never said if she went to any of those places.

Lawton asked Mrs. Krycki if she ever saw Jean drunk. Mrs. Krycki said, "Never." Lawton asked her if she ever saw Jean take a drink at all. Mrs. Krycki revised her Jean-the-Teetotaler line. She said Jean had a few glasses of sherry in the evening.

Lawton asked Mrs. Krycki if Jean ever confided her troubles. Mrs. Krycki said she mentioned her ex-husband once in a while. Lawton asked her about Jean's men friends. Mrs. Krycki denied that such friends existed.

Dr. Langhauser excused Mrs. Krycki.

Deputy Vic Cavallero took the stand and described the crime scene at Arroyo High School.

Margie Trawick was sworn in. She described the events she witnessed at the Desert Inn. She said the suspect looked like a man who'd had all his teeth pulled. He was just that thin in the jaw.

Jack Lawton testified. He summarized the Ellroy case three weeks in.

He said the victim appeared to be drunk at Stan's Drive-in. He said several people thought they'd seen the victim that Saturday night. Their information was unverified. Margie Trawick, Lavonne Chambers and Myrtle Mawby were their only verified eyewitnesses.

He said they'd run down a good bunch of suspects. He said all of the men were cleared. The investigation was still going forward.

Dr. Langhauser excused the jury. They returned with a verdict fast:

"Asphyxia, due to strangulation by ligature, inflicted on the deceased by a person or persons unknown to this jury at this time; and from the testimony introduced at this time, we find the death of the deceased was homicidal, and that the unknown person or persons was criminally responsible therefor."


Salvador Quiroz Serena was an ex-Airtek machinist. He was a 35-year-old Mexican. He was 5'6", 160 pounds, with black hair and brown eyes. His pal Enrique "Tito" Mancilla ratted him off for the Jean Ellroy snuff. Serena was known to drive a '55 Olds sedan.

Sheriff's Homicide caught the call. Hallinen and Lawton were incommunicado. Sergeant Al Sholund handled the tip.

He sent a teletype to the State Records Bureau. They replied fast. Serena had a full-page rap sheet.

One burglary pop. One ADW pop. One bigamy conviction. The suspect was registered as a resident alien and a resident ex-con.

Sholund teletyped the state DMV. They replied fast.

Serena owned a '54 Olds coupe. His last known address: 952 Westmoreland, L.A.

The address didn't match the address Mancilla gave him. Sholund drove to Airtek and braced Mancilla.

Mancilla said he knew Serena for two years—during and after his Airtek stint. Serena was pals with two other Airtek guys: Jim Foster and George Erqueja.

Serena was down in Mexico recently. He returned to L.A. last month. Jim Foster found him a pad at his apartment house in Culver City.

Mancilla visited Serena on or about June 23rd. He said, "Did you hear what happened to Jean?" Serena said, "No." Mancilla told him that Jean had been murdered. Serena did not seem surprised.

Serena said he danced with Jean at a company picnic last year. He said, "I could have had her if I wanted to."

Serena showed up at Mancilla's house seven or eight days later. He wanted to borrow Tito's car. Mancilla turned him down. Serena returned that night. He said he was moving to Sacramento.

Sholund found Jim Foster and George Erqueja on the premises. They supplied identical stories: Serena moved to Sacramento and got a job with the Aerojet Company. Sholund drove back to the Hall of Justice and laid out a detailed memo for Jack Lawton.

Lawton got the memo. He called Aerojet and talked to the personnel manager. The man said Salvador Quiroz Serena was most likely a recent hire named Salvador Escalante. Lawton said he'd be driving up to talk to him. He told the personnel man to keep that confidential.

The personnel man said he'd cooperate. Lawton called Jim

Bruton and ran the Escalante thing by him. They decided to drive up to Sacramento.

They made the drive that night. They got a motel room and went to Aerojet the next morning—July 17th.

The security boss delivered Serena AKA Escalante. Lawton and Bruton drove him to the Sacramento County Sheriff's Office and grilled him.

He was built stocky. He didn't really look like their guy.

He said he got married in Mexico on June 3rd. He moved back to California three weeks or so later. He heard a radio report on the murder while he was driving through El Centro. He ran into Tito Mancilla the next day. They discussed the nurse who got clipped.

He said his wife was his alibi. She didn't speak English, though.

Bruton called the local Border Patrol Office and nailed down an interpreter. They met him at the Escalante residence.

They talked to Elena Vivero Escalante. She alibied her husband up convincingly. They were in Mexico on June 21st. Salvador was never out of her sight. She corroborated all her husband's statements.

The suspect was released.


Sheriff's Homicide was a centralized division. It was made up of thirteen sergeants, two lieutenants and a captain. The squad room was above the County Morgue. A stench wafted up sometimes.

Murders were assigned on a rotating basis. There were no regular partnerships—the men were teamed up catch-as-catch-can. The unit was handpicked and elite. They handled sticky extortion cases under Sheriff Biscailuz's direct orders. Gene Biscailuz shot his top-secret shit straight to Homicide.

The unit handled suicides, industrial accidents and 35 to 50 murders a year. Twelve substations and a flock of contract cities fed them victims. Most of the men kept bottles in their desks. They drank in the squad room and hit the Chinatown bars on their way home.

Ward Hallinen was 46. Jack Lawton was 40. Their styles contrasted and clashed.

Ward was known as "the Silver Fox." He was a small man with light blue eyes and wavy gray-white hair. He wore slender-cut suits better than a window mannequin. He was soft-spoken, authoritative, meticulous. He did not like to carry a gun and disdained the rowdier aspects of police work. He did not like working with impatient and impetuous partners. He was married to former Sheriff Traeger's daughter. They had a girl in high school and a girl in her first year of college.

Jack was mid-sized, heavyset and balding. He was hard-charging, hardworking, thorough. If you gave Jack grief, he would kick the shit out of you in two seconds flat. He loved kids and animals. He routinely rescued dogs and cats found at crime scenes. He cut his homicide teeth in the army—investigating Jap war crimes. He dug the gravity of his work. It meshed with the volatile and protective parts of his nature. He had a tendency to fly off the handle. He was married and had three young sons.

Ward and Jack got along okay. They deferred to each other when they had to. They never let their conflicting styles fuck up a case.


The Ellroy case was stalled out. They weren't coming up with shit on the blonde and the dark man.

Court commitments interrupted them. Hallinen caught a Mexican knife killing on July 24th.

A punk named Hernandez got shivved. Three pachucos got popped at the scene. It all pertained to youth gang intrigue or somebody fucking somebody's sister.

Sheriff's Narco logged an Ellroy tip on August 1st. The tipster was a nurse named Mrs. Waggoner.

She said she answered a lovelorn ad and met a Mexican man named Joe the Barber. He was 45 years old, 5'11", 200 pounds. He drove a light green '55 Buick. Mrs. Waggoner had an affair with Joe the Barber. He tried to get her to steal narcotics from the hospital where she worked. He told her that he sold marijuana.

A Narco deputy liked the nurse angle. He forwarded the tip to Homicide. Joe the Barber was interviewed and crossed off as a suspect.

The El Monte PD logged a tip on August 3rd. Two Mexican men and a white woman reported it in person.

They said they were drinking at a Mexican place in La Puente. They met a man who offered to drive them wherever they wished to go. He was white, 25 to 30, 5′9″, 150 pounds, with dark brown hair and blue eyes. They got into his '39 Chevy Tudor.

He drove them to the San Dimas Wash. A '46 Ford truck pulled up behind them. The driver was white, 30 years old, 5′10″, 180 pounds, with blond hair and blue eyes.

They all stood around the Wash. The Chevy man grabbed the woman's necklace. He said if she wasn't careful she'd get it like that nurse in El Monte. The truck man did this "I hate Mexicans" number. One of the Mexican guys jumped him. The other Mexican guy and the woman escaped. The first Mexican guy beat up the truck man and joined them.

The informants left their names with the desk officer. He typed up a report and placed it in Captain Bruton's box.

The Ellroy case was stalled out. Hallinen caught a wife-stabs-husband job on August 29th.

Lillian Kella slashed Edward Kella—fatally good. She said he slapped her in the head once too often. The case was routine late-summer stuff.

Temple Patrol logged in a weird occurrence on September 2nd. It started outside the Kit Kat bar in El Monte.

Two deputies spotted a woman named Willie Jane Willis. She was leaning against a phone booth in a dazed condition. The Kit Kat's janitor said he saw Willie Jane get out of a yellow cement truck. The driver chased her around the truck, gave up the chase and drove off. Willie Jane showed the deputies a bump on her head.

The deputies drove Willie Jane to the Falk Medical Center. A doctor placed her on an examination table. Willie Jane started to rant. She said, "Carlos, don't kill her. I saw him kill her and dump her body by the school."

One of the deputies asked her if she meant Arroyo High.

Willie Jane attacked him and tried to run out a rear door. The deputies caught her and placed her in their patrol car. The emergency room doctor thought she was high on narcotics.

The deputies drove Willie Jane to the Temple City Station. She mumbled hysterically en route. The deputies heard her say, "I saw him kill her. He choked her and dumped her body by the school. I saw her face, it was purple, how horrible."

Willie Jane tried to jump out of the car. The deputies prevented her. Willie Jane said, "Don't take me back to that school, please don't make me go back there."

They arrived at the station. The deputies escorted Willie Jane inside. A detective interviewed her and forwarded a memo to Homicide.

Hallinen and Lawton wrote it off as bullshit.


The tips and nut reports died out. The Ellroy case moved into limbo.

Lawton caught a business-dispute killing on October 9th. Hallinen caught wife-shoots-husband jobs on the 12th and the 14th. A sex creep named Harvey Glatman was arrested on October 27th.

The CHP bagged him down in Orange County. He was struggling with a woman on a roadside near the Santa Ana Freeway. They fell out of Glatman's car and wrestled for the gun he pulled on her. A Highway Patrol guy saw the incident and made the arrest.

The woman's name was Lorraine Vigil. She was a pinup model from L.A. Glatman lured her out on a photo-session pretext. He said he had a studio in Anaheim.

Glatman was booked at the Orange County Sheriff's Office. They charged him with attempt rape and ADW. Deputies found clothesline cord, a camera, several rolls of film and a box of .32-caliber shells in his car. They checked old teletypes and missing persons reports and got three potential clicks.

8/1/57:

A pinup model named Judy Ann Dull disappeared. She was last seen with a photographer named Johnny Glynn. The two left Miss Dull's West Hollywood apartment and were never seen again. Harvey Glatman matched Johnny Glynn's description.

3/8/58:

A woman named Shirley Ann Bridgeford disappeared. She left her house in the San Fernando Valley with a man named George Williams. The two were never seen again. Miss Bridgeford belonged to a lonely-hearts club. Williams contacted her through the club directory. Harvey Glatman matched George Williams' description.

7/20/58:

A pinup model named Angela Rojas AKA Ruth Rita Mercado disappeared—and was never seen again.

Harvey Glatman agreed to take a polygraph test. The operator asked him questions pertaining to the three missing women. His responses indicated guilty knowledge. The operator pointed this out to him. Glatman said he killed the three women.

Bridgeford and Rojas were LAPD missings. Judy Ann Dull was an L.A. Sheriff's case. The Orange County cops notified both agencies.

Two LAPD detectives drove down to Orange County. Jack Lawton drove down to represent Sheriff's Homicide. Captain Jim Bruton came with him.

The interrogations ran long. Glatman had his details down pat.

Lawton questioned him regarding victim Dull. Sergeant Pierce Brooks questioned him regarding victim Bridgeford. Sergeant E. V. Jackson questioned him regarding victim Rojas.

Glatman said he saw a newspaper ad in late July '57. It offered pinup models at hourly rates. He called the number included and talked to a woman named Betty Carver. Miss Carver invited him over to view her portfolio.

The apartment was on North Sweetzer. Glatman arrived and asked Miss Carver if she was free for a session now. Miss Carver said she was busy. Glatman saw a photograph of her roommate Judy Dull. He asked if *she'd* be interested.

Miss Carver said she probably would be.

Glatman left and called back the next day. He talked to Judy Ann Dull and gave his name as Johnny Glynn. Miss Dull agreed to a two-hour session. Glatman drove to her apartment and picked her up.

They drove to his apartment in Hollywood. Glatman told her he wanted to sell some bound-and-gagged shots to *True Detective*. Miss Dull let him bind and gag her.

Glatman photographed her. Glatman pulled a gun on her. Glatman fondled her and raped her and forced her to pose in the nude with her legs spread.

They spent six hours at his apartment. Judy Ann did not resist his assaults. Glatman said she was actually eager. She told him she was a nympho and couldn't control herself around men.

Glatman tied her wrists and led her down to his car. It was 10:30 p.m.

He drove her east on the San Berdoo Freeway—90 miles or so out of L.A. They hit that big desert pocket around Indio. He turned off on a desolate switchback. He stopped the car and walked her off the road. He tied her ankles and placed her facedown in the sand.

He tied the slack end of the ankle cord around her neck. He stepped on her back. He yanked the middle of the cord and strangled her. He stripped her down to her panties and scooped sand over her body.

He got the itch again in March '58. He saw a lonely-hearts-club ad in the paper. He went out to the office, paid a fee and joined. He said his name was George Williams.

The director gave him some phone numbers. He made a date with a girl and went over to her place to check her out. She wasn't his type. He called Shirley Ann Bridgeford and arranged a date for Saturday night, March 8th.

He picked her up in full view of her whole goddamn family. He suggested a drive instead of a movie. Shirley Ann agreed.

Glatman drove her south, into San Diego County. They had dinner at a cafe and necked in the car. Shirley Ann said she had to be getting home.

Glatman drove her east. They parked off the freeway and necked a little more. Glatman pulled his gun and forced her into the backseat.

He raped her. He tied her hands and shoved her into the

front seat. He drove her farther east and stopped the car on a pitch-black desert road. He marched her out a good two miles and hogtied her and gagged her.

The sun came up. Glatman got out his camera and flash equipment.

He laid a blanket down. He photographed Shirley Ann bound and gagged. He cinched her neck to her ankles. He pulled the middle of his rope and strangled her.

He drove back to L.A. He developed the Shirley pictures. He put them in a metal box beside his Judy shots.

He got the itch again in July. He saw a cheesecake-model ad in the paper and called the number. Angela Rojas invited him over to her studio/pad on Pico.

Glatman showed up. Angela said she wasn't feeling good and asked him to take a raincheck. Glatman agreed. He came back the following night, uninvited.

Angela let him in. Glatman pulled his gun and forced her into her bedroom. He tied her feet and ankles and fondled her. He untied her and raped her. He held his gun to her back and marched her out to his car.

He drove her straight to the desert. He found a nesting spot around dawn.

He camped out with her all day. He raped her and photographed her. He drove her to a more isolated spot after dark.

He told her he wanted to take some more pictures. He walked her out into the toolies and set up his camera and flash gear.

He tied her up and gagged her and shot some film. He placed her facedown on a blanket and noosed her up neck-to-ankles. She kicked and thrashed and strangled herself to death. Glatman tossed some shrubs on the body and drove back to L.A.

Lawton mentioned the Jean Ellroy murder. Glatman said he didn't do it. He didn't know where El Monte was. He only killed the three women he just copped to. He didn't kill any redheaded nurse.

Glatman was booked on three counts of murder one. The cops and the Orange County DA discussed filing logistics.

Judy Ann Dull was murdered in Riverside County. Shirley Ann Bridgeford and Angela Rojas were murdered in San Diego County. Glatman assaulted Lorraine Vigil down in Orange. Harvey was fucked—his trial priority wasn't essential.

Glatman had two sex-assault priors. He spent five years in Sing Sing and two years in the Colorado State Pen. He was thirty years old and worked as a TV repairman. He was skinny. He looked like an undernourished little putz.

Lawton, Brooks and Jackson took a Harvey Glatman murder-site tour. Photographers, DAs and various deputy sheriffs went with them. Glatman led them straight to the bones of victim Bridgeford and victim Rojas.

Judy Dull's remains were found in December '57. They were Jane Doe-tagged at the Riverside County Coroner's Office.

The tour ended at Glatman's apartment. The cops examined his photograph collection.

He had dozens of mail-order smut pictures. They all featured bound-and-gagged women. He had pictures of bound-and-gagged women shot off his own TV screen. Glatman said he always watched TV with his camera in his lap. You got some good bonus shots that way.

He had pictures of girls he photographed in Denver. They were bound and gagged in their panties and bras. He said the girls were all alive and well.

He kept his special pictures in a metal box. The cops went through them one by one.

Judy Dull's brassiere was stretched below her breasts. Her gag flattened out her cheeks and distorted her whole face. Her legs-apart poses were fatuous and obscene.

She didn't look scared. She looked like a jaded adolescent. Maybe she thought she could outsmart this nebbish. Maybe she thought compliance equaled poise. Maybe she possessed a skewed pinup-girl bravado: all men are weak and easily moved with the right combination of flattery and pussy.

Angela Rojas looked dazed. Her desert backdrop was beautifully lit.

Shirley Ann Bridgeford knew her life was over. Glatman's camera caught her tears and contortions and the scream the gag in her mouth was holding mute.

The pictures shocked Jack Lawton. Glatman sickened him. He knew he didn't kill Jean Ellroy.

Hallinen and Lawton caught a case together on November 8th. A man named Woodrow Harley raped his 13-year-old step-daughter and smothered her with a chloroform-soaked pillow.

They spent a week wrapping it up. They visited Armand Ellroy and his son right before Thanksgiving.

The boy had grown a bit. He was very tall for a kid his age.

Hallinen and Lawton took Ellroy and his son down to Tiny Naylor's Drive-in. The kid ordered an ice cream concoction. Hallinen and Lawton ran their Mom's-boyfriend riff by him again.

He rehashed the stuff he already told them. He couldn't dredge up any new studs.

They went back to the apartment. Ellroy told the kid to go outside and play. He needed to talk to the gentlemen alone.

The kid walked out and tiptoed back down the hallway. He heard his father and the cops talking in the kitchen.

His father was calling his mother a promiscuous drunk. The cops were saying their case was dead. Jean was such a goddamn secretive woman. Her life just didn't make sense.

# Part II

## THE KID IN THE PICTURE

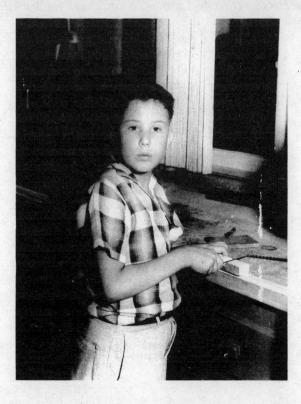

*You fooled people. You gave yourself out in small increments and reinvented yourself at whim. Your secret ways nullified the means to mark your death with vengeance.*

*I thought I knew you. I passed my childish hatred off as intimate knowledge. I never mourned you. I assailed your memory.*

*You fronted a stern rectitude. You cut it loose on Saturday nights. Your brief reconciliations drove you chaotic.*

*I won't define you that way. I won't give up your secrets so cheaply. I want to learn where you buried your love.*

**6**

My father put me in a cab at the El Monte depot. He paid the driver and told him to drop me at Bryant and Maple.

I didn't want to go back. I didn't want to leave my father. I wanted to blow off El Monte forever.

It was hot—maybe ten degrees more than L.A. The driver took Tyler north to Bryant and cut east. He turned on Maple and stopped the cab.

I saw police cars and official-type sedans parked at the curb. I saw uniformed men and men in suits standing in my front yard.

I knew she was dead. This is not a revised memory or a retrospective hunch. I knew it in the moment—at age ten—on Sunday, June 22nd, 1958.

I walked into the yard. Somebody said, "There's the boy." I saw Mr. and Mrs. Krycki standing by their back door.

A man took me aside and kneeled down to my level. He said, "Son, your mother's been killed."

I knew he meant "murdered." I probably trembled or shuddered or weaved a little bit.

The man asked me where my father was. I told him he was back at the bus station. A half-dozen men crowded around me. They leaned on their knees and checked me out up-close.

They saw one lucky kid.

A cop split for the bus station. A man with a camera walked me back to Mr. Krycki's toolshed.

He put an awl in my hand and posed me at a workbench. I held on to a small block of wood and pretended to saw at it. I faced the camera—and did not blink or smile or cry or betray my internal equilibrium.

The photographer stood in a doorway. The cops stood behind him. I had a rapt audience.

The photographer shot some film and urged me to improvise. I hunched over the wood and sawed at it with a half-smile/half-grimace. The cops laughed. I laughed. Flashbulbs popped.

The photographer said I was brave.

Two cops led me to a patrol car and put me in the backseat. I scooted over to the left-hand window and looked out. We took Maple to a side street to Peck Road southbound. I stuck my head out the window and registered odd things.

We turned west on Valley Boulevard and pulled up in front of the El Monte Police Station. The cops walked me inside and sat me down in a small room.

I wanted to see my father. I didn't want the cops to hurt him.

Some uniformed men kept me company. They were gentle and deferred to my status as a now motherless child. They kept a line of friendly chatter going.

My father picked me up Saturday morning. We took a bus to L.A. and went to see a movie called *The Vikings*. Tony Curtis got his hand chopped off and started wearing a black-leather stump guard. I had a nightmare about it.

Cops drifted in and out of the room. They kept handing me cups of water. I drank it all. It gave me something to do with my hands.

Two men walked into the room. The friendly cops walked out. One man was heavyset and almost bald. The other man had wavy white hair and light blue eyes. They were wearing sports jackets and slacks.

They asked me questions and wrote down my answers in small pocket notebooks. They had me describe my weekend with my father and asked me to name my mother's boyfriends.

I mentioned Hank Hart and Peter Tubiolo. My mother went out with Hank back in Santa Monica. Tubiolo was a teacher at my school. He dated my mother at least a couple of times.

I asked the men if my father was in trouble. They told me he wasn't. They said I would be released to his custody.

The white-haired cop gave me a candy bar and told me I could see my dad now. They let me out of that little square room.

I saw my father standing in the hallway. He saw me and smiled.

I ran straight to him. The impact knocked him back a little. He gave me his standard bear hug that showed off how strong he was.


A cop drove us to the El Monte depot. We caught a late bus to Los Angeles.

I sat next to the window. My father kept an arm around me. The San Berdoo Freeway was dark and full of glittery taillights.

I knew I should cry. My mother's death was a gift—and I knew I should pay for it. The cops probably judged me for not crying back at the house. If I didn't cry, it meant I wasn't normal. My thoughts were just that convoluted.

I let my clenched-up nerves go. I let the pure fucking awe I'd been feeling for hours slip free.

It worked.

I cried. I cranked tears out all the way to L.A.

I hated her. I hated El Monte. Some unknown killer just bought me a brand-new beautiful life.


She was a farm girl from Tunnel City, Wisconsin. I cared for her solely in conjunction with my father. When she broke the marriage off she made me his son exclusively.

I started hating her to prove my love for my father. I was afraid to acknowledge the woman's edgy will and courage.

My father was mistakenly diagnosed with cancer in 1956. My mother broke the news to me—but withheld the he'll-be-all-right punch line for dramatic effect. I wept and punched out our living-room sofa. My mother calmed me down and told me it was ulcers, not cancer—and I needed a little trip to get over the shock.

We drove down to Mexico. We got a hotel room in Ensenada and ate a lobster dinner at a nice restaurant. My mother wore an off-one-shoulder dress. She looked startlingly fair-skinned and redheaded. I was aware that she was performing.

I went swimming in the hotel pool the next morning. The water was visibly dirty. I came out with blocked ears and a throbbing headache.

The headache worked its way down to my left ear. The pain grew more localized and more intense. My mother examined me and told me I had a severe ear infection.

The pain was godawful. I cried and ground my teeth until my gums bled.

My mother bundled me up in the backseat of her car and drove us north to Tijuana. The pharmacies there sold medicine and hard narcotics over-the-counter. My mother found a place and purchased a bottle of pills, a vial of dope and a hypodermic syringe.

She fed me water and pills. She prepped a spike and shot me up right there in the car. My pain died instantaneously.

We drove straight back to L.A. The dope warmed me and lulled me to sleep. I woke up in my bedroom and saw strange new colors drifting out of the wallpaper.

I withheld the incident from my father. The omission was instinctive and precociously derived. I'll ascribe motive 40 years after the fact.

My mother protected me with decisively great style. I knew my father wouldn't want to hear her praised. I played to his fear. I didn't tell him she looked good in that dress. I didn't tell him how good that dope felt. I didn't tell him she owned my heart for a little while.

My parents excelled at appearances. They were a great-looking cheap couple, along the lines of Robert Mitchum and Jane Russell in *Macao*. They stayed together for 15 years. It had to be sex.

He was 17 years her senior. He was tall and built like a light heavyweight. He was drop-dead handsome and possessed a massive wang.

He was an ineffectual man who came off dangerous at first reading. She bought the physical package and the charm that went with it. I don't know how long the honeymoon lasted. I don't know how long it took them to get disillusioned and cede their marriage to dry rot.

They both moved west in the late '30s. They met, sizzled, wed and settled in L.A. She was a registered nurse. He was a noncertified accountant. He inventoried drugstore stock and prepared income tax returns for Hollywood people. He had a three-or-four-year run as Rita Hayworth's business manager and arranged her wedding to Aly Khan in 1949. Redhaired women ruled his postwar years.

I made the scene in '48. The novelty of a kid sent them gaga for a while. They moved out of their place in Beverly Hills and found a larger apartment in West Hollywood. It was a Spanish-style pad with brushed-stucco walls and arched doorways. I grew into a warped state of cognizance there.

Rita Hayworth fired my father, circa '52. He took occasional drugstore jobs and hogged the living-room couch most standard workdays. He loved to read and sleep. He loved to smoke cigarettes and watch sporting events on our bubble-screen TV. The couch was his all-purpose forum.

My mother hustled to and from work. She had a full-time gig at St. John's Hospital and wet-nursed a dipsomaniacal actress named ZaSu Pitts on the side. She brought home the bulk of the money and bugged my father to get a permanent job.

He put her off with vague vows and cited his Hollywood connections. He was pals with Mickey Rooney and a schlock producer named Sam Stiefel. He knew people with pull. He could parlay his friendships into something sweet.

I spent a lot of time on the couch with my father. He drew pictures for me and taught me to read when I was three and a half years old. We sat side by side and read separate books.

My father favored historical novels. I dug kid's animal stories. My father knew that I couldn't stand to see animals mistreated or killed. He skimmed the books he bought for me and shitcanned the ones he knew I'd find disturbing.

My father grew up in an orphanage and had no blood

family. My mother had a younger sister in Wisconsin. My father hated his sister-in-law and her husband, a Buick dealer named Ed Wagner. My father said Uncle Ed was a draft dodger and a kraut. He killed lots of krauts in the First World War and had no use for them.

The Wagners thought my father was a bum. My father told me my cousin Jeannie tried to scratch my eyes out once. I don't recall any such incident.

My parents' friends conformed to a type: older people naively impressed with them. My parents looked good and hobnobbed with Hollywood swingers. They dazzled in the short run and only fought, carped and bickered in the privacy of their own home. They kept up a united front and limited their offensive broadsides to one witness—me.

Their life together was one long skirmish. She attacked his sloth; he attacked her nightly booze intake. Their squabbles were strictly verbal—and the absence of physical violence made them that much more protracted. They argued in measured tones, rarely yelled and never screamed. They did not break flowerpots or hurl dishes. Their lack of overt theatrics cloaked the fact that their collective will to reason and reconcile did not exist. They fought a self-suppressed war. They worked themselves into the picayune state of the perpetually aggrieved. Their hatred escalated over years and peaked at a level of low fury.

It was '54. I was six years old and in the first grade at West Hollywood Elementary School. My mother sat me down on our living-room couch and told me she was divorcing my father.

I took it hard. I threw tantrums for weeks running. My histrionics were fevered and a cumulative response to years of chickenshit parental battling. TV had taught me that divorce was permanent and binding. Divorce stigmatized little kids and fucked them up for life. The mother got custody of all minor children.

My mother kicked my father out of the apartment. She tolerated my hurt-child routine for a few weeks, gave me a concise whack in the head and told me to stop it.

I stopped it. I got a crazy little-kid notion to forge an all-powerful separate thing with my father.

My mother hired a lawyer and filed for divorce. A judge granted her temporary custody and allowed me to spend weekends with my father. He rented a bachelor pad a few blocks from his old apartment.

I holed up with him for a string of Fridays-to-Sundays. We cooked burgers on a hot plate and made meals out of CheezWhiz and crackers. We read books side by side and watched TV fight cards. My father began to systematically poison my mind against my mother.

He told me she was a drunk and a whore. He told me she was fucking her divorce lawyer. He said he had a shot at gaining custody of me—if he could prove my mother morally deficient. He urged me to spy on her. I agreed to snoop out my mother's indiscretions.

My father got a job in downtown L.A. I snuck out and met him on his way home from work every chance I got. We rendezvoused at a drugstore on Burton Way and Doheny. We ate ice cream and talked a little bit.

My mother discovered this treachery. She called my father and threatened him with custody injunctions. She hired a baby-sitter to watchdog me after school.

I ditched my school bus the next morning. I hid out in the courtyard by my father's apartment. I wanted to see my father wicked bad. I was afraid of the Salk vaccine shots scheduled at school that day.

My mother found me. She drove me to school and arranged to inject me with the Salk vaccine herself.

She shot me up in her nurse's uniform. She was skilled with a needle—it didn't hurt at all. She looked good in white seersucker. It offset her red hair alluringly.

The divorce case went to court. I had to testify in closed session. I hadn't seen my father in a while. I spotted him outside the courtroom and ran to him.

My mother tried to intercede.

My father whisked me into a men's room and hunkered down to talk to me. My mother stormed in and dragged me out. My father let it happen. A man standing at a urinal with his dick in his hand observed the whole transaction.

I testified. I told a kindly judge that I wanted to live with my father. He ruled otherwise. His decree stipulated a weekday/ weekend split: five days with her, two days with him. He sentenced me to a bifurcated life divvied up between two people locked in an intractable mutual hatred.

I caught both sides of that hatred. It was resolutely scornful and eloquently expressed. My mother portrayed my father as weak, slovenly, lazy, fanciful and duplicitous in small ways. My father had my mother categorized more concisely: She was a Lush and a Whore.

I lived by the divorce decree. Weekdays meant restricted drudgery. Weekends meant freedom.

My father fed me tasty food and took me to cowboy movies. He told me World War I stories and let me leaf through his girlie magazines. He said he had several sweet deals cooking. He convinced me we were just moments shy of great wealth. Big money meant big-time lawyers and big-time legal pull. Those lawyers had detectives who could dig up dirt on the Lush and the Whore. They could get him full-time custody of me.

My mother moved us to a smaller apartment in Santa Monica. She quit St. John's and got an industrial nurse job at Packard-Bell Electronics. My father moved to a one-bedroom pad on the Hollywood-Wilshire District border. He didn't own a car and transported me by bus. He was well into his fifties and starting to look like a gigolo past his prime. People probably thought he was my granddad.

I transferred to a private school called Children's Paradise. It was unaccredited and set my mother back 50 bucks a month. The place was a dump site for kids from broken homes. Passing grades were guaranteed—but the hours of confinement stretched from 7:30 a.m. to 5:00 p.m. daily. The teachers were shrill or beaten-down passive. My father had a theory about the long school hours. He said they were calculated to give single moms time to fuck their boyfriends after work. He said this was not all bad.

Children's Paradise straddled some prime west-side real estate. A dirt yard jammed with play equipment faced Wilshire Boulevard. The yard was three times the size of the main classroom building. A swimming pool was positioned at the west flank.

I daydreamed my way through the third and fourth grades there. My reading skills eclipsed my retarded comprehension of arithmetic. I was a big kid. I flaunted my size and bluffed my way through minor kid confrontations. It was the genesis of my efficacious "Crazy Man Act."

I was afraid of all girls, most boys and selected male and female adults. My fear derived from my apocalyptic fantasy apparatus. I knew that all things went chaotically bad. My empirical training in chaos was unassailably valid.

My Crazy Man Act got me the attention that I craved and warned aggressors not to fuck with me. I laughed when nothing was funny, picked my nose and ate my snot, and drew swastikas all over my school notebooks. I was the poster boy for the If-You-Can't-Love-Me-Notice-Me chapter in all child psychology textbooks.

My mother was drinking more. She'd crank highballs at night and get pissed off, maudlin or effusive. I found her in bed with men a couple of times. The guys had that '50s lounge-lizard look. They probably sold used cars or repossessed them.

I told my father about the men. He said he had private eyes tailing my mother. I started scanning my blind side everywhere I went with her.

My mother quit Packard-Bell and hired on at Airtek Dynamics. My father worked drugstore jobs free-lance. I continued my education at Children's Paradise. My Crazy Man Act kept me tenuously afloat.

My parents were unable to talk in a civil fashion. They did not exchange words under any circumstances. Their expressions of hatred were reserved for me: *He's* a weakling; *she's* a drunk and a whore. I believed him—and wrote her accusations off as hogwash. I was blind to the fact that her broadsides carried a greater basis in truth.

'57 faded out. My mother and I flew to Wisconsin for Christmas. Uncle Ed Wagner sold her a spiffy red-and-white Buick. We drove it home the first week of '58. We settled back into our work and school routine.

My mother sat me down late in January and cozied me up for a big lie. She said we needed a change of scenery. I was almost ten years old, and I'd never lived in a house. She said she knew a nice place called El Monte.

My mother lied poorly. She tended to formalize and overstate her lies and often embellished them with expressions of parental concern. She always laid out her major lies half-drunk.

I was a good lie decoder. My mother did not credit me with this gift.

I told my father about the move. He found the notion dubious. He said El Monte was full of wetbacks. It was a skunk place by any and all standards. He figured my mother was ditching some West L.A. stud—or was running to some El Monte shitbird. You don't uproot and move 30-odd miles for no goddamn reason.

He told me to stay alert. He told me to report my mother's round-heeled stunts.

My mother wanted to show off El Monte. We cruised out there on a Sunday afternoon.

My father got me predisposed to hate and fear the place. He'd portrayed it accurately.

El Monte was a smoggy void. People parked on their lawns and hosed down their cars in their underwear. The sky was carcinogenic tan. I noticed lots of evil-looking pachucos.

We went by our new house. It was pretty on the outside—but smaller than our pad in Santa Monica.

We talked to our new landlady, Anna May Krycki. She was nervous and chatty and darty-eyed. She let me pet her Airedale dog.

A yard enclosed the Kryckis' house and our house. My mother said we could get a dog of our own. I told her I wanted a beagle. She said she'd get me one for my birthday.

We met Mr. Krycki and Mrs. Krycki's son from a previous marriage. We walked through our new house.

My room was half the size of my room in Santa Monica. The kitchen was no more than a crawl space. The bathroom was narrow and cramped.

The house justified the move. It cosmetically vouched my mother's Big Lie.

I knew it at the time.

We moved out early in February. I enrolled at Anne LeGore Elementary School and became my father's full-time spy.

My mother was drinking more. The kitchen smelled like her Early Times bourbon and L&M cigarettes. I sniffed the tumblers she left in the sink—to see what the allure was. The syrupy odor made me gag.

She didn't bring men home. My father figured she was shacking up on the weekends. He started calling El Monte "Shitsville, U.S.A."

I made the best of a bad place.

I went to school. I got friendly with two Mexican kids named Reyes and Danny. They shared a reefer with me once. I got dizzy and goofy ecstatic and went home and ate a whole box of cookies. I passed out and woke up convinced that I would soon become a heroin addict.

School was a drag. My arithmetic skills were subzero and my social skills were subpoor. Reyes and Danny were my only pals.

My father visited me at noon recess one day—a divorce decree violation. A kid shoved me for no reason. I kicked his ass in full view of my father.

My father was proud of me. The kid snitched me off to Mr. Tubiolo, the vice-principal. Tubiolo called my mother and suggested a conference.

They met and talked. They went out on a couple of dates. I reported the details to my father.

My mother got me a beagle puppy for my tenth birthday. I named her "Minna" and smothered her with love.

My mother laid a mind fuck on me in conjunction with the gift. She told me I was a young man now. I was old enough to decide who I wanted to live with.

I told her I wanted to live with my father.

She slapped me in the face and knocked me off the living-room couch. I banged my head on a coffee table.

I called her a drunk and a whore. She hit me again. I made up my mind to fight back next time.

I could brain her with an ashtray and negate her size advantage. I could scratch her face and ruin her looks so men wouldn't want to fuck her. I could smash her with a bottle of Early Times bourbon.

She pushed me over a very simple line.

I used to hate her because my father did. I used to hate her to prove my love for him.

She just bought my own full-tilt hatred.

El Monte was prison camp. Weekends in L.A. were brief paroles.

My father took me to movies on Hollywood Boulevard. We caught *Vertigo* and a string of Randolph Scott westerns. My father laid out the straight dope on Randolph Scott: He was one notorious homo.

He took me by the Hollywood Ranch Market and gave me a crash course in homos. He said fruits wore mirrored shades to measure crotch bulges covertly. Fruits served one good purpose. Their presence expanded the pool of available women.

He wanted to know if I liked girls yet.

I told him I did. I didn't tell him that full-blown women jazzed me more. Divorced mothers were more precisely my type.

Their bodies had these neat imperfections. Heavy legs and bra-strap markings drove me crazy. I liked pale-skinned, redhaired women especially.

The concept of motherhood excited me. I was up-to-date on the facts of life and was titillated by the fact that motherhood began with fucking. Women with kids had to be good at it. They were practiced. They developed a taste for sex during holy matrimony and couldn't live without it when their ordained unions went kaput. Their need was dirty, shameful and thrilling.

Like my curiosity.

Our bathroom in El Monte was tiny. The bathtub faced the toilet at a right angle. I caught a glimpse of my mother drying off after a shower one night.

She saw me looking at her breasts. She told me that the tip of her right nipple got infected after my birth and had to be removed. Her tone was in no way provocative. She was a registered nurse explaining a medical fact.

I had pictures in my mind now. I wanted to see more.

I spent hours in the bathtub, feigning interest in a toy submarine. I saw my mother half-nude and nude and stripped to her slip. I saw her breasts sway. I saw her good nipple pebbled up from the cold. I saw the red between her legs and the way steam made her skin flush.

I hated her and lusted for her.

Then she was dead.

# 7

Monday, June 23rd, 1958. A bright summer day and the start of my sunny new life.

A nightmare woke me up.

My mother did not appear. Tony Curtis and his black stump guard did. I shook the image off and let things sink in.

The boo-hoo stuff was behind me. I spilled some tears on the bus—and that was that. My period of mourning lasted half an hour.

I've got the look of that day memorized. It was incandescent powder blue.

My father told me the Wagners were coming out in a few days. Mrs. Krycki had agreed to look after my dog for a while. The funeral was next week—and my attendance was not mandatory. The Sheriff's Crime Lab was set to shoot him the Buick. He planned to sell it for my mother's short-term equity—if the provisions of her will did not bar the sale.

Mrs. Krycki told my father that I stabbed her banana trees to death. She demanded restitution—pronto. I told my father that I was just playing a game. He said it was no big thing.

He was coming off somber. I could tell he was really happy and in some state of serendipitous shell-shock. He was closing out his ex with postmortem minutiae.

He told me to amuse myself for a while. He had to go downtown and identify the body.

*

The Wagners arrived in L.A. a few days later. Uncle Ed was composed. Aunt Leoda was near distraught.

She worshipped her big sister. A style gap separated the Hilliker girls—Jean had the looks, the red hair and the sexy career. Her husband was superficially dashing and hung like a mule.

Ed Wagner was fat and stolid. He brought home the bacon. Aunt Leoda was a Wisconsin hausfrau. She was slow to rile and a good grudge holder. Her sister lived an alternative life that she found compelling. The explicit details of that life would undoubtedly shock her no end.

My father and I saw the Wagners several times. No discernible Ellroy-Wagner hatred surfaced. Ed and Leoda chalked my calm emotional state up to shock. I kept my mouth shut and let the adults do the talking.

The four of us drove out to El Monte. We stopped at the house and took a last walk through it. I hugged and kissed my dog. She licked my face and pissed all over me. My father goofed on the Kryckis—he thought they were geeks. Ed and Leoda picked up my mother's personal papers and memorabilia. My father tossed my clothes and books into brown paper bags.

We stopped at Jay's Market on our way out of town. A checker fussed over me—she knew I was the dead nurse's kid. My mother started a fight with me in that market just a few weeks back.

Something got her going on my poor scholastic progress. She wanted to show me my potential fate. She hustled me out of the market and drove me down to Medina Court—the heart of the El Monte taco belt.

Mexican punks were out walking that slick walk I admired. There were no houses—just shacks. Half the cars lacked axles and wheels.

My mother pointed out harrowing details. She wanted me to see what my lazy ways would get me. I didn't take her warnings seriously. I knew my father would never let me turn into a wetback.

*

I didn't go to the funeral. The Wagners went back to Wisconsin.

My father took possession of the Buick and sold it to a guy in our neighborhood. He managed to pocket my mother's down payment. Aunt Leoda became the executrix of my mother's estate. She held the purse strings on a fat insurance policy.

A double-indemnity clause boosted the premium up to 20 grand. I was the sole beneficiary. Leoda told me she was putting the money in trust for my college education. She said I could extract small amounts for emergencies.

I settled in to enjoy my summer vacation.

The cops came by a few times. They quizzed me on my mother's boyfriends and other known associates. I told them all I knew.

My father kept some newspaper clippings on the case. He told me the basic facts and urged me not to think about the murder itself. He knew I had a vivid imagination.

I wanted to know the details.

I read the clippings. I saw a picture of myself at Mr. Krycki's workbench. I nailed down the Blonde and Dark Man scenario. I got a spooky feeling that it was all about sex.

My father found out that I'd been through his clippings. He gave me his pet theory: My mother balked at a three-way with the Blonde and the Dark Man. It was part of a larger riddle: Why did she run to El Monte?

I wanted answers—but not at the expense of my mother's continued presence. I diverted my curiosity to kid's crime books.

I stumbled onto the Hardy Boys and Ken Holt series. Chevalier's Bookstore sold them for a dollar apiece. Adolescent detectives solved crimes and befriended crime victims. Murder was sanitized and occurred off-page. The kid detectives came from affluent families and tooled around in hot rods, motorcycles and speedboats. The crimes went down in swanky resort locations. Everybody ended up happy. The murder victims were dead—but were implicitly having a blast in heaven.

It was a literary formula preordained directly for *me*. It let me remember and forget in equal measure. I ate those books up wholesale and was blessedly unaware of the internal dynamic that made them so seductive.

The Hardy Boys and Ken Holt were my only friends. Their sidekicks were my sidekicks. We solved perplexing mysteries —but nobody got hurt too severely.

My father bought me two books every Saturday. I went through them fast and spent the rest of the week suffering withdrawal pangs. My father held the line at two a week, no more. I started shoplifting books to fill my reading gaps.

I was a sly little thief. I wore my shirttail out and stuck the books under my waistband. The folks at Chevalier's probably thought I was a cute little bookworm. My father never mentioned the size of my library.

The summer of '58 sped by. I rarely thought about my mother. She was compartmentalized and defined by my father's current indifference to her memory. El Monte was an aberrant non sequitur. She was *gone*.

Every book I read was a twisted homage to her. Every mystery solved was my love for her in ellipses.

I didn't know it then. I doubt if my father knew it. He was scheming his way through the summer with his redheaded demon in the ground.

He bought ten thousand Jap surplus "Tote Seats" at ten cents apiece. They were inflatable cushions to sit on at sporting events. He was convinced he could sell them to L.A. Rams and Dodgers organizations. The first batch would get him going. He could get the Japs to churn more Tote Seats out on a consignment basis. His profits would zoom from that point on.

The Rams and Dodgers brushed my father off. He was too proud to hawk the Tote Seats street-vendor style. Our shelves and closets were crammed with inflatable plastic. You could have blown the cushions up and floated half the county out to sea.

My father wrote off the Tote Seat venture and went back to drugstore work. He put in crash hours: noon to 2:00 or 3:00 a.m. He let me stay alone while he was gone.

Our pad was un-air-conditioned and soaked in summertime

heat. It was starting to smell—Minna defied housebreaking and urinated and defecated all over the floors. Dusk cooled the place off and diffused the stink a little. I loved being alone in the apartment after dark.

I read and skimmed the TV dial for crime shows. I looked through my father's magazines. He subscribed to *Swank, Nugget* and *Cavalier.* They were full of nifty pictures and risqué cartoons that went over my head.

I stared at my father's World War I medals—miniatures encased in glass. The aggregation marked him one big hero. He was born in 1898 and was three months shy of 50 when I was born. I kept wondering how much time he had left.

I liked to cook for myself. My favorite meal was hot dogs scorched on a coil burner. My mother's canned spaghetti dinners were nowhere near as good.

I always watched TV with the lights off. I got hooked on Tom Duggan's Channel 13 gabfest and tuned in every night. Duggan was half hipster, half right-wing blowhard. He abused his guests and talked about booze constantly. He portrayed himself as a misanthrope and a lech. He struck a deep chord in me.

His show ended around 1:00 a.m. My summer '58 rituals got scary then.

I was usually too agitated to sleep. I started imagining my father's death by homicide and car crash. I waited up for him in the kitchen and counted the cars that went by on Beverly Boulevard. I kept all the lights off—to show that I wasn't afraid.

He always came home. He never told me that sitting in the dark was a strange thing to do.


We lived poor. We had no car and relied on the L.A. bus system for transport. We consumed an all-grease-sugar-and-starch diet. My father did not touch alcohol—but compensated for it by smoking three packs of Lucky Strikes a day. We shared a single bedroom with our malodorous dog.

None of this bothered me. I was well fed and had a loving father. Books provided stimulation and a sublimated dialogue on my mother's death. I possessed a quietly tenacious ability to exploit what I had.

My father gave me free run of the neighborhood. I explored it and let it fuel my imagination.

Our apartment building stood at Beverly Boulevard and Irving Place. It was the edge of Hollywood and Hancock Park—a significant juncture of styles.

Small stucco houses and walk-up apartment buildings ran to the north. They ended at Melrose Avenue and the Paramount and Desilu Studio lots. The streets were narrow and grid-straight. Spanish-style facades dominated.

Beverly to Melrose. Western Avenue to Rossmore Boulevard. Five blocks north to south and seventeen blocks east to west. Movie studios to modest houses to a row of stores and cocktail pits to the Wilshire Country Club. Half of my wandering turf—about half the size of El Monte.

The eastern edge featured wood-framed houses and garish new apartment dumps. The western edge was a mid-L.A. Gold Coast. I dug the high-rise Tudor fortresses with doormen and wide entry ports. The Algiers Hotel-Apartments stood at Rossmore and Rosewood. My father said the place was a glorified "fuck pad." The bellboys ran a string of good-looking hookers.

My northern roaming flank was topographically diverse. I liked to watch the view decline west to east. Odd blocks were nicely tended. Odd blocks were dirty and run-down. I liked the Polar Palace Skating Rink at Van Ness and Clinton. I liked the El Royale Apartments—because they sounded like "Ellroy." The Algiers was thrilling. Every woman walking in and out was potentially a hooker.

I liked my northern roaming flank. Sometimes it scared me—kids riding by on their bikes would swerve my way or flip me the finger. Small confrontations would drive me south for days.

My southern roaming flank stretched from Western to Rossmore and Beverly to Wilshire Boulevard. The eastern edge had one draw: the public library at Council and St. Andrews. It was negligible prowl turf.

I *loved* to prowl due south and southwest. 1st Street, 2nd

Street, 3rd Street, 4th Street, 5th Street, 6th Street, Wilshire. Irving, Windsor, Lorraine, Plymouth, Beachwood, Larchmont, Lucerne, Arden, Rossmore.

Hancock Park.

Large Tudor houses and French chateaus. Spanish mansions. Broad front lawns, trellised arbors, tree-lined curbsides and an air of time-warp containment. Perfectly circumscribed order and wealth a few blocks from my shit-encrusted home.

Hancock Park hypnotized me. The landscape held me spellbound.

I roamed Hancock Park. I walked and gawked and strolled and trolled. I cinched Minna to her leash and let her pull me down Irving to Wilshire three or four times a day. I prowled the shops on Larchmont Boulevard and boosted books at Chevalier's.

I developed crushes on houses and girls glimpsed in windows. I constructed elaborate Hancock Park fantasies. My father and I would crash Hancock Park and make it our own kingdom.

I did not covet Hancock Park from any kind of aggrieved perspective. I owned the place with my imagination. It was enough—for a while.

The summer of '58 ended. I enrolled in the sixth grade at Van Ness Avenue Elementary School. My roaming jaunts were drastically curtailed.

Van Ness Avenue School was genteel. Nobody offered me marijuana. My teacher pampered me a little. She probably knew my mom was a murder victim.

I was becoming quite a large kid. I was foulmouthed and spouted profane lingo on the schoolyard. My father's favorite expression was "Fuck you, Fritz." His favorite expletive was "cocksucker." I mimicked his language and reveled in its shock value.

I was refining my Crazy Man Act. It kept me miserably lonely and sealed up in my own little head.

My reading tastes were growing more sophisticated. I'd

gone through all the Hardy Boys and Ken Holt books and was tired of pat plots and simple closures. I wanted more violence and more sex. My father recommended Mickey Spillane.

I stole some Spillane paperbacks. I read them and got titillated and scared. I don't think I followed the plots very well—and I know it didn't hinder my enjoyment. I dug the shooting and the sex and Mike Hammer's anti-Communist fervor. The total package was just hyperbolic enough to keep me from getting *too* frightened. It wasn't rock-bottom blunt and horrific—like my mother and the Blonde and the Dark Man.

My father was permitting me more freedom. He told me I could go to the movies by myself and take Minna out for her late walks.

Hancock Park by night was another separate world.

Darkness made colors recede. Corner streetlamps put out a nice glow. Houses became backdrops for window lights.

I stood out in the darkness and looked *in*. I saw draperies, blank walls, blips of color and passing shapes. I saw girls in private-school uniforms. I saw some beautiful Christmas trees.

Those late-night walks were spooky and enticing. Darkness reinforced my claim on the turf and pumped up my imagination. I started prowling backyards and looking in back windows.

The prowling was a thrill in itself. Back windows gave me intimate views.

Bathroom windows were the best. I saw half-dressed women and women and girls in robes. I liked to watch them putter in front of their mirrors.

I found a catcher's mitt on a picnic table. I stole it. I found a real leather football behind another house. I stole it and cut it open with a pocket knife to see what was inside.

I was still preadolescent. I was a thief and a voyeur. I was headed for a hot date with a desecrated woman.

**8**

She came to me in a book. An innocent gift burned my world down.

My father gave me the book for my eleventh birthday. It was a nonfiction ode to the Los Angeles Police Department. The title was *The Badge*. The author was Jack Webb—the star and brains behind the *Dragnet* TV show.

The show derived from LAPD case files. The cops talked in monotones and treated suspects with brusque contempt. The suspects were cowardly and bombastically verbose. The cops bought none of their bullshit.

*Dragnet* was the saga of dead-end lives up against authority. Suppressive police methods insured a virtuous L.A. The show talked a stern game and oozed subtextual self-pity. It was the epic of isolated men in an isolating profession, deprived of conventional illusions and traumatized by their daily contact with scum. It was '50s-style male angst—alienation as a public-service announcement.

The book was the TV show unchained. Jack Webb detailed police procedures and whined about the LAPD's white male burden at great length. He compared criminals to Communists without irony. He served up real-life anecdotes to illustrate the terrors and prosaic satisfactions of police work. He ran down some snappy LAPD cases—free of TV censorship strictures.

The Club Mecca firebomb job was a scorcher.

Four creeps were ejected from a neighborhood tavern on April 4, 1957. They returned with a Molotov cocktail and torched the joint to the ground. Six patrons died. The LAPD tracked the killers down within a few hours. They were tried, convicted and sentenced to death.

Donald Keith Bashor was a pad burglar. He hit small apartments in the Westlake Park District. Two women interrupted his pad crawls. Bashor beat them dead. He was captured, tried and convicted. He went to the gas chamber in October '57.

Stephen Nash was a gap-toothed psychopath. He was pissed off at the world. He beat a man to death and slashed a ten-year-old boy under the Santa Monica Pier. The LAPD nabbed him in '56. He copped to nine more murders and tagged himself "the King of the Killers." He was tried, convicted and sentenced to death.

The stories were deadpan horrific. The villains looked stupid and nihilistically inclined.

Stephen Nash killed on impulse. His murders lacked a quality of calculation and were not perpetrated with an eye for full-blown horror. Nash did not know how to harness his rage into symbolic gestures and inflict them on a living human being. He lacked the will or inclination to commit murders that inspired great public fascination.

The Black Dahlia killer knew what he didn't. He understood mutilation as language. He murdered a beautiful young woman and thus insured his anonymous celebrity.

I read Jack Webb's account of the Black Dahlia murder case. It sent me way off the deep end.

The Black Dahlia was a girl named Elizabeth Short. Her body was found in a vacant lot in January 1947. The dump site was four miles due south of my apartment.

Elizabeth Short was cut in two at the waist. The killer scrubbed her body clean and left her naked. He placed her two inches off a city sidewalk with her legs spread wide.

He tortured her for days. He beat her and sliced her with a sharp knife. He stubbed cigarettes out on her breasts and cut the corners of her mouth back to her ears.

Her suffering was horribly attenuated. She was systematically abused and terrorized. The killer probed and rearranged her internal organs postmortem. The crime was pure misogynist insanity—and thus ripe for misinterpretation.

Betty Short died at twenty-two. She was a flaky kid living out flaky kid fantasies. A reporter learned that she dressed solely in black and named her "The Black Dahlia." The tag nullified her and vilified her and turned her into a sainted lost daughter and a slut.

The case was a huge news event. Jack Webb steeped his twelve-page summary in the ethos of the time: Femme fatales die hard and are complicitous in attracting death by vivisection. He didn't understand the killer's intentions or know that his gynecological tampering defined the crime. He didn't know that the killer was horribly afraid of women. He didn't know that he cut the Dahlia open to see what made women different from men.

I didn't know those things then. I did know that I had a story to run to and run from.

Webb described the Dahlia's last days. She was running to and from men and stretching her mental resources schizophrenically thin. She was looking for a safe place to hide.

Two photographs accompanied the story.

The first one showed Betty Short at 39th and Norton. Her legs were half visible. Men with guns and pocket notebooks were standing over her body.

The second one showed her in life. Her hair was swept up and back—like a 1940s portrait shot of my mother.


I read the Dahlia story a hundred times. I read the rest of *The Badge* and stared at the pictures. Stephen Nash, Donald Bashor and the firebomb guys became my friends. Betty Short became my obsession.

And my symbiotic stand-in for Geneva Hilliker Ellroy.

Betty was running and hiding. My mother ran to El Monte and forged a secret weekend life there. Betty and my mother were body-dump victims. Jack Webb said Betty was a loose girl. My father said my mother was a drunk and a whore.

My Dahlia obsession was explicitly pornographic. My imagination supplied the details that Jack Webb omitted. The murder was an epigram on transient lives and impacted sex as death. The unsolved status was a wall I tried to break down with a child's curiosity.

I applied my mind to the task. My explication efforts were entirely unconscious. I simply told myself mental stories.

That storytelling worked counterproductively. My daytime tales of death by saw and scalpel gave me terrible nightmares. They were devoid of narrative lines—all I saw was Betty being cut, slashed, poked, probed and dissected.

My nightmares had a pure raw force. Vivid details burst out of my unconscious. I saw Betty drawn and quartered on a medieval torture rack. I saw a man drain her blood into a bathtub. I saw her spread-eagled on a medical gurney.

Those scenes made me afraid to sleep. My nightmares came steadily or at unpredictable intervals. Daytime flashes complemented them.

I'd be sitting in school. I'd be bored and prey to odd mental wanderings. I'd see entrails stuffed in a toilet bowl and torture gadgets poised for business.

I did not willfully conjure the images. They seemed to spring from somewhere beyond my volition.

The nightmares and day flashes continued through the spring and summer. I knew they were God's punishment for my voyeur prowls and thievery. I stopped stealing and peeping Hancock Park windows. The nightmares and day flashes continued.

I went back to stealing and watching. A man caught me in his yard and chased me out. I quit voyeurizing altogether.

The nightmares and day flashes continued. Their power dwindled through sheer repetition. My Black Dahlia obsession assumed new fantasy forms.

I rescued Betty Short and became her lover. I saved her from a life of promiscuity. I tracked down her killer and executed him.

They were strong, narrative-based fantasies. They took the queasy edge off my Dahlia fixation.

I was set to enter junior high in September '59. My father told me I should start taking buses by myself. I exploited that new freedom in the name of formal Dahlia research.

I took bus trips downtown to the Main Public Library. I read

the 1947 *Herald-Express* on microfilm rolls. I learned all about
the life and death of the Black Dahlia.

Betty Short came from Medford, Massachusetts. She had
three sisters. Her parents were divorced. She visited her dad
in California in 1943. She got hooked on Hollywood and men in
uniform.

The *Herald* called her a "playgirl" and a "party girl." I
decoded the terms to read "whore." She wanted to be a movie
star. She was concurrently engaged to several army flyboys. A
guy named Red Manley drove her up from San Diego a week
before her death. She had no fixed Los Angeles address. She'd
been bouncing around between rooming houses and cheap
apartments for months. She frequented cocktail bars and
cadged drinks and dinners off strange men. She told whopping
lies routinely. Her life was indecipherable.

I instinctively understood that life. It was a chaotic collision
with male desire. Betty Short wanted powerful things from
men—but could not identify her needs. She reinvented herself
with youthful panache and convinced herself that she was
something original. She miscalculated. She wasn't smart and
she wasn't self-aware. She recast herself in a cookie-cutter
mold that pandered to long-prescribed male fantasies. The
new Betty was the old Betty bushwhacked by Hollywood. She
turned herself into a cliché that most men wanted to fuck and
a few men wanted to kill. She wanted to get deep dark down
and cozy with men. She sent out magnetic signals. She met a
man with notions of deep-dark-down-and-cozy cloaked in rage.
Her only complicitous act was a common fait accompli. She
made herself over for men.

The *Herald* ran the Dahlia story for 12 solid weeks. It played
up the massive investigation rife with fruitless leads and
weirdo suspects. False confessions and other tangential
offshoots got front-page coverage.

The lesbian theory was hot for a while: Betty Short might
have traveled in dyke circles. The smut-picture theory had
a good run: Betty might have posed for pornographic
snapshots.

People ratted their neighbors off as the killer. People ratted
off lovers who jilted them. People went to psychics and sought

out the Dahlia's spirit. Elizabeth Short's death inspired a minor hysteria.

Postwar L.A. coalesced around the body of a dead woman. Hordes of people fell sway to the Dahlia. They weaved themselves into her story in bizarre and fantastical ways.

The story thrilled me and moved me. It filled me with a perverse sense of hope.

The Dahlia defined her time and place. She claimed lives from the grave and exerted great power.


Stephen Nash went to the gas chamber in August '59. He spit some chewing gum at a chaplain right before they strapped him in. He sucked down the cyanide fumes with a big shit-eating grin.

I enrolled at John Burroughs Junior High School a few weeks later. Harvey Glatman went to the gas chamber on September 18th. I hit my father up for a bicycle. We conned a C-note out of my aunt and bought a candy-apple-red Schwinn Corvette.

I customized that bike to the nines. I added gooseneck handlebars, plastic saddlebags, rhinestone-studded mud flaps and a speedometer that tapped out at 150 miles an hour. My father called my bike a "nigger wagon." It was beautiful—but very heavy and slow. I had to walk it up hills.

I had a vehicle now. My new school was three miles from my pad. My roaming turf expanded exponentially.

I rode my bike down to 39th and Norton several times. Houses covered the vacant lot where Betty Short was found. I tore them down with my imagination. I laid bicycle skid marks on the sidewalk near that hallowed spot.

I still had Dahlia nightmares. I conjured the Dahlia up to combat schoolroom boredom. I kept rereading *The Badge*. It kept me zeroed in on L.A. crime.

1949: the Brenda Allen vice scandal. Call girls jungled up with corrupt cops. Colorful mobster Mickey Cohen. The 1951 "Two Tonys" snuff. Marie "the Body" McDonald and her fake kidnap caper. The "Bloody Christmas" police brutality scandal.

I was developing a tabloid sensibility. Crime jazzed me and scared me in roughly equivalent measure. My brain was a police blotter.

I followed the Ma Duncan case on TV. Ma Duncan had a possessive passion for her son Frank. Frank married a hot young nurse and made Ma jealous. Ma hired two Mexican winos to rub the nurse out. They abducted her on November 17, '58. They drove her into the Santa Barbara hills and strangled her. Ma shortchanged the guys on their hit fee. Ma shot her mouth off and told a friend about the whole thing. The Santa Barbara fuzz busted Ma and the Mexicans. They were currently embroiled in legal proceedings.

I followed the Bernard Finch/Carole Tregoff case. Finch was a playboy physician. Tregoff was his slinky girlfriend. Finch had a lucrative West Covina practice. His wife was filthy rich—and Finch was her sole heir. Finch and Tregoff faked a burglary and snuffed Mrs. Finch in July '59. The case was a local sensation.

I followed Caryl Chessman's fight to beat the gas chamber. My father told me Chessman bit a woman's nipples off and drove her insane.

My father co-signed my crime obsession. He never tried to derail my one-track tendency. I could read what I wanted to and watch unlimited TV. He talked to me like a pal. He shot me choice gossip gleaned from his years as a Hollywood bottom-feeder.

He told me Rock Hudson was a fag and Mickey Rooney would fuck a woodpile on the off-chance a snake might be inside. Rita Hayworth was a nympho—he knew that from personal experience.

We were poor. Our apartment reeked of dogshit. I ate cookies and milk for breakfast every morning and hamburgers or frozen pizza for dinner every night. I wore ratty clothes. My father talked to himself and told TV commentators to "fuck off" and "suck my dick." We hung around in our undershorts. We subscribed to skin magazines. Our dog bit us occasionally.

I was lonely. I was friendless. I had a hunch that my life wasn't quite kosher.

But I *knew* things.

*

My parents named me Lee Earle Ellroy. They sentenced me to a life of tongue-tripping *l*'s and *e*'s—and "Leroy"s by default. I hated my given names. I hated being called "Leroy." My father conceded that the "Lee Earle" and "Ellroy" combo stunk. He said it was a nigger-pimp name.

He employed a part-time alias himself. He went by "James Brady" and worked some drugstore gigs under that name as a tax-evasion measure. I made up my mind early: Someday I'd ditch the "Lee Earle" and keep the "Ellroy."

My name brought me grief at school. Bullies knew the way to get my goat. They knew I was a timid kid. They didn't know that hurled "Leroy"s turned me into Sonny Liston.

There weren't many bullies at John Burroughs Junior High School. A few punk confrontations killed the "Leroy" epidemic.

John Burroughs was known as "J.B." It stood at 6th and McCadden—the southwestern edge of Hancock Park. I honed my warped cognizance there.

The student body was 80% Jewish. Rich Hancock Park kids and general kid riffraff formed the other 20%. J.B. had a hot reputation. A brilliant bunch of youngsters matriculated there.

My father called Jews "pork dodgers." He said they were smarter than regular people. He told me to stay alert—Jewish kids were competitive.

I stayed alert in school. I manifested my alertness perversely.

I teamed up with some fellow losers. We smuggled in skin magazines and jerked off in adjoining toilet stalls. We tormented a retarded kid named Ronnie Cordero. I gave oral book reports on books that did not exist—and hipped selected kids in my English class to the ruse. I took a controversial classroom stand on the capture of Adolf Eichmann. I compared Eichmann to the Scottsboro Boys and Captain Dreyfuss.

I coveted my Jew-baiter rep. I took my mother's antipapist line and ragged John Kennedy's presidential efforts. I cheered Caryl Chessman into the gas chamber. I urged my classmates to dig the atom bomb. I drew swastikas and Stuka airplanes all over my notebooks.

My antics were meant to shock. They were inspired by the brightness and erudition I encountered at school. My reactionary fervor was kinship twisted inside-out.

That brightness rubbed off on me. I got good grades with minimum effort. My accountant father did my math homework and prepared test crib sheets for me. I was free to read and dream away my off-school hours.

I read crime novels and watched crime TV shows. I went to crime movies. I built model cars and blew them up with firecrackers. I stole books. I crashed a ban-the-bomb rally in Hollywood and chucked eggs at pinko placard wavers. I developed a big throbbing love of classical music.

Dahlia nightmares came in intermittent bunches. My day flashes cohered around one image.

Betty Short was pinned to a revolving target board. A man's hand spun the board and slashed Betty with a chisel.

The image was subjectively viewed. The image made *me* the killer.

The Dahlia was always with me. Real girls vied for my heart. A killer was stalking all the schoolgirls I grooved on. Jill, Kathy and Donna lived in great peril.

My rescue fantasies were richly detailed. My intercessions were swift and brutal. Sex was my only reward.

I stalked Jill, Kathy and Donna around school. I lurked near their homes on the weekend. I never talked to them.

My father was getting real action. His pal George told me he was fucking two check-stand girls at the Larchmont Safeway. I came home unexpectedly one day and caught him in the sack.

It was a hot afternoon. Our apartment door was open. I walked up the outside stairs and heard groaning. I tiptoed inside and peeped through the bedroom doorway.

My father was pouring the pork to a zaftig brunette. The dog was on the bed with them. She was dodging legs and trying to sleep on a bouncing mattress.

I watched for a while and tiptoed back outside.

I was wising up to my father. If he *really* won all those medals, he'd be as famous as Audie Murphy. If he had *real* drive and talent, we'd be living fat in Hancock Park right now. He was too proud to hand-sell his ten thousand Tote Seats—but not too proud to scam money off my mother's insurance policy.

My teeth needed straightening. I hit my Aunt Leoda up for orthodontic treatment money and overquoted the amount required. My father paid the dentist's initial bill and pocketed the balance. He fell behind on his maintenance payments and paid a cut-rate oral surgeon 20 bucks to cut the hardware off my teeth.

Aunt Leoda was easily conned. I snow-jobbed her regularly. I was trashing my college education fund. The thought didn't faze me one iota.

I hated Ed and Leoda Wagner and my cousins Jeannie and Janet. My father hated the Wagner clan big-time. My hatred was his hatred carbon-copied.

Leoda thought my father killed my mother. My father got a kick out of the notion. He told me Leoda suspected him from the start.

I dug the Dad-as-killer concept. It subverted my awareness of my father's passive nature and gave the man some panache. He killed my mother to gain custody of me. He knew that I hated her. He was a killer and I was a thief.

My father harped on Aunt Leoda's suspicions. He enjoyed the implicit drama. He pushed me back to that stack of newspaper clippings.

I reread them. I matched my father's face to a police sketch of the Dark Man. There was no resemblance whatsoever. My father did not murder my mother. He was with me when the crime occurred.

Spade Cooley beat his wife to death in April '61. He was hopped up on amphetamines. Ella Mae Cooley wanted to ditch Spade and join a free-love cult. She wanted to screw younger men.

I followed the case. Spade Cooley copped a plea and beat the gas chamber. Ella Mae got fucked out of a just vengeance.

I was 13 years old. Dead women owned me.

**9**

I lived in two worlds.

Compulsive fantasies ruled my inner world. The outside world intruded all too often. I never learned to hoard my thoughts and hold them for private moments. My two worlds clashed continually.

I wanted to crash the outside world. I wanted to wow the outside world with my sense of drama. I knew that access to my thoughts would make people love me. It was a common teenaged conceit.

I wanted to take my thoughts public. I possessed exhibitionist flair—but lacked stage presence and control of my effects. I came off as a desperate clown.

My performing repertoire mirrored my private obsessions. I liked to spiel on crime and Nazi fiends in hiding. "Kiddie Noir" was my metier.

My forums were classrooms and schoolyards. I ran my spiels to doofus kids and exasperated teachers. I learned an old vaudeville truth: You hold an audience only as long as you make them laugh.

My fantasies were dark and serious. My audiences had a low tolerance for vivisected women. I learned to topically digress for yucks.

The early '60s were good comic fodder. I took contrary stands on the A-bomb, John Kennedy, civil rights and the Berlin Wall brouhaha. I yelled "Free Rudolf Hess!" and advocated the reinstatement of slavery. I did wicked JFK imitations and stumped for the nuclear annihilation of Russia.

A few teachers took me aside and told me my shtick wasn't funny. My classmates were laughing *at* me—not *with* me. I caught their implied message: You are one fucked-up kid. They caught my message up-front: Laugh at me or with me—just *laugh.*

My fantasies made for marginal stand-up routines. My fantasies were a schizoid bridge between my two worlds.

I fantasized endlessly. I got up a head of fantasy steam and rode my bike through red lights. I sat in theaters and ran fantasy riffs off the movies I was seeing. I turned boring novels into enthralling ones by adding extemporaneous subplots.

My one great fantasy theme was CRIME. My one great hero was myself, transformed. I mastered marksmanship, judo and complex musical instruments in a microsecond. I was a detective—who just happened to be a violin and piano virtuoso. I rescued the Black Dahlia. I zoomed around in sports cars and bright red Fokker tri-planes. My fantasies were richly anachronistic.

And sex-saturated.

Jean Ellroy-type women craved me. I took 40-ish redheads glimpsed on the street and gave them my mother's body. I plowed through them in the course of my adventures. I settled into marriage with the last schoolgirl to goose my heartbeat. I always left the Jean Ellroy substitutes bereft.

My fantasies were persistently one-note. They were a hedge against schoolday boredom and my wretched home life.

I had my father's number now. At 14 I was taller than him. I figured I could kick his ass. He was a weakling and a bullshit artist.

We were bound by a sticky kind of need. "We" were all we had. The "we" thing made my father all gooey. I bought the "we" thing in weak moments and bridled at it most of the time. The old man's love for me was cloying and at odds with his profane take on life. I loved him when he called President Kennedy "a Catholic cocksucker" and hated him when he wept at the national anthem. I dug his fuck-pad-hotel riffs and squirmed when he embellished his World War I exploits. I couldn't acknowledge a simple truth: The redhead was a better single-parent proposition.

The old man's health was fading. He was coughing up lungers and weaving behind dizzy spells. He'd make a small bundle at tax time, laze around the pad and deplete his roll. He'd look for drugstore work when he got down to his last ten scoots. His get-rich-quick fervor raged on.

He managed a stage show at the Cabaret Concert Theatre. The show featured young comedians and singers. My father got tight with a comic named Alan Sues.

The show bombed. My father and Alan Sues opened a hat shop. Sues designed the hats. My father kept the books and flogged the hats by mail order. The venture went bust quicksville.

My father segued to sporadic drugstore gigs. He was pushing sixty-five. He guzzled Alka-Seltzer for his ulcers at the same rate my mother downed bourbon. We were dead-assed broke throughout most of '62.

I conned coin out of Aunt Leoda. The "I need dental work" pitch worked wonders. Fifty-dollar handouts floated us for weeks. I stole from my father to augment my private income.

He sent me to the store to buy our food. I shoplifted a good portion of it and pocketed the price of the items. I carried a wad of one-dollar bills in a Vegas-style money clip.

I rode my top-heavy bike up to Hollywood and out to the beach. I rode it to the downtown public library. I liked to ride and sync my fantasies to street scenes. I liked to cruise by the places where Jill, Kathy and Donna lived.

I thieved as I rode. I copped books at the Pickwick Shop and boosted school supplies from Rexall Drugs. I stole without hesitation or shudders of remorse.

I cut a wide two-wheeled swath. I was a geeky minor miscreant-about-town. I stood 6'1" and scaled in at 130 pounds. Pimples comprised the bulk of my weight. My super-customized bicycle drew jeers and catcalls.

L.A. at large meant freedom. My neighborhood meant self-restriction. My immediate outside world was still rigidly circumscribed: Melrose to Wilshire to Western to Rossmore. That world was packed with my baby-boom peers.

I wanted to be with them. I knew a few from school and a few from neighborhood collisions. I knew all their names and most of their reputations. I craved their friendship and degraded myself to get it.

I tried to buy their affection with Jap surplus Tote Seats—and got laughed out en masse. I invited a few kids to my pad—and watched them recoil at the stench of dogshit. I tried to conform to their standards of normal behavior and betrayed myself with foul language, poor hygiene and expressed admiration for George Lincoln Rockwell and the American Nazi Party.

My exhibitionist flair was purely self-destructive. I couldn't tone down my act. I was programmed to grandstand and alienate. My efforts to adapt triggered an internal backlash. I cut myself off at the pass and remained a teenage leper.

Other lepers dug my act and fell in behind my banner. I ruled my leper colony imperiously. I didn't respect the kids who thought I was cool. My school friendships burned out quick. Most of my buddies were Jewish and predisposed to distrust my Nazi shenanigans.

My friendships began with nihilistic bonhomie and ended with ineffectual fistfights. I won kids over with shock tactics and blew them out with my overall loser vibe. The pattern was endlessly repetitive.

I made friends with a neighborhood kid. We started jacking each other off. It was my first sexual contact. It was shameful, exciting, loathsome and motherfucking scary.

We jacked each other off at his pad and at my pad and on apartment-house rooftops. We spread *Playboy* magazines out and looked at them while we labored. We knew we weren't fags. Our mutual-masturbation limits were easily adhered to.

I knew I wasn't a homo. My fantasy life proved it. I sought out the Kinsey Report for validation.

Doc Kinsey called youthful fag activity commonplace. He failed to address my real fears:

Can mutual jackoffs turn you into a fruit? Does the mere indulgence stigmatize you in recognizable ways?

I was a horny little shitbird. Mutual jackoffs were better than self-propelled jackoffs. My friend and I jacked each other off several times a week. I loved it and hated it. It was driving me fucking crazy.

I was afraid my father would catch us. I was afraid I'd start emitting fruit vibes. I was afraid that God would turn me into a fruit— just punishment for all my years of stealing.

My fear escalated. I felt people boring into my mind. I turned up the heat on my heterosexual daydreams—a strategy to thwart the people tuning in to my brainwaves.

I was afraid I'd talk in my sleep and alert the old man to my fruit potential. I dreamed that I was on trial for fruitness. Those dreams were scarier than my worst Black Dahlia nightmares.

I quit hanging out with my friend. A few weeks went by. My friend called me and asked me to take his Sunday-morning paper route—he wanted to go to Lake Arrowhead with his family.

I agreed. I slept late Sunday morning, rode over to his house and dumped his stack of *Herald*s in a trash can. My friend braced me at school the next day.

I accepted his challenge to fight. I stipulated a six-round bout—with boxing gloves, referee and judges. My friend agreed to the terms.

We scheduled the fight for the following Sunday. Our will to mayhem proved we weren't fruits.

I recruited a ref, three judges and a timekeeper. Ellie Beers' front lawn served as a ring. A few spectators showed up. It was *the* neighborhood kid event of late spring '62.

My friend and I wore twelve-ounce gloves. We were both stick-skinny and over six feet tall. We possessed no boxing skills whatsoever. We heaved, lurched, thrashed, flailed and powder-puff-punched the shit out of each other for six three-minute rounds. We ended up dehydrated and falling-down dizzy and unable to lift our arms.

I lost via split decision. The fight occurred around the time of the second Emíle Griffith–Benny "Kid" Paret bout. Griffith beat Paret dead. Griffith allegedly hated Paret. Paret allegedly went around calling Griffith a fruit.

I knew I wasn't a fruit. The fight proved it. Nobody was tapping into my brainwaves. It was a stupid fucking notion.

*

I lived by notions—stupid and otherwise. I soaked up crackpot ideas wholesale. Books and movies fed me storylines to revise from a warped perspective.

My mind was a cultural sponge. I was devoid of interpretive powers and possessed no gift for abstraction. I took in fictive plots, historical facts and general minutiae—and built a crazy world-view from odd bits of data.

Classical music got my brain perk-perk-perking. I got lost in Beethoven and Brahms. Symphonies and concertos hit me like complex novels. Crescendos and soft passages formed narrative through lines. Alternating fast and slow movements sent me into mental free-fall.

The nightly news gave me facts. I wove them into a sweeping form and contextualized them to suit my momentary fancy. I connected non-sequitur events and anointed heroes on perverse whim. A liquor-store heist might play into Nazis picketing the film *Exodus*. All murders were attributed to the Black Dahlia killer—currently stalking Jill, Kathy and Donna. I unraveled the hidden threads connecting seemingly disparate occurrences. I worked out of a Hancock Park mansion. I was surrounded by flunkies—say, Vic Morrow in *Portrait of a Mobster* or that tall British guy in *Mr. Sardonicus*.

I hijacked popular culture and furnished my inner world with the clutter. I spoke my own specialized language and viewed the outside world with x-ray-eyeglasses. I saw crime everywhere.

CRIME linked my worlds—inside and outside. Crime was clandestine sex and the random desecration of women. Crime was as banal and rarefied as a young boy's brain perk-perk-perking.

I was a committed anti-Communist and a somewhat more tenuous racist. Jews and Negroes were pawns in the world-wide Commie Conspiracy. I lived by the logic of sequestered truth and hidden agendas. My inner world was obsessively realized and as curative as it was debilitating. It rendered the outside world prosaic and made my daily transit in that world passably bearable.

The old man ruled my outside world. He ruled permissively and kept me in line with occasional outbursts of scorn.

He thought I was weak, lazy, slothful, duplicitous, fanciful and painfully neurotic. He was unhip to the fact that I was his mirror image.

I had his number. He had mine. I started shutting him out. It was the same extrication process I utilized with my mother.

Some neighborhood kids got my number and let me into their clique. They were outcasts with good social skills. Their names were Lloyd, Fritz and Daryl.

Lloyd was a fat boy from a broken home. His mother was a Christian wacko. He was as foulmouthed as I was and loved books and music just as much. Fritz lived in Hancock Park. He dug movie soundtracks and Ayn Rand novels. Daryl was an ass-kicker, athlete and borderline Nazi of half-Jewish parentage.

They let me into their clique. I became their subaltern, court jester and stooge. They thought I was a big-time laugh riot. My raunchy home life shocked and delighted them.

We rode our bikes to movies in Hollywood. I always lagged a hundred yards behind—my Schwinn Corvette was just that heavy and hard to propel. We listened to music and spritzed on sex, politics, books and our preposterous ideas.

I couldn't hold my own intellectually. My sense of discourse was internally directed and channeled into narrative. My friends thought I wasn't as smart as they were. They teased me and ragged me and made me the butt of their jokes.

I took their shit and kept coming back for more. Lloyd, Fritz and Daryl had a keen instinct for weakness and were skilled at male one-upmanship. Their cruelty hurt—but not enough to make me drop their friendship.

I was resilient. Small slights would make me cry and undergo intense grief for ten minutes maximum. Emotional thrashings left my wounds cauterized and ready to be reopened.

I was a case study in teenage intransigence. I held an iron-clad, steel-buffed, pathologically derived and empirically valid hole card: the ability to withdraw and inhabit a world of my own mental making.

Friendship meant minor indignities. Raucous laughs with the guys meant assuming a subservient role. The cost felt negligible. I knew how to reap profit from estrangement.

I didn't know that costs accrue. I didn't know that you always pay for what you suppress.


I graduated from junior high in June '62. I read, stole, masturbated and fantasized my way through the summer. I enrolled at Fairfax High School in September.

The old man insisted on Fairfax. It was 90-odd-% Jewish and safer than Los Angeles High School—the joint I was supposed to attend. L.A. High was full of tough Negro kids. The old man figured they'd kill me the first time I opened my mouth. Alan Sues lived a few blocks from Fairfax. The old man borrowed Alan's address and plopped his Nazi son down in the heart of the West L.A. shtetl.

It was a dislocating cultural experience.

John Burroughs Junior High felt safe. Fairfax felt dangerous. Lloyd, Fritz and Daryl were matriculating elsewhere. My Hancock Park acquaintances were off at prep school. I was a stranger in a strange fucking land.

Fairfax High kids were ferociously bright and sophisticated. They smoked cigarettes and drove cars. I parked my Schwinn Corvette on the first day of school and got roundly razzed.

I knew that my act wouldn't fly here. I retreated and scoped out the turf long-distance.

I attended classes and kept my mouth shut. I ditched my Ivy League threads and aped the sartorial style of Fairfax hipsters: tight slacks, alpaca sweaters and pointy-toe boots. The makeover didn't work. I looked like a frightened child cum lounge-singer-manqué.

Fairfax High seduced me. Fairfax Avenue seduced me. I dug the insular Yiddish vibe. I dug the oldsters yakking it up in a wild-assed guttural language. My reaction confirmed the old man's theory: "You only talk that Nazi shit to get attention."

I worked hard at school and tried to assimilate. The methodology eluded me. I knew how to rile, provoke, act like a buffoon and generally make a spectacle of myself. The concept of a simple social contract between equals was completely foreign to me.

I studied. I read shitloads of crime novels and went to crime movies. I fantasized and tailed girls home from school on my bike. The assimilation bit grew stale. Magnanimity ate shit. I was tired of being an anonymous Wasp in Jewville, U.S.A. I couldn't stand being ignored.

The American Nazi Party established an outpost in Glendale. The American Legion and Jewish War Vets wanted them out. I rode my bicycle to their office and bought 40 dollars' worth of hate goodies.

I got a Nazi armband, several issues of *Stormtrooper* magazine, a record called "Ship Those Niggers Back" by Odis Cochran and the Three Bigots, a few dozen racist bumper stickers and two hundred "Boat Tickets to Africa"—a gag item entitling all Negroes to a oneway trip to the Congo on a leaky barge. I was delighted with my new swag. It was hilarious and cool.

I wore the armband around my pad. I painted swastikas on the dog's water dish. My father started calling me "Der Führer" and "you Nazi cocksucker." He got ahold of a Jewish beanie and wore it around the pad to bug me.

I rode up to Poor Richard's Bookshop and purchased an assortment of far-right-wing tracts. I mailed them to the girls I was obsessed with and stuck them in mailboxes all over Hancock Park. Lloyd, Fritz and Daryl booted me out of their clique. I was just too weird and pathetic.

My father was knee-deep in a work slump. We fell behind on the rent and got booted out of our apartment. The landlord said the pad would have to be fumigated. A five-year accumulation of dog effluvia had rendered the place uninhabitable.

We moved to a cheaper crib a few blocks away. The dog went to work on it. I debuted my Nazi act at Fairfax High School.

Classroom declarations earned me scorn and quite a few laughs. I talked up my intention to establish a Fourth Reich in Southern California, deport all jigaboos to Africa and genetically engineer a new master race with my own seed. I was not perceived as a threat. I was one ineffectual Führer.

I kept it up. A few teachers called my father and ratted me off. The old man told them to ignore me.

Spring '63 marked my blitzkrieg. I disrupted classes, passed out hate tracts and sold Boat Tickets to Africa for ten cents a pop. A big Jewish kid cornered me in the rotunda and kicked my ass soundly. I got one decent shot in—and sprained all the fingers in my right hand.

The beating validated my act and left me undeterred. I would not be ignored.

The summer of '63 passed in a blur. I read crime novels, went to crime movies, concocted mental crime scenarios and stalked Kathy around Hancock Park. I stole books, food, model airplane kits and "Hang-Ten" swimming trunks to sell to rich-ass surfers. My Nazi hard-on abated. It was no fun without a captive audience.

My mother was five years dead. I rarely thought about her. Her murder had no place in my crime pantheon.

I still had occasional Black Dahlia nightmares. I still obsessed on the Dahlia. She was the heart of my crime world. I didn't know that she was the redhead transmogrified.

School reconvened in September. I went back to my Nazi routine. It played to a bored audience.

The gap between my inner world and outside world was stretching. I wanted to ditch school forever and live out my obsessions full-time. Formal education was worthless. I was destined to become a great novelist. The books I loved were my real curriculum.

The *Fugitive* TV show debuted in September. I got hooked on it fast.

It was mass-market noir. A doctor was running from a trumped-up murder charge and the electric chair. He hit a different town every week. The coolest woman in the town fell in love with him, unfailingly. A prissy psycho cop was chasing the doctor. Authority figures were corrupt and twisted by their power. The show sizzled with sexual longing. The female guest stars grabbed my gonads and did not let go.

They were 30-ish and more handsome than pretty. They responded to male stimulus with wariness and hunger. The show reeked of real sex just around the corner. The women were troubled and complex. Their desires carried psychic weight. TV gave me Jean Ellroy every Tuesday night at 10:00.

The fall of '63 progressed. I came home from school on November 1st and found my father sitting in a pool of urine and feces. He was twitching and weeping and babbling and drooling. His taut musculature had gone slack in the course of a day.

It was a horrifying sight. I started crying and babbling myself. The old man just looked at me. His eyes were huge and way out of focus.

I cleaned him up and called his doctor. An ambulance arrived. Two medics hustled my father out to the Veterans Administration Hospital.

I stayed home and cleaned up the remains of his mess. A doctor called me and told me my father had suffered a stroke. He wasn't going to die and he might well recover. His left arm was partially paralyzed and his speech was indecipherable for now.

I was afraid he'd die. I was afraid he'd live and kill me with those big wet eyes.

He started to recover. His speech capability improved within days. He got some movement back in his left arm.

I visited him every day. His prognosis was good—but he wasn't the same man.

He used to be a virile bullshit artist. He became a soft child in a week's time. The transformation ripped my heart out.

He had to read kiddie primers to get his tongue and palate working in sync. His eyes said, "Love me, I'm helpless."

I tried to love him. I lied about my progress in school and told him I'd support him when I scored big as a writer. My lies cheered him up the way his lies cheered me up years back.

His condition continued to improve. He came home on November 22nd—the day JFK bought it. He went back to smoking two packs a day. He went back to Alka-Seltzer. He talked his old raunchy talk with just a slight slur—but his fucking eyes gave him away.

He was terrified and defenseless. I was his shield against death and a slow fade in a charity nursing home. I was all he had.

The old man went on Social Security. We downscaled our lifestyle accordingly. I stole most of our food and cooked most of our high-salt, high-cholesterol meals. I ditched school most of the time and flunked the eleventh grade.

I knew my father was a dead man. I wanted to care for him and see him dead simultaneously. I didn't want him to suffer. I wanted to be alone in my all-pervasive fantasy world.

The old man was now stiflingly possessive. He was convinced that my mere presence could divert strokes and other acts of God. I chafed at his demands. I ridiculed his slurred speech. I stayed out late riding around L.A. with no destination in mind.

I couldn't get away from his eyes. I could not fucking negate their power.

I got busted for shoplifting in May '64. A floorwalker caught me boosting six pairs of swimming trunks. He detained me and hassled me for hours. He jabbed me in the chest and made me sign a guilt waiver. He cut me loose at 10:00 p.m.—way past my prescribed time to be home.

I rode to the pad and saw an ambulance in front of the building. My father was strapped in the back. The driver told me he just had a mild heart attack.

My father zapped me with his eyes. They said, "Where *were* you?"

He recovered and came home. He went back to smoking and sucking down Alka-Seltzer. He was hellbent to die. I was hellbent to live *my* way. Life was the Lee Ellroy Show. It played to unimpressed and vexed crowds in and out of school.

I provoked fights with smaller kids. I broke into the shed behind the Larchmont Safeway and stole 60 dollars' worth of empty pop bottles. I made obscene phone calls. I called in bomb threats to high schools throughout the L.A. basin. I burglarized a hot-dog stand, stole some frozen meat and tossed it down a sewer hole. I went on kleptomaniacal missions and sulked, skulked and nazified my way through a second pass at grade 11.

I turned 17 in March '65. I was now a full-grown 6'3". My pantlegs terminated several inches above my ankles. My shirts were stained with blood and pus from cystic acne explosions. I wanted OUT.

The old man deserved a quick out himself—just like the redhead.

I knew he'd hang on and die slow. I knew I didn't want to see it.

I threw a Nazi tantrum in English class and got suspended from school for a week. I went back and did it again. I got expelled from Fairfax High for good.

Faraway places beckoned. Paradise loomed just outside L.A. County. I told the old man I wanted to join the army. He gave me his permission and let me enlist.

The army was a big mistake. I knew it the moment I took the oath.

I called my father from the induction center and told him I was in. He broke down and sobbed. A little voice in my head said, "You killed him."

I got on a plane with a dozen other enlistees. We flew to Houston, Texas, and caught a connecting flight to Fort Polk, Louisiana.

It was early May. Fort Polk was hot, humid and overrun with flying and crawling bugs. Hard-ass sergeants formed us into lines and harangued the shit out of us.

I knew that my freewheeling life was over. I wanted OUT immediately.

A sergeant got us squared away and settled into a reception center barracks. I wanted to say, "I changed my mind—please let me go home." I knew I couldn't take the hard work and discipline upcoming. I knew I had to get OUT.

I called home. The old man was incoherent. I panicked and buttonholed an officer. He heard me out, checked me out and walked me to the infirmary.

A doctor examined me. I was frantically agitated and into a performance mode already. I was afraid for my father and afraid of the army. I was calculating advantages in the middle of a panic attack.

The doctor shot me up with a high-powered tranquilizer. I weaved back to my barracks and passed out on my bunk.

I woke up after evening chow. I was woozy and my speech was slurred. A notion took tenuous hold.

All I had to do was crank my fear for my father's safety up a few notches.

I started stuttering the next morning. I was convincing from the first tangled syllable on. I was a Method actor tapping into real-life resources.

My platoon sergeant bought the act. I was a stage ham—but not quite a scenery chewer. I wrote the sergeant a note and expressed grave concern for my father. The sergeant called him and told me, "He don't sound good."

I was assigned to a unit: Company A, 2nd Battalion, 5th Training Brigade. I was tagged as a probable nut case my first day in uniform. The company commander heard my tortured speech and said I was unfit for this man's army.

Real fear shaped my performance. An innate dramatic sense honed it. I could have snapped *for real* in a hot second. My long twitchy body was a great actor's tool.

I began basic training. I endured two days of marching and general army jive. My fellow trainees shined me on—I was a stuttering geek from Mars.

The company commander called me into his office. He said the Red Cross was flying me home for two weeks. My father just had another stroke.

The old man looked surprisingly good. He was sharing a room with another stroke victim.

The guy told me all the nurses were in awe of my dad's jumbo whanger. They giggled about it and scoped it out while he was sleeping.

I visited my father every day for two weeks running. I told him I was coming home to take care of him. I meant it. The *real* outside world scared me back to loving him.

My furlough was a blast. I festooned my uniform with war surplus insignia and bopped around L.A. like I was King Shit. I wore paratrooper's wings, the combat infantry badge and four rows of campaign ribbons. I was the most self-decorated buck private in military history.

I flew back to Fort Polk late in May. I resumed my stuttering act and ran it by an army psychiatrist. He recommended me for immediate discharge. His report cited my "over-dependence on supportive figures," "poor performance in stressful situations" and "marked unsuitability for military service."

My discharge was approved. The paperwork would take a month to process.

I did it. I fooled them and duped them and made them believe me.

The Red Cross called a few days later. My father just had another stroke.

I saw him one last time. The Red Cross got me back right before he died.

He was emaciated. He had tubes in his nose and his arms. He was stuck full of holes and smeared with red disinfectant.

I held his right hand to the bed rail and told him he'd be fine. His last discernible words were, "Try to pick up every waitress who serves you."

A nurse hustled me into a waiting room. A doctor walked in a few minutes later and told me my father was dead.

It was June 4, 1965. He outlived my mother by less than seven years.

I walked over to Wilshire and caught a bus back to my motel. I forced myself to cry—just like I did with the redhead.

**10**

The army cut me loose in July. I got a general discharge "Under Honorable Conditions." I was free, white and 17. I was draft-exempt just as Vietnam started to percolate.

My fellow trainees were headed for advanced infantry training and probable Vietnam duty. I dodged their bullet with Method-actor aplomb. I spent my last month at Fort Polk wolfing down crime novels. I stuttered and lurked around the Company A mess hall. I scammed the entire U.S. Army.

I flew back to L.A. and beelined to the old neighborhood. I found a one-room pad at Beverly and Wilton. The army sent me home with five hundred dollars. I forged my father's name to his last three Social Security checks and cashed them at a liquor store. My bankroll increased to a grand.

Aunt Leoda promised to shoot me a C-note a month. She warned me that my insurance money wouldn't last forever. She signed me up for Social Security and VA benefits— surviving-child stipends that would terminate on my 18th birthday. She urged me to go back to school. Full-time students could collect the coin up to age 21.

She was glad my father was dead. It probably assuaged her grief for my mother.

School was for geeks and spastics. My motto was "Live Free or Die."

The dog was kenneled up. My old apartment was locked and boarded. The landlord had seized my father's belongings in lieu of back rent. My new crib was great. It featured a bathroom, tiny kitchenette and 12′ × 8′ living room with a Murphy bed. I papered the walls with right-wing bumper stickers and Playmate of the Month foldouts.

I strutted around in my uniform for a week. I stood over my father's grave and flaunted my army greens replete with unearned regalia. I boosted a new wardrobe from Silverwoods and Desmonds'. It was pure Hancock Park: madras shirts, crew-neck sweaters, thin-wale cord pants.

L.A. looked bright and beautiful. I knew I'd pursue some kind of swinging fucking destiny right here in my own hometown.

I stuck my roll in the bank and looked for work. I got a job passing out handbills and quit from boredom one week later. I got a bus-boy job at L.A.'s flagship Sizzler steakhouse and got fired for dropping shitloads of dishes. I got a kitchen job at a Kentucky Fried Chicken joint and got fired for picking my nose in front of customers.

I ran through three jobs in two weeks. I shrugged my failures off and opted for a work-free summer.

Lloyd, Fritz and Daryl rediscovered me. I had a pad of my own now. This made me a viable flunky.

They let me back into their clique. A brilliant kid named George made us a fivesome. Fritz and George were USC- and Caltech-bound. Lloyd and Daryl were stuck with another year of high school.

The clique met at my place and George's place. George's father, Rudy, was a highway patrolman and a certified right-wing crackpot. He got drunk every night and defamed liberals and Martin Luther Coon. He dug my Boat Tickets to Africa and took a fatherly interest in me.

It was great to have friends. I blew my thousand-dollar roll taking them out to steak dinners and movies. We bombed around in Fritz's '64 Fairlane. Bicycle jaunts were behind us.

I stole most of my food. I was on an all-steak diet and filched T-bones and rib-eyes at nearby supermarkets. Two clerks jumped me outside the Liquor & Food Mart early in August. They held me down, plucked a steak out of my pants and called the fuzz.

The LAPD arrived. Two cops drove me to the Hollywood Station, booked me for shoplifting and turned me over to a juvenile officer. The guy wanted to contact my parents. I told him they were dead. He said kids weren't allowed to live alone prior to age eighteen.

A cop drove me down to the Georgia Street Juvenile Facility. I called Lloyd and told him where I was. The cop processed my arrest papers and dumped me in a dormitory filled with hardcased juvies.

I was scared. I was the biggest kid in the dorm—and recognizably the most defenseless. I was seven months shy of legal age. I figured I'd be stuck here all that time.

Tough Negro and Mexican kids sized me up. They asked me about my "beef" and laughed at my answers. They talked gangsterese and ridiculed me for not speaking their language.

I stayed calm until lights-out. Darkness jump-started my imagination. I put myself through a string of jail horrors and cried myself to sleep.

Rudy got me out the next day. He cooked up a deal to get me six months probation and "emancipated juvenile" status. I could live solo—with Rudy as my informal guardian.

It was one sweet deal. I needed a ticket out of jail and Rudy needed an audience for his tirades. Lloyd, Fritz and Daryl heard him out reluctantly. I soaked up his shit with abandon.

Rudy was tight with a bunch of crazy cop ideologues. They passed around mimeographed copies of "The Nigger's 23rd Psalm" and "Martin Luther Coon's Welfare Handbook." Rudy and I yukked it up for a string of consecutive nights. The Watts riot interrupted us.

L.A. was burning. I wanted to kill all the rioters and turn L.A. into Cinder City myself. The riot thrilled me. This was crime writ large—crime on a big plot-extrapolatable scale.

Rudy was called to duty. Lloyd, Fritz and I skirted the periphery of the riot zone. We carried BB pistols. We mouthed racist jive and cruised south until some cops made us go home.

We did it again the next night. Live history was groovy. We watched the riot from the Griffith Park telescopes and saw strips of Los Angeles sizzling. We drove out to the valley and saw some rednecks burn a cross in a Christmas-tree lot.

The riot fizzled out. It reconflagrated in my head and ruled my thoughts for weeks.

I ran stories from diverse perspectives. I became both riot cop and riot provocateur. I lived lives fucked over by history.

I spread my empathy around. I distributed moral shading equitably. I didn't analyze the cause of the riot or prophesy its ramifications. My public stance was "Fuck the niggers." My concurrent narrative fantasies stressed culpable white cops.

I never questioned the contradiction. I didn't know that storytelling was my only true voice.

Narrative was my moral language. I didn't know it in the summer of 1965.


Rudy didn't care what I did. My probation officer ignored me. I continued to steal and dodge work.

I craved free time. Free time meant time to dream and cultivate my sense of potent destiny. Free time meant time to fall prey to impulse.

It was a hot day in mid-September. I got an urge to get drunk.

I walked down to the Liquor & Food Mart and stole a bottle of champagne. I took it over to Robert Burns Park, popped the top and guzzled the whole thing.

I went ecstatic. I went hyper-effusive. I crashed a group of Hancock Park girls and told them crazy lies. I blacked out and woke up on my bed drenched in vomit.

I knew I'd *found* something.

The discovery thrilled me. I started stealing booze and experimenting with it.

Heublein premixed cocktails were good. I dug sweet Manhattans and tart and tangy whisky sours. Beer quenched your thirst—but lacked the blastoff potential of hard liquor. Straight scotch was too strong—it burned going down and brought up bile in its wake. I avoided straight bourbon and bourbon highballs. Bourbon reminded me of the redhead.

Vodka and fruit juice was great. You got a fast push out of

the gate with minimum gag action. Gin, brandy and liqueurs induced dry heaves.

I drank for stimulation. Booze sent me stratospheric.

It jacked up my narrative powers. It gave my thoughts a physical dimension.

Booze made me talk to myself. Booze made me spritz my fantasies aloud. Booze made me address scores of imaginary women.

Booze altered my fantasy world—but did not change the basic subject matter. Crime remained my dominant obsession.

I had a big crime backlog to embellish.

The Watts riot was recent and hot. The Ma Duncan case was a slick golden oldie. I walked Ma to the gas chamber a hundred fantasy times.

Doc Finch and Carole Tregoff were rotting in prison. I saved Carole from jailhouse dykes and made her my woman. I snuck into Chino and snuffed Spade Cooley. Ella Mae got her vengeance at last. I committed Stephen Nash's murders and pulled B&Es with Donald Keith Bashor.

Booze gave me prime verisimilitude. Details blipped off my brain pan in vivid new colors. Narrative twists emerged unexpectedly.

Booze gave me crime hyperbolized and rendered more subtle. It gave me the Black Dahlia on a broad historical scale.

I drank by myself and screened crime and crime-sex fantasies for hours. I drank with Lloyd and got him hooked on the Dahlia. We discussed the case at great length. My occasional Dahlia nightmares ceased altogether.

I stole most of my liquor and found an adult to purchase some for me legally. He was a Negro wino living under a freeway embankment. He called himself Flame-O. He said the cops dubbed him that because he tended to torch himself when he got drunk.

Flame-O bought me bottles. I paid him in short dog jugs of Thunderbird wine. He told me I was wino bait myself. I didn't believe him.

Lloyd and Fritz reintroduced me to weed. I dug it ferociously. It added a surreal edge to my fantasies and made food a rich sensual pleasure. I knew it wouldn't turn me into a junkie. That was strictly a 1958 illusion.

1965 faded out. It was one motherfucker of a year.

Rudy kissed me off. He figured out I was worthless and not a sincere right-winger. I turned 18 in March '66. I was now a street-legal adult.

And an unemployed petty thief about to lose his government handout.

I unkenneled the dog and brought her home. She went to work on the floors immediately. I pondered my future. I concluded that I couldn't live without my survivor's dole.

I had to go back to school to keep the dough coming. Lloyd was going to a freako Christian high school. The freight was $50 a month. My dole came to $130. I could attend a few classes and retain a net profit of 80 bucks monthly.

Lloyd and I discussed the matter. He told me I'd have to take a convincing dive for Jesus. I memorized some Bible verses and went in to see the principal of Culter Christian Academy.

I put on a good show. I strutted my new faith in high histrionic style. I believed what I was saying for the length of time I was saying it. I possessed a chameleon soul.

I enrolled at Culter Academy. The place was packed with born-again psychos and doper malcontents. I attended secular classes and Bible study groups. It was brain-deadening rebop straight down the line. I knew I couldn't take this shit five days a week.

I attended school sporadically. The Culter staff cut me some slack—I was a tormented but sincere young Christian. I stiffed them for two months' tuition and dropped out completely. My brief conversion netted me $260.

My government benefits stopped. My income dropped to a C-note a month. My rent was $60. I could stretch the remaining $40—if I stole *all* my food and liquor and scrounged dope off my friends.

I did it. I extended my shoplifting range and hit markets and liquor stores way north and way west. I was bone-skinny. I jammed steaks and bottles under my pants and did not display telltale bulges. I wore my shirttails out. I bought small items to justify my presence in stores.

I was a pro.

Lloyd, Fritz and Daryl could score dope. I couldn't. I had an adult-free pad they could kick back in. They supplied me with grass and pills.

I didn't like Seconal and Nembutal. They made you goofy and near-catatonic. LSD was okay—but the attendant trans-cendental message left me cold. Lloyd and Fritz popped acid and went to see epics like *Spartacus* and *The Greatest Story Ever Told*. I went with them a few times and ditched the movies midway through. Sandals and resurrection—Snoresville. I sat in the lobby and hallucinated on candy-counter girls.

Fritz knew some Dr. Feelgoods who dispensed ampheta-mines. The stuff kept him hyper-focused during long study sessions. USC was tough going. Fritz said the uppers gave him an edge.

He dumped his excess stash on me. Dexedrine and Dexamyl jacked my fantasy life up six levels.

My narrative skills expanded sixfold. Speed-induced palpi-tations kineticized the whole process.

Speed highs went through my brain and lodged in my virgin genitalia.

Speed was sex. Speed gave my sex fantasies a new coherent logic. Speed gave me 40-ish redheads and Hancock Park girls. Speed gave me epic jackoff sessions.

I pounded my pud for 12 to 18 hours straight. It felt so *gooooood*. I'd lie on my bed with the dog asleep beside me. I'd slam the ham with my eyes shut and the lights out.

Amphetamine comedowns terminated my fantasies. The dope passed through my system and left me depressed and sleep-deprived. I drank myself into a nether world then. Booze ascended while speed receded. I always passed out grasping for some woman.


Fritz lost his speed connection. I lost mine by default. I got gnawingly hungry for real love and sex.

I wanted a girlfriend *and* unlimited poontang. Fritz's sister set me up with her friend Cathy.

Cathy went to Marlborough—an exclusive Hancock Park girl's school. She was plain-featured and chubby. We went to see *The Sound of Music* on our first date. I lied and told Cathy that I really liked the movie.

Cathy was socially dense and love-starved. I found it appealing. She disdained formal date activities. She craved park-the-car make-out action.

Which meant hugging and kissing sans tongues.

We "made out" several weekend nights running. The no-tongue/no-skin policy drove me insane. I begged for more contact. Cathy refused. I begged some more. Cathy threw a big diversion at me.

She planned a string of get-togethers with her school chums. The diversion got me inside looks at several juicy Hancock Park pads.

I liked the plush furnishings. I liked the big rooms. I liked the wood panels and oil paintings. This was my old voyeur prowl world—close-up and intimate.

Cathy introduced me to her friend Anne. Anne was 6'1", blond and strapping. She never got dates.

I called Anne up and asked her out. We went to a movie and necked in Fern Dell Park. She shot me some tongue. It was *gooooood*.

I called up Cathy and broke our thing off. Anne called me and told me to stay out of her life. I called Fritz's sister Heidi and asked her out. She told me to buzz off. I called Heidi's friend Kay and asked her out. She told me she was a committed Christian and only went out with saved guys.

I wanted more love. I wanted sex with no schoolgirl limits. I wanted to see some more Hancock Park pads.

Fritz maintained a little room adjoining his garage. He kept his records and stereo shit there. It was his hideout. He never let his parents or sister in. Lloyd, Daryl and I had keys.

The room was 20 yards from the main house. The house tantalized me. It was my favorite sex-fantasy backdrop.

I broke in one night. It was late '66.

Fritz and his family were out somewhere. I got down on the ground beside the kitchen door and stuck my left arm through a pet-access hole. I tripped the inside latch and let myself in to the house.

I walked around. I kept the lights off and prowled upstairs and down. I checked the medicine cabinets for dope and filched a few painkillers. I poured myself a double scotch and popped the pills right there. I washed the glass I used and put it back where I found it.

I walked through Heidi's bedroom. I savored the smell of her pillows and went through her closet and drawers. I buried my face in a stack of lingerie and stole a pair of white panties.

I left the house quietly. I didn't want to blow a shot at re-entry. I knew I'd touched another secret world.

Kay lived directly across the street. I broke into her house a few nights later.

I called the house from Fritz's back room and got no answer. I walked over and checked entry points.

I found an open window overlooking the driveway. It was covered by a screen secured with bent nails. I pried two bottom nails loose, removed the screen and vaulted into the house.

It was strange turf. I turned a few lights on for a second to acclimate myself.

There was no liquor cabinet. There was no good shit in the medicine chests. I hit the refrigerator and stuffed myself with cold cuts and fruit. I explored the house upstairs and down—and saved Kay's bedroom for last.

I looked through her school papers and stretched out on her bed. I examined a clothes hamper stuffed with blouses and skirts. I opened dresser drawers and held a table lamp over them for light. I stole a matching bra and panties.

I replaced the window screen and bent the nails back to hold it in place. I walked home very high.

Burglary was voyeurism multiplied a thousand times.

*

Kathy lived in a big Spanish house at 2nd and Plymouth. She was my longtime secret love.

She was tall and slender. She had dark brown hair, brown eyes and freckles. She was intelligent, sweet-natured and altogether gracious. I was afraid of her for no justifiable reason.

I broke into her house. It was a very cold night in early '67.

I called her number and got no answer. I walked over to the house and saw no lights on and no cars in the driveway. I walked around to the back and tried to slide some windows open. The third or fourth one was unlatched.

I pulled myself inside. I stumbled around the first floor and turned lights on for a split second. I found a liquor sideboard and guzzled out of every bottle on it. I got a slam-bang-heavy booze rush and walked upstairs.

I couldn't tell whose bedroom was whose. I lay down on all the beds and found female undergarments in an armoire and chest of drawers. The sizing on the bras and panties confused me. I stole two sets to make sure I had Kathy's.

I found some prescription downers in a medicine chest. I stole three and chased them with a weird-ass liqueur. I went out that back window, weaved home and passed out on my bed.


I kept doing it. I went at it with uncharacteristic restraint.

I quit popping pills at the scene. I only stole fetishistic booty. I went back to Heidi's, Kay's and Kathy's houses at odd intervals and stayed inside no more than 15 minutes. I aborted my mission if I found my entry points secured.

The thrill was sex and other worlds briefly captured. Burglary gave me young women and families by extension.

I burglarized my way through '67. I never strayed outside Hancock Park. I tapped the homes of my dream girls exclusively.

Heidi, Kay and Kathy. Missy at 1st and Beachwood. Julie three doors down and across the street from Kathy. Joanne at 2nd and Irving.

Secret worlds.

*

Daryl moved up to Pordand in early '68. Fritz transferred to UCLA. Lloyd was attending L.A. City College. He was almost as booze-and-dope-addled as I was.

Lloyd possessed the balls that I lacked. He had a bent for tortured women hooked up with abusive men. He tried to rescue them and got into fights with dope-dealer sleazebags. He had a big heart and a big brain and a wickedly nihilistic sense of humor. He lived with his religious-nut mother and her second husband—a produce merchant with a couple of fruit stands out in the valley.

Lloyd had a taste for Hollywood lowlife. He knew how to talk to hoodlum types and hippies. I tagged along on a few of his Hollywood excursions. I met bikers, fruit hustlers and Gene the Short Queen— a 4'10" transvestite. I stumbled around Hollywood, took weird drug combinations and woke up in parks and Christmas-tree lots.

The peace-and-love era was booming. Lloyd had one foot in that cultural door and one foot back on the edge of Hancock Park. He had his own dual-world scheme going. He postured and copped dope in Hollywood and came home to his crazy mother.

Hollywood scared me and vexed me. Hippies were faggot shitheads. They loved degenerate music and preached specious metaphysics. Hollywood was a pus pocket.

Lloyd disagreed. He told me the real world frightened me. He said I only knew a few square miles.

He was right. He didn't know I supplanted my knowledge with things he'd never know.

I kept burglarizing. I went at it cravenly and cautiously. I kept reading crime novels and brain-screening crime fantasies. I kept stealing and eating an all-steak diet. I lived off a C-note a month.

The dog disappeared. I came home and found my door open and Minna long gone. I suspected my dog-hater landlord.

I searched for Minna and put a lost-dog ad in the *L.A. Times*. Nothing came of it. I blew two months' rent money on dope and got locked out of my pad.

Aunt Leoda refused to advance me some coin. I spent a week crashed out in Fritz's back room and got evicted by his father. I moved into Lloyd's bedroom and got evicted by his mother.

I moved into Robert Burns Park. I stole some blankets from a Goodwill box and slept in an ivy patch for three weeks. A nocturnal sprinkling system doused me at irregular intervals. I had to gather up my blankets and run for dry spots.

Outdoor living ate shit. I went to the California State Employment Office and got some job referrals. A Serbo-Croatian psychic hired me as a handbill distributor.

Her name was Sister Ramona. She preyed on poor blacks and Mexicans and spread her message via mimeographed flyer. She healed the sick and dispensed financial advice. Poor people flocked to her door. She soaked the stupid cocksuckers for all they were worth.

Sister Ramona was a racist and right-wing fanatic. Her husband drove me to poverty pockets and dropped me off with newspaper bags full of handbills. I slid them under doors and stuffed them in mailboxes. Little kids and dogs followed me around. Teenagers laughed at me and flipped me the bird.

The husband gave me two bucks a day lunch money. I spent it on T-Bird and muscatel. Flame-O was right: I turned into a full-fledged wino.

I put a roll together and got my pad back. I quit my Sister Ramona job.

A high-school acquaintance introduced me to a woman who needed a place to stay. She said she'd devirginize me in exchange for a roof. I eagerly accepted her offer.

She moved in. She devirginized me under duress. I didn't turn her on and my acne-scarred back repulsed her. She fucked me four times and told me that was all I was getting. I was crazy about her and let her stay anyway.

She bewitched me. She dominated me completely. She stayed with me for three months and announced that she was a lesbian. She'd just met a woman and was moving in with her.

I was heartbroken. I went on a long vodka bender and blew my rent money. My landlord evicted me again.

I moved back into Robert Burns Park and found a

permanent dry spot by a toolshed. I started to think that outdoor living wasn't *that* bad. I had a safe spot to sleep, and I could hang out with Lloyd and read in public libraries all day. I could shave in public restrooms and take occasional showers at Lloyd's place.

I got my rationale straight and proceeded on that course. I switched my diet from steaks to luncheon meat and haunted branch libraries all over L.A. I drank in library men's rooms and went through Ross Macdonald's entire oeuvre my first few weeks on the street. I kept a change of clothes at Lloyd's pad and bathed there occasionally.

It was fall '68. I met a freak at the Hollywood Public Library. He told me about Benzedrex inhalers.

They were an over-the-counter decongestant product encased in little plastic tubes. The tubes held a wad of cotton soaked in a substance called prophylhexedrine. You were supposed to stick the tube in your nose and take a few sniffs. You *weren't* supposed to swallow the wads and fly on righteous ten-hour speed highs.

Benzedrex inhalers were legal. They cost 69 cents. You could buy them or boost them all over L.A.

The freak said I should steal a few. I dug the idea. I could tap into a speed source without dope connections or a doctor's prescription. I stole three inhalers at a Sav-On drugstore and hunkered down to chase them with root beer.

The wads were two inches long and of cigarette circumference. They were soaked in an evil-smelling amber solution. I gagged one down and fought a reflex to heave it back up. It stayed down and went to work inside half an hour.

The high was *gooooood*. It was brain-popping and groin-grabbing. It was just as good as a pharmaceutical-upper high.

I went back to my spot in Robert Burns Park and jacked off all night. The high lasted eight solid hours and left me dingy and schizzy. T-Bird took the edge off and eased me into a fresh euphoria.

I'd found something. It was something I could have at will.

I went at it willfully. I stole inhalers and flew every third or fourth day for a month. I chugged down inhalers in library men's rooms and buzzed back to Burns Park with my head scraping the moon. The speed continuum gave me my most textured crime and sex fantasies. I stole a flashlight and some skin mags and worked them into my scene.

Outdoor life was good. I told Aunt Leoda to send my monthly C-note care of Lloyd. She thought I was bunking in with a buddy. I didn't tell her I was now a perpetual camper.

I forgot to factor rain into my outdoor-life equation. Some drizzles sent me looking for shelter. I found a deserted house at 8th and Ardmore and moved in.

It was a two-story job with no interior lights and no running water. The living room featured a moldy faux-leather couch. The couch was good for sleeping and sustained jackoff action.

I settled into the house. I kept the front door unlocked and hid my stuff in a closet when I went out. I figured I was being discreet. I was mistaken.

It went down in late November. Four cops kicked my door in and charged me with shotguns.

They threw me to the floor and handcuffed me. They stuck those big 12-gauge pumps in my face. They threw me in a car, drove me to Wilshire Station and booked me for burglary.

My cellmate was a black guy popped for armed robbery. He held up a liquor store, got away clean and saw that he'd dropped his Afro comb at the scene. He went back to get it. The proprietor recognized him. The cops bagged his ass right there.

I was scared. This was worse than Georgia Street Juvie.

A detective interviewed me. I told him I was sleeping in the house—not burglarizing it. He believed me and knocked the beef down to plain trespassing. A jailer moved me over to the misdemeanor side of the tank.

My fear subsided a bit. My cellmates said trespassing was chickenshit stuff. I'd probably get cut loose at arraignment.

I spent Saturday and Sunday at the Wilshire holding tank. They fed us two TV dinners and two cups of coffee a day. I was in with a bunch of drunks and wife beaters. We all lied about our crime exploits and the women we'd fucked.

A Sheriff's bus hauled us to court early Monday morning. It

dropped us off at the Lincoln Heights Division—home of the famous Lincoln Heights drunk tank.

We waited to see the judge there. The tank was forty yards square and jam-packed with male lowlife. Deputies lobbed lunch sacks into the crowd. You had to fight for your food. I was tall enough to snag my chow straight out of the air.

The day stretched. A dozen winos suffered alcoholic seizures. We went before the judge ten or so at a time. The judge was a woman named Mary Waters. The guys in the tank said she was a nasty old cunt.

I stood before her and pled guilty. She said I looked like a draft dodger. I told her I wasn't. She ordered me held without bail—pending a probation workup. I was due back in court on December 23rd.

It was December 2nd. I was headed for three weeks in stir.

I tamped down my composure. A deputy hooked me up to a 12-man shackle chain. Another deputy herded us out to a big black & white bus.

The bus took us to the Main County Jail. It was a huge facility a mile northeast of downtown L.A. The induction process took 12 hours.

Deputies skin-searched us and sprayed us with delousing solution. We traded our street clothes for jail denims. We got blood-tested and inoculated for various diseases. We spent hours moving from one barred pen to another. I got to my actual cell at 2:00 or 3:00 a.m.

It was a four-man cell overpacked now to six. A deputy told me to slide my mattress under the left bottom bunk. I scooted down there and passed out from complete exhaustion.

I woke up for 6:00 a.m. chow. A deputy called off some names on an intercom—my name included. We were being "rolled up" to the Hall of Justice Jail.

An inmate said this was everyday stuff. You processed in at the "New" County and got rolled up elsewhere. The Hall of Justice Jail was known as the "Old" County.

A deputy shackled me to some guys. Two deputies herded us out to a van and drove us to the Old County. We elevatored up to a tank on the thirteenth floor.

My tier was packed to double capacity. A deputy said the

new guys had to sleep on the catwalk. You had to roll your mattress up in the morning and drift between cells until lights-out.

I had twenty days of this coming. An inner voice hipped me to the basic gestalt.

You are big—but not tough. You commit crimes—but are not a *real* criminal. Watch how you act. Watch what you say. Be careful, be calm and hold your breath for twenty days.

I fed myself that message instinctively. I did not verbalize the thought. I didn't know that my mere presence shouted: fool, chump, geek, ineffectual kid.

I kept my mouth shut. I programmed myself to be stoic. I tried not to betray my fear overtly. My fellow inmates laughed at the plain sight of me.

Most of them were felons awaiting trial in Superior Court. They understood and disdained male weakness.

They laughed at my twitchy walk and shortened my two names to the hated "Leroy." They called me "the Nutty Professor." They never put their hands on me. They considered me beneath that kind of contempt.

Lloyd visited me. He said he called my aunt and told her I was in jail. My insurance money was running out. The old girl was set to advance me 200 scoots anyway. Lloyd knew a flop I could get for 80 a month—the Versailles Apartments on 6th and St. Andrews.

I counted off my 20 days. A probation officer came to see me. He said Judge Waters was set to release me. I would get a suspended sentence and three years' formal probation. I would have to get a job.

I said I'd look for work pronto. I promised that I'd walk the straight and narrow.

I kept my mouth shut on the tier—and listened. I learned that Romilar-CF cough syrup gave you a righteous high and that strips of tape along window panes denoted alarm systems. The guy at Cooper's Donuts knew all the hot black hookers. You could score dope at three Norm's Coffee Shops. the place at Melrose and La Cienega was called Fag Norm's. The place at Sunset and Vermont was called Normal Norm's. The place on the south side was called Nigger Norm's.

Marijuana grew wild in certain parts of Trancas Canyon. Ma Duncan's son was now a hot criminal lawyer. Doc Finch was up for parole soon. Carole Tregoff turned lez in the joint. Caryl Chessman was a punk—all the guys at Quentin hated him. That Susan Hayward flick *I Want to Live* was bullshit. Barbara Graham really did beat Mabel Monahan to death.

I listened and learned. I read a beat-up copy of *Atlas Shrugged* and came to the unsound conclusion that I was a superman. I stayed booze- and dope-free and added ten pounds of jail-food muscle.

Mary Waters released me two days before Christmas. I boosted some inhalers on my way back to Burns Park.


I got a one-room pad at the Versailles and signed up with a temp agency. They sent me out on some mailroom jobs. My probation officer found my work life satisfactory. He liked my short hair and Ivy League threads. He told me to avoid hippies. They were all strung out on mind-altering substances.

So was I.

I worked my temp gigs Monday to Friday. I killed a half-pint of scotch for breakfast and chased it with Listerine mouthwash. Cruise control got me through to lunch and some wine and/or weed. I got drunk every night and took inhaler trips on the weekends.

Romilar was a good B&E drug. It made common things seem surreal and full of hidden truth. I went on a righteous burglary run behind it. I hit Kathy's house, Kay's house and Missy's house—and concentrated on the medicine chests. I popped every inviting pill I saw on top of my cough syrup. I blacked out and woke up on my bed two times out of three.

I liked appearing clean-cut and cosmetically wholesome. Every freak in '69 L.A. was a fuzz magnet. They wore long hair and fruitcake clothes and sent out "Bust Me" vibes. I didn't. I bopped around in my co-existing worlds with relative impunity. I was good at giving people what they wanted to see.

I turned 21 in March. I gave up my pad and moved to a cheap hotel in Hollywood. I got a long-term temp job at KCOP-TV.

I worked in the mailroom. People responded to ads for shit like *64 Country Hits* and sent folding money and coins in through the mail. The heft of quarters and dimes gave those envelopes away. I started raking in a lot of extra money.

I spent it all on booze, dope and pizza. I moved to a better place—a bachelor pad at 6th and Cloverdale. I got hopped up on some women there and followed them around the neighborhood.

My insurance money ran out. My mailroom thefts more than covered the loss. I got in a fender bender with the company van and had to admit I had no driver's license. KCOP fired me. I got some short-term temp gigs and lived ultra-cheap. I got desperate. I broke into Missy's house and broke a cardinal rule.

I stole all the money in her mother's purse. There was no going back to that sweet house at 1st and Beachwood.

My pad prowls were starting to scare me more than thrill me. I felt the law of chance on my tail. I'd broken into places maybe twenty times total. My jail stint taught me things that fed my sense of caution.

House burglary was first-degree burglary. It was a penitentiary offense. I knew I could handle county jail time. Prison time would eat me up whole.

The Tate-LaBianca snuffs occurred in August. I felt the ripples all through Hancock Park.

I noticed some tape around Kathy's windows. I saw more private patrol cars out trawling. I saw security-service signs on front doors.

I stopped B&E'ing cold turkey. I never did it again.

I spent the next year in fantasy limbo. I held down temp gigs and a job at a pornographic bookstore. Hard-core packaged smut was now legal. Unpainted hippie girls were spread out nude in full-color magazines.

The girls didn't look jaded or degraded. They looked like they were posing for chuckles and some bread. They were engaged in an ugly pandering business. They betrayed their awareness of it with little frowns and glazed eyes.

They reminded me of the Black Dahlia—sans heavy makeup and noir baggage. The Dahlia choked on movieland illusions. These girls were deluded on some junk metaphysical plane.

They bored straight into my heart. I was the porno bookstore clerk out to save them from pornography and take his reward in sex. I hoarded their pictures the way Harvey Glatman hoarded pix of his victims. I gave my girls names and prayed for them every night. I sicced the Dahlia killer on them and saved them as his blade descended. They spread their legs and talked to me when I flew on Benzedrex inhalers.

I didn't fall for ones with perfect shapes and pert faces. I loved the smiles that didn't quite work and the sad eyes that couldn't lie. Mismatched features and oddly shaped breasts hit me hard. I was looking for sexual and psychological gravity.

I stole that bookstore blind. I examined every sex mag that came in and ripped out pictures of the most wrenching women. I worked midnight to 8:00 a.m., tapped the till and went to a bar that screened beaver flicks all day. I got drunk and looked at more hippie girls—and I always studied their faces more than their bodies.

My pornographic season passed too quickly. The bookstore boss got hip to my thefts and fired me. I went back to temp work, built up a surplus roll and went on a gargantuan two-month bender.

I socked in a case of vodka, a load of steaks and a load of inhalers. I gorged myself on fantasy, fantasy sex, cholesterol, and the work of Raymond Chandler, Dashiell Hammett and some junk crime writers. I stayed inside for days running. I lost and gained and lost weight and worked myself into a near-insane frenzy.

I stiffed my landlord for two months' rent. He started banging on my door and talking eviction. I didn't have enough money to muzzle him. I had enough to secure a cheaper pad for a month.

I found a place by the Paramount Studio. It was a genteel dive called the Green Gables Apartments. A small bachelor rented for 60 a month—very cheap for 1970.

Lloyd helped me move. I packed my stuff into his car and pulled a classic late-night rent dodge. I got squared away at the Gables and looked for work.

I didn't find any. The low-skill job market was soft. I took a series of inhaler trips and started seeing and hearing things that might or might not be real.

The tenant next door smirked at me when we passed in the hall. He banged on my window when I inhaler-tripped. He knew what I was doing. He disapproved. He read my lips and deciphered all my dirty sweet nothings. He read my thoughts through the wall that separated us.

He hated my porno books. He knew I murdered my mother and killed my father with neglect. He thought I was a freak and a pervert. He wanted to destroy me.

I flew and crashed, flew and crashed, flew and crashed. My paranoia raged in proportion to the dope in my system. I heard voices. Sirens on the street sent me hate messages. I jacked off in the dark to deceive the man next door.

He *knew* me.

He put bugs in my icebox. He poisoned my wine. He hooked my fantasies up to his TV set.

I bolted midway through an inhaler trip.

I left my clothes and fuck books behind. I ran out of the apartment and fast-walked three miles northeast. I saw a For Rent sign in front of a building at Sunset and Micheltorena.

I rented a convenience room for $39 a month. The building was filthy and reeked of spilled garbage.

My room was half the size of a six-man jail cell. I moved in with the clothes on my back and a short dog of T-Bird.

I popped some inhalers the next morning. New voices assailed me. The tenant next door started hissing through my air vents.

I was afraid to leave my bed. I knew the heat coils in my electric blanket were microphones. I ripped them out. I pissed in the bed and tore the pillows apart. I stuffed foam rubber in my ears to muffle the voices.

I bolted the next morning. I headed straight for Robert Burns Park.


It went bad from there. It went bad with self-destructive logic.

It went bad slowly.

The Voices came and went. Inhalers let them in. Liquor and enforced sobriety stifled them. I understood the problem intellectually. Rational thought deserted me the second I popped those cotton wads in my mouth.

Lloyd called the voices "amphetamine psychoses." I called them a conspiracy. President Richard M. Nixon knew I murdered my parents and ordered people to stalk me. They hissed into microphones wired to my brain. I heard the Voices. Nobody else did.

I couldn't stop taking inhalers. I heard the Voices for five years.

I spent most of that time outside. I lived in parks, backyards and empty houses. I stole. I drank. I read and fantasized. I walked all over L.A. with cotton stuffed in my ears.

It was a five-year daily sprint.

I'd wake up outside somewhere. I'd steal liquor and lunchmeat. I'd read in libraries. I'd go into restaurants, order drinks and meals and ditch out on the check. I'd hit apartment-house laundry rooms, break into washers and dryers and steal the coins inside. I'd take inhalers and notch some nice moments before the Voices claimed me.

I'd walk.

Wilshire Boulevard cut straight to the beach. I'd walk it out and back in the course of one inhaler trip. I had to keep moving. Traffic noise deflected the Voices. Lack of movement made the Voices cacophonous.

I walked five years away. They went by in a slow-motion blur. My fantasies ran through them at fast-forward counter-point. Street scenes served as backdrops for the Voices and my own internal dialogue.

I didn't babble or betray my state of mind overtly. I always shaved and wore dark cords to hide accumulated grime. I stole shirts and socks as I needed them. I doused myself with cologne to kill the stench of outdoor life. I showered at Lloyd's place occasionally.

Lloyd was headed nowhere at a nice sedate rate. He was drinking, using drugs and making stabs at college. He flirted with danger and lowlife and kept his mom's house as a backup option.

Lloyd walked me through some bad dope withdrawals. He disrupted me with little jolts of the truth. The LAPD disrupted me and force-fed me jail time.

They hassled me and arrested me. They popped me for plain drunk, drunk driving, petty theft and trespassing. They detained me as a suspicious late-night pedestrian and kicked me out of deserted houses and Goodwill bins. They held me at various station houses and shot me to the Sheriff's for an aggregate total of four to eight months county time.

Jail was my health retreat. I abstained from booze and dope and ate three square meals a day. I did push-ups and worked trusty details and got a little muscle tone going. I hung out with stupid white guys, stupid black guys and stupid Mexican guys—and swapped stupid stories with them. We had all committed daring crimes and fucked the world's most glamorous women. An old black wino told me he fucked Marilyn Monroe. I said, "No shit—I fucked her too!"

I worked the trash-and-freight detail at the New County Jail and the library at Wayside Honor Rancho. My favorite jail was Biscailuz Center. They fed you big meals and let you read in the latrines after lights-out. Jail was no big fucking traumatic deal.

I knew how to ride short stretches. Jail cleaned out my system and gave me something to anticipate: my release and more booze and dope fantasies.

Crime fantasies. Sex fantasies.

The redhead was 15 years dead and somewhere far away. She ambushed me in the summer of 1973.

I was living in a dive hotel. I took inhaler trips in a communal bathtub down the hall from my room. I ran warm water and hogged the tub for hours. Nobody complained. Most of the tenants took showers.

I was in the tub. I was jacking off to a cavalcade of older women's faces. I saw my mother naked, fought the image and lost.

I jerry-rigged a story straight off.

It was '58. My mother didn't die in El Monte. She wasn't a drunk. She loved me woman to man.

We made love. I smelled her perfume and cigarette breath. Her amputated nipple thrilled me.

I brushed her hair out of her eyes and told her I loved her. My tenderness made her cry.

It was the most impassioned and loving story I'd ever perpetrated. It left me ashamed and horrified of what I had inside me.

I tried to live the story again. My mind wouldn't let me. All the dope in the world couldn't bring the redhead back.

I abandoned her one more time.

I blew my rent money and lost my hotel room. I moved back to Burns Park.

I took inhaler trips and fought a war within myself. I tried to conjure up my mother and devise a way to let her stay. My mind failed me. My conscience shut the whole business down.

The Voices got very specific. They said you fucked your mother *and* killed her.

I had a huge prophylhexedrine tolerance. It took ten to twelve cotton wads to get me off the ground. The shit was fucking up my lungs. I woke up congested every morning.

I developed chest pains. Every breath and heartbeat doubled me over. I took a bus to the County Hospital. A doctor examined me and told me I had pneumonia. He admitted me and put me on antibiotics for a week. They killed my infection dead.

I left the hospital and went back to outdoor life, booze and inhalers. I got pneumonia again. I got it cured. I went on a year-long T-Bird-and-inhaler run and ended up with the DTs.

Lloyd was living in West L.A. I camped out on the roof of his building. The first hallucinations hit me in his bathroom.

A monster jumped out of the toilet. I shut the lid and saw more monsters seep through it. Spiders crawled up my legs. Little blobs hurled themselves at my eyes.

I ran into the living room and turned the lights out. The little blobs went fluorescent. I raided Lloyd's liquor stash and drank myself senseless. I woke up on the roof—dead scared.

I knew I had to quit drinking and taking inhalers. I knew they'd kill me in the fucking near future. I stole a short dog and hitchhiked to the County Hospital. I killed my bottle on the front steps and turned myself in.

A doctor processed me into the drunk ward. He said he'd recommend me for the Long Beach State Hospital program. Thirty days there would boil me clean and set me up to live sober.

I wanted it. It was that or die young. I was 27 years old.

I spent two days at the drunk ward. They zonked me out on tranquilizers and sedatives. I didn't see any monsters or blobs. I wanted to guzzle booze as much as I wanted to kick it. I tried to sleep around the clock.

Long Beach said they'd take me. I was slated to go down there with three guys on the ward. They were old drunks with years on the rehab circuit. They were professional alcoholic recidivists.

We went down in a hospital van. I liked the look of the place.

Men and women bunked in separate dorms. The cafeteria looked like a restaurant. The rec rooms looked like something out of summer camp.

The program featured AA meetings and group therapy. "Rap" sessions were not mandatory. The patients wore khakis and numbered wristbands—like the trusties in the L.A. County Jail system.

Antabuse was mandatory. Eagle-eyed nurses made the patients take it every day. You got deathly ill if you drank on top of it. Antabuse was a scare tactic.

I started to feel better. I rationalized the DTs away as a freak non sequitur. I was dormed-up with drunks from all walks of life. The men scared me. The women turned me on. I started to think I could beat booze and dope on my own terms.

The program commenced. I daydreamed in the AA meetings and ran my mouth during group therapy. I invented sexual exploits and directed my tales to the women in the room. It hit me a week or so in: You're just here for three hots and a cot.

I went along with the program. I ate like a pig and put on ten pounds. I spent all my spare time reading crime novels.

I was coughing a lot. A staff nurse braced me about it. I told her I'd had a recent string of lung ailments.

She had a doctor check me out. He shot me up with a muscle relaxant and stuck a tube with a penlight attached down my throat. He peered down a scope device and wiggled the little beam around my lungs. He said he didn't see anything wrong.

My cough persisted. I endured the program and wondered what I'd do for an encore. All my options scared me.

I could find a crummy job and stay clean with Antabuse. I could stay off booze and inhalers and use other drugs. I could smoke weed. Weed goosed your appetite. I could put on some weight and build muscle. Women would dig me then. Weed was my ticket to a healthy, normal life.

I didn't really believe it.

Inhalers were sex. Booze was my fantasy core. Weed was strictly for giggles and hot dates with doughnuts and pizza.

I completed the program. I stayed on Antabuse and moved back to Lloyd's roof with thirty-three days sober.

My cough was getting worse. My nerves were shot and my attention span topped out at three seconds. I slept for ten-hour stints or tossed all night.

My body wasn't mine.

The roof landing was my refuge. I had a nice perch by the fire door. It went all-the-way bad right there.

It was mid-June. I got up from a nap and thought, "I need some cigarettes." My mind went dead then. I couldn't recall or retrieve that one simple thought.

My brain hit blank walls. I couldn't say the thought or visualize it or come up with words to express it. I spent something like an hour trying to form that one simple thought.

I couldn't say my own name. I couldn't think my own name. I couldn't form that one simple thought or any thoughts. My mind was dead. My brain circuits had disconnected. I was brain-dead insane.

I screamed. I put my hands over my ears, shut my eyes and screamed myself hoarse. I kept fighting for that one simple thought.

Lloyd ran up to the landing. I recognized him. I couldn't

come up with his name or my name or that simple thought from an hour ago.

Lloyd carried me downstairs and called an ambulance. Paramedics arrived and strapped me to a gurney.

They drove me to the County Hospital and left me in a crowded hallway. I started hearing voices. Nurses walked by and yelled at me telepathically. I coughed and bucked against my restraints. Somebody stuck a needle in my arm—

I woke up strapped to a cot. I was alone in a private hospital room.

My wrists were raw and bloody. Most of my teeth felt loose. My jaw hurt and my knuckles stung from little abrasions. I was wearing a hospital smock. I'd pissed all over it.

I reached for that one simple thought and caught it on the first bounce. I remembered my nigger-pimp name: Lee Earle Ellroy.

It all came back. I recalled every detail. I started crying. I prayed and begged God to let me keep my mind.

A nurse came into the room. She undid my restraints and walked me to a shower. I stayed under the water until it turned cold. Another nurse dressed my cuts and abrasions. A doctor told me I'd have to stay here a month. I had an abscess on my left lung the size of a big man's fist. I needed thirty days of intravenous antibiotics.

I asked him what went wrong with my mind. He said it was probably "post-alcohol brain syndrome." Sober drunks went through it sometimes. He said I was lucky. Some people went crazy for good.

My lung condition might or might not be contagious. They were isolating me to be sure. They hooked me up to a drip gizmo and started pumping me full of antibiotics. They fed me tranquilizers to lull down my fear.

The tranks kept me woozy. I tried to sleep all day every day. Normal waking consciousness scared me. I kept imagining permanent brain malfunctions.

Those few insane hours summarized my life. The horror rendered everything that went before it irrelevant.

I reprised the horror all my waking hours. I couldn't let it go. I wasn't telling myself a cautionary tale or gloating over my survival. I was simply replaying the moments my entire life had worked toward.

The horror stayed with me. Nurses woke me out of blissful sleep to fuck with my drip gadget. I couldn't run my mind in long-prescribed fantasy patterns. The horror wouldn't let me.

I imagined permanent insanity. I punished myself with my now splendidly functioning brain.

The fear got unbearable. I checked out of the hospital over my doctor's protests and caught a bus to Lloyd's place. I stole a pint of gin, guzzled it and passed out on his floor. Lloyd called the paramedics again.

Another ambulance arrived. The paramedics woke me out of my stupor and led me down to it. They drove me straight back to the hospital. I was readmitted and placed in a four-man room on the lung ward.

A nurse hooked me up to another drip gadget. She gave me a big bottle to spit sputum in.

I was afraid I'd forget my name. I wrote it on the wall behind my bed as a reminder. I wrote "I will not go insane" beside it.

11

spent a month hooked up to a needle. A respiration therapist beat on my back every day. It loosened big globs of sputum. I spat them in the jar by my bed.

The abscess went. My fear stayed.

My mind was functioning normally. I played memory games to test-fire it. I memorized magazine ads and slogans on milk cartons. I was building mind muscle to fight potential insanity.

I went insane once. It could happen again.

I couldn't let the fear go. I fed on it all day every day. I didn't analyze why I drove myself to the point of brain malfunction. I addressed the problem as a physical phenomenon.

My brain felt like an external appendage. My lifelong plaything was in no way indigenous to me. It was a specimen in a bottle. I was a doctor poking it with a stick.

I knew that booze, drugs and my tenuous abstention from them caused my brain burnout. My rational side told me that. My secondary response derived straight from guilt. God punished me for mentally fucking my mother.

I believed it. My fantasy was just that transgressive and worthy of divine intervention. I tortured myself with the concept. I exhumed the midwestern Protestant ethic my mother tried to outrun—and used it for self-flagellation.

My new mental kick was mental self-preservation. I did mental tricks to keep my mind limber. It fed my fear more than it buttressed my confidence.

My lung abscess healed completely. I checked out of the

hospital and cut a deal with God.

I told him I wouldn't drink or pop inhalers. I told him I wouldn't steal. All I wanted was my mind back for keeps.


The deal jelled.

I went back to Lloyd's roof. I didn't drink or pop inhalers or steal. God kept my mind in sound working order.

The fear stayed.

I knew it could happen again. I understood the preposterous aspect of all divine contracts. Booze and inhaler residue could lurk in my cells. My brain wires could sputter and disconnect without warning. My brain could blow tomorrow or in the year 2000.

Fear kept me sober. Fear taught me no moral lessons. My days ran long and sweaty and anxious. I sold my plasma at a skid-row blood bank and lived off ten dollars a week. I haunted libraries and read crime novels. I memorized whole passages to keep my mind running strong.

A guy in Lloyd's building worked as a golf caddy. He told me it was good tax-free money. You could work or not work as you pleased. Hillcrest Country Club was high-class. The members tossed you some good coin.

The guy brought me to Hillcrest. I knew I just got lucky.

It was a prestigious Jewish club south of Century City. The golf course was hilly and deep green. The caddies congregated in a "caddy shack." They drank, played cards and told obscene stories. Drunks, dopers and compulsive gamblers ruled the shack. I knew I'd fit in.

Caddy jobs were called "loops." Caddies were also called "loopers." I knew jackshit about golf. The caddy master told me I'd learn.

I started out packing one bag only. I stumbled through my first dozen loops and moved to two-bag duty. The bags weren't that heavy. Eighteen holes of golf ran four hours. The standard two-bag fee was 20 dollars. It was good 1975 money.

I worked Hillcrest six days a week. I made good daily pay and got myself a room at the Westwood Hotel. The place was equidistant to Hillcrest and the Bel-Air, Brentwood and Los

Angeles country clubs. Loopers rented most of the rooms. The place was a caddy shack adjunct.

Looping took over my life. The rituals deflected my fear and eased it into a fadeout.

I loved the golf course. It was a perfectly self-contained green world. Caddy work was mentally undemanding. I let my mind wander and earned a living simultaneously.

The milieu stimulated me. I invented back stories for Hillcrest members while I walked beside them, and ran gag riffs on lowlife loopers. The culture clash of wealthy Jews and caddies with one foot in the gutter was a constant laugh riot. I made friends with a smart young caddy going to college part-time. We discussed the Hillcrest membership and the caddy experience endlessly.

I spent time with a diverse bunch of people. I listened to them and learned how to talk to them. Hillcrest felt like some kind of way station en route to the real world.

People told me stories. I took a master class in country-club lore. I heard tales of self-made men who clawed their way out of the shtetl and tales of rich drunks who succumbed to caddy life. The golf course was a picaresque education.

Most of the loopers smoked weed. Weed didn't scare me like booze and inhalers did. I kissed off four sober months with some Thai Stick.

It was *goooood*. It was the best shit I'd ever smoked. I started buying it and smoking it all day every day.

I figured it wouldn't fuck up my lungs or shut down my brain. It wouldn't spark incestuous fantasies and piss God off. It was the manageable and controllable drug of the 1970s.

So I rationalized.

I smoked weed for a year and a half. It was *goooood*—but not great. It was like trying to reach the moon in a Volkswagen.

I didn't drink or take inhalers. I sucked down marijuana and lived as a more subtle full-time fantasist.

I took my fantasies outdoors. I took them to Hillcrest and other golf courses at night. I hopped the fence at L.A. Country Club and fantasy-walked the north course for hours.

I played with my Hillcrest cast of characters and worked them into a crime story. I worked in an alcoholic hero. He hailed from the sad edge of Hancock Park. He nursed a lifelong obsession with the Black Dahlia case.

I worked in the Club Mecca torch and classical music. I worked in the DTs. My hero wanted to find a woman and love her to death.

My 18-year fantasy backlog telescoped into this one story. I began to see that it was a novel.

I got fired from Hillcrest. A member's son mouthed off to me in front of a good-looking woman. I decked him in full view of the putting green. A security guard escorted me off the premises.

I was bombed on weed. Weed hit me unpredictably.

I got a caddy gig at Bel-Air Country Club. The members and loopers there were just as seductive as the Hillcrest crew. The golf course was even more beautiful.

I stayed bombed at Bel-Air. I bought a tape player for my room and spent hours jacked up on weed and the German Romantic composers. I roamed golf courses at night and wrestled with that one emerging story.

Lloyd moved into the Westwood Hotel. He was off of booze and hard dope and on marijuana maintenance himself. He was flirting with the notion of *real* sobriety. I told him I wasn't interested.

I lied.

I was almost 30. I wanted to do things. I wasn't stealing. I wasn't lusting for my mother. I had my brain back on permanent loan from God or other cosmic sources. I did not hear voices. I was not as fucked-up as I used to be.

And I was not a civilized human being.

Marijuana maintenance filled me out physically. I ate a lot, lugged golf bags and cranked hundreds of daily push-ups. I was big, strong and hulking. I had beady brown eyes and wore bead-enhancing wire-rimmed glasses. I was stoned all the time. I looked like a crazy man consumed by interior monologue. Strangers found me disturbing.

Women found me scary. I tried to pick a few women up in bookstores and frightened the shit out of them. I knew I came off desperate and socially unkempt. My hygiene was markedly substandard.

I was hungry. I wanted love and sex. I wanted to give my mental stories to the world.

I knew I couldn't have those things in my current condition. I had to renounce all forms of dope. I couldn't drink. I couldn't steal. I couldn't lie. I had to be a locked-down, uptight, pucker-assed motherfucker. I had to repudiate my old life. I had to build a new life from the sheer desiccated force of my old one.

I liked the concept. It appealed to my extremist nature. I liked the self-immolation aspect. I liked the air of total apostasy.

I danced with the concept for weeks. It blitzed my storytelling drive and soured my taste for dope. I wanted to change my whole life.

Lloyd cleaned up in AA. He told me total abstinence was better than booze and dope at its best. I believed him. He was always smarter and stronger and more resourceful than me.

I followed his lead. I said "Fuck it" and shrugged off my old life.

AA was wild. The late-'70s scene was craaaaaazy. It was redemption and sex and God and big stupid pratfalls. It was my sentimental education and road back to the world.

I met a lot of people who'd lived my life with their own variations. I heard stories that topped mine for sheer horror. I made friends. I learned moral precepts and developed a plainly expressed faith in God that was no more complex and just as heartfelt as a kid in Sunday school's.

My initial entry hurt. AA meetings taxed me. The people talked ambiguous juju. I only stuck around to hold hands with women during the Lord's Prayer.

The women magnetized me and kept me coming back. I returned "one day at a time" for some hand holding. Lust and my apostolic will kept me sober.

AA did a subtle job on me. The literature critiqued alcoholism and drug addiction brilliantly. I saw that I carried one strain of a common plague. My story was banal in that context. Only a few incidental details made me unique. The critique gave AA principles a strong moral kick. I found them wholly credible and trusted in their efficacy.

The principles won me over. The people made me capitulate.

I got tight with some guys. I unclenched around women and cut my ego loose at AA lecterns. I became an accomplished public speaker fast. My self-destructive exhibitionism turned around full-circle.

Westside AA swung hard. The demographic makeup was young, white and horny. Booze and dope were out. Sex was in. The Westside mandate was Stay sober, trust God and fuck.

People went to "Hot Tub Fever" after meetings. A guy threw sober wife-swapping parties. Men and women met at meetings and got married in Vegas two hours later. Nude pool parties reigned. Women hit on men blatantly. Annie "Wild Thing" B. flashed her breasts at Kenny's Deli after every Thursday-night Ohio Street meeting.

I got laid. I went through one-, two- and three-night stands and wrenching stabs at hard-line monogamy. I let detoxing smack addicts crash on my floor while I boogied to late dates at Hot Tub Fever. I made 300 a week at the golf course and spent most of it on women. I picked up junkie prostitutes, took them to AA meetings and fed them the Black Dahlia story to scare them out of hooking. It was a frenetic, often joyous profligacy.

I lived out most of my dope-fueled sex dreams sober.

The real world eclipsed my fantasy world. My one persistent fantasy was that story I knew was a novel.

It haunted me. It invaded my thoughts at strange times. I didn't know if I had the stones to write it. I was enjoying a season of comfort. I didn't know that I was running from old things.

My mother was 20 years dead. My father was dead 13. I dreamed about him. I never dreamed about her.

My new life was long on fervor and short on retrospection. I knew I abandoned my father and hastened his death and paid the debt off in increments. My mother was something else.

I knew her only in shame and loathing. I plundered her in a fever dream and denied my own message of yearning. I was afraid to resurrect her and love her body-and-soul.

I wrote my novel and sold it. It was all about L.A. crime and me. I was afraid to stalk the redhead and give her secrets up. I hadn't met the man who'd bring her home to me.

# Part III

## STONER

*You were a ghost. I found you in shadows and reached out to you in terrible ways. You didn't censure me. You withstood my assaults and let me punish myself.*

*You made me. You formed me. You gave me a ghostly presence to brutalize. I never wondered how you haunted other people. I never questioned my sole ownership of your spirit.*

*I wouldn't share my claim. I remade you perversely and sealed you off where others couldn't touch you. I didn't know that simple selfishness rendered all my claims invalid.*

*You live outside of me. You live in the buried thoughts of strangers. You live through your will to hide and dissemble. You live through your will to elude me.*

*I am determined to find you. I know I can't do it alone.*

# 12

His ghosts were all women. They ran through his dreams interchangeably.

The decomp off Route 126. The waitress in the Marina. The teenager stunned mute by rape and blunt-force trauma.

Dream logic distorted the details. Victims moved between crime scenes and displayed conflicting signs of death. They came to life sometimes. They looked older or younger or just like they did when they fell.

Daisie Mae was sodomized like Bunny. Karen took the sap shots that knocked Tracy to her knees. The sap was homemade. The killers stuffed ball bearings into a length of garden hose and taped the ends shut.

The instant resurrections were unnerving. The women were supposed to stay dead. Murder brought them to him. His love began the moment they died.


He was dreaming a lot. He was giving up the chase and going through some kind of early withdrawal. It was time to get out. He gave it all he had. He wanted out unequivocally.

He was leaving debts unpaid. Karen would be sending him reminders. He failed her because the connections weren't there and other murders scattered his obligations. He was a victim of confusion and chance—just as she was.

He'd try to pay her off with the love he still carried.

*

His name was Bill Stoner. He was 53 years old and a homicide detective with the Los Angeles County Sheriff's Department. He was married and had twenty-eight-year-old twin sons.

It was late March '94. He was leaving the job in mid-April. He'd served 32 years and worked Homicide for the past 14. He was retiring as a sergeant with 25 years in grade. His pension would sustain him nicely.

He was leaving the job intact. He wasn't a drunk and he wasn't obese from liquor and junk food. He stayed with the same woman for 30-plus years and rode out the rough times with her. He didn't go the bifurcated route so many cops did. He wasn't juggling a family and a series of girlfriends in the new gender-integrated law-enforcement community.

He didn't hide behind the job or revel in a dark world-view. He knew that isolation spawned resentment and self-pity. Police work was inherently ambiguous. Cops developed simple codes to insure their moral grounding. The codes reduced complex issues to kick-ass epigrams. Every epigram boiled down to this: Cops know things that other people don't. Every epigram obfuscated as much as it enlightened.

Homicide taught him that. He learned it gradually. He saw slam-dunk cases through to successful adjudication and did not understand why the murders occurred. He came to distrust simple answers and solutions and exulted in the few viable ones that he found. He learned to reserve judgment, shut his ego down and make people come to him. It was an inquisitor's stance. It gave him some distance on himself. It helped him tone down his general temperament and rein in some shitty off-the-job behavior.

The first 17 years of his marriage were a brush war. He fought Ann. She fought him. It stayed verbal out of luck and a collective sense of boundary. They were equally voluble and profane and thus evenly matched. Their demands were equally selfish. They brought equal reserves of love to the war.

He grew up as a homicide detective. Ann grew up as a registered nurse. She entered her career late. Their marriage survived because they both grew up in the death business.

Ann retired early. She had high blood pressure and bad allergies. Their bad years put some bad mileage on her.

And him.

He was exhausted. Hundreds of murders and the rough stretch with Ann made for one big load. He wanted to drop the whole thing.

He knew how to let things go. The death business taught him that. He wanted to be a full-time husband and father. He wanted to see Ann and the boys up-close and permanent.

Bob was running an Ikea store. He was married to a solid woman and had a baby daughter. Bob toed the line. Bill Junior was more problematic. He was lifting weights, going to college and working as a bouncer. He had a son with his Japanese ex-girlfriend. Bill Junior was a brilliant kid and an inveterate fuckhead.

He loved his grandchildren to death. Life was a kick in the head.

He had a nice house in Orange County. He had his health and money socked away. He had a good marriage and a separate dialogue with dead women. It was his own take on the *Laura* Syndrome.

Homicide detectives loved the movie *Laura.* A cop gets obsessed with a murder victim and finds out she's still alive. She's beautiful and mysterious. She falls in love with the cop.

Most homicide cops were romantics. They blasted through lives devastated by murder and dispensed comfort and counsel. They nursed entire families. They met the sisters and female friends of their victims and succumbed to sexual tension hot-wired to bereavement. They blew their marriages off behind situational drama.

He wasn't that crazy or hooked on theatrics. The flip side of *Laura* was *Double Indemnity:* A man meets a woman and flushes his life down the toilet. Both scenarios were equally fatuous.

Dead women fired up his imagination. He honored them with tender thoughts. He didn't let them run his life.

He was set to retire soon. Things were running through his head fast and bright.

He had to drive out to the Bureau. A man was meeting him at 9:00. His mother was murdered 30-some years back. The man wanted to see her file.

\*

The January earthquake wrecked the Hall of Justice. Sheriff's Homicide moved to the City of Commerce. It was an hour's shot north of Orange County.

He took the 405 to the 710. Freeway runs were half of any given homicide job. Freeway runs exhausted him.

L.A. County was large, topographically diverse and traversable only by freeway. Freeways streamlined body-disposal problems. Killers could zip to remote canyons and dump their victims fast. Freeways and freeway embankments were four-star drop zones. He rated freeways by their body-dump past and body-dump potential. Every stretch of L.A. freeway marked a dump site or the route to a crime scene. Every on- and off-ramp led him to some murder.

Bodies tended to stack up in the worst parts of the county. He knew every mile of freeway to and from every skunk town with a Sheriff's Homicide contract. The mileage accrued and weighed his weary ass down. He wanted to get off the Drop Zone Expressway forever.

Orange County to downtown L.A. was a hundred miles round trip. He lived in Orange County because it wasn't L.A. County and one big map of past and present murder. Most of Orange County was white and monolithically square. He fit in superficially. Cops were hellions masquerading as squares. He liked the Orange County vibe. People got outraged over shit he saw every day. Orange County made him feel slightly disingenuous. Cops flocked to places like Orange County to live the illusion of better times past and pretend they were somebody else. A lot of them carried reactionary baggage. He dumped his a long time ago.

He lived where he did to keep his two worlds separate. The freeway was just a symbol and a symptom. He'd always be running back and forth—one way or another.

Sheriff's Homicide was working out of a courtyard industrial complex. They were squeezed in between toolmaking and computer-chip firms. The setup was temporary. They were supposed to move to permanent digs soon.

The Hall of Justice oozed style. This place didn't look remotely coplike. The exterior was plain white stucco. The interior was plain white drywall. The main room featured a hundred desks pushed together. The place looked like a phone sales front.

The Unsolved Unit was walled off separately. A storeroom lined with shelves adjoined it. The shelves were stuffed with unsolved homicide files.

Each file was marked with the letter Z and a six-digit number. Stoner found Z-483-362 and carried it back to his desk.

He spent seven years at Unsolved. The unit had a simple mandate: Check Z-files for workable leads and assess new information coming in on unsolved murders. The job was public relations and anthropological study.

Unsolved cops rarely solved murders. They fielded phone tips, perused files and got hooked on old killings. They ran checks on old suspects and talked to old detectives. Unsolved entailed a lot of desk work. Older men rotated in before they retired.

Stoner was ordered in young. Captain Grimm had a special job for him. Grimm thought the *Cotton Club* murder was workable. He told Stoner to work it full-time.

The job took four years. It was a high-profile, career-defining glory case.

It kicked his ass. It put a lot of freeway miles on him.

Stoner looked through the Z-file he pulled. The autopsy photo was gruesome. The Arroyo High shots were almost as ugly. He'd prepare the man first.

Cops cruised by his desk and ragged him about his retirement. His partner, Bill McComas, just had a quadruple bypass. The guys wanted a progress report.

Mac was tenuously okay. He was set to retire next month— less than intact.

Stoner kicked his chair back and daydreamed. He was still seeing things fast and bright.

*

He was a California boy. His people split Fresno and bopped to L.A. County during the war. His parents fought like cougars. It pissed him off and scared his sisters.

He grew up in South Gate. It was flat, hot and postwar stucco. Transplanted Okies reigned. They liked hot rods and barn music. They worked industrial jobs and snagged boom-economy paychecks. The old South Gate spawned blue-collar squares. The new South Gate spawned dope fiends.

He grew up hooked on girls and sports and nursed a vague sense of adventure. His father was a foreman at the Proto-Tool plant. It was lots of work for marginal pay and zero adventure. He tried Proto-Tool himself. It was boring and hard on the body. He tried junior college and pondered a teaching career. The notion didn't really send him.

His sisters married cops. He had one brother-in-law on the South Gate PD and one on the Highway Patrol. They told him enticing stories. The yarns dovetailed with some other notions he'd been kicking around.

He wanted adventure. He wanted to help people. He took the entrance test for the Los Angeles County Sheriff's Department the day after his twenty-first birthday.

He passed it. He passed the physical and the background check. He was assigned to the Sheriff's Academy class of December '61.

The Department was shorthanded. He was pre-assigned to the Hall of Justice Jail. He met some celebrated killers straight off.

He met John Deptula. Crazy John burglarized a bowling alley and woke up a live-in handyman named Roger Alan Mosser. Deptula beat Mosser to death and carted his body out to the Angeles National Forest. He decapitated Mosser and stuck his head down a campground porta-toilet. Ward Hallinen cleared the case for Sheriff's Homicide.

He met Sam LoCigno. LoCigno popped Jack "The Enforcer" Whalen. It was a contract hit. It occurred at Rondelli's Restaurant in December '59. The hit was botched six ways from Sunday.

His tier featured drag queens and badass armed robbers. He listened to them and learned things. He entered the

Academy and devoured a four-month course in criminal justice. He met a good-looking blonde named Ann Schumacher. She was working at the Autonetics plant in Downey. They made plans to go out on his graduation night.

He graduated the Academy in April '62. He took Ann to the Crescendo on the swinging Sunset Strip. Ann looked good. He looked good. He was packing a .38 snub-nose. He was twenty-one years old and unassailably cool.

He wanted to work a prowl-car beat. The Sheriff's were running patrol units out of fourteen stations. He wanted full-time action.

He got jail duty.

They assigned him to the Wayside Honor Rancho. It was sixty-five miles from his pad. The job initiated his long and ugly relationship with freeways.

Wayside knocked some youth out of him. Wayside was a good course in pre-breakdown American justice.

Wayside housed inmates sentenced to county time and Hall of Justice Jail overflow headed to the joint. Whites, Negroes and Mexicans hated each other but refrained from racial warfare. Wayside was an efficient cog in a still-operational system. The system worked because criminal numbers were far short of stratospheric and most criminals did not employ violence. Heroin was the big bad drug of the era. Heroin was a well-contained dope epidemic. Heroin made you pull B&Es and pimp your girlfriend to support your habit. Heroin made you nod out. Heroin did not make you freak out and chop up your girlfriend—like crack would twenty years later. The system worked because felons and misdemeanants plead guilty most of the time and did not file nuisance appeals routinely. The system worked because pre-breakdown jail time was doable. Criminals were pre-psychologized. They accepted authority. They knew they were lowlife scum because they saw it on TV and read it in the papers. They were locked into a rigged game. Authority usually won. They took pleasure in picayune triumphs and reveled in the game's machinations. The game was insiderism. Insiderism and fatalism were hip. If you stayed shy of the gas chamber, the worst you'd get was penitentiary time. Pre-breakdown joint time was doable. You could drink pruno and fuck sissies in the ass. The system worked because America was yet to buck race riots and assassinations and environmental bullshit and gender confusion and drug proliferation and gun mania and religious psychoses linked to a media implosion and an emerging cult of victimhood—a 25-year transit of divisive bad juju that resulted in a stultifying mass skepticism.

He became a cop at just the right time. He could cleave to simple notions with a clear conscience. He could kick ass with legal impunity. He could postpone aspects of his cop education and come of age as a homicide detective.

He bought the whole illusion back in 1962. He knew the system worked. Jail duty was doable. He got a twisted kick out of the inmates. They played their roles according to the script of the time. The jailers did, too.

He married Ann in December '62. He transferred to Norwalk Station a year later. He spent his first anniversary out in a patrol car. Ann was hurt and pissed.

They started fighting. Ann wanted all of his time. He wanted all of her time precisely synced to his schedule. The L.A. County Sheriff's demanded most of his time. Something had to give.

They fought. His marriage turned into his parents' marriage with the volume up and lots of "Fuck you"s. Ann had this abandonment complex. Her mother left her and shacked up with an armed robber. The guy took Mom with him on a cross-country heist spree. Ann had this overtly screwed-up childhood.

They fought. They reconciled. They fought. He resisted scads of cop-chaser women out to throw him some trim. The LASD hovered as his potential divorce co-respondent.

He loved patrol work. He loved the flow of unexpected events and the daily mix of new people in trouble. Norwalk was a "gentlemen's station." The population was white and the pace was slow. The county ding farm was on his beat. The dings wandered off and pulled amusing stunts stark naked. The Norwalk deputies ran a ding taxi service. They were always running some ding back to the farm.

He enjoyed his Norwalk tour of duty. The system worked

and crime was containable. Some of the older guys saw hard times coming. The Miranda decision was fucking things up. The balance of power had shifted from cops to criminal suspects. You couldn't log confessions with sweat-box tricks and phone-book shots to the kidneys.

He didn't hold with those tactics. He didn't pack black-leather sap gloves with 16-ounce palm weights. He wasn't a violent guy. He tried to reason with unruly types and only fought when he had to.

He flipped his patrol car in mid-pursuit and almost died on the spot. He tangled with a teenage glue sniffer and took some heavyweight lumps. He responded to an accident call and swooped down a two-vehicle pile-up. A man was dead in his truck. His head smashed into the radio dials and kicked the volume way up. You could hear the song "Charade" for blocks around.

Norwalk gave him some wild moments. They were bush league compared to Watts in August '65.

Ann was eight months pregnant. They were driving north on the Long Beach Freeway. Their view was high and expansive. They saw a dozen fires blazing.

He pulled off the freeway and called Norwalk Station. The watch commander told him to suit up and report to Harvey Aluminum. Harvey was deep in a labor-management conflict. The LASD had a command post set up there already.

He dropped Ann off and blasted over to Harvey. The parking lot was jammed with black & whites and deputies in full riot gear. The command post was dispatching four-man units. He grabbed a 12-gauge shotgun and three temporary partners.

The deal was 12-hour shifts. The deal was go bust looters and firebugs. The deal was scour Watts and Willowbrook—the flashpoint of all this nigger voodoo.

He went into it in broad daylight. The heat was somewhere up in the 90s. The fires added some heat. His riot gear added some more. South L.A. was all heat and frenzy.

Looters were gutting liquor stores. Looters were guzzling brand-name stuff right there. Looters were pushing shopping carts down the street. The carts were chock-full of booze and TV sets.

Gunshots popped continuously. You couldn't tell who was shooting who. The National Guard was out in force. They looked young and dumb and scared and plain trigger-happy.

You couldn't patrol logically. Too much came at you too fast. You had to snag looters at random. You had to work by whim and the stimulus of the moment. You couldn't gauge the direction of gunshots. You couldn't trust the guardsmen not to spray rounds and kill you with ricochets.

It was uncontainable disorder. It grew in direct proportion to their attempts to control it. A deputy was pushing a crowd back. A looter grabbed his shotgun. It discharged and blew his partner's brains out.

It went on and on. The action dispersed and reconstellated unexpectedly. He worked three whole days of it. He shagged dozens of looters and lost weight from heat exposure and adrenaline overload.

The action tapped out from some kind of mass exhaustion. Maybe the heat wore the rioters down. They made their statement. They brightened up their shitty lives. They gorged themselves with cheap booty and convinced themselves they'd gained more than they lost.

The cops lost their collective cherry.

Some denied it. They attributed the riot to a specific series of criminally spawned events. Their logic of cause-and-effect went no deeper.

A lot of cops went into default mode. Unruly niggers were unruly niggers. Their inbred criminal tendencies should now be suppressed even more rigorously.

He knew better. The riot taught him that suppression was futile. You don't burn down your own world for no good reason. You couldn't shut people down or keep people out. The more you tried, the more chaos would supersede order. The revelation thrilled him and scared him.

The twins were born a month after the riot. His marriage ran smooth for a while. He studied for the sergeant's exam and worked Norwalk Patrol. He pondered the lessons of Watts.

He lived in two worlds. His family world was uncontrollable. The lessons of Watts failed him at home. He knew how to handle criminals. He couldn't handle the volatile woman he loved.

The novelty of kids wore off. They started fighting again. They fought in front of the boys and felt bad about it.

He made sergeant in December '68 and transferred to Firestone Station. Firestone was high-density, high-crime, all black. The pace was frantic. He learned to work at triple his Norwalk rate.

He worked as a patrol supervisor. He ran from Code 3 call to Code 3 call every shift. Firestone was dope and armed robbery and brutal domestic calls. Firestone was a riot zone back in '65. The folks there had their own post-riot revelations going. Firestone was sidewalk crap games and guns. Firestone was the child who climbed into the dryer and got burned and spun to death. Firestone was decelerated chaos. Firestone could blow fast.

He spent four years there. He finished his patrol tour and went on the station detective squad. He did some community relations work. Anything that bridged the cop-civilian gap was good for business. The LAPD had fucked cop-civilian relations to an all-time fare-thee-well. He didn't want the Sheriff's to follow their lead.

He transferred to the auto-theft detail. He developed sound detective skills and reveled in the specific nature of the work. Theft crimes were cut-and-dried. They boiled down to violated ownership. They were isolated problems that ended with the apprehension of specifically guilty parties. He didn't have to pop harmless kids for marijuana. He didn't have to referee domestic disputes and dispense marital advice like he knew what he was talking about.

Detective work was his calling. He had the social skills and the temperament for it. Patrol work was a breathless sprint with no fixed finish line. Detective work was sedately paced by comparison. He plugged into suspects one-on-one and co-opted their knowledge. He moved deeper into the cop-criminal matrix.

He came to Firestone as a policeman. He left as a detective. He went to Internal Affairs Division and hounded other cops.

Cops who stole money. Cops who leaned too hard on their

nightsticks. Cops who used dope. Cops who jacked off at porno movies. Cops who gave blow jobs to inmates in county holding tanks. Cops who were ratted off for imagined offenses out of pure spite.

IA was brutal. The moral turf was hazily defined. He did not enjoy hassling fellow cops. He sought out the literal truth pertaining to their situations and stressed mitigating factors. He felt empathy for some very twisted men. He knew how the job undermined family contracts. A fair portion of the cops he knew were functioning alcoholics. They were no better or worse than cops accused of smoking dope.

He had a handle on his own shortcomings. He used them to illustrate the big bottom line. *You* don't steal or use dope or engage in perverted activities. *You* don't exploit your cop status for illegal gain. *You* have to impose those restrictions on the cops you investigate.

It was a morally valid line. It was an ego-driven simplification.

His marriage was dead stalled. He wanted out. Ann wanted out. They kept waiting for the other one to get up some guts and end it. They bought a house and sunk their hooks in each other deeper. He fought a persistent urge to chase women.

He left IA in '73. He went to the Lakewood Station squad and worked auto theft and auto burg for two years. He went to Metro in '75.

Metro worked county-wide. He ran a five-man surveillance team all over the county map. L.A. County expanded for him. He saw crime booming in poverty pockets where people had just enough coin for drugs and cheap pads. The landscapes there were flat and polluted. The people lived in operational squalor. They moved between smoggy towns like rats in a maze. Freeways spun them around in circles. Drugs were a closed circuit of brief ecstasy and despair. Burglary and robbery were drug-adjunct crimes. Murder was a common by-product of drug use and illegal drug trafficking. Drug enforcement was a futile closed circuit. Drug use was an insane and entirely understandable reaction to life in bumfuck L.A. County. He learned these things driving elevated freeways.

He worked Major Frauds in '78 and moved to VOIT in '79. VOIT stood for Violent Offender Impact Team. It was a small unit mandated to apprehend serial armed robbers. The job crossed over to Homicide.

Ann got a calling. She obeyed it on instinct. She entered nursing school and excelled at the work. Her stab at independence resurrected their marriage.

He respected her profession. He respected her pursuit of a career at age forty. He liked the way her calling meshed with his new calling.

He wanted to work Sheriff's Homicide. He wanted to investigate murders. He wanted it with a passionate sense of commitment.

He called in some favors and got it. It brought him to the body off the roadside and the body in the Marina. It brought him to the girl stunned mute by rape and blunt-force trauma.

His ghosts.

# 13

He learned some things about murder early on. He learned that men killed with less provocation than women. Men killed because they were drunk, stoned and pissed off. Men killed for money. Men killed because other men made them feel like sissies.

Men killed to impress other men. Men killed so they could talk about it. Men killed because they were weak and lazy. Murder sated their lust of the moment and narrowed down their options to a comprehensible few.

Men killed women for capitulation. The bitch wouldn't give them head or give them her money. The bitch overcooked the steak. The bitch threw a fit when they traded her food stamps for dope. The bitch didn't like them pawing her 12-year-old daughter.

Men did not kill women because they were systematically abused by the female gender. Women killed men because men fucked them over just that rigorously and persistently.

He considered the rule binding. He didn't want the rule to be true. He didn't want to see women as a whole race of victims.

The issue of free will perplexed him. Many female murder victims put themselves in harm's way and passively co-signed their death warrants. He didn't want to concede the point. He had a gender-wide crush on women. It was big and random and essentially idealistic. It kept him faithful when his marriage strayed bad.

His first victim was female.

Billy Farrington broke him in at Sheriff's Homicide. Billy was a black fashion plate. Billy wore custom suits to crime scenes replete with stiffs purging stomach gas and feces. Billy taught him to read crime scenes very slowly and deliberately.

Billy was 55 and near the end of his law-enforcement career. Billy had a big block of vacation time accrued. Billy let him work the Daisie Mae case solo.

It was a body dump up in Newhall. A man spotted a burning bundle and extinguished the flames. He called the Newhall Sheriff's Station. The watch commander called Sheriff's Homicide.

Stoner rolled out. He sealed off the crime scene and examined the body.

The victim was fully clothed. She was white and elderly. Her face was contorted. She looked almost mongoloid.

She was wrapped in a U.S. flag and some baby blankets. The bundle was cinched with electrical cord. The blankets were soaked in gasoline or a similar noxious accelerant. She looked like she took some bludgeon shots to the head.

Stoner walked the area. He saw no footprints, no tire tracks and no discarded bludgeon tools. The area was hilly and brush-covered. The killer probably carried the body up from a nearby access road.

A coroner's team arrived. They went through the victim's scorched clothing.

They found no identification. Stoner found a gold chain necklace. It looked like a peace sign or some kind of weird-ass symbol.

Stoner bagged it. The coroner's team removed the body.

Stoner drove to the Hall of Justice and checked recent missing persons reports. Nothing matched his Jane Doe. He put out a teletype. It stressed the victim's necklace and said she might be mentally retarded. He called the Information Bureau and told them to put out the word on Jane.

Channel 7 News ran a TV spot that night. Stoner got a call a few minutes later.

A man said he made the necklace. The pendant was an AA symbol. He sold the necklaces at AA meetings in Long Beach.

Stoner drew a picture of the necklace and wrote up the

facts on his case beneath it. He added his name and number at Sheriff's Homicide. He mimeographed a hundred copies and distributed them at every AA meeting in the Long Beach area.

A man named Neil Silberschlog saw the flyers and called him. He said the victim sounded like an old AA girl. She was known as Daisie Mae. She was running with a young guy named Ronald Bacon. Silberschlog lived near Bacon. Bacon was driving Daisie Mae's '64 Impala. Daisie Mae was nowhere around. Silberschlog thought the deal was hinky.

Stoner drove to Long Beach and met the informant. Silberschlog ID'd a morgue photo of the victim. He said she wasn't retarded. She was just a crusty old drunk.

Daisie Mae lived nearby. Silberschlog walked Stoner down to her pad.

It was a dive. An old drunk named One-Eyed Betty was crashed out in the front room. Betty said she saw Daisie Mae's car in front of Ronnie Bacon's place. Ronnie had Daisie Mae's watch. He changed the strap and gave it to his 16-year-old girlfriend. Ronnie just got popped for burglarizing a drugstore. He was in the Main L.A. County Jail.

Stoner drove to the jail and interviewed Ronald Bacon. He was 25 years old and stone white trash. He said he went to AA for friendship. He knew Daisie Mae—but he sure didn't kill her.

Stoner drove back to Long Beach. He searched Bacon's pad and found an empty gas can. A neighbor said Bacon sold him a blood-soaked couch.

Stoner talked to One-Eyed Betty again. She recounted Daisie Mae's last day on earth.

Daisie Mae just got her welfare check. She wanted to buy a TV set. One-Eyed Betty and Ronald Bacon wanted to help her spend her money. They drove her around looking for cheap TVs.

They were in Daisie Mae's car. Bacon made Daisie Mae cash her welfare check. One-Eyed Betty went home. Bacon and Daisie Mae drove off alone.

Stoner requested a warrant on Ronald Bacon. A deputy DA heard him out and filed homicide charges. Bacon was held to answer for one count of murder one.

A woman called Stoner at the Bureau. She told him her

daughter used to date Ronald Bacon. Bacon wrote her daughter a very suspicious letter.

The tone was sniveling. Bacon said he just stole some money and was "here in the car with her." He beat an old woman to death. He started grubbing for sympathy before he torched her body.

A handwriting expert examined the letter and confirmed that Ronald Bacon wrote it. Bacon was tried, convicted and sentenced to life in prison with a no-parole stipulation. Stoner solved his first murder. He learned that men killed women and ran to other women in self-pity.

A Norwalk man shot his wife. He aimed above her head and caught her right between the eyes. The man was just letting off steam. He stashed his marijuana plants before he reported the incident. Stoner popped him for murder two. He learned that men killed women out of boredom.

A black woman shot and killed her husband. She buzzed Lennox Station and placed an anonymous prowler call after the fact. The dispatcher sent a car by her building. The deputies didn't see any prowler. The woman called Lennox Station back. She told the dispatcher she shot her husband by mistake. He came in the window unexpectedly. She thought he was a prowler. She didn't know that all incoming station calls were tape-recorded.

The dispatcher called Sheriff's Homicide and explained the situation. Stoner rolled to the crime scene and confronted the woman. She admitted that she shot her husband before she made the first call. She said he'd been beating her up. She showed off her bruises to prove it. Stoner arrested her and ran her husband's name by the Lennox detective squad. The guys were glad she offed the fucker. They were getting ready to pop him for a string of robberies.

Stoner talked to the woman's neighbors. They said the heist man beat his wife up regularly. He lazed around the crib while she worked. He spent her money on liquor and dope.

The woman remained in custody. Stoner went to the DA

and talked mitigation. The DA agreed to plea-bargain her beef down.

The woman got probation. She called Stoner and thanked him for his kindness. He learned that women killed men when that last blow to the head tipped them just a bit off-center.


Homicide was a learn-as-you-go proposition. The Dora Boldt job was a big education.

He caught it with Billy Farrington. Billy split on another vacation and let him run crazy with it. The job was a two-week tornado.

Dora and Henry Boldt lived in Lennox Division. They were white holdouts in a black neighborhood. They were frail and almost 80 years old.

Their son found them.

Dora was dead in the living-room hallway. A pillowcase was wrapped around her head. It was soaked with blood and brain fluids.

Henry was alive in the bedroom. Somebody beat him and kicked him unconscious.

The house had been ransacked. The phone lines were cut. The son ran next door and called 911.

Patrol units arrived. An ambulance arrived. Henry Boldt regained consciousness. A deputy asked him to hold up one finger if the killer or killers were white and two fingers if they were black. Henry held up two fingers. The ambulance took him away.

Stoner and Farrington arrived. A lab crew showed up. Everybody thought the same thing.

It was two guys. They beat the old lady to death. They did it with their fists, their feet and flashlights.

The lab guys dusted for prints. They found glove marks all over the house. Stoner found a half-eaten piece of cheese on the kitchen floor. A photo man stepped on it and destroyed the teethmarks.

Stoner talked to Dora Boldt's family. They inventoried the house and helped him compile a list of stolen items. They gave him serial numbers for a missing crockpot and TV set.

Billy Farrington went on vacation. Stoner went to the Lennox detective squad, the Inglewood PD squad and the LAPD's West L.A. Bureau. He talked to a dozen burglary cops. He talked to some guys at LAPD Homicide. He told them about his case. They described 40 similar B&Es with three murders attached.

The victims were old white women. They were beaten to death. The perpetrators always cut the phone lines and ate food out of the icebox. They bludgeoned their victims. They ransacked their houses and stole their cars 30% of the time. All the victims were elderly whites. All the cars were abandoned within a small radius out in West L.A. All the beatings were savage. One woman lost an eye. The perpetrators were going out every third or fourth night.

Stoner categorized the crimes and wrote up a detailed report. He put out an urgent county-wide bulletin. He went back to the Lennox, Inglewood and West L.A. squads and laid out his information. Everybody thought the same thing: They had to go proactive immediately.

The Beverly Hills PD called Stoner. They saw his bulletin. They had two suspects for him.

Their names were Jeffrey Langford and Roy Benny Wimberly. They were male blacks in their mid-20s. The BHPD got them for two burglaries. They were sentenced to three years state time. They might be out of prison now.

Stoner called the State Parole Bureau and the State DMV. He learned that Wimberly and Langford were paroled a month before the burglaries started. Langford lived in West L.A.— near the spot where the stolen cars were abandoned.

Stoner called in a Metro team and put them under surveillance. Wimberly and Langford cruised in Langford's jeep three days running. They cruised by two houses in West L.A. and a house in Beverly Hills. Old white people lived in the houses.

Stoner called in the LAPD. A burglary cop named Varner put surveillance teams on the two West L.A. houses. Stoner called in the BHPD. They put a team on the house in their jurisdiction and moved the old people out.

Varner covered two houses. He moved the people out of

House #1. The people in House #2 refused to leave. Varner boarded up the living room and planted two cops with shotguns there. The people agreed to hide out under 24-hour guard.

Wimberly and Langford started cruising House #2 exclusively.

Stoner knew they'd hit soon. He set up a helicopter and two street surveillance teams and distributed walkie-talkies. Langford's house was covered. House #2 was covered. The chopper was set to tail the suspects from a safe distance. Stoner set up a command post at Lennox Station. He was directly linked to House #2 and all mobile units.

The suspects left Langford's house at 1:00 a.m., 7/3/81.

They drove to the alley behind House #2. The chopper pinned down every move they made.

They parked their jeep. They walked to House #2 and jumped the back fence. They cut the outside phone wires. They started prying at the back bedroom windows.

The windows were boarded shut. The old folks did it as an added precaution. They forgot to tell the cops.

Wimberly and Langford kept prying. The walkie-talkie lines inside House #2 went dead. Stoner contacted his mobile units. They were parked a block from House #2.

Wimberly and Langford kept prying. They kept making big fucking noise. They were bold and stupid. The Big Picture eluded them.

A firecracker went off somewhere down the block. The mobile units thought it was a shot. They hit their lights and sirens and swooped down on Wimberly and Langford.

Wimberly and Langford ran. The mobile units closed the alley off and apprehended them.

Stoner interviewed them at Lennox Station. They wouldn't cop out to the burglaries or murders. Stoner told them Henry Boldt died. They didn't react. Stoner told them he made them for five murders total. They played the whole interrogation sullen.

Billy Farrington got back from vacation. He helped Stoner interview the suspects. Langford called Billy a nigger. Stoner got between them and kept things from escalating.

Wimberly and Langford refused to cop out. Stoner searched their houses. Cargo trucks hauled off stolen merchandise. Stoner executed a search warrant on Wimberly's parents' house. He recovered lawn mowers, beauty supplies and a gold-plated mirror. He found Dora Boldt's crockpot. There were no fingerprints on it. The number on the bottom was not a serial number. The crockpot had no evidentiary value.

The stolen merchandise was stored at Parker Center. Victims identified it. Wimberly and Langford were indicted on 18 counts of first-degree burglary. No verifiable items stolen from the Boldt house or the houses of the other murdered women were recovered. Stoner couldn't file murder charges on Wimberly and Langford. He wanted to kill the fucking photo man who squashed that piece of cheese.

Wimberly and Langford were tried and convicted. Langford got 17 years. Wimberly got 20 to 25. Langford got paroled early. The Feds popped him with two kilos of cocaine. Langford got life with no-parole stipulated.

Stoner went for multiple homicides and settled for burglary one. The Wimberly-Langford job left him pent up and afraid for his parents. Wimberly and Langford grew up middle-class. They were not abused at home. Stoner learned that men killed women for lawn mowers and crockpots.


A man kidnapped a 60-year-old woman. He tried to force her to get cash at some ATMs. The woman kept punching in the wrong code numbers. The man got frustrated and shot her to death.

He dumped her in a church parking lot. He stole her credit cards and bought a pair of size-10 Kinney boots. The Riverside County Sheriff's chased him down on an old parole warrant. He heard the knock on the door. He hid out in bed underneath his three-hundred-pound girlfriend.

The Riverside cops popped him two days later. He told them he had the goods on an L.A. County murder. A biker told him he whacked an old broad and dumped her behind a church. He could find the biker for them—if they let him out.

The Riverside cops called Stoner and relayed the man's story. Stoner asked them if the man was wearing size-10 Kinney boots. The cops said he was. Stoner said he'd be right over with a murder warrant.

The man confessed. Sheriff's Robbery made him for some holdups. His girlfriend was his driver. The man refused to snitch her off. Men killed women and got gooey over women in a heartbeat.

A Cambodian man moved to Hawaiian Gardens. He had two kids from a previous marriage. His first wife died in the war. He had two kids with his new wife. They were hard-working Cambodian-Americans.

The man learned his wife was cheating on him. He stabbed their two kids to death and stabbed himself to death. Stoner learned that men killed women by proxy.

An angel dust addict went prowling in his bathrobe. He broke into a trailer and stabbed an old man in the eyes. Deputies followed blood spots back to his pad. The kid was trying to flush his bathrobe down the toilet. He said he didn't know why he went out prowling.

Stoner figured he was looking for a woman.

Karen Reilly was a body dump. A guy got a flat tire on the 126 freeway and saw his hubcap fly off into a field. He looked for it. He smelled something dead and almost tripped over Karen.

She was badly decomposed and chewed up by animals. Critters got her hyoid bone. There was no way to determine strangulation. There was no way to run serology or toxicology tests. There was no way to attribute cause of death.

Stoner and Farrington worked the crime scene. The temperature was pushing three digits. They found some jewelry on the body and tagged it.

Stoner checked missing-persons reports. He found a two-week-old LAPD case and contacted the assigned detectives. They told him his decomp sounded like their girl. They picked up the jewelry found on the body and showed it to Karen Reilly's parents. Her parents ID'd it.

Two private detectives were working the case already.

Karen's parents hired them a few days after Karen disappeared. They met with Stoner and Farrington and gave them a progress report.

Karen Reilly was 19. She liked liquor and unsavory young dudes. She lived with her parents in upscale Porter Ranch.

She signed up at a temp agency. She met a young male Latin named John Soto. Soto worked at the agency. He lived with his common-law wife and kid and his brother Augie and Augie's 16-year-old girlfriend. Karen was fucking John Soto. Her parents disapproved.

Karen was home right before she vanished. She was drinking jellybeans with a girlfriend. She got zorched. She ranted against John Soto and his "wife." She said they were crummy parents. She said she wanted to rescue their kid.

Karen left the house alone. Her mom and dad never saw her again.

The Soto brothers furnished the rest of the story.

Karen walked to a main drag and started hitchhiking. Two guys picked her up. The driver asked her for her phone number. Karen gave it to him. The guys dropped her outside the Soto brothers' building.

The Soto guys let her in. Karen verbally attacked John's common-law wife and ran out of the apartment. The wife chased her. They traded insults on the sidewalk at 2:00 in the morning. John Soto ran down. He made his wife go upstairs. Augie Soto and his girlfriend walked outside and talked to Karen. Karen said she was going to hitchhike home or hitch to Los Banos Lake.

Augie and his girlfriend walked upstairs. John gave them the keys to his car and told them to go find Karen. It was 2:30 a.m.

Augie and his girlfriend cruised around. They didn't spot Karen. They drove over to the local 7-Eleven. They bullshitted with a clerk there. They stayed until dawn. They never saw Karen again.

Karen's parents called the Sotos repeatedly. John Soto told them the same story he told the detectives. Karen's brother kicked the Sotos' door in and slapped John and Augie around. They stuck to the story they told the detectives. The Reilly family thought the Soto brothers killed Karen. The detectives disagreed. They figured Karen went hitchhiking and met some fuckhead freak.

Stoner interviewed Karen Reilly's parents and brother. They condemned the Soto boys. Stoner interviewed John and Augie and their women. They all stuck to their story. Stoner interviewed the 7-Eleven clerk. He disputed Augie's account of their late-night bullshit session.

Augie said they dropped in around 3:00 a.m. The clerk said they showed up at 5:00. Stoner went back to John and Augie and asked them to take polygraph tests. The brothers agreed.

John passed his test. Augie's test came back inconclusive. John's wife and Augie's girlfriend refused to be tested.

Karen Reilly's mother called Stoner. She said Karen's high-school boyfriend tried to kidnap her daughter a few months ago. He grabbed Karen at the house and forced her into his car. Karen's mother interceded. The boy drove away.

Stoner interviewed the ex-boyfriend. He said he was still in love with Karen. He didn't want her hanging out with low-rent beaners. He forced Karen into his car to talk some sense to her. The kid agreed to take a polygraph test. His mother intervened and refused to allow it.

Stoner went back to the 7-Eleven. He found out the clerk moved to Vegas and got snuffed in a drug contretemps.

Other homicides occurred. They demanded fast attention. The Karen Reilly case was rife with unindictable suspects. There was no conclusive cause of death.

Say the Soto boys beat the polygraph. Say the old boyfriend killed her. Say a man picked her up hitching. They share some bad dope and Karen ODs. The man strips the body and dumps it. A pervert picks Karen up. He rapes her in his car and offs her to cover a rape bust. A serial killer was out strangling female hitchhikers. Say he ran into Karen.

Stoner worked his fresh cases. He worked the Reilly case in his dreams.

He saw Karen alive and Karen shriveled red-black from heat and decomposition. He saw the ways she might have died. He always woke up trying to pinpoint the moment she crossed that line.

The 7-Eleven guy saw her fucking John Soto in the backseat of his car. The car was bouncing on its rocker beams right there in the parking lot. John's wife caught the show and created a big ruckus.

Karen invited Augie Soto out to Los Banos Lake. Augie showed up with some buddies. Karen's aunt and uncle wouldn't let them in their cabin. Karen camped out with her Mexican friends.

Karen was drinking too much. Karen loved to shock her friends and her uptight parents. Karen was living out a predictably rebellious pattern.

She left her house drunk. She'd just announced her new career goal to a drunken girlfriend. She wanted to be a hooker. She left her house to rouse some unfit parents and rescue their neglected child.

She was confused and stupidly guileless. She was 19. She could have pulled out of her tailspin as easily as she crossed that line.

Stoner couldn't let her go.

Stupid rebellious girls had limited options. Life favored stupid rebellious boys. Stupid rebellious girls repulsed and titillated. Their act was aimed at this big world out to ignore them. Sometimes the wrong man caught their act in a too-perfect incarnation.

Stoner learned that men killed women because the world ignored and condoned it.


He worked dozens of homicides. He maintained a salutary solve rate. He spent time with his victims' families. He neglected his own family. His sons grew up fast. He spent half their birthdays at crime scenes. The Los Angeles County murder rate kept escalating. He hacked at his paperwork backlog and sat in stalled freeway traffic. He picked up fresh murders and juggled old murders and went on suicide and industrial-accident calls. He solved nineteen out of twenty-one cases in one calendar year. He worked with good partners and did half the work. He worked with bad partners and did all the work. Some cases jazzed him. Some cases bored him. He worked a million mom-kills-pop and pop-kills-mom murders. He worked two million Mexican bar killings where all 40 eyewitnesses were in the bathroom and claimed they didn't see nothing. Some cases got him musing on some wild fucking topics. Some cases put him to sleep like a big meal and a bad movie. He chased leads on the "Night Stalker" case. He solved the "Mini-Manson" case and took down some fiends killing fag hustlers. Murders accumulated. It sent him into Murder Commitment Exhaustion. He went on vacation and suffered Murder Commitment Withdrawal. He worked all his cases with the same commitment and discriminated in his head and heart. Court dates accumulated. They circumscribed a wide array of murders. Some were recent. Some were old. He juggled a wide array of facts and rarely fucked up on the witness stand.

He spent eight years on the Drop Zone Expressway. He had no desire to exit. His one dream was simple and altogether silly.

He wanted to limit *his* murders to a meaningful few.

He got his dream. He got it because Bob Grimm got this wild bug up his ass. Grimm wanted to clear the *Cotton Club* case. He moved Stoner into the Unsolved Unit early in '87.

Stoner protested the transfer. Unsolved was an old man's job. He was only forty-six. He wanted to work fresh cases. Grimm told him to shut up and do as he was told.

The *Cotton Club* job was famous. The victim was a show-biz sleazebag named Roy Radin. He was killed in '83. His death purportedly derived from dope intrigue and Hollywood flimflam. It all connected to a shitty flick called *The Cotton Club*.

Grimm told Stoner he'd be working with Charlie Guenther. It was good news. Guenther was the man who *really* broke the Charles Manson case. He worked the Gary Hinman job for Sheriff's Homicide and busted two freaks named Mary Brunner and Bobby Beausoleil. They wrote "Pig" and "Political Piggy" on Hinman's walls after they killed him. Similar slogans were scrawled at the Tate-LaBianca crime scenes. Guenther went to the LAPD and laid out the Hinman murder. Brunner and Beausoleil were in custody during the Tate-LaBianca time frame. Guenther told the LAPD to check out their pals at the Spahn Movie Ranch. The LAPD ignored Guenther's advice. They solved Tate-LaBianca by fluke luck several months later.

Guenther was on vacation now. Grimm told Stoner to get acclimated at Unsolved and study the initial *Cotton Club* file. Stoner browsed old files to get the Unsolved gestalt. Something led him to Phyllis (Bunny) Krauch—DOD 7/12/71.

The case was semi-famous. A reporter ran it by him years back. The Bunny Krauch job caused havoc at Sheriff's Homicide.

Bunny West grew up rich in Pasadena. She married a man named Robert Krauch in the late '50s and had four kids by him. Krauch was a reporter for the *L.A. Herald*. His father was a big cheese with the paper.

Bunny Krauch was beautiful. She was kindhearted and pathologically cheerful. Robert Krauch was possessive and ill-tempered. Everybody liked Bunny. Nobody liked Robert.

The Krauches moved to Playa del Rey in the early '60s. They bought a beautiful beachfront home. Robert developed a bad reputation. People considered him eccentric. He rode his bicycle around Playa del Rey and put out hostile vibes.

Marina del Rey was the new hip enclave. It was just a mile north of Playa. It featured boat slips and yachts and lots of groovy bars and restaurants.

Charlie Brown's opened up in '68. It was a freewheeling bar and steakhouse with a swinging clientele. The waitresses were all stone foxes. They wore lowcut tops and short dresses. The manager dug the L.A. Lakers. He sucked up to the players and got his girls dates with them. Charlie Brown's became a big sports hangout.

Bunny Krauch got a waitress job there. She worked the late shift and quit around midnight. She started living a separate life a mile away from her family.

Charlie Brown's swung hard. The waitresses were always dodging passes. Bunny Krauch got pawed and groped every night.

This Don guy was the King of the Gropers. He worked as a bug exterminator. He was unattractive and well into his fifties.

The waitresses loathed him. He became Bunny Krauch's lover. Nobody could figure them out.

Don was 20 years older than Bunny. Don was disgusting. Don was a flagrant ass-pincher and a drunk.

The affair went on for three years. Don and Bunny met at a motel on Admiralty Way. They met at Charlie Brown's and other restaurants in the Marina. They were not discreet. Bunny's friends knew the score. Robert Krauch did not.

Robert got a vasectomy. Bunny said she wanted to stay on the pill. The pill regulated her period.

Robert did not get the picture.

Bunny died in her car. It was parked in a cul-de-sac near Charlie Brown's. Somebody strangled her. They tied two Charlie Brown's napkins around her neck and pulled. Somebody raped her and sodomized her. Her dress was pushed up and her blouse was ripped open. She left Charlie Brown's at midnight and died soon after. She died in her Charlie Brown's outfit.

A private patrol guard found her. Sheriff's Homicide took over.

Don had an alibi. Robert Krauch said he was asleep at home when the murder occurred. A witness saw a man on a bike near the crime scene. Robert Krauch said it wasn't him. Robert Krauch said he didn't know his wife was cheating on him.

The patrol guard was a red-hot suspect. A woman said the man and his cousin raped and sodomized her two years ago. It was her word against theirs. The cops believed them. The matter went no further.

Detectives leaned on the guard. He denied the earlier sex beef and denied killing Bunny Krauch. He took a polygraph test and passed it.

A half-dozen detectives were assigned to the case. Dozens more volunteered. The case became the rage of Sheriff's Homicide. It featured a beautiful victim and a rocking milieu. It was *Laura* updated to a promiscuous era. Bunny Krauch bewitched all the guys. They wanted to find her killer and fuck him over good. They wanted to meet all the Charlie Brown's girls. They wanted to shake up the Marina.

They hit the area hard. They turned Charlie Brown's upside down and hassled every creep who ever pawed Bunny Krauch. They interviewed the L.A. Lakers and Bunny's waitress pals. They leaned on tit pinchers and registered sex offenders. They chased Bunny's ghost.

Some drank too much. Some fell in love. Some got righteously laid. A few took the big plunge behind sex and murder and flushed their family lives down the shitter for women they just met.

Bunny Krauch put a hex on Sheriff's Homicide. Stoner loved her for it. He was sorry some other women got hurt. He knew how to keep things straight. He knew how to keep his thing with women sealed up inside him.

He fell hard for Bunny. He wished the guys who took the big plunge knew how to love like he did.

He clicked with Charlie Guenther. They both liked to work full-tilt.

They read the *Cotton Club* file individually and together. They talked to the surviving investigator and got their facts straight.

It started as an LAPD missing-persons case. Roy Radin's assistant reported Radin missing. Radin was staying at a hotel-apartment complex in West Hollywood. He walked out the door on 5/13/83. He got into a limo with a female coke dealer named Laney Jacobs. Radin and Jacobs were pissed off at each other. Jacobs thought Radin got one of her minions to steal some dope and money from her. Radin and Jacobs were hooked up with a has-been producer named Robert Evans. They were haggling over the *Cotton Club* film project. It was acrimonious bullshit.

Radin and Jacobs were meeting to hash out their disputes. They were supposed to dine at La Scala in Beverly Hills. Radin feared foul play. He told his pal Demond Wilson to tail Laney's limo. Wilson was a has-been actor. He used to star in the *Sanford and Son* TV show.

Radin split with Laney. Wilson blew his tail. Radin dropped off the face of the earth.

The LAPD couldn't find Laney Jacobs. Bob Evans didn't know where Roy Radin was. The LAPD had Radin pegged as a fly-by-night cokehead. They figured he'd turn up sooner or later. They dropped their investigation.

Radin turned up dead five weeks later. A beekeeper found his body in Caswell Canyon up near Gorman. It was badly decomped. Twenty-two-caliber shell fragments were scattered all around it. Somebody stuck dynamite in Radin's mouth postmortem. The explosion failed to obliterate his teeth. Forensic techs ID'd the body from dental charts.

Gorman was in L.A. County. Carlos Avila and Willy Ahn caught the case for Sheriff's Homicide.

They studied the LAPD missing-persons file. They tagged Laney Jacobs as a major coke dealer. They learned that she was tight with a strongarm man named Bill Mentzer. They located Jacobs in Aspen, Colorado. They decided not to jerk her chain just yet. They couldn't locate Mentzer.

Months passed. Willy Ahn got sick. He learned he had a potentially fatal brain tumor. He worked the Radin case anyway. Carlos Avila checked the LAPD computer and learned that Bill Mentzer was suspected of a recent contract hit.

The victim was named June Mincher. She was an ugly, two-hundred-pound black woman. Most people thought she was a drag queen or a man. She was a prostitute, phone-sex entrepreneur and shakedown artist.

She was hassling a wealthy family. The grandson was one of her tricks. The family hired a private eye named Mike Pascal to teach her a lesson. Pascal farmed the job out to Bill Mentzer. Mentzer pistol-whipped June Mincher and a trick she was fucking at her pad. Mincher kept bugging the family. She was shot to death on 5/3/84. Mentzer was their number-one suspect. They had jackshit for proof.

Avila couldn't find Mentzer. Months went by. Avila worked fresh murders and came back to the Radin case when his workload thinned out. Willy Ahn was now gravely ill.

An LAPD narc named Freddy McKnight shot his mouth off to a guy in the DA's Office. McKnight said he had the inside scoop on the Roy Radin job. He was going to bust a big Sheriff's case himself.

The DA's man called Bob Grimm. Grimm called his top contact at LAPD and told him to squeeze McKnight. The squeeze worked. McKnight told Grimm and Avila his story.

McKnight had a snitch named Mark Fogel. He popped Fogel with a big load of Laney Jacobs' coke. Fogel ran a limo service. Bill Mentzer and a guy named Bob Lowe drove for him part-time. Fogel said that Mentzer and Lowe were in on the Radin snuff. Fogel just clued McKnight to a big coke deal. Mentzer and Lowe were bringing two kilos in to the L.A. airport. It was Laney Jacobs' dope. McKnight was set to bust Mentzer and Lowe right there at LAX.

Avila joined the arrest team. The bust went down smoothly. They took two kilos off Mentzer and Lowe. Mentzer and Lowe refused to discuss the Radin snuff. They bailed out of custody fast.

Mentzer and Lowe shared an apartment in the Valley. Avila got a warrant and searched it. He found a snapshot of Mentzer and two unknown men in the desert. It looked like the spot where Roy Radin's body was found. Avila found some car registration papers. Laney Jacobs gave Bob Lowe a Cadillac the very day Roy Radin disappeared.

Avila revisited the Radin crime scene. The photo was shot right there. Avila ran the photo by his witnesses. Nobody knew the two men with Mentzer.

Willy Ahn died. Mentzer and Lowe beat the dope rap on a search-and-seizure glitch. Avila braced the DA. The DA read his Radin case summary and declined to file. He said the case was weak.

Avila caught some fresh murders. He ran the Radin case by the DA's Office every so often. Nobody wanted to file. Two years and some months passed.

Stoner knew they could break it. They had to make the right people talk.

It was all there.

Radin vanished in a limo. Mentzer and Lowe drove limos part-time. Mentzer worked for Laney Jacobs. Laney hated Roy Radin. Mentzer was an amateur hit man.

Stoner wanted to move. Guenther wanted him to study another case first. The Tracy Lea Stewart job was Guenther's bête noir. He knew the killers. He wanted to pop the main guy before he retired. He wanted to get Stoner hooked on Tracy.

Stoner read the file. He got hooked instantly.

Tracy Stewart was 18. She lived with her parents and kid brother in Carson. She was quiet and shy and easily frightened.

She disappeared 8/9/81. She met a boy named Bob at Redondo Beach that day. Bob was about 21. He was nice-looking. He asked Tracy out. Tracy told him to call her.

Bob called at 6:00 p.m. He suggested a drive and a few games of pool at a nice bowling alley. Tracy said sure. Bob said he'd be right over. Tracy told her mother she was going out on a date. Her mother told her to call home at least once.

Bob picked Tracy up. Tracy called her mother one hour later. She called from a bowling alley in Palos Verdes. She said she'd be home by midnight or 1:00 a.m.

She didn't come home. Her parents waited up. They called the Carson Sheriff's Station in the morning.

A deputy went by the bowling alley. He talked to some people on duty last night. They recalled Tracy and Bob. They didn't know who Bob was.

The case was bounced to Sheriff's Missing Persons. Sergeant Cissy Kienest talked to Tracy's friends and dozens of beach habitués. Nobody knew Bob. Nobody saw Tracy or Bob the night of 8/9/81.

Tracy's parents distributed flyers and ran newspaper ads. Tracy remained missing. The case lay dormant for four years.

A man named Robbie Beckett assaulted his girlfriend in 1985. He was arrested in Aspen, Colorado. He was sentenced to two years in the Colorado State Penitentiary. Sergeant Gary White handled the case for the Aspen PD.

White and Beckett had a cordial relationship. Robbie told White he wanted to buy some time off his sentence. He knew about a murder in L.A. The date was August '81. The victim was a girl he picked up. Her first name or middle name was Lee. He forgot her last name.

White said he couldn't promise any deals. Robbie laid out his story anyway.

His father was named Bob Beckett Sr. He used to live with him in Torrance—down by Redondo Beach and Palos Verdes. His father was an artist. He ran a rinky-dink art school and made extra cash as a strongarm enforcer. He collected money for some mob-connected guys in San Pedro. His father was 6'4", 270. His father knew karate. His father was in the Society for Creative Anachronisms—this group where people acted out this weird medieval shit. His father hung out with a faggy guy named Paul Serio. Paul Serio was a big shot in that weird society. His father was forty-five years old now. His father was a baaad son-of-a-bitch.

His father had a girlfriend named Sharon Hatch. She broke off their relationship in May '81. Bob Beckett Sr. went crazy. He stalked Sharon and threatened her. He told Robbie to round up some bikers to gang-rape her.

Robbie loved and feared his dad. Robbie hated to see him hurt and angry. He rounded up some guys to rape Sharon. He called it off at the last moment. Robbie liked Sharon. He didn't want to hurt her. He figured his dad would outgrow this whole vengeance thing.

Bob Beckett Sr. stayed hurt and angry. He dropped his Sharon fixation and developed a new one. He told Robbie to find him a young girl. He could rough up the girl and get back at Sharon that way.

Robbie stalled him. He figured his father would outgrow the young-girl fixation. Bob Beckett Sr. persisted. Robbie gave in.

He met that girl Lee at the beach. He got her number. He called her and asked her out. He took her to a bowling alley and shot some pool with her. They necked and drank some beer. He told her he had to stop someplace before he took her home.

The girl said okay. Robbie took her to his father's apartment. The lights were off. Bob Beckett Sr. was waiting in the bedroom. Robbie left the girl in the living room and walked in. His father said, "Did you bring me something?" Robbie delivered the girl.

Bob Beckett Sr. pawed her and raped her. Robbie got blind

drunk in the living room. Bob Beckett Sr. spent two or three hours alone with the girl.

He told her he'd drive her home. He told her to take a shower first. He locked her in the bathroom. He told Robbie they had to kill her.

Robbie didn't want to kill her. Bob Beckett Sr. grabbed a homemade sap and insisted. Robbie gave in.

Bob Beckett Sr. unlocked the bathroom and told the girl to get dressed. She did it. Robbie and Bob Beckett Sr. walked her down to their van. It was 2:00 or 2:30 a.m.

Robbie swung the sap. It caught on a tree branch. The blow stunned the girl and ripped her face. Robbie couldn't dredge up the guts to hit her again.

Bob Beckett Sr. hit her and threw her in the back of the van. He got in and pinned her down with his knees. He strangled her barehanded and wrapped a plastic garbage bag over her head.

They drove the body south on the 405 freeway. They took some weird roads out to the boonies. They dumped the girl in some bushes near a fence.

They drove home and sweated out exposure. The papers ran some missing-girl stories. Bob Beckett Sr. told Robbie to gut the van. Robbie replaced the paneling and bought a new set of tires. No cops came around. Robbie figured coyotes ate the body.

Robbie lived scared for a while. He moved out of his father's apartment and moved in with his mother. Bob Beckett Sr. gave the van to Robbie's brother David. Time dragged by. Bob Beckett Sr. married a woman named Cathy. Cathy had two daughters. Bob Beckett Sr. started molesting her twelve-year-old.

Robbie told a few friends what happened. They thought he was bullshitting. Robbie was a boozer and a brawler and a sometime fruit hustler. His friends didn't feature him as a murder-victim procurer.

Bob Beckett Sr. moved to Aspen. He got a job with his old karate buddy Paul Hamway. Robbie moved to Aspen and settled in near his father.

Gary White bought most of the story. Robbie threw in a little teaser. He said his father did a contract hit in Florida. He knew the details—but refused to divulge them.

Gary White called Sheriff's Homicide. He ran Robbie's story by Charlie Guenther.

Guenther consulted the Missing Persons Unit. Cissy Kienest said "Lee" might be Tracy Lea Stewart. Guenther sent a Tracy Stewart photo to Aspen. Gary White placed it in with a dozen shots of other young women. He showed them to Robbie Beckett. Robbie pointed to Tracy.

White called Charlie Guenther and told him he hit paydirt. Guenther and Cissy Kienest flew to Aspen.

Bob Beckett Sr. visited Robbie in prison. Robbie told him he snitched him off for the dead girl. Bob Beckett Sr. convinced him to retract his story. He laid on threats and recriminations and stressed plain old father-son loyalty. Robbie kowtowed to his dad like he always did.

Charlie Guenther and Cissy Kienest tried to interview Robbie. Robbie pissed backwards. He said the story he told White was bullshit. He wouldn't issue a formal statement confirming it. He wouldn't testify against his father.

Robbie wouldn't budge. They couldn't arrest him or Bob Beckett Sr. without a sworn statement and some kind of formal arrangement with the L.A. DA's Office.

White laid a side trip on Guenther. Daddy Beckett's step-daughter just accused him of fondling her. She told a social services counselor. It wasn't a criminal matter yet.

Guenther decided to fuck with Bob Beckett Sr. He found him and goosed him with his stepdaughter's story. Beckett flexed his muscles and stayed frosty. Guenther wanted to rumble. Bob Beckett Sr. probably sensed it.

That was 18 months ago.

Stoner read the Stewart file a half-dozen times. The case was as workable as the *Cotton Club* job. They knew who killed Tracy. They knew who killed Roy Radin. They couldn't do a fucking thing about it right now.

Charlie got him hooked on Tracy Stewart. Bob Grimm got him hooked on *The Cotton Club*. He had a brilliant partner. Two cases constituted a manageable few.

They had to make some people talk.

*

They knew ex-wives were good talkers. They knew Bill Mentzer had an ex-wife named Deedee Mentzer Santangelo. Her father was a heavyweight Teamster. They contacted him. They told him they were checking out Deedee's lowlife ex.

The old man hated Mentzer. He called Deedee and told her to cooperate. Stoner and Guenther met with her. She examined the photo that Carlos Avila found. She ID'd the two men standing with Mentzer.

One man was named Alex Marti. He was from Argentina. He was a scary, violent guy. Deedee saw him provoke a couple of fights. She was afraid of him.

The other man was an ex-cop named Bill Rider. He used to be tight with Larry Flynt, the porno king. He was married to Flynt's sister. He used to be Flynt's security boss. Rider was back in Ohio now. He was engaged in litigation against Flynt.

Stoner got Rider's number and called him. He told Rider he needed to know the exact spot where that photo was taken. It pertained to an active homicide investigation. Rider said he'd think about it and call Stoner back.

He called back the next day. He was pissed. He'd talked to Deedee Mentzer Santangelo. He knew the cops were after Bill Mentzer. Stoner should have leveled with him.

Stoner acted apologetic. Rider said he'd fly out if the Sheriff's Department paid for his airfare and lodging. Bob Grimm okayed the expenditure. Rider flew out and talked to Stoner and Guenther. He dropped little tidbits on the Mincher killing and the Radin job straight off.

He took Stoner and Guenther out to Caswell Canyon. He said Mentzer and Marti bragged about the Radin hit. Bob Lowe did the job with them. Marti was a psycho punk with Nazi tendencies. He was selling dope out of a pad in Beverly Hills now.

Rider shot his mouth off and started acting regretful. He said he was afraid of Mentzer and Marti. He had a family. Mentzer and Marti knew it. Stoner said he could supply protection. Stoner told Rider the catch.

Rider had to make Mentzer and Lowe talk. They had to talk in a closed-in, buggable venue. Rider said he'd go home and think about it.

Gary White called Charlie Guenther and broke some good news.

Robbie Beckett got out of prison. He got popped for another assault and was looking at a solid dime. Robbie called White. Robbie said he'd make a formal signed statement. Robbie made that statement. Robbie gave up Daddy Beckett for Tracy Stewart and a lot more.

Robbie Beckett was suicidally talkative. He laid himself out as his father's full-time slave and onetime murder accomplice. The best deal he could get for handing up Bob Beckett Sr. was murder two and 20 to life. His second assault conviction would have cost him five years net. Robbie torched his whole life to fuck Daddy Beckett.

Robbie put his story in writing. He tacked on the story of Bob Beckett Sr. and the Susan Hamway hit.

Bob Beckett Sr. worked for Paul Hamway. Susan Hamway was Paul's estranged wife. Paul and Susan were fighting a divorce war. Susan was living in Fort Lauderdale, Florida. She had custody of their 18-month-old daughter.

Paul hated Susan. He asked Bob Beckett Sr. if he knew any professional killers. Bob Beckett Sr. said he'd set it up for ten thousand dollars.

Paul Hamway told him to do it. He added one stipulation. Somebody should call him after the hit. He'd concoct a way to rescue his baby daughter then.

Bob Beckett Sr. called Paul Serio and arranged a rendezvous in Miami. Serio flew out. Bob Beckett Sr. met him. He brought a knife, a gun and a dildo. They rented a car and drove to Susan Hamway's house.

They knocked on the door. Susan opened up. She recognized her husband's friend Bob Beckett Sr.

Susan let the men in. Her baby was asleep in the bedroom.

Bob Beckett Sr. hit her in the head with his gun. Paul Serio strangled her with a telephone cord. Bob Beckett Sr. stabbed her in the back with a kitchen knife. Serio helped him remove her clothes and pull down her panties. They couldn't get up the nerve to stick the dildo in her vagina.

The baby slept through the murder. Paul Serio and Bob Beckett Sr. left the house in broad daylight.

They drove to a causeway near Miami Beach. They tossed their weapons in. Bob Beckett Sr. called Paul Hamway and told him his ex was dead. He said he made it look like a random sex killing.

Hamway was supposed to call one of Susan's neighbors and express concern for Susan's whereabouts. The neighbor would find the body. The neighbor would give him an alibi and rescue his daughter.

Serio flew back to L.A. Bob Beckett Sr. flew back to Aspen. Nobody rescued the baby.

The baby starved to death. She pulled big tufts of her hair out before she expired. The Fort Lauderdale PD investigated the Hamway murder. They hung the rap on a retarded man who lived nearby.

His name was John Purvis. He was tried, convicted and sentenced to life in prison. His sentence carried a strict no-parole clause.

Stoner and Guenther flew to Aspen. Robbie Beckett's lawyer wouldn't let them interview Robbie. He wanted a written deal with the L.A. DA first. Stoner called Deputy DA Dale Davidson. Davidson contacted Robbie's lawyer and offered him murder two—if Robbie testified against Bob Beckett Sr. The lawyer accepted the deal. He told Robbie not to waive extradition just yet. He told him to get a good L.A. lawyer. Robbie said he'd sit tight and await instructions.

Stoner and Guenther flew to Miami. They looked for Laney Jacobs and came up empty. They drove to Fort Lauderdale and researched the Susan Hamway case.

The prosecutor was a judge now. He admitted the case against John Purvis was shaky. Stoner and Guenther told him Robbie Beckett's story. The judge said he'd look into it. Stoner and Guenther flew back to L.A.

A Fort Lauderdale detective called Stoner. He gave him some details on the Hamway investigation. Stoner caught the gist: The cops wheedled a bogus confession out of a mentally deficient suspect.

Stoner ran down Robbie Beckett's version. The detective

acted shocked. He said he'd talk to Robbie—after he testified against his father.

Stoner and Guenther talked to Daddy Beckett's ex-wife and daughter Debbie. The ex said Daddy was bugging David Beckett. He wanted him to dump that van he gave him. She said David refused.

Debbie Beckett was dying of AIDS. She said her father used to molest her. She said he beat up David and Robbie regularly. She said he ruled by terror.

The van was crucial. Stoner and Guenther found David Beckett and sweet-talked him. His father told him to burn the van. David said no. Stoner and Guenther impounded the van. A lab team went through it. They found no hair, blood or fibers attributable to Tracy Lea Stewart.

Stoner and Guenther interviewed Mark Fogel. He fingered Laney Jacobs as a major coke dealer and played dumb on the Roy Radin murder. Stoner and Guenther drove to Taft, California. They told Tracy Stewart's parents that their daughter was dead.

They took it hard. They wanted details. Stoner and Guenther supplied them. Mrs. Stewart said she renewed Tracy's driver's license every year. Stoner said they'd try to recover her body.

Both their cases were in limbo. The Radin reinvestigation was almost a year old. They were waiting for Bill Rider to help them entrap their suspects. They were waiting for Robbie Beckett to waive extradition.

Stoner and Guenther located Laney Jacobs. She was married to a dope dealer named Larry Greenberger. They were living in Okeechobee, Florida. Stoner and Guenther decided to let Laney sit.

They located a string of her dope associates. Most of the people talked. They said Laney was vain, shallow, greedy, ruthless and conniving. She was Florida Panhandle trash. She was cheap ambition personified. She started out as a dope lawyer's secretary. She met dope dealers, fucked them and learned the trade. She was a plastic-surgery freak. She'd had her face and most of her body altered to strict specifications.

She buzzed around in Stoner's head. She joined Bunny Krauch and Tracy Stewart.

Bunny tried to live two lives a mile apart. Her tyrant husband drove her toward an unknown killer. Tracy was the quintessential female murder victim. She was killed for sex and quick disposability. Laney was lower than snakeshit. She killed a man for money and a two-second movie credit.

Robbie Beckett waived extradition. Gary White flew him out to L.A. Stoner and Guenther met the plane. They told Robbie they wanted to find Tracy's body. Robbie studied maps of Riverside and San Diego Counties. He pinpointed a few locations.

Stoner and Guenther drove him around for 14 hours. Robbie checked out various landscapes and said he couldn't be sure. They didn't spot any shredded clothes or human remains. Stoner and Guenther drove Robbie to the Main County Jail and processed him in.

Robbie talked to his public defender. The PD conferred with Dale Davidson. They cut a formal deal. Stoner and Guenther were free to bust Bob Beckett Sr.

Gary White ran a public-utilities check and found him. He was living in Tustin with his new wife. Tustin was Orange County. Stoner called the Tustin PD and arranged for three backup patrol units.

The bust was a nonevent.

Stoner and Carlos Avila knocked on the door. They asked Frau Beckett where Bob Beckett Sr. was. Bob Beckett Sr. walked out and placed his hands in handcuff position.

Stoner and Avila drove him to the Main County Jail. Charlie Guenther was ecstatic. He was set to retire soon. They nailed Daddy Beckett on the home stretch.

The Stewart case was closed. The *Cotton Club* case was in limbo. The reinvestigation was 14 months old.

Bill Rider called Stoner. He said he was living in San Pedro. He wanted to help Sheriff's Homicide. He wanted to spend time with Stoner and Guenther to see if he could trust them.

The process took three months. Stoner and Guenther met Rider two dozen times. Rider fed them tidbits on Mentzer and

Marti. It was good background stuff. It wasn't crucial information.

Rider said he had the gun that killed June Mincher. He lent it to Mentzer and got it back a few days later. He did not know it would serve as a murder weapon.

He let Stoner and Guenther borrow the gun. They took it to the crime lab and had it test-fired. They compared the rounds to the rounds from the Mincher killing. They matched perfectly.

Charlie Guenther retired. Carlos Avila replaced him. Stoner and Avila went to Bob Grimm and explained the Rider deal.

Rider was a "security consultant." He had to earn a living. He had to stay out of sight to avoid reprisals from Mentzer and Alex Marti. Rider was essential to the case. He deserved a monthly paycheck.

Grimm talked to Sheriff Block. Block okayed $3,000 a month. Rider took the money. He agreed to formally snitch off the *Cotton Club* killers. The next step was entrapment.

Rider called Bob Lowe in Maryland. He was working a bartender gig there. Rider dropped some obfuscation on Lowe. He said he was coming to Washington to do a surveillance job. He needed a backup man. Lowe said he'd love to help.

Stoner, Avila and Rider flew to Maryland. The Maryland State Police bugged Rider's car and hotel room. Rider called Lowe to set up the surveillance job. Lowe said he was busy and recommended his pal Bob Deremer. Stoner and Avila hit the roof. Rider said they should tape Deremer anyway. He used to bunk with Bill Mentzer. They were tight throughout the *Cotton Club*/June Mincher time frame. Deremer might spill some good shit.

Rider faked two surveillance jobs with Deremer. The State Police taped one car and one hotel-room surveillance. Deremer said Mentzer did the Radin hit. Bob Lowe was part of the team. He got paid seventeen grand and a Cadillac.

Deremer said he drove Mentzer around after the Mincher hit. Rider asked him how much Mentzer paid him. Deremer said three months' free rent.

Rider braced Bob Lowe at a bar. He was wearing a full-body

wire. Lowe said he drove for Mentzer twice. He saw Mentzer clip the fat nigger woman. They shot Radin with .22 hollow points. Exploded .22s looked like shotgun pellets. They tossed the guns in a lake near Miami—3,000 miles from Caswell Canyon.

Stoner and Avila flew back to L.A. They had to let things sit for a while. They couldn't bulldoze Rider through a fast bug string. He had to connect with their suspects at a relaxed and believable pace.

Months dragged by. John Purvis was still in prison. Robbie Beckett and Daddy Beckett were engaged in pretrial motions. The Fort Lauderdale cops were waiting for Robbie to testify. Convincing testimony would exonerate John Purvis. They could go after Daddy Beckett and Paul Serio then. They could nail them for Susan Hamway.

Robbie Beckett and Daddy Beckett were housed in different jails. They met during a botched court transfer. Daddy talked to Robbie. He convinced him to retract his sworn statement. Robbie called Dave Davidson and told him the deal was off. He wouldn't testify against his father. Davidson told Robbie he'd be tried for murder one. Robbie said he didn't care.

The DA's Office lost their case against Bob Beckett Sr. They released him from custody.

Stoner and Avila talked to two dozen people close to Mentzer and Jacobs. They stayed away from Mentzer and Jacobs deliberately.

They conducted their interviews. They put the *Cotton Club* story together from the ground up.

Roy Radin's father produced schlock stage shows. He died young. Roy took over his operation at age seventeen. He got rich working his own crass variation of the business.

He put on police and civic benefit shows. They featured washed-up stars like Milton Berle and Joey Bishop. Charity benefits were regulated by strict state laws. Radin broke those laws. He took egregiously large percentage fees and embezzled money earmarked for charity.

Radin weighed three hundred pounds. Radin was a cocaine addict. Radin threw wild parties at his Long Island estate. Radin almost got in big trouble circa '78.

An actress named Melonie Haller stumbled away from a Radin soiree. She was half-nude and bombed out of her gourd. She told the cops that Radin and some other freaks gang-raped her. The cops investigated. They popped Radin on a gun-possession charge. Radin paid a fine and stopped throwing wild parties. He got an itch to crash the movie biz and moved west in '82.

He met Laney Jacobs at a party. He started buying coke from her. Laney used a limo company partially owned by Bob Evans. She favored a driver named Gary Keys. Keys told Laney that Evans was looking for money. He wanted to make a movie about the Cotton Club—the Harlem nightspot popular in the '30s. Laney told Keys she had money to invest in the right movie project.

Laney worked for a coke magnate named Milan Bellachaises. He sent her out to L.A. to distribute his West Coast supply. Her dope runner was a redneck named Tally Rogers. They were selling 30 kilos a month. They were making a half-million-dollar monthly profit.

Laney was a cocaine addict. She wanted to be a movie producer. Gary Keys told Bob Evans she had money to burn.

Laney and Bob got together. They started partying and fucking. Laney rented an apartment in Beverly Hills and turned it into an orgy pad.

Evans told her *The Cotton Club* was big-budget stuff. He needed 50 million dollars minimum. Laney said she knew a guy named Roy Radin. He had lots of money and wanted to break into movies. Evans told her to set up a meeting. Laney set it up fast.

Radin tumbled. He told Evans he'd sell his house and tap into some filthy-rich investors. Evans promised Laney a $50,000 finder's fee.

Radin contacted a banker friend down in Puerto Rico. The banker was close to the territorial governor. He got the governor hot for the *Cotton Club* deal. He hit him up for 50 million dollars in government money. The governor said he'd pop for 35 only. Radin accepted his terms. He flew to New York to discuss the deal with Bob Evans.

They met at Evans' apartment. Laney showed up. She told

Radin she was getting 5% of the *Cotton Club* profits for putting the deal together. Radin objected to her percentage. Evans sided with Laney. Radin threw a tantrum and stormed out.

Laney flew back to L.A. She got into another ruckus straight off.

Tally Rogers wanted more money. He was driving dope up and down the coast and making relative chump change. Laney refused to up his wages.

Tally's wife, Betty Lou, showed up. She flew in from Tennessee unannounced. Laney showed her some L.A. hotspots. Tally convinced Laney to take her to Vegas.

Laney and Betty Lou split. Tally raided Laney's garage. He stole 12 kilos and $250,000 in cash.

The maid called Laney. She said she saw Tally poking around in her garage. Tally called Betty Lou and told her to disappear. Betty Lou caught a cab to the Vegas airport.

Laney flew back to L.A. She called Milan Bellachaises. He told her to get the dope and money back.

Laney knew this guy Bill Mentzer. He'd allegedly do anything for money. Laney called Mentzer and hired him to find Tally Rogers.

Mentzer rounded up Alex Marti and Bob Lowe. They flew to Memphis and kidnapped Tally's best friend. He showed them Tally's known haunts. They didn't spot Tally. They released his friend and flew to Miami. They discussed the Tally problem with Milan Bellachaises. Nobody came up with anything constructive.

Mentzer called Mike Pascal. He gave him the names of Laney's tight friends and told him to check their toll-call records. They might get a lead on Tally that way.

Pascal called Mentzer back two days later. He knew Mentzer wanted results. He knew Laney hated Roy Radin. He knew Radin partied with Tally Rogers.

Pascal lied to Mentzer. He said Tally called Radin right after he stole the money and dope. Radin was calling the Bahamas a lot. Tally was probably hiding out there.

Mentzer flew back to L.A. Laney was in L.A. Milan Bellachaises told her to obey Mentzer's orders. Radin was in L.A. Laney called him. She accused him of stealing her dope and money. She said he was trying to fuck her out of her *Cotton Club* percentage.

Radin denied the theft. He said he didn't know where Tally Rogers was. He was telling the truth.

Mentzer told Laney his plan.

She lures Radin into a limousine. Bob Lowe is driving. She tells Lowe to stop for cigarettes. A car is tailing them. Mentzer and Marti jump out and jump in the limo. Laney gets lost. The boys take Radin somewhere and torture the shit out of him. He talks when the pain gets bad.

The *Cotton Club* story was ridiculous and petty. The killers were clowns. The victim was a greedy piece of shit. The supporting players were parasitic slime.

Stoner kept reaching for Bunny Krauch and Tracy Stewart.


Mentzer and Marti were in L.A. Lowe was in Maryland. Laney was in Okeechobee, Florida, with Larry Greenberger. Stoner and Avila turned up the heat.

Bill Rider called Mentzer and told him he was in L.A. He invited him over to the Holiday Inn. Rider's room was bugged. Stoner and Avila were stationed next door.

Rider talked up his lawsuit against Larry Flynt. Mentzer talked up the Radin snatch.

Three black & whites pulled up behind the limo. Mentzer thought they were cooked. Marti stuck his gun in Radin's crotch. Mentzer stuck his gun in Radin's mouth. The black & whites sped past them—ha, ha, ha!

Mentzer segued to other topics. Stoner and Avila needed more incriminating talk. They had to bug Rider and Mentzer again.

They decided to stage a dope buy. They called in Sheriff's Narco and worked out a plan.

They wired up a room at the Long Beach Holiday Inn. Rider called Mentzer. He said he was making a dope buy and needed a bodyguard. He offered Mentzer $200. Mentzer took the job.

They staged the buy in a parking lot near the hotel. They used real dope. Sheriff's deputies portrayed coke dealers.

Rider brought Mentzer up to his room after the buy. Stoner and Avila were hooked up to headphones next door.

Mentzer ran his mouth nonstop.

He had a load of guns and C-4 explosive stashed in a public storage locker. They shot Roy Radin with soft-point .22s. The stupid cops thought he was shotgunned.

C-4 was pure combustion. Public storage was a public health hazard. Stoner wanted the shit contained. He gave Rider an old safe and told him to call Mentzer. Rider called Mentzer and offered him the safe. Mentzer accepted the gift. Rider and Mentzer hauled the safe to the storage shack and put the guns and C-4 in it. Rider was wearing a body wire.

Mentzer said Larry Greenberger was dead. He shot himself accidentally. It happened in Okeechobee. Mentzer thought the deal was suspicious.

Stoner called the Okeechobee cops. They thought the deal was suspicious. Laney Jacobs was hiding out behind legal counsel. Stoner knew she shot Greenberger.

The Okeechobee cops called Stoner back. They told him Laney Jacobs was running. Stoner started tracking her by her credit card receipts.

It was time to hit hard.

Stoner went to Deputy District Attorney David Conn. He told him the entire story. He played the Rider-Lowe and Rider-Mentzer tapes. Conn gave him the green light.

Charges were filed. Warrants were secured. Stoner cooked up a plan with the Okeechobee cops.

They said they'd help him pin down Laney Jacobs. They'd call her lawyer and set up a meet and promise not to bust her for Larry Greenberger's death. They'd say they just wanted to question her. They'd question her and bust her on a California warrant abstract. They'd hold her for the L.A. County Sheriff's.

It was a great fucking plan.

Stoner set up a command post. It was midway between Marti's house and Mentzer's apartment. Stoner set up two SWAT teams to hit them.

Carlos Avila flew to Maryland to arrest Bob Lowe. Bob Deremer was on a long-haul truck job. Nobody knew where he was.

10/2/88.

The Okeechobee cops arrest Laney Jacobs. The SWAT teams hit Mentzer and Marti simultaneously.

They cut their phone lines and patch in calls on a closed circuit. They tell Mentzer and Marti to look out the window and see all the cops with guns. Mentzer and Marti look out their windows and walk outside with their hands up.

Search teams are deployed. Dope-and-bomb-sniffing dogs go with them. They rip through Marti's house and Mentzer's apartment.

Carlos Avila busts Bob Lowe. Local cops snag Bob Deremer in Lafayette, Indiana.

Deremer waives extradition. He's transported to L.A. and arraigned on accessory charges. Laney Jacobs and Bob Lowe fight extradition. They remain in custody back east.

Carlos Avila is exhausted. Bill Stoner is exhausted. He's still hooked on Tracy Lea Stewart. He still has a big hard-on for Bob Beckett Sr.


Laney Jacobs waived extradition at Christmas. She was transported to Los Angeles and held at the Sybil Brand Institute for Women. Robbie Beckett went to trial in February '89.

The trial lasted a week. The jury was out one hour. Robbie was found guilty and sentenced to life in prison. Daddy Beckett was scot-free. John Purvis was still in prison. The Fort Lauderdale cops gave up on the Hamway case.

Fuck John Purvis. He was already convicted. They had no case against Daddy Beckett, Paul Serio and Paul Hamway. They needed Robbie Beckett. Robbie would not betray his father.

It took three years to adjudicate the *Cotton Club* case. Prelims, motion hearings and the jury-selection process ate up months. The trial lasted fourteen months. The penalty phase dragged on. Carlos Avila retired. Bill Stoner worked for the prosecution team full-time. He flew around the country. He interviewed a hundred witnesses. He logged in thousands of airplane miles and thousands of freeway miles. The *Cotton Club* case consumed four and a half years of his life.

The jury came back on 7/22/91. Mentzer, Marti, Lowe and Jacobs were found guilty. They all got life with no shot at parole. Stoner still didn't know exactly why they killed Roy Radin.

Mentzer said their torture plans went screwy. Marti goaded Radin in the limo. Marti kept calling him a fat Jew. Marti shot him the moment they hit Caswell Canyon.

Marti told a different story. So did Lowe. Stoner was way past caring.

A Fort Lauderdale cop called Stoner in January '93. He said John Purvis's mother just hired a lawyer. The lawyer was going on some nighttime TV show. He intended to start a big ruckus. The Fort Lauderdale PD was reopening the Hamway case.

Stoner wished him well. The Fort Lauderdale cops reopened the case and mishandled it again.

They misidentified Paul Serio. They confused Daddy Beckett's pal with a Vegas hit man of the same name. They figured the Vegas guy and Paul Hamway set the Susan hit up. They offered Daddy Beckett full immunity if he testified against them. Daddy Beckett accepted the deal and testified before a Florida grand jury. The grand jury handed down indictments against Paul Hamway and Paul Serio. Daddy Beckett told the cops that his Paul was not a Vegas hit man. His Paul was a schoolteacher currently living in Texas.

John Purvis was released from prison. The Fort Lauderdale cops popped the real Paul Serio. Serio contradicted Daddy Beckett's account of the Hamway snuff and laid all the guilt on Daddy. Serio's account was worthless. Daddy Beckett was exempt from prosecution.

John Purvis joined his mother and lawyer on the Phil Donahue show. Donahue screened some lively footage. It was Daddy Beckett's taped confession to the Fort Lauderdale cops.

There's Daddy Beckett. He's showing the cops how he strangled Sue Hamway. There's Daddy Beckett—exempt from prosecution. Daddy walked on the Stewart caper. Daddy breezed on Sue Hamway and her baby.

Robbie Beckett saw the show in Folsom Prison. He saw Daddy Beckett stage the Hamway snuff with true brio. He saw Daddy's eyes. He knew he was reliving the moment he killed Tracy.

Robbie called Bill Stoner and told him he wanted to talk. Stoner and Dale Davidson flew up to Folsom. Robbie gave them a formal statement and agreed to testify against his father. He told them he wouldn't piss backwards this time. Stoner and Davidson believed him.

Davidson drew up a warrant. It charged Robert Wayne Beckett with the murder of Tracy Lea Stewart. Stoner located Daddy Beckett in Las Vegas. He called in a Vegas PD fugitive team and arrested him in his front yard.

Daddy wanted to cut a deal. Stoner told him to get fucked. Daddy saw a judge. The judge said no bail. The L.A. courts were brutally backlogged. The cocksucker wouldn't get to trial before 1995.


Stoner was daydreaming a lot. He was seeing things fast and bright. He was spending lots of time with his dead women.

He was exhausted. He was retiring next month. A funny little thought kept running through his head.

He wasn't sure he could give up the chase completely.

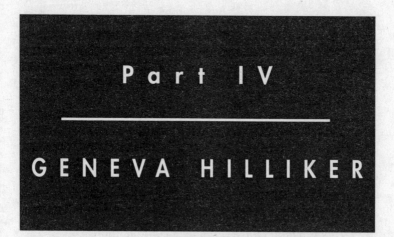

# Part IV

## GENEVA HILLIKER

*You're poised to run. You've got time and stealth on your side. Time favors runners. Their tracks disappear. You can't tell how they hid before they vanished.*

*You don't want me to know. Your secret life was designed to shut certain men out. You ran from men and to men and cut yourself down to nothing. You possessed runner's guile and wore runner's camouflage. Your runner's passion killed you.*

*You can't run from me. I ran from you for too long. This is where I force a runner's confrontation.*

*It's our time now.*

# 14

I flew out to L.A. to see my mother's murder file. My motives were ambiguous at best.

It was March '94. Jean Ellroy was 35 years and 9 months dead. I was 46 years old.

I was living in high-line Connecticut. I had a big house like the ones I used to break into. I flew out a day early and got a suite at the Mondrian Hotel. I wanted to hit the file with a clear head and a cold heart.

It started six weeks back. My friend Frank Girardot called me. He said he was writing a piece on old San Gabriel Valley murders. The piece would be published in the San Gabriel Valley *Tribune* and the Pasadena *Star-News*. It would spotlight five unsolved killings—my mother's included. It would spotlight the L.A. Sheriff's Unsolved Unit.

Frank would view my mother's file. He would read the reports and see the crime scene photos. He would see Jean Ellroy dead.

It hit me immediately. It hit me hard and fast and on two distinct levels.

*I* had to see the file. I had to write about the experience and publish the piece in a major magazine. It would stir up publicity for my next novel.

I called my editor at *GQ* and pitched him. He jumped on the idea and talked to his boss. The boss green-lighted me. I called Frank Girardot and asked him to brace his men at Sheriff's Unsolved. Frank contacted Sergeant Bill McComas and Sergeant Bill Stoner. They said I could view the file.

I made travel arrangements. The big L.A. earthquake hit and diverted me for weeks. The Hall of Justice was condemned. Sheriff's Homicide moved out. Their files were stuck in transit. The delay gave me some time to dance with the redhead.

I knew it was time to confront her. An old photograph told me why.

My wife found the picture in a newspaper archive. She bought a duplicate copy and framed it. I'm standing at George Krycki's workbench. It's 6/22/58.

You can't discern my state of mind. I might be bored. I might be catatonic. I'm not giving anything up.

It's my life at ground zero. I'm too stunned or relieved or lost in calculation to evince signs of simple grief.

That picture was 36 years old. It defined my mother as a body on a road and a fount of literary inspiration. I couldn't separate the her from the me.

I like to hole up in hotel suites. I like to turn off the lights and crank the AC. I like temperature-controlled and contained environments. I like to sit in the dark and let my mind race. I was set to meet Bill Stoner the next morning. I ordered a room-service dinner and a big pot of coffee. I turned out the lights and let the redhead take me places.

I knew things about us. I sensed other things. Her death corrupted my imagination and gave me exploitable gifts. She taught me self-sufficiency by negative example. I possessed a self-preserving streak at the height of my self-destruction. My mother gave me the gift and the curse of obsession. It began as curiosity in lieu of childish grief. It flourished as a quest for dark knowledge and mutated into a horrible thirst for sexual and mental stimulation. Obsessive drives almost killed me. A rage to turn my obsessions into something good and useful saved me. I outlived the curse. The gift assumed its final form in language.

She hot-wired me to sex and death. She was the first woman on my path to the brilliant and courageous woman I married. She gave me an enduring puzzle to ponder and learn from. She gave me the time and place of her death to extrapolate off. She was the hushed center of the fictional world I'd created and the joyful world I lived in—and to date I had acknowledged her in an altogether perfunctory manner.

I wrote my second novel—*Clandestine*—in '80. It was my first confrontational swipe at Jean Ellroy. I portrayed her as a tortured drunk with a hyperbolically tortured past in hicktown Wisconsin. I gave her a nine-year-old son and an evil ex-husband who physically resembled my father. I threw in autobiographical details and set the bulk of the book in the early '50s to spotlight a Red Scare subplot. *Clandestine* superficially addressed Jean Ellroy. It was *all* about her son at age 32. The hero was an ambitious young cop. He was out to fuck women and ascend at all costs. I was an ambitious young writer. I was hot to ascend.

Ascension meant two things. I had to write a great crime novel. I had to attack the central story of my life.

I set out to do that. I implemented my conscious resolve in an unconscious fashion. *Clandestine* was richer and more complex than my first book. The mother and son were vividly etched. They failed only by real-life comparison. They were not my mother and I. They were surrogate fictions. I wanted to get them out of the way and move on. I thought I could paint my mother with cold details and banish her that way. I thought I could dump a few boyhood secrets and sign myself off. Jean Ellroy was not my preferred murder victim. Elizabeth Short was. I dumped the redhead for the Dahlia again.

I wasn't ready for Elizabeth yet. I wanted to address her as a seasoned novelist. I wanted to extend my dialogue with women first.

I split L.A. in '81. It was too familiar and too easy. AA was too easy. I wanted to ditch all the people hooked on therapy and 12-step religion. I knew I could stay sober anywhere. I wanted to blast out of L.A. and limit my L.A. intake to the fictional L.A. in my head. *Brown's Requiem* was coming out in October. *Clandestine* was set to be published some time in '82. I had a third book finished. I wanted to start over in a sexy new locale.

I moved to Eastchester, New York—20 miles north of the Apple. I got a basement apartment and a caddy gig at Wykagyl Country Club. I was 33. I thought I was extremely hot shit. I wanted to prove myself in New York. I wanted to get heavy with the Dahlia and find the transcendental real-life woman I knew I'd never find in L.A.

New York was pure crystal meth. It meshed with my dual-world lifestyle. I wrote in my pad and lugged golf bags for a maintenance bankroll. Manhattan was a heartbeat away. Manhattan was full of provocative women.

My male friends disdained my taste in women. Movie stars and fashion models left me bored. I dug career women in business attire. I dug that one skirt seam about to pop from 15 extra pounds. I dug stern character. I dug radical and non-programmatic world-views. I disdained dilettantes, wannabes, incompetents, rock & rollers, therapy freaks, weirdo ideologues and all women who did not exemplify a sane version of the midwestern-Protestant/profligate balance I inherited from Jean Ellroy. I dug handsome women more than women other men deemed beautiful. I dug punctuality and passion and considered the two equal virtues. I was a moralistic and judgmental zealot operating on a time-lost/life-regained dynamic. I expected my women to toe the hard-work line and submit to the charismatic force I thought I possessed and fuck me comatose and make me submit to their charisma and moral rectitude on an equitable basis.

That's what I wanted. It's not what I got. My standards were slightly unreasonable. I revised them every time I met a woman I wanted to sleep with.

I remade those women in the image of Jean Ellroy sans booze, promiscuity and murder. I was a tornado sweeping through their lives. I took sex and heard their stories. I told them my story. I tried to make a string of brief and more extended couplings work. I never tried as hard as the women I was with.

I learned things in the process. I never downscaled my romantic expectations. I was a chickenshit cut-and-run guy and a heartbreaker with a convincingly soft facade. I took the ax to most of my affairs. I dug it when women got my number and grabbed the ax first. I never axed my romantic expectations. I never took a soft line on love. I felt bad about the women I fucked over. I went at women less ferociously over time. I learned to disguise my hunger. That hunger went straight into my books. They got more and more obsessive.

I was burning a lifelong torch with three flames.

My mother. The Dahlia. The woman I knew God would give me.

I wrote four novels in four years. I kept my Eastchester and Manhattan worlds separate. I got better and better. I attracted a cult following and built up a four-star review scrapbook. My writing wages improved. I retired my caddy cleats. I locked myself up for a year and wrote *The Black Dahlia*.

The year flew by. I lived with one dead woman and a dozen bad men. Betty Short ruled me. I built her character from diverse strains of male desire and tried to portray the male world that sanctioned her death. I wrote the last page and wept. I dedicated the book to my mother. I knew I could link Jean and Betty and strike 24-karat gold. I financed my own book tour. I took the link public. I made *The Black Dahlia* a national bestseller.

I told the Jean Ellroy–Dahlia story ten dozen times. I reduced it to sound bites and vulgarized it in the name of accessibility. I went at it with precise dispassion. I portrayed myself as a man formed by two murdered women and a man who now lived on a plane above such matters. My media performances were commanding at first glance and glib upon reappraisal. They exploited my mother's desecration and allowed me to cut her memory down to manageable proportions.

*The Black Dahlia* was my breakthrough book. It was pure obsessive passion and a hometown elegy. I wanted to stay in the '40s and '50s. I wanted to write bigger novels. I felt the call of bad men doing bad things in the name of authority. I wanted to piss on the noble-loner myth and exalt shitbird cops out to fuck the disenfranchised. I wanted to canonize the secret L.A. I first glimpsed the day the redhead died.

*The Black Dahlia* was behind me. My tour closed out a 28-year transit. I knew I had to surpass that book. I knew that I could return to L.A. in the '50s and rewrite that old nightmare to my own specifications. It was my first separate world. I knew I could extract its secrets and contextualize them. I could claim the time and place. I could close out that nightmare and will myself to find a new one.

I wrote three sequels to *The Black Dahlia* and called the collective work "The L.A. Quartet." My critical reputation and public profile snowballed. I met a woman, married her and divorced her within three years. I rarely thought about my mother.

I closed out L.A. in the '50s and traded up to America in Jack Kennedy's era. The jump goosed my geographic and thematic scope and pushed me halfway though a wild new novel. L.A. in the '50s was behind me. Jean Ellroy wasn't. I met a woman. She pushed me toward my mother.

The woman's name was Helen Knode. She wrote for a lefty rag called the *L.A. Weekly*. We met. We coupled. We wed. It was extravagant love. It was two-way recognition running at 6,000 RPM.

We flourished. It got better and better. Helen was hyper-brilliant. Helen was high rectitude and profane laughter. Our imaginations melded and collided.

Helen was obsessed with the whole perplexing man-woman question. She dissected it and satirized it and de- and reconstructed it. She played it for laughs and lampooned my melodramatic take on the subject.

She zoomed in on my mother. She called her "Geneva." We concocted scenarios featuring my mother and some celebrated men of her era. We laughed our tails off. We put Geneva in bed with Porfirio Rubirosa and critiqued misogynist America. Geneva turned Rock Hudson straight. Geneva pussy-whipped JFK and turned him monogamous. We riffed on Geneva and my dad's monolithic whanger. We wondered why the fuck I didn't marry a redhaired woman.

Helen found that picture. Helen urged me to study it. She was my mother's advocate and agent provocateur.

She knew me. She quoted a dead playwright and called me a bullet with nothing but a future. She understood my lack of self-pity. She knew why I despised everything that might restrict my forward momentum. She knew that bullets have no conscience. They speed past things and miss their marks as often as they hit them.

She wanted me to know my mother. She wanted me to find out who she was and why she died.

**15**

I parked outside the Homicide Bureau. I drank some coffee in my car and stalled a little. I thought about the crime scene photos.

I'd see her dead. I'd see her for the first time since I saw her alive. I kept no pictures of her. All I had were mental portraits of her clothed and nude.

She was tall. I was tall. I had her features and my father's coloring. I was going gray and bald. She died with a full head of brilliant red hair.

I walked up and rang the bell. A speaker above the door crackled. I asked for Sergeant Stoner.

The door clicked open. Bill Stoner walked up and introduced himself.

He ran about 6' and 180. He had thin brown hair and a big mustache. He was wearing a dark suit and a striped shirt-and-tie ensemble.

We shook hands and walked back to Unsolved. Stoner flashed a copy of my book *White Jazz*. He asked me why all the cops were extortionists and perverts. I said good cops made for bad fiction. He pointed to the dust jacket photo. My bull terrier was sprawled across my lap.

He said the dog looked like a bleached pig. I said his name was Barko. He was a smart motherfucker. I missed him. My ex-wife got custody.

Stoner laughed. We sat down at adjoining desks. He passed me a brown accordion folder.

He said the crime scene shots were graphic. He asked me if I wanted to see them.

I said yes.

We were alone in the office. We started talking.

I said I did some county time in the '60s and '70s. We discussed the merits and drawbacks of Biscailuz Center and Wayside Honor Rancho. I said I loved the stuffed bell peppers on the county lunch menu. Stoner said he ate them when he worked Wayside.

He had a soft inquisitor's voice. He laced his monologues with brief pauses. He never interrupted. He held steady eye contact.

He knew how to draw people out. He knew how to extract intimacies. I felt him leading me. I didn't resist. I knew he'd nailed my exhibitionist side.

I was stalling. The brown folder scared me. I knew Stoner was leading me up to it.

We talked. We traded L.A. crime tales. Stoner's perceptions were sharply lucid and devoid of commonly held police ideology. He called the LAPD a racist institution and spun stories with a vivid sense of drama and theme. He said "fuck" as routinely as I did and used profane language to peak effect. He described the Beckett case and took me straight into Tracy Stewart's terror.

We talked for two hours. We stopped almost on cue.

Stoner left the room. I quit stalling.

The file contained envelopes and teletype sheets and odd notes scrawled on odd slips of paper. It contained a Sheriff's Homicide "Blue Book." The book ran fifty pages. It contained typed reports in chronological order.

The dead body report. The coroner's report. Reports on exonerated suspects. Three interviews transcribed verbatim.

The Blue Book was flimsy and musty. Two names were typed on the cover. I didn't recognize them. Sergeants John G. Lawton and Ward E. Hallinen.

The men who asked me who my mother was fucking. One of them bought me a candy bar a million years ago.

The file was badly maintained. It was bulging with loose note slips dropped in and forgotten. The sloppy look offended me and hit me as symbolic. This was my mother's lost soul.

I imposed order on it. I formed a line of neat paper stacks. I put the envelope marked "Crime Scene Picts." off to one side. I skimmed the first set of Blue Book reports and noted odd details.

My El Monte address was 756 Maple. Two witnesses saw my mother at the Desert Inn bar. The name stunned me. The papers said she went to a local cocktail lounge. They never got more specific.

I skimmed a few reports. A Desert Inn witness called my mother's male companion a Mexican. The fact surprised me. Jean Ellroy was right-wing and obsessed with appearances. I couldn't see her out in public with a cholo.

I skimmed the back section and saw two handwritten letters. Two women snitched off their ex-husbands. They wrote to John Lawton and detailed their rationales.

Woman #1 wrote in 1968. She said her ex worked with Jean at the Packard-Bell plant. He had affairs with Jean and two other Packard-Bell women. He acted suspicious after the killing. Woman #1 asked him where he was that night. He hit her and told her to shut up.

Woman #2 wrote in 1970. She said her ex had a grudge against Jean Ellroy. Jean refused to process an injury claim he submitted. It sent him "off the deep end." Woman #2 included a postscript: Her ex torched a furniture store. They repossessed a dinette set he bought and sent him "off the deep end" again.

Both letters read vindictive. John Lawton attached a memo slip to letter #2. It said both tips were checked out and judged invalid.

I zigzagged through the book. I caught little blips of data.

Harvey Glatman was questioned and cleared as a suspect. I remembered the day he went to the gas chamber. A Desert Inn witness disputed the Mexican bit. She said the guy with the blonde and the redhead was a "Swarthy White Man." My mother worked at Airtek Dynamics from 9/56 on. I thought she was still at Packard-Bell then. The autopsy report noted semen in my mother's vagina. There was no mention of internal bruising or vaginal abrasions. There was no speculation on rape versus consensual sex. My mother was menstruating. The autopsy surgeon found a tampon in her vagina.

Facts hit me rapid-fire. I knew I had to contain the barrage. I got out my pen and notebook and flipped to the transcribed statements. The first one blew me out the fucking door.

Lavonne Chambers hopped cars at Stan's Drive-in—five blocks from the Desert Inn. She served my mother and her male companion twice that Saturday night and Sunday morning.

She said the man was Greek or Italian. He was driving a two-tone '55 or '56 Olds. He brought my mother in around 10:20 p.m. They ate in the car. They talked. They left and returned at 2:15 a.m.

The man was quiet and sullen. My mother was "quite high." She "chatted gaily." The top of her dress was down and one breast was half-exposed. She looked "slightly disheveled." The man "acted bored with her."

It was hot new information. It blew my old theory to hell.

I thought my mother left the bar with the Swarthy Man and the Blonde. They tried to force her into a three-way. She resisted. It went way bad.

He was "bored." She was "disheveled." He probably fucked her and wanted to dump her. She wanted more of his time.

I used to frequent the Stan's Drive-in across from Hollywood High. The carhops wore red-and-gold outfits. The "Krazy Dog" was great. The burgers and fried chicken were famous.

I read the statement three times. I wrote down the key facts. I braced myself and opened the first envelope.

It contained three snapshots. I saw Ed and Leoda Wagner, circa 1950. I saw my father at age 45 or 46. The photos were marked "Vic's sist. & husb." and "Vic's ex-husb." My father looked fit and handsome.

The third photo was marked "Vic, August '57."

She was wearing a white dress. I remembered it. She was holding a drink and a cigarette. Her hair was up—the way she always wore it. People were frolicking behind her. It looked like a company picnic.

She looked bad. Her face was haggard and puffy. She looked older than 42 years and 4 months. She looked like a drunk putting up a losing front. The picture was inimical to the picture I held in my mind.

That picture was all wish fulfillment. I freeze-framed my mother at a lusty forty. The lines on her face displayed strength—not dissipation. That picture was all buried yearning. I succumbed to that picture and made love to her those few precious fantasy times.

I opened the second envelope. I saw two Identi-Kit portraits of the Swarthy Man. Portrait #1 showed a skinny Joe Blow. Portrait #2 showed a sadist with similar features.

I opened the third envelope. It contained 32 male mug shots. The men were registered sex offenders. Some were white and some were Latin. They all resembled the Identi-Kit portraits.

They were questioned and cleared. They all had that flashbulb-blind sleazy pervert look. They wore neckboards from previous sex rousts. The boards listed their arrest dates and various penal code numbers. The dates covered '39 to '57. The numbers covered rape and sex mayhem and a half-dozen passive offenses. Most of the men were unkempt. A few of them were wincing like they just got hit with a phone book. Their collective vibe was repellent. They looked like a venereal smear or a come stain on a shithouse wall.

I opened the last envelope. I saw my mother dead at Arroyo High School.

Her cheeks were bloated. Her features had thickened. She looked like a sick woman sleeping.

I saw the sash cord and stocking cinched around her neck. I saw the insect bites on her arms. I saw the dress she had on. I remembered it. I looked at the black & white photos and remembered that the dress was light and dark blue.

The dress was below-the-knee length. Someone pulled it above her hips. I saw her pubic hair. I looked away fast and made it a blur.

The last picture was an autopsy shot. My mother was prone on a morgue slab. Her head was propped up on a black rubber block.

I saw her deformed nipple and the dry blood on her lips. I saw a sutured abdominal incision. They probably cut her open at the crime scene. They probably took a liver reading before she turned dead cold.

I examined all the crime scene pictures. I memorized details. I felt perfectly calm. I put everything back in the folder and handed it to Stoner.

He walked me out to my car. We shook hands and said goodbye. Stoner was subdued. He knew I was someplace far off.


I went to bed early that night. I woke up way before dawn. I saw the pictures before I opened my eyes.

I felt a little gear click in place. It was like saying "Oh" to acknowledge a big revelation.

Now you know

You thought you knew. You were wrong. Now you know for real. Now you go where she leads you.

They went back to Stan's Drive-in. It was 2:15 a.m. He was bored. They just had sex. He wanted to ditch this desperate woman and get on with his life. The combustion occurred because she wanted MORE. More sex or more male attention. The promise of a next time with flowers and a ritzier venue.

I trusted my new theory. It made me feel this big wave of love for my mother.

I was her son. I was hooked on MORE as bad as she was. Gender bias and my time favored me. I got to drink and fuck with a sanction she never dreamed of. Luck and a coward's circumspection saved me. I saw the road she went down. She force-fed me the survivor's instinct she never developed herself. Her pain was greater than mine. It defined the gap between us.


I went back to Connecticut and wrote my piece for *GQ*. It wasn't cathartic. It didn't click that little gear off. She was always right there with me.

It was a clumsy embrace and a reunion. It was a reckless pass. It was a blind date that Helen and Bill Stoner set me up on.

Now you go where she leads you.

The concept confused me. I pledged my devotion on blind faith.

**16**

She pointed me toward her secrets. Her lead was a taunt and a dare. She challenged me to discover how she lived and died.

I decided to expand my *GQ* piece 50-fold and turn it into a book. My publisher bought the idea. Bill Stoner retired in April. I contacted him and made him an offer. I said I wanted to reinvestigate my mother's homicide. I'd pay him a percentage of my book advance and cover all expenses. We would team up and attempt to find the Swarthy Man—dead or alive. I knew we were bucking stratospheric odds. I didn't care. The redhead was my primary target.

Stoner said yes.

The *GQ* piece was published in August. It emphasized my mother and me and our shared lust for MORE. I turned in my novel and rented an apartment in Newport Beach, California. Stoner said our job could run a year or more.

I flew out on Labor Day. The people on my flight were talking O.J. Simpson nonstop.

The case was three months old. It was the premier woman killing of all time already. The Black Dahlia case was big and quintessentially L.A. The Simpson case eclipsed it fast. It was huge. It was epic performance art. It was a disingenuously staged multimedia circus based on the shaky premise of a botched hack-and-run job. Everybody knew O.J. did it. Pundits riffed off that consensus and went nuts looking for hidden truth and empirical precedents. Media hacks hit the truth harder. They saw the O.J. job as a crass microcosm. It was cocaine and tit jobs. It was health club narcissism and the two-way bondage of five-figure monthly alimony payments. The bottom-level audience defined the crime. They wanted O.J.'s meretricious lifestyle. They couldn't have it. They settled for a skanky morality play that told them that lifestyle was venal.

O.J. and the Swarthy Man. Nicole and Geneva.

My mother was a very private woman. I was a showboat and a seasoned opportunist. I always craved attention. My instincts said she never did. I wanted to give her to the world. You could call me a memory rapist and point to my previous exploits to prove it.

You'd be right. You'd be wrong. I'd cop a plea behind my newfound passion.

She was dead. She was insensate. It was ridiculous to wonder if she'd understand or not. I had a crass show-and-tell side. She was the heart of my story.

The issue troubled me. I respected her privacy and was setting out to destroy it. I saw only one way out.

I had to submit to her spirit. If I hurt her, I'd feel her censure.

Stoner met me at the airport. We drove straight to Arroyo High School.

It was my second visit. A film crew shot me here once. I breezed through the interview. I hadn't seen the pictures. I couldn't point to the exact spot and place my mother there.

Stoner parked near the spot. It was hot and humid. He turned on the air conditioning and rolled up the windows.

He said we had to talk about my mother. We had to talk truthfully and bluntly. I told him I could handle it. He said he wanted to reconstruct the crime the way he thought it happened.

I mentioned my new theory. Stoner said he didn't buy it.

He said the Swarthy Man wanted some pussy. Jean was menstruating and refused to give it up. They were necking and fondling. The Swarthy Man wanted more. Jean wanted to cool him down. She said, Let's go back to Stan's Drive-in.

They drove back to Stan's. Lavonne Chambers served them again. Jean was half-drunk and lighthearted. The Swarthy Man was horny and pissed off at her. He knew this secluded road by Arroyo High School.

They finished their snack. The Swarthy Man suggested a drive. Jean said okay. The Swarthy Man drove her straight here and demanded some cunt.

Jean said no. A verbal fight ensued. The Swarthy Man hit Jean in the head five or six times. He used his fists or a small metal tool he had in the car.

Jean went unconscious. The Swarthy Man raped her. Lubrication explained the absence of vaginal abrasions. They necked and fondled a while back. Jean got turned on. She was still wet. The Swarthy Man made a smooth penetration. The rape itself was clumsy and frenzied. The coroner found a tampon at the rear of Jean's vagina. The Swarthy Man's penis jammed it down there.

Jean remained unconscious. The Swarthy Man got his rocks off and panicked. He was stuck in his car with an unconscious woman. She could ID him and nail him on a rape charge. He decided to kill her.

He had a sash cord in his car. He wrapped it around Jean's neck and strangled her. The cord broke. He pulled off Jean's left stocking and strangled her with it. He hauled her body out of the car and dumped it in the ivy. He got out of the area fast.

I shut my eyes and replayed the whole reconstruction. I ran some graphic close-ups.

I started shaking. Stoner turned the air conditioning off.

**17**

My apartment came furnished. The chairs and couch were dipped in synthetic stain-repellent. The rental agency supplied bedding and cooking utensils. The previous tenant left me some bug spray and Old Spice cologne.

The rental folks installed a telephone. I hooked up an answering machine. The pad was low-class by my current standards. The living room and bedroom were small. The walls were blank white. I rented the place on a month-to-month open-end lease. I could cut out at a moment's notice.

I moved in. I started missing Helen fast.

The place looked like a good obsession chamber. It was tightly contained and cavelike. I could close the curtains. I could turn off the lights and chase the redhead in darkness. I could buy a CD player and some music. I could listen to Rachmaninoff and Prokofiev and spin off that point where lyrical flights go discordant.

Bill's house was twenty minutes away. Bill carried a reserve badge and a gun permit. He was working for the DA's Office on an ad-hoc basis. They were building their case against Bob Beckett Sr. Bill had carte blanche at Sheriff's Homicide. He had access to all the files and communications equipment. Our investigation was sanctioned by Sheriff's Homicide. Bill would share information with the Unsolved crew. He had the Jean Ellroy file out on permanent loan. He said we had to study every scrap of paper in it.

I bought a large corkboard and nailed it to my living-room wall. I borrowed some file photos and made a collage.

I tacked up two shots of my mother in August '57. I tacked up the evil portrait of the Swarthy Man. I wrote a question mark on a Post-it note and placed it above the three pictures. I selected five pervert mug shots and placed them below the spread.

My desk faced the display. I could look up and see my mother moving into her tailspin. I could see the final result. I could blitz my memory of her younger and softer.

Bill called me. He said I should meet him at the Sheriff's Academy. He wanted to show me some evidence.

I drove out and met him in the parking lot. Bill said he had some fresh news.

Sergeant Jack Lawton died in 1990. Ward Hallinen was still alive and living down in San Diego County. He was 83 now. Bill talked to him. He didn't recall the Ellroy case at all. Bill explained our situation. Hallinen got excited and told him to bring the file down. Something in it might spark his memory.

We walked to the evidence warehouse. A small office adjoined it. Three clerks were standing around. They were deep into topical bullshit. A white guy said O.J. did it. Two black guys disagreed. Bill flashed his badge and signed an evidence form.

A clerk took us back to the warehouse. It was wicked hot and roughly the size of two football fields placed sideways. It was lined with heavy-duty steel shelving.

The ceiling was 30 feet high. The shelves ran all the way up. I saw 20 or 30 rows packed with plastic bundles.

Bill drifted off. I stood by a desk near the door. The clerk brought me a bundle. It was marked Z-483-362.

It was transparent plastic. I saw four small plastic bags inside. I opened the outer bag and placed the smaller bags on the desk.

The smallest bag contained minute dust and fiber samples. A tag listed their origin: "1955 Oldsmobile/MMT-879/6/26/58." The second bag held three small envelopes. They were sealed.

They were marked with my mother's name and Z-file number. The contents were listed separately below:

"Vic's fingernails (sample)."

"Vic's hair (sample)."

"Vic's pubic hair (sample)."

I didn't open them. I opened the third bag and saw the dress and brassiere my mother wore to her death.

The dress was light and dark blue. The brassiere was white with a lace bodice. I held them and put them to my face.

I couldn't smell her. I couldn't feel her body in them. I wanted to. I wanted to recognize her scent and touch her contours.

I ran the dress over my face. The heat was making me sweat. I got the lining a little bit wet.

I put the dress and brassiere down. I opened the fourth bag. I saw the cord and nylon stocking.

They were twisted up together. I saw the point where the cord frayed and snapped around my mother's neck. The two nooses were intact. They formed perfect circles no more than three inches across. My mother's throat was constricted to just that dimension. She was asphyxiated with just that much force.

I held the ligatures. I looked at them and turned them around in my hands. I held the stocking to my face and tried to smell my mother.

# 18

I drove out to El Monte that night. It was soaringly hot and humid.

The San Gabriel Valley always ran hot. My mother died in an early-summer heat wave. It was just that hot now.

I followed an old homing instinct. I kept my windows down and let hot air in the car. I passed the El Monte Police Station. It was right there in its 1958 location. The building looked different. It might have had a face-lift. My car felt like a fucking time machine.

I turned north on Peck Road. I remembered a long walk back from a movie. I sat through *The Ten Commandments*. I got home and found my mother blitzed to the gills.

I turned west at Peck and Bryant. I saw a 7-Eleven store on the southwest corner. The customers were Latin. The counterman was Asian. White El Monte was long gone. I turned on Maple and parked across the street from my old house.

It was my third visit in 36 years. Media people accompanied me the first two times. I was glib on both occasions. I pointed out anachronisms and riffed on what subsequent tenants did to the property. This was my first nighttime visit. Darkness covered the alterations and returned the house to me as it was then. I remembered the night I watched a rainstorm from my mother's bedroom window. I stretched out on her bed and turned the lights off to see the colors better. My mother was out somewhere. She caught me in her bedroom once before and reprimanded me. I snuck around her bedroom and checked out her lingerie drawer every time she split for the evening.

I swung back to Peck Road and drove down to Medina Court. It was exponentially more run-down than it was in '58. I saw four sidewalk dope buys in the course of three blocks. My mother drove me down Medina Court a few weeks before she died. I was a lazy little boy. She wanted to show me my future as an Anglo-Saxon wetback.

El Monte was a shit town now. El Monte was a shit town in 1958. It was a genteel shit town indigenous to its era. Dope was clandestine. Guns were scarce. El Monte was running at 10% of its current population and $\frac{1}{30}$th of its current crime rate.

Jean Ellroy was a freak El Monte victim. El Monte appealed to her honky-tonk side. She thought she found a good place to hide. It met her safety standards. It included a weekend playground. She'd see the danger here today. She'd stay away. She brought her own danger here in 1958.

She sought this place out. She made it her separate world. It was 14 miles from my fictional and real L.A.

El Monte scared me. It was the bridge between my separate real and fictional worlds. It was a perfectly circumscribed zone of loss and full-blown random horror.

I drove to 11721 Valley. The Desert Inn was now Valenzuela's Restaurant. It was a white adobe building with a terra-cotta roof.

I parked in the back. My mother parked her Buick in the same spot that night.

I walked into the restaurant. The layout shocked me.

It was narrow and L-shaped. A service counter faced the door. It looked exactly like the fantasy image I'd held for 36 years.

The booths. The low ceiling. The base of the L off to my right. Everything matched my old mental print.

Maybe she brought me here. Maybe I saw a picture. Maybe I just walked into a weird psychic matrix.

I stood in the doorway and looked around. All the waitresses and customers were Latin. I got half a dozen who-the-fuck-are-you looks.

I walked back to my car. I drove up Valley to Garvey. I

cruised the parking lot on the northeast corner.

Stan's Drive-In was here then. An abandoned coffee shop was here now. Stan's was six blocks from the Desert Inn. The Desert Inn was a mile and a half from 756 Maple. 756 Maple was a mile and a half from Arroyo High School.

It was all tight and local.

I drove to Arroyo High. The sky was hazy black. I couldn't see the mountains two miles north of me.

I parked on King's Row. I hit my high beams and framed the crime scene.

I assumed the Swarthy Man's perspective. I transposed my lust for MORE into his lust to fuck my mother. I put all my rage to surmount my past into his rage to destroy my mother's resistance. I nailed his determination and the blood in his eyes. I fell short on his will to inflict pain in pursuit of pleasure.

I remembered a sad incident. It happened in '71 or '72.

It was 2:00 or 3:00 a.m. I was coming off inhalers in Robert Burns Park. I thought I heard a woman scream.

I wasn't quite sure. I was jacked up on amphetamine. I was hearing the Voices.

The scream scared me. I knew it came from the apartments on the west side of the park. I wanted to run away and hide. I wanted to save the woman. I hesitated and ran toward the sound.

I scaled the park fence. I made a lot of noise.

I looked into a bright bedroom window. I saw a woman putting on a robe. She looked in my direction. She turned the light off and screamed. The scream didn't sound like the scream I thought I heard. I jumped back into the park and ran off down Beverly Boulevard. The Voices followed me. They told me to find the woman and assure her I intended no harm. I figured out that the first scream wasn't a scream. It was a woman making love.

I got drunk the next morning. The Voices subsided. I never apologized to the woman.

The incident spooked me. I scared that woman. I knew she'd never understand my good intentions.

*

I drove back to Newport Beach. I checked my machine and caught a message from Bill Stoner.

He said he had urgent news. He said to call him regardless of the time.

I called him. Bill said he found an old Unsolved file that blew his fucking mind.

The date was 1/23/59. The victim was named Elspeth "Bobbie" Long. She was beaten. She was strangled with a nylon stocking. She was dumped on a road in La Puente—four miles from El Monte. The Long case and the Ellroy case were point-by-point twins.

**19**

A night owl called it in. The San Dimas desk logged it at 2:35 a.m. The guy said he was out coon hunting. He saw a body by the road at Don Julian and 8th. His name was Ray Blasingame. He lived and worked in El Monte. He was calling from the gas station at Valley and 3rd.

The desk man buzzed a patrol unit. Deputy Bill Freese and Deputy Jim Harris rolled to Valley and 3rd. They followed Ray Blasingame to the dump site. He was driving a Ford pickup with four coon dogs in the back.

The site was secluded. The road was paved with crushed rock. A dirt shoulder and a barbed-wire fence ran behind it. The road led to a water pump station.

It was cold. It was dark. The Puente Hills were due south. Valley Boulevard was one half-mile north.

The woman was laid out face-up. She was stretched flat on the dirt between the road and the fence. She was wearing a charcoal-gray and black sweater, a black skirt and open-toed black shoes. A red overcoat covered her legs. A horse-and-jockey pin was attached to the left shoulder. A black plastic purse was propped up by the fence.

She was white. She was medium-sized. She had short blond hair. She was 45 to 50 years old.

Her face was bruised. A nylon stocking was lashed around her neck.

Harris radioed the San Dimas Station. The desk man called

Sheriff's Homicide. Lieutenant Charles McGowan, Sergeant Harry Andre and Sergeant Claude Everley rolled out. A patrol lieutenant and a print deputy arrived two minutes later.

Andre saw the Jean Ellroy crime scene. He told Everley that this one looked similar. The Ellroy killer tossed the victim's coat across her legs. This guy did the same thing.

A morgue car arrived. A photo car arrived. A coroner's assistant checked out the body. A photo deputy lit the crime scene and shot it.

The morgue man noted signs of early rigor mortis. The victim's head and neck were stiff. Everley pulled up her outer garments and examined her underclothes. She was wearing a red slip, a red bra and a red pantie girdle. Her legs were bare.

Andre emptied the purse. He found a pair of glasses, $1.32, a pack of Camel cigarettes, a hair brush, a pair of light-blue wool or wool-cotton-blend gloves, a tin of aspirin, a plastic key fob, a ballpoint pen, a pocket mirror and a brown leather wallet with a white-and-silver horse embossed on the front. The wallet contained snapshots of the victim, a bus ticket stub, a clipping from a horse racing scratch sheet and identification cards for Elspeth Evelyn Long and Bobbie Long. The cards listed addresses in New Orleans, Miami, and Phoenix, Arizona. The cards listed the victim's DOB as 7/10/06 and 7/10/13. An insurance ID card listed an L.A. address: 2231½ West 52nd Street. The card was dated 2/18/57.

The morgue crew removed the body. Andre called Sheriff's Homicide. He told the desk man to send some guys out to the victim's address. Everley got his flashlight and searched the area. He didn't spot any tire tracks or discarded weaponry.

Ray Blasingame went home. The photo man took some more shots. The sun came up. Andre and Everley walked the road in full daylight.

They didn't see anything new.


The victim lived in a small apartment house. Her place was at the bottom floor rear. Ward Hallinen, Ray Hopkinson and Ned Lovretovich tossed it.

They woke the manager up and badged him. He let them

into the apartment and went back to bed. They tossed both rooms. They found a box of nylon stockings and a stack of silver dollars and half-dollars. They found a stack of newspaper articles on horse racing. They found a camera with the dial set at exposure #6. They found an address book. They found a payroll check for $37.00. It was dated 1/21/59. It was issued by Bill's Cafe—1554 West Florence Avenue. They found some horse racing programs and scratch sheets and letters from a horse-race tipster.

The apartment was clean. The victim's belongings were neatly arranged. The stockings totaled up to even pairs.

They grabbed the camera and the address book. They woke the manager up and told him to keep the place locked. He said they should talk to a woman named Liola Taylor. She lived next door. He hardly knew Bobbie Long himself. Liola knew her better.

They found Liola Taylor and questioned her. She said Bobbie Long lived next door for four years or so. She worked at a restaurant on Florence. She knew lots of men. She wasn't loose. She liked male companionship. She was going out with a rich guy. She said she was after his money. She never mentioned his name. She never mentioned her own family.

Hallinen, Hopkinson and Lovretovich drove to Bill's Cafe. They talked to the boss—William Shostal. He said Bobbie Long was a good waitress. She was friendly. She loved horse racing. She hung out with a waitress named Betty Nolan.

Shostal gave the cops Betty's address. They drove to her house and questioned her.

She said she saw Bobbie at work on Tuesday. That was three days ago. Bobbie said she was going to the track on Thursday. That was yesterday. Bobbie knew a guy named Roger. Bobbie knew a guy who worked at the Challenge Creamery. Betty said she didn't know their last names. Betty said she didn't know any "rich guy." A man brought Bobbie to work two weeks ago. He had slicked-back hair and a mustache. He was driving a white-and-turquoise car. Betty said she didn't know his name. She never saw him before or since. She said they should contact Fred Mezaway—the cook at Bill's Cafe. Fred dropped off Bobbie's paycheck Wednesday or Thursday.

Hallinen called Bill Shostal and got Mezaway's address. Shostal said he'd probably be home now. Hallinen, Hopkinson and Lovretovich drove to the address and questioned Mezaway.

He said he planned to drop off Bobbie's check early Wednesday night. He got involved in a card game and postponed the errand. He dropped the check off Thursday morning. Bobbie scolded him. She said he had no business playing cards.

Mezaway said Bobbie dated around. He couldn't supply any names. She owed a bookie $300. He didn't know the bookie's name. He didn't know any "rich guy" or any guy named Roger or any guy with slicked-back hair or any guy who worked at the Challenge Creamery.

The cops drove back to Bobbie Long's apartment. They went through Bobbie's address book and started calling her friends. They got a string of no-answers. They reached a woman named Freda Fay Callis. Freda Fay said she saw Bobbie on Tuesday. They got together and picked up their friend Judy Sennett. They ran Bobbie by her doctor's office. Bobbie was having bad headaches. She bumped her head on an iced-tea dispenser at work. The doctor x-rayed Bobbie's head and took a blood sample.

The girls drove out to Rosemead. They dropped Judy off at her son-in-law's place. Freda Fay drove Bobbie back to L.A. and dropped her at her apartment. Bobbie called her yesterday morning. She said, Let's go to the races. Freda Fay said she was broke and declined the invitation.

Freda Fay said Bobbie was a racetrack fanatic. She took the bus out to Santa Anita habitually. Sometimes she'd meet strangers and get rides home. Bobbie was friendly. She wasn't man crazy. She liked men with money. Freda Fay didn't know any "rich guy" or any guy named Roger. She didn't know Bobbie's bookie. She didn't know any guy with slicked-back hair or any guy who worked at the Challenge Creamery.

The cops made some more calls. They reached Bobbie's friend Ethlyn Manlove. She said Bobbie never mentioned any family. Bobbie told her she was married a long time ago. She got married in New Orleans and divorced in Miami. Ethlyn

Manlove said Bobbie dated around. She couldn't supply any names. She didn't know any "rich guy." She didn't know Bobbie's bookie. She didn't know any guy with slicked-back hair or any guy who worked at the Challenge Creamery. The name Roger tweaked her. Roger might be this married guy Bobbie palled around with.

It was 2:00 p.m. The Long snuff made the afternoon papers. A man walked into the LAPD's 77th Street Station. He said his name was Warren William Wheelock. People called him Roger. He read about the Bobbie Long murder. He knew Bobbie. He thought the cops might want to talk to him.

The desk sergeant called Sheriff's Homicide. The watch commander called Bobbie Long's apartment and talked to Ray Hopkinson. Hopkinson called 77th Street and talked to Warren William Wheelock.

Wheelock said he met Bobbie at Hollywood Park Racetrack in May '58. He said he went by her apartment Wednesday morning—two days ago. He invited Bobbie down to San Diego. He was going down there with his wife. Bobbie brushed him off. She said she wanted to go to the track on Thursday. Wheelock and his wife went down to Dago. They visited his brother-in-law. They went to the jai alai games down in T.J. He had a ticket for game #7—dated last night.

Wheelock said he didn't know Bobbie's bookie. He didn't know any "rich guy" or any guy with slicked-back hair or any guy who worked at the Challenge Creamery. Hopkinson thanked him and said he'd be in touch.

Hallinen, Hopkinson and Lovretovich drove to the Hall of Justice. They checked the bus ticket in Bobbie Long's purse. Lovretovich called the L.A. Transit Authority. He explained his situation and read off the numbers on the ticket. His contact did some checking and called back. He said the ticket was issued yesterday— 1/22/59. It was purchased at 6th and Main in downtown L.A. Their stub was the unused portion. Somebody took an M-line bus to Santa Anita Racetrack and did not take the bus home.

Hallinen walked down to the morgue. Deputy Coroner Don H. Mills ran the autopsy by him.

Bobbie Long died of acute asphyxiation. She took some bad

shots to the head. Her skull was fractured in four places. One fracture wound was crescent-shaped. The killer might have hit her with a crescent wrench. Her sixth cervical vertebra was fractured and separated. She had partially digested beans, rice and cornmeal in her stomach. She had semen in her vagina. Her external genitalia were not bruised or abraded. Her blood alcohol registered at 0%. She died cold sober.

A teletype went out that night.

BROADCAST NO. 76   1/23/59   FILE NO. Z-524-820

MURDER INFORMATION WANTED   EMERGENCY

FOUND AT APPROX 2:30 AM 1/23/59 VICTIM
BOBBIE LONG FWA 45-50 5/5½ 135 LBS., BLUE
EYES, SHORT DISHWATER BLOND HAIR. DRESSED IN
CHARCOAL AND BLACK BLOUSE, BLACK FELT
SKIRT, BRIGHT RED FULL LENGTH COAT WITH
COSTUME JEWELRY HORSE PINNED ON LEFT
SHOULDER. VICTIM'S PANTIE GIRDLE, BRA, AND
SLIP WERE ALSO BRIGHT RED. WORE OPEN-TOE
BLACK SHOES AND CARRIED BLACK PURSE. VICTIM
WAS FOUND LYING ON BACK BESIDE A DIRT ACCESS
ROAD NEAR A PUMP HOUSE OFF DON JULIAN ROAD
AND 8TH AVE., LA PUENTE AREA, FULLY CLOTHED,
STRANGLED WITH A NYLON STOCKING. HAD ALSO
BEEN BEATEN ON THE HEAD WITH AN INSTRUMENT
LEAVING CRESCENT-SHAPED MARKS. HAD HAD
INTERCOURSE OR HAD BEEN RAPED. ATTENDED
RACES AT SANTA ANITA ON 1/22/59. PURSE
CONTAINED GLASSES AND CAMEL CIGARETTES,
PLUS USUAL FEMININE EFFECTS. SUSPECT'S CAR
MAY HAVE BLOODSTAINS. PLEASE CHECK YOUR
FIELD INTERROGATION CARDS FOR THE AFTERNOON
AND EVENING UP TO 12:00 MIDNIGHT OF 1/22/59.
ATTN/TEMPLE STATION
ATTN/SAN DIMAS STATION

ATTN/SAN GABRIEL VALLEY POLICE DEPTS.
ATTN/SAN GABRIEL VALLEY AREA CHP
REFER MCGOWAN, ANDRE, EVERLEY HQ DB
HOMICIDE DETAIL
FILE Z-524-820

PETER J. PITCHESS, SHERIFF DC SNDG 600 PM

Ward Hallinen met Harry Andre and Claude Everley at the Bureau. They discussed the Long case 14 hours in. They all thought it resembled the Jean Ellroy job.

Jean Ellroy was probably raped. Bobbie Long most likely engaged in sex willingly. Her undergarments were properly in place. That fact implied consensual sex.

Both women sustained head wounds. The body dump locations were six miles apart. Santa Anita was two miles north of Arroyo High School. Both victims were divorcees. The crime scenes looked almost identical. The Ellroy killer dropped the victim's coat on her legs. The Long killer did the same thing. Bobbie Long was blond. Jean Ellroy was seen with a blond woman. Jean Ellroy ate chili at Stan's Drive-in. Bobbie Long ate Mexican food. The time lag between homicides was seven months and one day.

The Ellroy killer used a sash cord *and* a nylon stocking. The Long killer used a stocking only. Nylon stockings were common strangulation tools. The MO might link the two murders. The MO might not.

Andre and Everley called every police department in the San Gabriel Valley. They laid out their case. They asked patrol supervisors to check field interrogation cards and traffic reports. Bobbie Long was out with a man last night. They were looking for possible sightings.

They removed an ID photo from Bobbie Long's wallet. They canvassed the restaurants and bars near the dump site. They hit some joints along Valley Boulevard. They tried the French Basque, Tina's Cafe, the Blue Room, the Caves

Cafe, Charley's Cafe and the Silver Dollar Cafe. They came up empty.

They hit the Canyon Inn. They heard a guy talking up their case way too loud. They braced him. The guy was drunk. He was trying to impress some women.

Andre and Everley called it quits and went home. Ward Hallinen dropped Bobbie Long's camera off at the crime lab and told a tech man to develop the film. Ned Lovretovich worked late at the Bureau. He kept calling the names in Bobbie Long's address book.

He talked to Edith Boromeo. She said she knew Bobbie 20-some years. They waitressed together in New Orleans. Bobbie was married to a laundry truck driver. He used to beat Bobbie up. She didn't remember his name. She didn't know Bobbie's bookie or any "rich guy" or any guy with slicked-back hair or any guy who worked at the Challenge Creamery.

He talked to Mabel Brown. She said she used to waitress with Bobbie. Bobbie was very outspoken and rude. She went to the track with Bobbie quite a few times. Bobbie blew all her money on bets and never chipped in for gas. Bobbie accepted rides from strange men all the time. She didn't know Bobbie's bookie. She didn't know any "rich guy." She didn't know any guy with slicked-back hair. She didn't know any guy who worked at the Challenge Creamery.

He talked to Bill Kimbrough. The guy said he owned a grocery store near Bobbie Long's apartment. He saw Bobbie at the bus stop yesterday. She was alone. She said she was going to the track. Lovretovich drove back to Bobbie Long's apartment. He tossed it again. He found two liquor bottles stashed below the kitchen sink.

The Long job was one day old. Everybody thought the same thing.

Bobbie met some freak at the track. He cooked her some chow at his pad or took her to a restaurant. He fucked her at his pad or fucked her at a motel or raped her at the crime scene and forced her to put her undies back on. They had to canvass Santa Anita. They had to hit all the restaurants and motels in the San Gabriel Valley.

Andre and Everley drove out to the track. They contacted the concessions boss and showed him their Bobbie Long snapshot. The guy said she looked familiar. He saw a girl like that on Thursday. She was kissing a man with thin blond hair and a big bulbous nose. She was wearing some kind of dark outfit. She wasn't wearing a coat. There were five checkrooms at the track. Maybe she checked her coat.

Santa Anita was big and spread out. The concessions guy showed Andre and Everley around. They hit all the check-rooms, bars, betting windows and lunch counters. They flashed Bobbie Long's picture. A dozen people said she looked familiar.

Andre called the Bureau. Blackie McGowan said they got an early-morning tip.

Somebody found a nylon stocking in a suit at Bedon Cleaners in Rosemead. The stocking guy read the morning paper. He knew Bobbie Long got choked. He figured the odd stocking had to be somewhere. He called the Temple City Station. A patrol unit picked up the stocking and rushed it to the Sheriff's Crime Lab. A technician examined it and compared it to the stocking that choked Bobbie Long. The stockings did not match.

Andre and Everley drove to the Bureau. They called in their sketch man, Jack Moffett. They told him to draw a picture of Bobbie Long in her snazzy red-and-black ensemble. They told him to draw it in full color and get some glossy prints made up.

Moffett went to work. Andre called Metro and requested two deputies. The duty sergeant sent Bill Vickers and Frank Godfrey over. They canvassed bars and restaurants on the Jean Ellroy job. Andre told them to blanket the San Gabriel Valley. Hit all the restaurants serving Mexican food and hit all the motels. Look for couples checking in Thursday night. Get their car license numbers and contact the DMV. Get complete registration stats. Contact the registered vehicle owners and find out who they shacked up with. Motel clerks were required to write down license numbers when their guests checked in. Get that information and follow it up.

Vickers and Godfrey rolled out. Ward Hallinen rolled out to El Monte. He found Margie Trawick. He showed her a photograph of Elspeth "Bobbie" Long. Margie said no. She wasn't the woman she saw with Jean Ellroy.

Claude Everley called the crime lab. He told a technician to photograph Bobbie Long's clothing and make up some color glossies. The man said he'd developed the film in Bobbie Long's camera. He got six shots total. They showed Bobbie alone and Bobbie with a few other women. One shot showed a woman and a two-tone '56 Olds.

Everley told Andre. Andre said the Ellroy suspect drove a two-tone Olds. Everley called the lab guy back. He told him to route the car photo to the Information Bureau. They could plant it in the L.A. papers. They might I.D. the car that way.

Andre liked the car bit. He figured the same guy choked Bobbie and that redheaded nurse.

Vickers and Godfrey canvassed motels and restaurants. Andre and Everley canvassed the track all weekend. Ned Lovretovich called the people in Bobbie Long's address book. They all said the same thing.

Bobbie loved horse racing. Bobbie was frugal. Bobbie disdained all forms of sex. Bobbie was married two to four times. Nobody knew when, where or who to. Nobody knew her bookie. Nobody knew the "rich guy" or the guy with slicked-back hair or the guy who worked at the Challenge Creamery.

Blackie McGowan assigned four more detectives. He told them to canvass full-time. The San Gabriel Valley was large and full of fuck-pad motels.

A tip came in on Monday—1/26/59. The tipster ran a hay mill out in La Puente.

He fingered a truck driver. The guy was shooting his mouth off. He said he screwed a girl at 8th and Don Julian. He said he screwed her *goooood*. He screwed her early Friday morning.

The truck driver was Mexican. He lived up in Beaumont.

Harry Andre called the Beaumont PD and told them to bring the man in. They did it. Andre and Everley drove up to Beaumont and grilled him.

He said he screwed the girl early *Thursday* morning. Her name was Sally Ann. He met her at Tina's Cafe on Simpson and Valley. He went to her pad before he screwed her. It was on 8th Avenue. He saw the name "Vasquez" on the mailbox.

The man stuck to his story. He said his pal Pete could verify it. Pete lived in La Puente.

Andre and Everley drove to La Puente. They talked to Pete. They found the house with the "Vasquez" mailbox. They talked to Sally Ann. They cleared the Mexican.

A tip came in on Tuesday—1/27/59. A man named Jess Dornan snitched off his neighbor Sam Carnes.

Sam was acting weird lately. Sam was a racetrack fool. Sam defaced his car upholstery two days ago. Maybe he was hacking out some bloodstains.

Andre questioned Sam Carnes. Sam had an alibi for last Thursday night.

Vickers and Godfrey canvassed. Andre and Hallinen canvassed. Sergeant Jim Wahlke and Deputy Cal Bublitz canvassed. Sergeant Dick Humphreys and Deputy Bob Grover canvassed. They hit the El Gordo Restaurant, Panchito's Restaurant, the El Poche Restaurant, the Casa Del Rey Restaurant, Morrow's Restaurant, the Tic-Toe Restaurant, the County Kitchen, the Utter Hut, Stan's Drive-In, Rich's Cafe, the Horseshoe Club, the Lucky X, Belan's Restaurant, the Spic & Span Motel, the Rose Garden Motel, the End-of-the-Trail Motel, the Fair Motel, the El Portal Motel, the 901 Motel, the Elmwood Motel, the Valley Motel, the Shady Nook Cabins, the 9331 Motel, the Santa Anita Motel, the Flamingo Motel, the Derby Motel, the Bradson Motel, the El Sorrento Motel, the Duarte Motel, the Filly Motel, the Ambassador Motel, the Walnut Auto Court, the Welcome Motel, the Wonderland Motel, the Sunkist Motel, the Bright Spot Motel, the Home Motel, the Sun View Motel, the Mecca Motel, the El Barto Motel, the Scenic Motel, the La Bonita Motel, the Sunlite Motel, the El Monte Motel, the Troy Motel, the El Campo Motel, the Garvey Motel, the Victory Motel, the Rancho Descanso Motel, the Rainbow Motel, the Mountain View Motel, the Walnut Lane Motel, the Covina Motel, the La Siesta Motel, the Stan-Marr Motel and the Hialeah Motel.

They got hazy information and no information. They checked 130 car registrations. They hit married couples and one-night couples and adulterous couples and prostitute-and-customer couples. They couldn't locate some people. They ran up a substantial call-and-clear list. They came up dead short on hard suspects.

A tip came in on Wednesday—1/28/59. A woman named Viola Ramsey snitched off her husband.

His name was James Orville Ramsey. He abandoned Mrs. Ramsey last month. He called her Monday night. He said, "If you want to put me on the goddamn spot, your ass is going to lay next to that waitress in the Puente Hills. If your friends miss you for three or four days, tell them they will find your ass laying in the sand next to hers."

James Orville Ramsey was 33 years old. He was a fry cook. Mrs. Ramsey said he hated waitresses. He thought they were cheap and no good. He liked horse racing and Mexican food. He was a drunk. He served time for burglary and GTA. He liked older women. He threatened to kill Mrs. Ramsey and "spit in her blood." He drove a '54 Chevy two-door. His last known place of employment was the Five Points Bowling Alley in El Monte. He was shacked up with a 19-year-old girl named Joan Baker. She waitressed at Happy's Cafe. Mrs. Ramsey waitressed at Jack's Bar in Monterey Park.

Claude Everley questioned James Orville Ramsey. The tip was vindictive bullshit.

The L.A. papers ran the car photo on Thursday—1/29/59. They ran a sidebar piece requesting information and listed the Sheriff's Homicide phone number. The Long case was six days old. It was going absolutely nowhere.

Andre and Everley canvassed the track again. A coffee-counter girl said she saw Bobbie Long last week. She pushed to the front of her line. She was quite rude.

Another coffee girl told the same story. Bobbie pushed to the front of her line. She was rude. She refused to wait in line like everybody else.

A cashier said he saw Bobbie last week. She cashed a ticket at his window. She "acted rummy."

A security guard said he saw Bobbie last Thursday. She was alone.

A bartender said he served Bobbie last week. She was "half drunk."

A bus driver said he saw a woman resembling Bobbie Long last week. She got into a '53 Ford with two male Negroes. The car was powder blue. The passenger door squeaked.

The lab guys did some good work. They hung Bobbie Long's coat, blouse and skirt on pegs and shot them in full color. Ward Hallinen picked up two dozen prints and drove out to the San Gabriel Valley. He left copies at the Temple City Sheriff's Station, the San Dimas Sheriff's Station and the Baldwin Park, Arcadia and El Monte PDs. He talked to five detective squad lieutenants. He asked them to run separate canvasses within their jurisdictions. They said they'd try to squeeze the work in.

Ethlyn Manlove came into the Bureau Thursday afternoon. Ray Hopkinson interviewed her. A stenographer transcribed her statement.

She said Bobbie Long lied about her age. She said Bobbie was married twice. Bobbie married a guy in New Orleans and a guy in Abilene, Kansas. She didn't know their names. Bobbie had two brothers and a sister. She didn't know their names. She said Bobbie had no need for love or sex. Bobbie loved money. Bobbie was "very mercenary."

Hopkinson asked Miss Manlove if Bobbie would trade sex for money. She said she would. She said a sea captain "kept" Bobbie during World War II. He paid for her clothes and apartment. He sent her $250 a month.

Miss Manlove said Bobbie would demand *good* money. She'd want $25 or $50 a throw. Maybe she put out for some guy. Maybe he stiffed her. Bobbie threw a fit. The guy killed her to shut her up and keep his money.

Hopkinson said it was possible.

A woman called Sheriff's Homicide on Friday—1/30/59. She identified herself as Mrs. K. F. Lawter and said she saw the picture in the papers. The woman was her former tenant Gertrude Hoven. Gertrude used to live in a building she owned.

Ward Hallinen called Mrs. Lawter. She said Gertrude Hoven lived in San Francisco now. The picture was taken outside her building in the Crenshaw District. The Oldsmobile belonged to Mrs. Henry S. Nevala. She still lived in the building.

Hallinen called Mrs. Nevala. She said she remembered the incident. Bobbie Long took the picture. It was cheeky behavior. Bobbie should have asked permission first.

They discussed Bobbie Long. Mrs. Nevala said Bobbie used to bet with a bookie named Eddie Vince. Eddie worked out of a restaurant at 54th and Crenshaw. He died in a car wreck last year. Another guy took over his business.

The Long case was one week old. It was all loose ends and misinformation.

They cleared all the motel guys. They checked reports on choke murders going back five years and came up empty. They hauled in some of the sex fiends from the Ellroy case and leaned on them again. They leaned on 22 brand-new registered sex offenders. They came up dead empty.

Other murders occurred. The Bobbie Long crew dispersed. They worked fresh cases and snagged occasional Bobbie Long tips.

They got a tip and identified the Challenge Creamery guy. His name was Tom Moore. He was working at the Challenge Creamery the night Bobbie got choked.

They got a tip on 2/14/59. Two East L.A. deputies popped a clown named Walter Eldon Bosch. He was holed up in a motel room. He was jacking off and making dirty phone calls. They checked him out and cleared him as a suspect.

They got a tip on 2/17/59. Norwalk Patrol popped a guy named Eugene Thomas Friese. Two deputies caught him dragging a woman into an alley. He had a rape jacket dating back to 1951. He took a polygraph test on the Bobbie Long case. The examiner called the result "inconclusive."

They got a tip on 3/29/59. The Temple City squad called it in. A woman named Evelyn Louise Haggin said a man named

William Clifford Epperly kidnapped her, raped her and performed sex perversions on her. Harry Andre interviewed Evelyn Louise Haggin. She said Epperly choked her unconscious. Her neck was unmarked. She said she had sex with Epperly two or three times before he raped her. Andre talked to Epperly. Epperly said he just served a year county time. He was in custody from 2/20/58 to 2/8/59. Andre confirmed the dates and cleared Epperly.

They found Eddie Vince's partner and cleared him. They traced Bobbie Long back to New Orleans and Miami and got no concrete answers. The Long case sputtered out and went inactive.

They got a tip on 3/15/60. Two creeps kidnapped a teenage girl. They forced her into their truck and drove her out to the boonies. They raped her, went down on her and forced her to blow them. They released her. She told her parents what happened. They called the San Dimas Station. The girl talked to two squad detectives. She described her assailants. One of the guys sounded like a local jerk named Robert Elton Van Gaasbeck. The detectives took the girl by Van Gaasbeck's pad. She identified Van Gaasbeck and his '59 Ford pickup. Van Gaasbeck snitched off his pal Max Gaylord Stout.

Harry Andre grilled Van Gaasbeck and Stout pro forma. He cleared them on Bobbie Long and Jean Ellroy.

They got a tip on 6/29/60. A male Mexican tried to rape a woman at a trailer park in Azusa. The victim's name was Clarisse Pearl Heggesvold.

The male Mexican entered her trailer and pulled her outside. He dragged her behind the trailer and pulled off her dress and slip. He stated, "I'm going to get some." The victim started yelling. Her neighbor Sue Sepchenko ran over. She started hitting the male Mexican with a broom handle. The male Mexican released Clarisse Pearl Heggesvold and ran toward Sue Sepchenko. Clarisse Pearl Heggesvold picked up several four-by-six masonry blocks and threw them at the male Mexican's car—a '55 red-and-white Buick two-door, license number MAG-780. She broke the windshield and two side windows. The male Mexican ran to his car and escaped. Sue Sepchenko called the San Dimas Sheriff's Station. She reported the incident and the suspect's license number. Patrol deputies traced the number and arrested the vehicle's owner: Charles Acosta Linares, AKA Rex.

Al Sholund handled the tip. He grilled Linares and cleared him fast. Linares was fat and overtly psychotic.

They got a tip on 7/27/60. A guy named Raymond Todd Lentz broke into a house in La Puente stark nude. He saw Donna Mae Hazleton and Richard Lambert Olearts asleep on the living room couch. Donna Mae and Richard woke up. Lentz ran outside. Richard called the San Dimas Station. Patrol deputies found Lentz and arrested him. Lentz said he'd been drinking with Donna Mae's ex-husband. He knew Donna Mae was a hot divorcee. He thought he could walk into the house and have sex with her. His own wife was pregnant and could not give him satisfaction.

Claude Everley interviewed Lentz. He cleared him in record time.


A woman was strangled in Baldwin Park in May '62. The case went unsolved. It was a manual strangulation. It looked like a quickie choke-and-run job. It didn't look like the Jean Ellroy and Bobbie Long murders.

An attempt rape occurred on 7/29/62. The victim was named Margaret Jane Telsted. The rape-o was named Jim Boss Bennett. They connected at the Torch Bar in Glendora.

Bennett and Miss Telsted drank some beer together. Bennett invited Miss Telsted to his pad in La Puente. They drove over in her car. They had a beer in the kitchen. Bennett maneuvered Miss Telsted into the bedroom and threw her down on the bed. He stated, "Come on now, you know what I want. You've been married." Miss Telsted said, "I am not a tramp." Bennett slugged her in the chest and tore off her capri pants, blouse and underpants. He disrobed himself and exposed his private parts. He said he wanted intercourse. He threw Miss Telsted down on the floor. He forced her legs apart and achieved a minor penetration. Miss Telsted struggled. Bennett banged her head on the floor. He failed to achieve a complete penetration.

Miss Telsted ran into a back bedroom and saw a man asleep on the bed. She ran to the kitchen. Bennett stopped her. She said she'd submit to sex if he let her get dressed and move her car. She said her ex-husband might be out lurking. She wanted to cover her tracks.

Bennett said okay. Miss Telsted put her clothes on and walked outside. Bennett followed her. Miss Telsted jumped in her car. Bennett tried to grab her. His dog ran out of the house and growled at him. Bennett backed off. The dog jumped into the car and sat down beside Miss Telsted. Miss Telsted drove to the West Covina Police Station and reported the incident. She took the dog home with her.

The West Covina cops called the San Dimas Sheriff's and relayed the complaint. Two detectives popped Jim Boss Bennett. They brought him to the San Dimas Station and grilled him. He disputed Miss Telsted's story. He said he never really got inside her. The detectives booked him. The detectives checked him out real good. They thought he looked like an old Identi-Kit portrait. They called Sheriff's Homicide and gave him up as a murder suspect.

Ward Hallinen drove out to the San Dimas Station. He stood behind a one-way mirror and observed Jim Boss Bennett. Bennett looked like the suspect in the Jean Ellroy murder. He ran Bennett through the DMV and CII.

He got two fast replies.

Bennett had no registered vehicles. Bennett had a two-page rap sheet.

He was 44. He was born in Norman, Oklahoma. He had assault convictions dating back to 1942. He got popped for drunk driving on 3/16/57 and 7/7/57. The second bust occurred in nearby Baldwin Park.

Bennett was driving a '47 Merc. He almost plowed six pedestrians outside the Jubilee Ballroom. A patrol unit chased him. He ran his car up on a dirt embankment. He stopped the car, stumbled out of it and almost fell to the ground. Two deputies grabbed him. He resisted arrest and was forcibly restrained.

Bennett got popped for battery on 2/22/58. The bust occurred at the VFW Hall in nearby Baldwin Park.

Bennett was dancing with a woman named Lola Reinhardt. He started yelling at Miss Reinhardt for no apparent reason. He told her he wanted to leave now. Miss Reinhardt refused to leave. Bennett dragged her outside and shoved her into his car.

He slapped her and yelled at her. He said, "I'll kill you or you'll kill me." A man named Lester Kendall approached the car. Bennett wrapped an arm around Miss Reinhardt's neck and tried to choke her. Kendall grabbed Bennett. Miss Reinhardt broke free. Someone called the Temple City Sheriff's. A patrol unit arrived. A deputy arrested Jim Boss Bennett.

Hallinen ran a public utilities check. He turned up six prior addresses for Jim Boss Bennett.

He lived in Baldwin Park, El Monte and La Puente. His employment record showed big gaps between jobs. He worked at Hallfield's Ceramics. He worked at United Electrodynamics. He was a laborer and a tractor driver and an electrical assembler. He was married to a woman named Jessie Stewart Bennett. They lived together on and off.

Hallinen interviewed Bennett. He never mentioned Bobbie Long or Jean Ellroy. He brought up the VFW caper. Bennett contradicted Lola Reinhardt's statement. He said a crazy guy smashed his car with a Coke bottle. Another guy smashed the windshield with his fist. Bennett's story made no sense.

Hallinen decided to run a five-man lineup.

He called Margie Trawick and told her to stand by. He located Lavonne Chambers in Reno, Nevada. She was dealing cards in a casino. She agreed to fly in. Hallinen told her the Sheriff's Department would cover all her expenses.

He found four county inmates who resembled the Identi-Kit portrait. They agreed to stand in a lineup.

Lavonne flew in. Hallinen picked her up and drove her to the Temple City Station. Margie Trawick arrived.

Five men were standing in an interview room. Jim Boss Bennett was standing in the #2 position.

Margie and Lavonne stood behind a one-way glass wall. They observed the five men separately.

Margie said, "Number 2 is the image of him. Face looks like

the face I saw that night. Hair looks like the man's, and his hairline and face looks a little thinner. He looks familiar, like the man I saw that night."

Lavonne pointed to Man #2. She said, "To me, that is the man I saw with the redheaded woman."

Hallinen talked to Lavonne and Margie individually. He asked them if they were absolutely sure. They hedged and equivocated and hemmed-and-hawed and said not absolutely.

Hallinen thanked them for their candor. Bennett was a good suspect/longshot hybrid. He looked like the Identi-Kit portrait. He did not look Greek or Italian or in any way Latin. He looked like skinny white trash.

They couldn't hold him any longer. They couldn't file a murder charge on him. The attempt rape case was flimsy. The complainant was a barfly. They had to cut Jim Boss Bennett loose.

They released him. Hallinen still tagged him as a viable suspect.

He talked to Bennett's wife and his known associates. They said Jim was bad—but not awful. He never told them Jim was a sex-murder suspect.

He had no proof. He had two shaky IDs. He ran Bennett in on an assault charge. He wanted to sweat him and lean on him.

Bennett bailed out. Hallinen decided to drop the whole thing. Nuisance tactics backfired routinely. Harassment was harassment. Hard-core suspects deserved it. Bennett missed that mark. Lavonne and Margie were solid. Lavonne and Margie weren't quite sure.

It was 9/1/62. The Long case stood inactive. The Ellroy case was four years, two months and ten days old.

## 20

The Bobbie Long digression stunned me. I spent four days alone with the file.

I put three crime scene photos up on my corkboard. I placed a shot of Bobbie Long alive beside a shot of my mother. I tacked up a Jim Boss Bennett mug shot. I centered the collage around three shots of Jean Ellroy dead.

The effect was more blunt than shocking. I wanted to undermine my mother's victimhood and objectify her death. There's the blood on her lips. There's her pubic hair. There's the cord and stocking on her neck.

I stared at the corkboard. I bought another board and placed the two together. I tacked up all the Long and Ellroy crime scene shots in contrasting order. I memorized the points of resemblance and the points of departure.

Two ligatures on Jean. One ligature on Bobbie. The purse by the barbed-wire fence. The ivy thicket and the dirt road by the water-pump station. The two overcoats identically discarded.

My mother looked her age and then some. Bobbie Long looked younger than hers. Jim Boss Bennett looked too countrified to be the Swarthy Man.

I studied the Long file. I studied the Ellroy file. I read the Long and Ellroy Blue Books and all the reports and note slips in both folders. I stared at my wall display. I wanted to de-eroticize my mother and get used to seeing her dead. I put the two cases together and built chronologies and narrative lines from odd bits of data.

My mother left the house between 8:00 and 8:30. She was seen at the Manger Bar "between 8:00 and 9:00." She was alone. The Manger Bar was near the Desert Inn and Stan's Drive-in. My mother and the Swarthy Man arrived at Stan's some time after 10:00. Lavonne Chambers served them. They left Stan's. They arrived at the Desert Inn some time after 10:30. The Blonde Woman arrived with them. Michael Whittaker crashed the party. Margie Trawick observed the group. She left the Desert Inn at 11:30. My mother, the Swarthy Man, the Blonde and Mike Whittaker were still seated together. My mother, the Swarthy Man and the Blonde left around midnight. A waitress named Myrtle Mawby saw my mother and the Swarthy Man at the Desert Inn around 2:00 a.m. They left. They arrived at Stan's Drive-In around 2:15. Lavonne Chambers served them again. They drove off around 2:40. My mother's body was discovered at 10:10 a.m. Her car was found behind the Desert Inn.

That was all witness-verified gospel. The chronological gaps formed theoretical vacuums. The Bobbie Long chronology was simple. Bobbie went to Santa Anita Racetrack. Her body was found in La Puente—eight miles southeast.

She met a man at the track. He fed her, fucked her and killed her. It was non-witness-verified gospel. I believed it. Stoner believed it. We couldn't prove it. The cops operated on that premise back in '59. It was indisputable today. My mother's last night alive defied strict interpretation.

She left the house in her car. She was at the Manger Bar alone. She met the Swarthy Man somewhere. She dropped her car off somewhere and got into his car. Lavonne Chambers served them in his car. They left Stan's Drive-In. They went to the Desert Inn. They picked up the Blonde en route. They went back to Stan's in his car. Her car was found behind the Desert Inn.

She could have met the Swarthy Man at his pad. She could have met him at a cocktail lounge. She could have left her car at either location. They went to Stan's in his car. She could have picked up her car right after. He could have picked up the Blonde. She could have picked up the Blonde. They could have met the Blonde outside the Desert Inn. They partied at the Desert Inn. They left together. They could have gone somewhere as a group. The Blonde could have gone off alone. My mother and the Swarthy Man could have kissed and fondled in his car or her car behind the Desert Inn. They could have gone to his pad. They could have kissed and fondled in the Desert Inn parking lot before that 2:00 a.m. nightcap. She could have turned off the sex in his car or her car. She could have shut him down at his pad. They could have gone to the Blonde's pad. She could have shut him down there. They went back to the Desert Inn. They could have gone back from the Blonde's place or the Swarthy Man's place or another cocktail lounge or any dark street in the San Gabriel Valley. My mother could have left her car at the Blonde's place or the Swarthy Man's place. She could have left it at either location during any one of the reconstructive time gaps in the evening. The Swarthy Man could have retrieved the car after he killed her. He could have dumped it in the Desert Inn parking lot at 3:00 or 4:00 a.m. The Blonde could have dumped it. They could have run a two-car convoy. They could have split the scene in the Blonde's car or the Swarthy Man's car.

It's 2:40 a.m. My mother and the Swarthy Man split Stan's Drive-in. Her car is parked behind the Desert Inn or parked somewhere else. He's bored and sullen. She's half-drunk and chatty. They go to his place or the Blonde's place or Arroyo High School or *someplace*. She shuts him down again or says the wrong thing or looks at him the wrong way or enrages him with a barely perceptible gesture.

Maybe it's rape. Maybe it's sex by consent. Maybe Stoner's reconstruction was valid. Maybe my MORE theory hit some factual chords. Maybe my mother balked at a three-way at some point in the evening. Maybe the Swarthy Man decided to coerce some solo action. Maybe Lavonne Chambers and Margie Trawick got their times wrong and fucked up the means to establish any kind of accurate time line. Maybe Myrtle Mawby got her time wrong. Maybe my mother and the Swarthy Man left the Desert Inn with the Blonde and did not return for that 2:00 a.m. nightcap. You had a killer and a victim. You had an unidentified woman. You had three female witnesses and a drunken male witness. You had a seven-hour time span and a geographically localized series of prosaic events that resulted in murder. You could extrapolate off the established facts and interpret the prelude in an infinite number of ways.

She might have met the Swarthy Man and the Blonde that night. She might have met them on some previous honky-tonk jaunt. She might have met them separately. The Blonde might have set her up with the Swarthy Man. The Blonde might be an old friend. The Blonde might have urged her to move out to El Monte. The Swarthy Man might be an old lover back for more.

He might be a former Packard-Bell or Airtek employee. He might be an old barroom flame passing through. He might have killed Bobbie Long seven months after he killed my mother.

There was no telephone at 756 Maple. The cops couldn't check my mother's toll calls. She might have called the Blonde or the Swarthy Man that evening or some time in the four months she lived in El Monte. Every call outside El Monte proper would register on her phone bills. The Blonde might have lived in Baldwin Park or West Covina. The Swarthy Man might have lived in Temple City. The cops never found my mother's purse. The cops didn't find an address book at 756 Maple. It was probably in my mother's purse. She carried her purse that night. The Swarthy Man got rid of the purse. His name might have been in the address book. The Blonde's name might have been in it.

It was 1958. Most people had telephones. My mother didn't. She was hiding out in El Monte.

I studied my mother's file. I studied the Long file. I picked up strange facts and a wrenching omission.

My mother left an unfinished drink in the kitchen. Maybe the Blonde called her up and suggested some fun. Maybe our cramped little house closed in on her and forced her to bolt. Bobbie Long might have been a closet juicer. A cop found two bottles in her kitchen. I always thought my mother fought the man who killed her. I always thought the cops found bloody skin under her nails. The autopsy report stated nothing of the kind. It was my heroic embellishment. I cast my mother as a redheaded tigress and carried the image for 36 years.

Jean and Bobbie. Bobbie and Jean.

Two murder victims. Near-identical crime scenes a few miles apart. A strong consensus at Sheriff's Homicide.

The guys thought one man killed both women.

Stoner leaned that way. I leaned that way with one reservation. I did not see the Swarthy Man as a serial killer.

I forced myself to stand back from the judgment. I knew my grounds for rejection were partially aesthetic. Serial killers bored me and vexed me. They were a real-life statistical rarity and a media plague. Novels, films and TV shows celebrated them as monsters and exploited their potential to spark simple suspense plots. Serial killers were self-contained evil units. They were perfect foils for clichéd cops on the edge. Most of them suffered horrific childhood trauma. The details made for good pop-psych drama and gave them a certain victimized panache. Serial killers were hopped-up eyeball fuckers and ravaged inner children. They were scary in the moment and as dismissible as an empty box of popcorn. Their hyperbolic drives sucked in readers and viewers and distanced them within their own ghoulish rapture. Serial killers were very unprosaic. They were hip, slick and cool. They talked wild Nietzschean rebop. They were sexier than the one twisted fuck who killed two women out of lust and panic and perfectly applied pressure on a two-time-only trigger.

I cashed in on serial killers myself. I consciously rejected them three novels back. They were good background fodder. They were silly literary shit from any other standpoint. I didn't think a serial killer killed my mother and Bobbie Long. I wasn't sure the same man offed both women. The Swarthy Man was out in public with the Blonde and my mother. His rage seemed to escalate as the night wore on. He knew Arroyo High School. He probably lived in the San Gabriel Valley. Calculating psychopaths don't shit where they eat.

The Blonde knew the Swarthy Man. She knew he killed my mother. He probably coerced her into silence. Bobbie Long was not the Blonde. Bobbie Long was just a low-rent victim waiting to happen.

She was cheap and avaricious. She was willful. She had a

bad history with men and reveled in her petty triumphs over the male gender. She had a bad fucking mouth.

Maybe she met the Swarthy Man at the track. He killed that goddamn nurse last year and his wig was still a bit loose. He took Bobbie someplace for dinner. He lured her back to his crib and promoted some pussy. Bobbie demanded payment. He balked. His wig blew all the way.

Maybe he learned from the redhead. Maybe she flipped his switch irrevocably. Maybe she drove him out of the closet and showed him that rape and consensual sex were incomplete without strangulation. Maybe he became a serial killer.

Maybe Jean and Bobbie flipped his switch the same way. Maybe he killed those two women and crawled back into some psychic black hole. Stocking strangulation was a common MO. The Swarthy Man choked my mother with a sash cord and a stocking. Bobbie Long was killed with a single ligature.

Maybe they were killed by two different men.

I stepped back from the issue. Stoner warned me not to lock into any given theory or hypothetical reconstruction.

I spent four days alone with the files. I locked myself up and focused on the reports and note slips and the pictures on my corkboards. Stoner had duplicate copies of the Long and Ellroy Blue Books. We called each other three or four times a day and discussed points of evidence and general case logic. We agreed that Jim Boss Bennett was not the Swarthy Man. He was too booze-addled and recognizably fucked up to seduce women over the course of a long evening or day at the track. Jim Boss Bennett was a stone juicehead. He chased overtly alcoholic women. He found them in rock-bottom venues. The Desert Inn was upscale by his standards. He went to beer and wine bars that served Eastside Old Tap Lager and T-Bird on the rocks. Stoner said he was probably a longtime date raper. He didn't penetrate Margaret Telsted. He probably penetrated a dozen other women. He probably blew a few rapes from alcoholic impotence and poor strategic planning. My mother liked cheap men. She possessed egalitarian standards. Jim Boss Bennett was too raggedy-assed and pathetic for her. She dug musky male lowlife. Jim Boss Bennett ran low on musk and high on body odor. He wasn't her type.

We discussed the two women who snitched off their ex-husbands. Woman #1 was named Marian Poirier. Her pussy-hound ex was named Albert. He allegedly had affairs with Jean Ellroy and two other women at Packard-Bell Electronics.

Mrs. Poirier admitted that she had no evidence. She said her husband knew two other murdered women. She said it was "too much of a coincidence." She didn't name the dead women. Jack Lawton wrote her a letter and asked her to name them. Mrs. Poirier wrote back and ignored Lawton's question. Stoner wrote the woman off. He said she sounded like a borderline fruitcake.

Woman #2 was named Shirley Ann Miller. Her ex was named Will Lenard Miller. Will allegedly killed Jean Ellroy. Will allegedly babbled, "I shouldn't have killed her!" in his sleep one night. Will allegedly painted his two-tone Buick a few days after the snuff. Will allegedly torched a furniture warehouse in 1968.

I found a stack of notes on Will Lenard Miller. Most of them were dated 1970. I saw Charlie Guenther's name a half-dozen times.

Guenther was Stoner's old partner. Bill said he was living up near Sacramento. He said we should fly up and run the Miller stuff by him.

We discussed Bobbie Long and my mother. We tried to plumb a through line to connect them in life.

They worked a few miles from each other. They fled bad marriages. They were secretive and self-sufficient. They were remote and superficially outgoing.

My mother was a drunk. Bobbie gambled compulsively. Gambling bored my mother. Sex left Bobbie cold.

They never met in life. All our through lines read like speculative fiction.

I spent some time with Bobbie. I turned off the living room lights and stretched out on the couch with pictures of her and my mother. I was close to a wall switch. I could think in the dark and tap the lights to look at Bobbie and Jean.

I resented Bobbie. I didn't want her to distract me from my mother. I held my mother's picture to keep Bobbie in her place. Bobbie was a tangential victim.

Bobbie storms to the front of the coffee line. Bobbie gambles herself into debt and rags a friend for playing cards. Gambling was a chickenshit obsession. The big thrill was the risk of self-annihilation and the shot at transcendence through money. Sex obsession was love six times or six thousand times removed. Both compulsions mortified. Both compulsions destroyed. Gambling was always about self-abnegation and money. Sex was a stupid glandular disposition and sometimes the route to big bad love.

Jean and Bobbie were sad and lonely. Jean and Bobbie were up on the same high ledge. You could sift through all the disparate bits of data in their files and say that they were the same woman.

I didn't believe it. Bobbie was looking to score. Jean was looking to hide and get out of herself and maybe give herself up for something weird or new or better.

Bobbie Long was not our real focus. She was a possible or probable related murder victim and a possible or probable lead on the Swarthy Man's deteriorating psyche. There were no Long case eyewitnesses. Bobbie's friends were mid-50-ish in 1959 and were probably all dead now. The Swarthy Man was probably dead. He was probably a hard-living bar habitué. He probably smoked. He probably drank whisky or pure grain spirits. He might have bellied up from cancer in 1982. He might be hooked up to an oxygen mask in scenic La Puente.

I sat in the dark and held the two Identi-Kit portraits. I turned on the lights and looked at them once in a while. I violated Stoner's rule and reconstructed the Swarthy Man.

Bill saw him as a smooth-talking salesman. I saw him as a slick blue-collar guy. He did odd jobs for extra money. He worked weekend gigs out of his beat-up '55 or '56 Olds. He carried a toolbox in the backseat. It contained a length of sash cord.

He was 38 or 39. He liked women older than him. They knew the score on one hand and fell for cheap romance on the other. He hated them as much as he liked them. He never asked himself why this was so.

He met women in bars and nightclubs. He beat a few women up over the years. They said things or did things that got under his skin. He took a few women the hard way. He came on scary and convinced them to give it up before he took it by force. He was fastidious. He was cautious. He could turn on the charm.

He lived in the San Gabriel Valley. He liked the nightspots. He liked the construction-boom scope of the place. He day-dreamed a lot. He thought about hurting women. He never asked himself why he was thinking such flat-out crazy shit.

He killed that nurse in June '58. The Blonde kept her mouth shut. He lived scared for six weeks, six months or a year. His fear fizzled out. He chased women and fucked women and beat up women once in a blue moon.

He aged. His sex drive abated. He quit chasing, fucking and beating up women. He thought about that nurse he killed way back when. He felt no remorse. He never killed another woman. He wasn't a raging psycho. Things never spun out of control like they did that night with the nurse.

Or:

He picked up Bobbie Long at Santa Anita. The nurse was seven months dead. He picked up a few women in the meantime. He didn't hurt them. He figured the nurse was some freak accident.

He screwed Bobbie Long. She said something or did something. He throttled her and dumped her body. He lived scared for a long fucking time. He was afraid of the cops and the gas chamber and afraid of himself. He lived with the fear. He grew old with it. He never killed another woman.

I called Stoner and pitched my reconstructions. He found the first one plausible and dismissed the second one. He said you don't kill two women and just stop there. I disagreed. I told Bill he was unduly tied to cop empiricism. I said the San Gabriel Valley was this deus ex machina. The people who flocked there flocked there for unconscious reasons that superseded the conscious application of logic and made anything possible. The region defined the crime. The region was the crime. You had two sex killings and one or two sex killers eschewing standard sex-killer behavior. The region explained it all. The unconscious San Gabriel Valley migration explained every absurd and murderous act that went down there. Our job was to pinpoint three people within that migration.

Bill listened to my pitch and got specific. He said we needed to comb my mother's file and start looking for old witnesses. We had to run DMV checks and criminal records checks. We had to evaluate the 1958 investigation. We had to trace my mother's steps from her cradle to her grave. Homicide jobs veered off in weird directions most of the time. We had to stay on top of our information and always stand ready to jump.

I said I was ready now.

Bill told me to turn off the lights and go back to work.

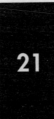

# 21

Ward Hallinen was 83. I saw him and remembered him immediately.

He gave me a candy bar at the El Monte Station. He always sat to the left of his partner. My father admired his suits.

His blue eyes took me back. I remembered his eyes and nothing else about him. He was frail now. His skin was covered with red-and-pink lesions. He was 46 or 47 in 1958.

He met us outside his house. It was a faux-ranch job enclosed by shade trees. A nice stretch of land adjoined it. I saw a barn and two horses grazing.

Stoner introduced me. We shook hands. I said something like, "How are you, Mr. Hallinen?" My memory was running at warp speed. I wanted to ignite his memory. Stoner said he might be senile. He might not remember the Jean Ellroy case.

We walked inside and sat down in the kitchen. Stoner placed our file on a free chair. I looked at Hallinen. He looked at me. I mentioned the candy bar moment. He said he didn't recall it.

He apologized for his bad memory. Stoner made a crack about his own advanced age and failing faculties. Hallinen asked him how old he was. Bill said, "Fifty-four." Hallinen laughed and slapped his knees.

Stoner mentioned some old Sheriff's Homicide men. Hallinen said Jack Lawton, Harry Andre and Claude Everley were dead. Blackie McGowan was dead. Captain Etzel and Ray Hopkinson were dead. Ned Lovretovich was still up and about. He retired a long time ago himself. He wasn't sure of the date.

He did some private security work and started breeding race horses. He'd notched a lot of pension time. He'd milked L.A. County for a nice piece of change.

Stoner laughed. I laughed. Hallinen's wife walked in. Stoner and I stood up. Frances Traeger Hallinen told us to sit down.

She looked fit and alert. She was old Sheriff Traeger's daughter. She sat down and tossed out some names.

Stoner tossed out some names. Hallinen tossed out a few. The names sparked little stories. I took a little cop nostalgia tour.

I recognized a few names. A hundred deputies dropped notes in the Ellroy and Long files. I tried to picture Jim Wahlke and Blackie McGowan.

Frances Hallinen brought up the Finch-Tregoff case. I said I followed it as a youngster. Ward Hallinen said it was his biggest case ever. I mentioned a few details. He didn't recall them.

Frances Hallinen excused herself and walked outside. Bill opened up the file. I pointed to the horses outside and segued to the Bobbie Long case and Santa Anita. Hallinen shut his eyes. I saw him fighting to bring it all back. He said he remembered going out to the track. He couldn't dredge up anything more specific.

Bill showed him the Arroyo High photos. I ran a concurrent crime scene narration. Hallinen stared at the pictures. He screwed up his face and fought. He said he *thought* he remembered the case. He said he *thought* he had a very good suspect.

I mentioned Jim Boss Bennett and the '62 lineup. Bill got out a stack of Jim Boss Bennett mug shots. Hallinen said he didn't recall the lineup. He stared at the mug shots for a good three minutes.

His face contorted. He held the pictures and clamped one hand down on the kitchen table. He dug his feet into the floor. He was fighting his incapacity full-bore.

He smiled and said he couldn't place the man. Bill handed him the Ellroy Blue Book and asked him to flip through the reports.

Hallinen read the dead body report and the autopsy report.

He read the transcribed witness statements. He read slowly. He said he remembered a few other cases he worked with Jack Lawton. He said the stenographer's name was familiar. He said he remembered the old El Monte police chief.

He stared at the crime scene photos. He said he knew he was there. He gave me a look that said, That's your mother—how can you look at these pictures?

Bill asked him if he kept his old case notebooks. Hallinen said he tossed them out a few years ago. He said he was sorry. He wanted to help. His mind wouldn't let him.

I gave Bill the cutoff sign. We packed up the file and said our goodbyes. Hallinen apologized again. I laid out a time-gets-us-all rap. It sounded patronizing.

Hallinen said he was sorry he didn't nail the bastard. I said he was up against a very cunning victim. I thanked him for his hard work and kindness.


Bill and I drove back to Orange County. We discussed our future plans all the way. Bill said we'd be fighting a failed-memory onslaught. We'd be talking to people who were middle-aged in 1958. We'd be sifting through memory gaps and chronologically skewed recollections. Old people concocted things unconsciously. They wanted to please and impress. They wanted to prove their mental solvency.

I mentioned Hallinen's notebooks. Bill said our file was short on supplemental reports. Hallinen and Lawton worked the case all summer. They probably filled up six notebooks. We had to reconstruct their initial investigation. They could have interviewed the Swarthy Man and never snapped to him as a suspect. I asked Bill if Jack Lawton was married. Bill said he was. Two of his sons worked as deputies for a while. Jack used to work with his old partner Billy Farrington. Billy would know if Jack's wife was still alive. He could contact her and see if she kept Jack's notebooks.

I called the notebooks a long shot. Bill agreed. I said it all came back to the Blonde. She knew the Swarthy Man. She knew he killed Jean Ellroy. She never came forward. She was afraid of reprisals or she had something to hide. I said she probably shot her mouth off anyway. She told people what happened. She bragged about her closeness to murder or phrased the story as a cautionary lesson. Time passed. Her fear abated. She told people. Two people or six people or a dozen people knew the story or elements of the story.

Bill said we had to take our case public. I said the Blonde told people who told people who told people. Bill said I was the fucking publicity scrounger supreme. I said we should install a toll-free tip line at my pad. Bill said he'd call the phone company and set it up.

We discussed the Long case. Bill said we had to call the Coroner's Office and see if they kept the semen samples they took from Bobbie Long and my mother. He knew a lab that ran DNA tests for $2,000. They could conclusively determine if Bobbie Long and my mother had sex with the same man.

I asked Bill to prioritize the Long case. He said it rated low. A random pickup killed Bobbie Long. My mother probably *knew* the Blonde and the Swarthy Man. She probably knew at least one of them *before* that night.

I mentioned the Swarthy Man's car and the IBM punch cards in the file. It looked like the cops only checked car registrations for the San Gabriel Valley. Lavonne Chambers pinpointed a '55 or '56 Olds. I figured the cops would check registrations for the whole fucking state. Bill said the punch-card run was confusing. Homicide jobs were full of weird inconsistencies.

I said it all came back to the Blonde. Bill said, "Cherchez la femme."

We flew up to Sacramento the next morning. We flew up behind some bad news.

Bill called the Coroner's Office. They said they tossed our semen slides. They tossed out old evidence routinely. They needed space to store new evidence.

We rented a car and drove to Charlie Guenther's house. Bill called Guenther last night and told him we were coming. He asked him some preliminary questions. Guenther said the case was vaguely familiar. He said the file might revive his memory.

We brought the file. I brought 50 potential questions.

Guenther was friendly. He came across 65 going on 40. He looked good. He had gray-white hair and blue eyes like Ward Hallinen. He ran an O. J. Simpson hate riff in place of standard hellos. He jumped to our case fast.

Bill ran the key points by him. Guenther said he remembered it now. He got called in with his partner Duane Rasure. Some woman snitched off her ex-husband. They checked the guy out. They didn't confirm or refute his guilt.

We sat down at a coffee table. I emptied the Will Lenard Miller envelope. It contained three photographs of Will Lenard Miller; reports from the Orange County Sheriff's Department; copies of Will Lenard Miller's 1957, 1958 and 1959 income tax returns; income tax withholding statements from 1957, 1958 and 1959; a finance company bill dated 5/17/65; an Orange County Sheriff's Department to El Monte PD teletype dated 9/4/70; a house escrow agreement signed by Will and Shirley Miller—dated 1/9/57; an investigatory checklist in Charlie Guenther's handwriting; a note sheet detailing Will Lenard Miller's criminal record—with two bad check charges in '67 and '69 and a credit card forgery in '70; a lawyer's letter dated 11/3/64—detailing alleged injuries that Will Lenard Miller suffered while working at the C. K. Adams Machine Shop on 3/26/62; an Orange County Municipal Court Probation Order dated 11/22/67; and a polygraph report on Will Lenard Miller—dated 9/15/70.

We looked at the paperwork. We put the income tax forms aside. We looked at the pictures of Will Lenard Miller.

He was dark-haired and heavyset. He had blunt facial characteristics. He did not look like the Swarthy Man.

Guenther examined his checklist. He said the notations pertained to standard procedure. He always did the same thing when he picked up old cases. Nothing juked his memory. The list was just a personal reminder.

We read the lawyer's letter. It itemized Will Lenard Miller's workplace grievances.

Miller took a spill and fucked up his left knee. He started having dizzy spells and blackouts. He fell down and fucked up his head. His physical injuries fucked up his psychological balance.

I mentioned a Blue Book report. Shirley Miller said my mother refused to process an injury claim her husband submitted. She said it sent him "off the deep end."

Guenther said Miller was a goddamn crybaby. Bill said he sure didn't look Latin.

We checked out the probation order. Will Lenard Miller bounced a few checks. He got a $25 fine and two years' probation. He had to make restitution. He had to see a financial counselor. He had to get permission to make purchases above $50.

We all agreed.

Will Lenard Miller was one sorry sack of shit.

We checked his tax statements. They confirmed our appraisal.

Will Lenard Miller went through jobs quick. He worked at nine different machine shops in three calendar years.

We read the Orange County Sheriff's reports. We put the basic story in perspective.

It was late August '70. The Orange County cops went looking for Will Lenard Miller. They wanted to pop him on a probation warrant. Deputy J. A. Sidebotham talked to Shirley Ann Miller. She said she broke up with Will Lenard Miller one year ago. She said he burned down a furniture warehouse in 1968. She said he murdered a nurse named Jean Hilliker in 1958.

Jean worked at Airtek Dynamics. She used to date Will Lenard Miller. She rejected a medical claim that Will Lenard Miller submitted. This enraged Will Lenard Miller. Jean Hilliker was murdered two weeks later. Shirley Miller read about it. Will Lenard Miller looked like a picture of the suspect. The papers said the suspect drove a Buick. Will Lenard Miller drove a '52 or '53 Buick. He painted it a few days after the murder. The McMahon Furniture Company repossessed some furniture that Will Lenard Miller bought. Somebody torched their warehouse a few weeks later. Shirley Miller read about it. She showed the article to Will Lenard Miller. Will Lenard Miller said, "I did it." Will Lenard Miller was mentally ill and a "psycho."

Sidebotham called the El Monte PD. They told him Jean Hilliker was Jean Hilliker Ellroy. The L.A. Sheriff's handled the case. The El Monte PD assisted.

Sidebotham arrested Will Lenard Miller. He booked him on the probation warrant and locked him down in the Orange County Jail. The El Monte PD contacted Sheriff's Homicide. Deputy Charlie Guenther and Sergeant Duane Rasure were told to reopen the Jean Ellroy case.

Guenther and Rasure interviewed Shirley Ann Miller. She told them the same story she told Deputy Sidebotham. Guenther and Rasure interviewed several Airtek people. The El Monte PD assigned two cops to assist them. Sergeant Marv Martin and Detective D. A. Ness interviewed more Airtek people. Guenther and Rasure and Martin and Ness interviewed Will Lenard Miller. Will Lenard Miller said he did not kill Jean Hilliker. Will Lenard Miller took a polygraph test and passed it.

Guenther said it was all coming back. He remembered Will Lenard Miller. They grilled him at the Orange County Jail. He was popping pills for some kind of heart condition. He looked like shit. They wanted to take him up to L.A. for his polygraph test. The DA refused to release him. Guenther said he didn't trust the Orange County polygrapher. He said he thought the test came back inconclusive.

We checked the polygraph transcript.

RE: *WILL LENARD MILLER*
Allegation: Involvement in Death of JEAN ELLROY During
          June, 1958, El Monte.

Subject: Polygraph Examination of WILL LENARD MILLER

By: FREDERICK C. MARTIN, Polygraph Examiner
    District Attorney's Office

*September 15, 1970*
  During pre-test interview after discussing with MILLER the circumstances surrounding the demise of JEAN ELLROY, and after showing him a picture consisting of four males and four females grouped around a table, he stated he did

not recognize any of the persons in the picture—especially that of ELLROY. In addition he stated he had never personally met or seen her in his life. He stated he was familiar with her only because his wife worked at the plant where ELLROY was a nurse, and that ELLROY would dispense medication to his wife. He stated in conversations between him and his wife he became aware of this, as well as observing her name on the medication bottle.

A series of physical and psychological test patterns was conducted on MILLER, and it was determined from these tests that MILLER was a capable subject for examination. The following relevant questions, and verbal answers thereto, were utilized during the examination:

1. Did you ever meet in person any of the females in the picture I have shown you? ANSWER: No.

2. Did you kill JEAN ELLROY during June, 1958? ANSWER: No.

3. Did you dispose of JEAN ELLROY's body in a field in El Monte during June, 1958? ANSWER: No.

4. Did you shoot JEAN ELLROY to death? ANSWER: No.

There were no reactions indicative of deception shown to any of the above relevant questions. Question No. 4 is a control question—no such act occurring or alleged.

> FREDERICK C. MARTIN, Polygraph Examiner
> District Attorney's Office

pc
Dictated 9-16-70


Bill said it looked like an incomplete test. Guenther said Miller was never a hard suspect. I said Shirley Miller got her facts wrong.

She worked at Airtek. Will Lenard didn't. There were no tax statements from Airtek. My mother drove a Buick. The Swarthy Man didn't. Miller's paint job meant nothing.

Bill said he'd call Duane Rasure and the two El Monte cops. They might have more information. Guenther said we had to find the Blonde. We were stone fucked without her.

*

We flew back to Orange County. Bill called me the next morning.

He said he'd talked to Rasure and the El Monte cops. Rasure remembered the case. He said he talked to four or five Airtek employees. The people said Will Lenard Miller worked at Airtek for real. They couldn't connect him to Jean Ellroy in any context. Rasure called the Miller deal a washout.

Marv Martin remembered the case. He said he discussed it with Ward Hallinen—back in that '70 time frame. Ward came out to the El Monte Station. They talked about Will Lenard Miller. Hallinen did not know that Miller existed. Martin threw out one bomb. He said he thought Will Lenard Miller hung himself in his cell right after they questioned him. D. A. Ness said Marv had it all wrong. He said Miller had a heart attack and died in his cell.

The suicide rumor shocked me. Bill said he didn't believe it. Somebody would have dropped a note in my mother's file. He said he just called Louie Danoff at the Bureau. Louie said he'd call the Orange County Sheriff's. Police agencies kept files on their in-custody deaths.

I called Will Lenard Miller an intergalactic long shot. Bill said I was being optimistic. He said we should go to the Bureau and run some witnesses.


I brought a list. Bill showed me three computer terminals.

One fed into the California State Department of Justice. It supplied personal statistics, aliases and CII numbers indicating criminal records. One fed into the California State DMV. It supplied driving records, personal statistics, previous addresses and your subject's current address. The "reverse book" computer stored statistics from eight western states. You fed in your subject's name. You got an address and phone number back.

I met Louie Danoff and John Yarbrough. They were working the Unsolved Unit. Danoff said Will Lenard Miller did not kill himself in the Orange County Jail. He just talked to his Orange County contact. The man checked around and said no go. Bill asked Yarbrough to trace Lavonne Chambers. She was 29 in 1958. She was employed by a Nevada casino in 1962.

I checked my witness list.

Mr. and Mrs. George Krycki, Margie Trawick, Jim Boss Bennett, Michael Whittaker, Shirley Miller, Will Lenard Miller, Peter Tubiolo. Margie Trawick's DOB was 6/14/22. Jim Boss Bennett's DOB was 12/17/17. Michael Whittaker was 24 in 1958. I knew the age stats would narrow down our search.

Bill ran the Kryckis first. He got no hit on the DMV and State DOJ. He got a reverse book hit. George and Anna May Krycki lived in Kanab, Utah. The computer printed out their address and phone number.

Bill ran Jim Boss Bennett. He got a State DOJ hit. The printout stated that Jim Boss Bennett's CII record was purged. Bill said Jim Boss Bennett was probably dead. The DOJ wiped dead people out of their main computer. He wanted to confirm Bennett's death. He said he knew a guy who could check Social Security records.

We ran Peter Tubiolo. We got a DMV hit. Tubiolo was 72 now. He lived in Covina.

We ran Shirley Miller. We got a DMV hit. Her address matched an address in the Will Lenard Miller file. An asterisk and the word "deceased" were printed below it.

We ran Will Lenard Miller. We got a DOJ hit and a purge listing. Bill said the fucker was dead.

We ran Margie Trawick. We got three negative hits. I remembered that Margie was married and divorced or widowed. Her maiden name was Phillips. Bill ran Margie Phillips and our established DOB. He got no DMV and DOJ hits. The reverse book supplied a long printout. Margie Phillips was a common name.

We ran Michael Whittaker. We got a DMV hit and a DOJ hit for a Michael *John* Whittaker. We got a 1986 address in San Francisco. The DOJ printout listed a CII number and a 1/1/34 date of birth.

I opened up my briefcase and checked the Ellroy Blue Book. Whittaker's middle name was John.

Bill wrote down the CII number and gave it to a clerk. She said she'd order a copy of Whittaker's rap sheet and his current address statistics.

John Yarbrough walked up. He handed Bill a memo slip. He said he called a guy on the Vegas PD. The guy called a guy on the Nevada Gaming Commission. They found Lavonne Chambers' casino employment record. They called the Nevada State DMV and got the whole ball of wax.

Lavonne Chambers was now Lavonne Parga. She just renewed her driver's license. She lived in Reno, Nevada.

## 22

Bill wanted to hit Lavonne Chambers clean. He didn't want to call and request an interview. He wanted to hit her before she had time to think and formulate answers.

We flew to Reno. We got two rooms at a Best Western. The desk clerk gave us a map. We rented a car and drove to Lavonne Chambers' last known address.

It was outside Reno proper. The area was semi-rural and semi-run-down. Everybody had a truck or a four-wheel-drive camper. The vehicles looked good. The houses looked bad.

We knocked on Lavonne Chambers' door. A man opened up. Bill badged him and explained our situation. The man said Lavonne was his mother. She was at the Washoe County Medical Center. She had these bad asthma attacks.

The man remembered the murder. He was just a toddler then. He said he'd call his mother and prepare her.

He gave us directions to the hospital. We got there inside ten minutes. A nurse walked us to Lavonne Chambers' room.

She was sitting up in bed. She had an oxygen tube in her nose. She didn't look sick. She looked tough and sturdy.

She looked astonished.

Bill and I introduced ourselves. Bill stated his police affiliation. I said I was Jean Ellroy's son. Lavonne Chambers stared at me. I shaved 36 years off of her and put her in a red-and-gold Stan's Drive-in outfit. I felt a little shaky. I took a chair uninvited.

Bill sat down beside me. The bed was a few feet in front of us. I got out a notepad and pen. Lavonne said my mother was beautiful. Her voice was strong. She didn't gasp or wheeze.

I thanked her. She said she felt so darn guilty. Carhops were supposed to jot down license plate numbers. The procedure helped the cops apprehend check dodgers. She never wrote down that plate number. My mother and the man looked respectable. She never regretted anything one iota as much.

I asked her how well she remembered that evening. She said she remembered it good. She used to replay her memories like a broken record. She wanted to be sure she remembered everything.

Bill asked her some background questions. I knew he was testing her. Her answers jibed with the background details in the file.

Bill said, Let's go back. Lavonne said okay. She described my mother and the Swarthy Man for starters. She said my mother had red hair. She said she served my mother and the Swarthy Man twice. She couldn't put their visits in chronological perspective. The cops thought the killer was local. She kept glancing around every night she worked at the drive-in. She kept her eyes peeled for years.

Bill mentioned the Bobbie Long murder. Lavonne said she didn't know it. I said the same man might have killed Bobbie Long. Lavonne asked me when she was killed. I said 1/23/59. Lavonne said she talked to the cops all that summer. They fell out of touch way before January.

Bill mentioned the '62 lineup. Lavonne's memories clashed with established Blue Book facts. She said it was a one-man lineup. She said she was the only witness. She confirmed her basic Blue Book statement. She wasn't sure the man she saw that day was the man with my mother.

Bill showed her two Jim Boss Bennett mug shots. She couldn't place Jim Boss in any context. I showed her the two Identi-Kit portraits. She placed them immediately.

Bill said, Let's go back. Lavonne said okay. She ran us through that night again. I interposed spatial questions. I wanted to know exactly where she was standing every time she saw the Swarthy Man. Lavonne said customers flashed their lights to signal for the check. I saw cars and darting high beams and Lavonne slinging trays and two-second profile blips of a man about to kill a woman.

I mentioned the Swarthy Man's car. Bill cut me off. He asked Lavonne how well she knew cars back then. Most carhops knew all the makes and models. Did she know cars that well?

Lavonne said she was bad at cars. She was no good at distinguishing different makes and models. I saw where Bill was going. I asked Lavonne how she identified the Swarthy Man's car.

Lavonne said she heard a news broadcast. The dead woman sounded like that redhead she served Saturday night. She stewed about it. She tried to remember the car the red-head was in. She talked to her boss. He pointed out different cars. She narrowed down the car that way.

I looked at Bill. He gave me the cutoff sign. He handed Lavonne a copy of the Jean Ellroy Blue Book and asked her to read through her statement. He said we'd be back later to discuss it.

Lavonne said we should come back after dinner. She told us to avoid the casinos. You just can't beat the house odds.


We ate dinner at a steakhouse in the Reno Hilton. We discussed the car issue at length.

I said Lavonne's car ID might be contaminated. Her boss might have confused her. Her Blue Book statement was emphatic. The Swarthy Man was driving a '55 or '56 Olds. Maybe Lavonne tagged the wrong car. Maybe the ID was faulty from the gate. Maybe Hallinen and Lawton got hip to the fact. Maybe that explained the low punch-card count in the file.

Bill said it was possible. Witnesses convinced themselves that certain things were true and stuck to their statements hell or high water. I asked him if we could check old car registration records. He said no. The information wasn't computerized. The hand-filed records were destroyed a long time ago.

We finished our dinner and walked through the casino. I got a wild urge to shoot craps.

Bill explained the bets to make. The combinations confused me. I said "Fuck it" and put a hundred dollars on the pass line.

The shooter made four straight passes. I won $1,600.

I gave the croupier a hundred dollars and cashed in the rest of my chips. Bill said I should change my name to Bobbie Long Jr.

Lavonne waited up for us. She said she read her old statement. It didn't spark any fresh recollections.

I thanked her for her diligence—then and now. She said my mother really was very beautiful.

The Reno trip taught me some things. I learned how to talk in a soft register. I learned how to rein in aggressive body language.

Stoner was my teacher. I knew I was shaping my detective persona to his exact specifications. He knew how to subordinate his ego and make people tell him things. I wanted to develop that skill. I wanted to develop it fast. I wanted old people to tell me things before they died or went senile.

A reporter from the *L.A. Weekly* called me. She wanted to do a story on the new investigation. I asked her if she'd include a toll-free tip-line number. She said she would.

Bill's Social Security contact reported. He said Jim Boss Bennett died of natural causes in 1979. Billy Farrington reported. He said Jack Lawton's widow was still alive. She promised to check her garage for Jack's old notebooks and call if she found them. The clerk at the Bureau called Bill. She said she received Michael Whittaker's rap sheet. The sheet ran ten pages. She ran down the details.

They were pathetic and horrific. Whittaker was 60 years old now. He was a hophead, a hype and a 30-year junkie. He danced with my mother at the Desert Inn.

I met Bill at the Bureau. We discussed Whittaker.

Bill said he was probably up in Frisco or in jail somewhere. I said he might be dead from AIDS or general attrition. Bill told the clerk to run a public utilities check. He wanted to pin

Whittaker down. We had to find him. We had to find Margie Trawick.

I got out our reverse book printout. I said I could call all our Margie Phillips numbers. Bill said we should run an employment check first.

I had the name and address memorized. Margie Trawick worked at Tubesales—2211 Tubeway Avenue. Bill checked a Thomas Guide. The address was five minutes away.

We drove over. The place was a big warehouse and office building combined. We found the personnel boss. We talked to her. She checked her files. She said Margie Trawick worked here from '56 to '71. She said all personnel files were strictly confidential.

We persisted. The woman sighed and wrote down Bill's home number. She said she'd call some old employees and ask them about Margie.

Bill and I drove back to the Bureau. We checked the Ellroy Blue Book and found three more names to run.

Roy Dunn and Al Manganiello—two Desert Inn bartenders. Ruth Schienle—the Airtek personnel director.

We ran the names through the DMV computer. We got four Roy Dunns, no Ruth Schienles and an Al Manganiello in Covina. We ran the names through the DOJ computer. We got three negative hits. We ran Ruth Schienle through the reverse book and got a possible hit in Washington State.

Bill called Al Manganiello. He got an extended dial tone. I called Ruth Schienle. A woman answered the phone.

She was 28 years old and unmarried. She had no relatives named Ruth Schienle.

Bill and I drove back to Orange County. We split up for the day. I took the file. I wanted to know every word in it. I wanted to forge connections that nobody else ever saw.

Bill called me that night. He said Margie Trawick died in 1972. She had terminal cancer. She was sitting in a chair at a beauty shop and collapsed from a brain hemorrhage.


We tracked Michael Whittaker down in San Francisco. We traced him to a dive in the Mission District. Bill called him. He said he wanted to discuss the Ellroy murder. Whittaker said, "All I did was dance with her!"

We took a cab to his hotel. Whittaker wasn't there. The desk clerk said he boogied out with his wife a few minutes ago. We waited in the lobby. Dopers and hookers bopped through. They gave us weird looks. They sat around and bullshitted. We heard a dozen riffs on O. J. Simpson. The consensus was split two ways: O.J. was framed and O.J. offed the bitch justifiably.

We waited. We saw a ruckus at the projects across the street. A black kid ran in and sprayed the playground with some kind of assault weapon.

Nobody got hurt. The kid ran off. He looked like a delighted child trying out a new toy. The cops came and poked around. The desk clerk said stuff like that happened every day. Sometimes the little humps shot each other.

We waited for six hours. We walked down to a doughnut shop and got some coffee. We walked back. The desk clerk said Mike and his wife just snuck upstairs.

We walked up and knocked on the door. I was pissed off and dead tired. Whittaker let us in.

He was bony and potbellied. He wore his hair in a biker ponytail. He didn't look scary. He looked weak. He looked like a freak who came to San Francisco to score dope and grow old on welfare.

The room was 9′ × 12′ tops. The floor was covered with pill vials and paperback crime novels. Whittaker's wife weighed about 300 pounds. She was sprawled on a narrow daybed. The room smelled. I saw bugs on the floor and a line of ants around the baseboard. Bill pointed to the books and said, "Maybe you've got some fans here."

I laughed. Whittaker stretched out on the bed. The mattress sagged and hit the floor.

There were no chairs. There was no bathroom. The sink smelled like a urinal.

Bill and I stood by the door. A breeze blew down the outside hallway. Whittaker and his wife came on obsequious. They started to justify their life and the pill bottles out in plain sight. I cut them off. I wanted to get to that night and hear

Whittaker's version. His formal statement made no sense. I wanted to take a hot knife to his brain.

Bill knew I was getting impatient. He gave me a let-me-talk sign. I moved back and stood in the doorway. Bill laid out a little I'm-not-here-to-judge-you/you're-in-no-trouble rap. He sucked Whittaker and his wife right in.

Bill talked. Whittaker talked. His wife listened and looked at Bill. I listened and looked at Whittaker.

He ran down his 44 arrests. He did time for every dope charge in the fucking penal code.

Bill took him back to June '58. Bill walked him to the Desert Inn that night. Whittaker said he went there with a "fat Hawaiian guy who knew karate." The fat Hawaiian guy "beat a few guys up." It was pure bullshit.

He didn't remember the Blonde or the Swarthy Man. He didn't remember the victim so good. He ran down his drunk arrest later that night. He said the cops questioned him the night after the murder and again two days or so later. He was on methadone now. Methadone fucked with his mind. He only went to that okie bar once. He never went back. The place put a hex on him. He had a pal named Spud then. He knew these guys the Sullivan brothers. They came from his hometown—McKeesport, Pennsylvania. His own brother died of cirrhosis. He had two sisters named Ruthie and Joanne—

I gave Bill the cutoff sign. He nodded and gave Whittaker a let's-slow-down-now gesture.

Whittaker stopped talking. Bill said we had to get to the airport. He pointed to me and said I was the dead woman's son. Whittaker oohed and aahed. His wife did a big gee-whiz number. I thawed out a little and slipped them a hundred dollars. It was crap-table money.

Billy Farrington reported. He said Dorothy Lawton couldn't find Jack's notebooks. He said he'd contact Jack's sons and see if they had them.

I got a 1-800 line hooked up to my regular phone line. I changed the message on my answering machine. It went, "If you have information on the murder of Geneva Hilliker Ellroy on June 22, 1958, please leave a message at the tone." I had two phone numbers and one answering machine. Every incoming caller got the murder message.

A producer from the *Day One* show called me. He said he read my *GQ* piece. He talked to some people at *GQ* and heard about the new investigation. He wanted to film a segment about it. It would run on prime-time network TV.

I said yes. I asked him if he'd run our tip number. He said yes.

I started to get a little queasy. The redhead was stepping out on a big new public scale. She lived in compartmentalized secrecy and shunned all public displays. Publicity was our most direct route to the Blonde. I had to justify my public displays that way.

Bill and I spent four days with the *L.A. Weekly* reporter. We spent a week with the *Day One* crew. We took them to Arroyo High and Valenzuela's Restaurant and the old stone cottage on Maple. We ate a lot of bad Mexican food. The folks at Valenzuela's wondered who the hell we were and why we were always here with camera people and that old file and all those gory black & white pictures. They didn't speak English. We didn't speak Spanish. We tipped extravagantly and made Valenzuela's our El Monte HQ. Bill and I called the place the Desert Inn. That was its righteous name. I started to love the place. That first nighttime visit scared me. My subsequent visits hit me sweet and soft. My mother danced on this spot. I was dancing with her now. The dance was all about reconciliation.

We met the man who owned my old house. His name was Geno Guevara. He bought the house in '77. A preacher sold it to him. The Kryckis were long gone already.

Geno loved the media people. He let them tromp around his yard and take pictures. I spent some time inside the house. The interior was altered and enlarged. I shut my eyes and tore down the alterations. I stood in my bedroom and my mother's bedroom the way they were then. I felt her. I smelled her. I smelled Early Times bourbon. The bathroom was intact from 1958. I saw her nude. I saw her run a towel between her legs.

Arroyo High became a public staging ground. The *Day One*

crew shot Bill and me there. The *L.A. Weekly* photographer shot her own crime scene pix. School kids buzzed around. They wanted to know the whole story. They laughed and tried to squeeze in front of the cameras. We hit Arroyo High five or six times in the course of two media weeks. The visits felt like violations and vulgarizations. I didn't want the place to lose its power. I didn't want to turn King's Row into a common access road and an everyday stop on the publicity track of my life.

El Monte was becoming benignly familiar. The metamorphosis was predictable and altogether disturbing. I wanted El Monte to stay elliptical. I wanted it to hide from me and teach me how she hid. I wanted to reclaim my old fear and learn from it. I wanted to strand myself in the few square miles of El Monte. I wanted to build a man-hunting instinct from that isolation.

Bill and I finished our first media run. We found Peter Tubiolo, Roy Dunn and Ellis Outlaw's daughter Jana. They ran us back to El Monte in 1958.

Tubiolo was 72 now. He was exactly half his current age then. He remembered me. He remembered my mother. He was heavyset and friendly then and now. I could have picked him out of a 50-man lineup. He'd aged in an absolutely recognizable fashion.

He was warm. He was gracious. He said he never went out with my mother. He never knew how the cops got that crazy idea.

I told them. It was true. I saw him pick my mother up in his blue-and-white Nash. I mentioned the Nash. Tubiolo said he loved that car. I didn't dispute his claim about my mother. The cops cleared him then. His appearance and his guileless manner cleared him now. He was a widower. He was childless. He looked prosperous and seemed happy. He left Anne LeGore School in '59. He became a big wheel in the L.A. County system. He lived a good life. He probably had some good years left.

He said he never went to the Desert Inn or Stan's Drive-in. He said I was a high-strung kid. He said the Mexican kids from Medina Court had a dodge back then. They ditched their shoes and came to school barefoot. Kids had to wear shoes to school. It was a heavyweight rule. Tubiolo sent barefoot kids home all the time. My friends Reyes and Danny worked that dodge. I smoked a reefer with them. It was craaaaazy, daddy-o. I saw *The Ten Commandments* with them. I laughed at all the sacred hoo-ha. Reyes and Danny made me shut up. They were Catholic. My mother hated Catholics. She said they took their orders from Rome. The Swarthy Man was a Latin-type Caucasian. He was probably Catholic. All my mental circuits returned to that night.

Roy Dunn and Jana Outlaw took us back to the Desert Inn.

We interviewed them at home. Dunn lived in Duarte. Jana Outlaw lived in El Monte. They were San Gabriel Valley lifers.

Dunn remembered the murder. Jana didn't. She was nine years old then. Dunn used to drink with Harry Andre. Harry drank at the Playroom Bar. Dunn worked at the Playroom and the Desert Inn. Ellis Outlaw paid good wages. Ellis choked to death on a piece of food in 1969. He was half-dead from booze already. Myrtle Mawby was dead. Ellis's wife was dead. The Desert Inn enjoyed a ten-year run. The joint fucking rocked. Spade Cooley played there—years before he beat his wife to death. Ellis brought in colored entertainers. Joe Liggins and some Ink Spot clones played the Desert Inn. The Desert Inn was a bookie front. Ellis ran card games and served liquor after-hours. Hookers worked the bar. The food was good. Ellis fed the El Monte cops at a sizable discount. He sold the Desert Inn to a guy named Doug Schoenberger. Doug renamed it The Place. He let gambling and bookmaking and prostitution flourish. Doug was tight with an ex-El Monte cop named Keith Tedrow. Keith saw the Jean Ellroy crime scene. He spread a stupid rumor about Jean Ellroy's body. He said the killer bit one nipple off. Keith quit the El Monte PD. He joined the Baldwin Park PD. He got murdered in '71. He was parked in his car. A woman shot him. She pled insanity and beat the rap. It looked like Keith was trying to shake her down for a head job. Doug Schoenberger sold The Place and moved to Arizona. He got murdered in the mid-'80s. The crime went unsolved. Doug's son was the #1 suspect.

Roy and Jana knew the Desert Inn. They had the place down cold. They fell short on hard information.

We needed names.

We needed the names of old Desert Inn regulars and San Gabriel Valley cocktail lounge trawlers. We had to find out who they knew in 1958. We had to establish a range of friendships and acquaintanceships. We had to find names to match the physical characteristics of the Blonde and the Swarthy Man. We had to create an ever-widening concentric circle of names. We had to find two names in a big place and a faraway time.

Roy and Jana gave us three names:

An old Desert Inn waitress now employed at a local Moose Lodge. An old Stan's carhop. An old Desert Inn bartender.

We found the waitress and the carhop. They didn't know shit about the Jean Ellroy case and couldn't supply any names. Roy and Jana got their time and venues wrong. The carhop worked at Simon's Drive-In. The waitress worked at The Place, not the Desert Inn. She knew a much younger crowd.

Bill and I discussed the Desert Inn. We placed it in the context of late June '58.

Ellis Outlaw was about to serve a drunk-driving sentence. He catered to local yokels and illegal off-track bettors. He catered to local hoods and satellite people with shit to hide from the cops. Margie Trawick saw the Blonde and the Swarthy Man one time only. Myrtle Mawby saw them one time only. Margie worked part-time. Myrtle worked part-time. The Swarthy Man was probably a local guy. The Desert Inn was *the* local spot. The Swarthy Man could have passed through before that night and left his image in a hundred memory banks. Hallinen and Lawton camped out at the Desert Inn all summer. They took down names and left them in their personal notebooks. Certain people could have lied to them. Certain people could have known. The Blonde could have owed Ellis Outlaw money. The Swarthy Man could have told certain people that the nurse was a goddamn cocktease. Certain people could have figured the cunt had it coming. Certain people could have lied to the cops.

Bill and I agreed.

Our crime played out within narrow boundaries. The

Blonde and the Swarthy Man got lucky and fell through the cracks.

We had to uncover two names and link them to a runner in hiding.

# 23

Kanab, Utah, was just above the Arizona border. The main drag was three blocks long. The local men wore cowboy boots and nylon parkas. It was 20 degrees cooler than Southern California.

The drive took us through Las Vegas and some sweet hill country. We got two rooms at a Best Western and crashed out early. We were set to see George and Anna May Krycki in the morning.

Bill called Mrs. Krycki two days in advance. I listened in on a bedroom extension. Mrs. Krycki was shrill in 1958. She sounded just as shrill today. My father used to goof on her jerky hand gestures.

She couldn't believe the cops were rehashing such an ancient case. She referred to me as "Leroy Ellroy." She said I was a spasticated boy. Her husband tried to teach Leroy Ellroy how to push a broom. Leroy Ellroy just couldn't learn.

Mrs. Krycki agreed to be interviewed. Bill said he'd drive up with his partner. He didn't say his partner was Leroy Ellroy.

Bill ragged me for two days straight. He called me Leroy. He kept saying, "Where's your broom?" Mrs. Krycki told the cops that Jean Ellroy never drank. I came home one night and found my mother and Mrs. Krycki tanked.

The Kryckis' house in Kanab looked like their house in El Monte. It was small and plain and well tended. Mr. Krycki was sweeping out the driveway. I remembered his posture more than his face. Bill said he had a great broom technique.

We got out of the car. Mr. Krycki dropped his broom and introduced himself. Mrs. Krycki walked out. She'd aged as recognizably as Peter Tubiolo. She looked strong and healthy. She walked up to us and invaded our collective body space. She ran some mile-a-minute greetings and agitated gestures like the ones my father satirized.

She walked us inside. Mr. Krycki stayed outside with his broom. We sat down in the living room. The furniture was garishly upholstered and mismatched. Plaids, stripes, geometric designs and paisleys worked against each other. The overall effect was agitation.

Bill stated his name and displayed his badge. I stated my name. I waited a beat and said I was Jean Ellroy's son.

Mrs. Krycki ran some gestures and sat on her hands. She said I got so big. She said I was the most spasticated boy she ever saw. I couldn't even push a broom. God knows her husband tried to teach me. I said broom work was never my forte. Mrs. Krycki didn't laugh.

Bill said we wanted to talk about Jean Ellroy and her death. He told Mrs. Krycki to be absolutely candid.

Mrs. Krycki started talking. Bill flashed me a let-her-talk sign.

She said the Mexican influx drove her and George out of El Monte. The Mexicans destroyed the San Gabriel Valley. Her son, Gaylord, was living in Fontana now. He was 49. He had four daughters. Jean had red hair. She cooked popcorn and ate it with a spoon. Jean answered a newspaper ad and rented their little back house. Jean said, "I think this place will be safe." She thought Jean was hiding in El Monte.

Mrs. Krycki stopped talking. Bill asked her to explain her last remark. Mrs. Krycki said Jean was cultured and refined. She was overqualified for El Monte. I asked her why she thought that. Mrs. Krycki said Jean read condensed books published by the Reader's Digest. She stood out in El Monte. She didn't belong there. She came to El Monte for some mysterious reason.

Bill asked her what Jean talked about. Mrs. Krycki said she talked about her nursing school adventures. I asked her to describe those adventures. She said that was all she recalled.

I asked Mrs. Krycki about my mother and men. She said Jean went out most Saturday nights. She never brought men home. She never bragged about men. She never talked about men at all. I asked Mrs. Krycki about my mother and liquor. She contradicted all her old statements.

George smelled liquor on Jean's breath one day. He found two empty bottles in the bushes outside. Jean brought bottles home in brown paper bags. Jean looked tired most of the time. They suspected that Jean was quite a heavy drinker.

Mrs. Krycki stopped talking. I looked directly at her and nodded. She ran a fast free-form riff.

Jean had a deformed nipple. She saw Jean's body at the morgue. They had her under a sheet. Her feet stuck out. She recognized them. Jean always walked around the yard barefoot. The cops ran up her phone bill. They never offered to pay for their calls.

Mrs. Krycki stopped talking. Bill eased her through 6/21 and 6/22/58. Her account matched our Blue Book reports.

Mr. Krycki walked in. Bill asked him to recount those two days. Mr. Krycki told the same basic story. I asked him to describe my mother. He said she was a good-looking woman. She wasn't the El Monte type. Anna May knew her better than he did.

Mr. Krycki looked uncomfortable. Bill smiled and told him we were fresh out of questions. Mr. Krycki smiled and walked outside.

Mrs. Krycki said there was one thing she never told the cops. I nodded. Bill nodded. Mrs. Krycki started talking.

It happened around '52. She was living on Ferris Road in El Monte. Gaylord was six or seven. She was separated from her first husband.

She shopped at a market nearby. A family named LoPresti owned it. This box boy played cupid with her. He said his uncle John wanted to take her out real bad. John LoPresti was about 30 then. He was tall. He had dark hair and an olive complexion.

She went out with him. He took her to the Coconino Club. They danced. He was a good dancer. He was "smooth and calculating."

They left the Coconino. They drove out to the Puente Hills. LoPresti stopped the car and made some very fresh moves. She told him to stop. He slapped her. She got out of the car. He grabbed her and shoved her in the backseat.

He pulled at her clothes. She resisted him. He climaxed and wiped his pants off with a handkerchief. He said, "You've got mustard" and "You've got nothing to worry about now." He drove her home. He didn't touch her again. She didn't call the cops. She was embroiled in a custody fight with her ex. She didn't want to raise a stink and tarnish her reputation. She saw LoPresti two more times.

She was out walking. He drove by her and waved. He asked her if she wanted a ride. She ignored him.

She saw him about two years later. She was at the Coconino with George. LoPresti asked her to dance. She ignored him. She warned Jean Ellroy about him—right before she went out that Saturday night.

The story played ugly and true. The coda played fictitious. It sounded contrived and way too coincidental.

LoPresti was local. LoPresti was Italian. LoPresti was a nightclub predator. I closed my eyes and replayed the Puente Hills scene. I added a vintage car and period clothing. I put the Swarthy Man's face on John LoPresti.

We had a real suspect.

We drove back to Orange County. We talked John LoPresti nonstop. John was a sex-assault bungler in 1952. Give him six years to refine his act and grow more twisted. Bill agreed. LoPresti was our first hot suspect.

The drive took 13 hours. We got back around midnight. We slept the trip off and drove to El Monte.

We hit the El Monte Museum. We checked the 1958 El Monte phone books. We found eight markets listed in the Yellow Pages.

Jay's on Tyler. Jay's on Central. The Bell Market on Peck Road. Crawford's Giant Country Store on Valley. Earp's Market and the Foodlane on Durfee. The Tyler Circle on Tyler. Fran's Meats on Garvey.

No LoPresti Market. No listings for Italian specialty stores.

We checked the White Pages. Most of the personal listings featured parenthetical addenda. They listed occupations and wives' first names. We turned to the L's and hit twice.

LoPresti, John (Nancy) (Machinist)—10806 Frankmont.

LoPresti, Thomas (Rose) (Salesman)—3419 Maxson.

Frankmont was near 756 Maple. Maxson was near Stan's Drive-in and the Desert Inn.

We drove to the Bureau. We ran all four LoPrestis through the DMV and DOJ computers. We got no hits on Thomas and Rose. We hit on John and Nancy.

Nancy had a valid California driver's license. The printout listed a current address and her old address on Frankmont. Her DOB was 8/16/14. John lived in Duarte. I pointed to some weird numbers by his address. Bill said it was a trailer park listing. John was 69 years old. He had blue eyes. He was 6'1" and 215 pounds.

I pointed to his height and weight. Bill pointed to his age and eye color. The cocksucker did not match the Swarthy Man's description.

Duarte was three miles north of El Monte. The trailer park was butt-ugly. The trailers were old and weather-stripped. They were jammed together with no space between them.

We found #16 and rang the buzzer. An old man opened the door. He matched our driver's license stats. He had blue eyes and thick features. His face exonerated him.

Bill badged him and asked him his name. The man said John LoPresti. Bill said we had some questions about an old murder. John said come on in. He didn't twitch or cringe or shake or admit or deny his guilt.

We entered his trailer. The interior was six feet wide tops. The walls were decorated with *Playboy* centerfolds. They were handsomely mounted and laminated with high-gloss shellac.

John sat down in an old recliner. Bill and I sat on the bed. Bill sketched out the Jean Ellroy case. John said he didn't recall it.

Bill said we were looking up the old El Monte crowd. We

wanted to dig the late-'50s scene. We knew he was living on Frankmont.

John said that wasn't him. That was his late uncle John and aunt Nancy. He lived in La Puente then. El Monte was his stomping grounds. His uncle Tom owned a market in El Monte. El Monte was a swinging location.

I asked him where he hung out. John said the Coconino and the Desert Inn. He went to the Playroom sometimes. It stood behind Stan's Drive-In. They served shots of whisky for 25 cents.

Bill asked him if he'd ever been arrested. John said he got popped for drunk driving. I came on skeptical. I said, What else? John said he got popped in 1946. Somebody said he pulled some dirty shit.

I said, What kind of shit? He said somebody stuck a dirty book under some woman's door. He got blamed for it.

Bill said we needed names. We wanted to find the old Desert Inn crowd. We wanted to find every lounge lizard who ever cruised Five Points.

John lit a cigarette. He said he was going in for open-heart surgery tomorrow. He needed all the pleasure he could get.

I said, Give us some names. John dropped eight or ten first names. I said, Give us some full names. John said, "Al Manganiello." Bill said we were looking for him. John said he was working at Glendora Country Club.

I pressed him for more names. Bill pressed him for more names. We named all the El Monte spots and told him to match some names to specific venues. John couldn't feed us one single name.

I wanted to fuck with him.

I said, We heard that you were one sharp dude with the ladies. John said this was true. I said, We heard you *really* liked women. John said, Oh, yeah. I said, We heard you got lots of pussy. John said he got more than his share. Bill said, We heard you mauled a woman named Anna May Krycki and shot your load prematurely.

John shook and twitched and cringed and denied his guilt. We thanked him and walked out the door.

# 24

We worked the case. We probed defective memory vaults. We logged information. We excavated names.

We dug up first names and last names and nicknames and full names and matching and nonmatching descriptions. We got names from the file. We got names from old cops. We got names from elderly barflies and El Monte lifers. We worked the case for eight months. We cultivated names and harvested names. We did not create an incrementally expanding concentric circle of names. We were up against a large place and a large block of time lost.

We kept going.

We found former deputy Bill Vickers. He remembered the two canvass jobs. They thought they had a two-time killer. They figured the same guy choked the nurse and the racetrack lady. We asked him for names. He didn't have any.

We found Al Manganiello. He gave us the same names Roy Dunn and Jana Outlaw gave us. He told us about an old carhop in Pico Rivera. We found her. She was senile. She didn't remember the late 1950s.

We found Jack Lawton's sons. They said they'd look for Jack's notebooks. They looked. They didn't find them. They figured their dad threw them out.

We found former LASD captain Vic Cavallero. He remembered the Jean Ellroy crime scene. He did not remember the investigation or the Bobbie Long snuff. He said he popped a guy in the late '50s. The guy was on the LAPD. He was bombing down Garvey double-fast. He had a woman with him. She hopped cars at Stan's Drive-in. She said the cop beat her up. She refused to file a complaint. The cop was fat and blond. Cavallero said he was one choice prick. He didn't remember his name.

We found ex-El Monte cop Dave Wire. We asked him for names. He said he had a suspect. His name was Bert Beria. He was dead now. He was an ex-El Monte reserve cop. Bert was a drunk. Bert was nuts. Bert beat up his wife and raced his police car on the San Berdoo Freeway. Bert looked like those old Identi-Kit pix. Bert drank at the Desert Inn. Bert would rape your pet turtle. Wire said we should check Bert out. Wire said we should talk to Keith Tedrow's ex-wife, Sherry. Sherry knew the El Monte bar scene.

We found Sherry Tedrow. She gave us three names. We looked up two Desert Inn barmaids and a fat cat named Joe Candy. Joe bankrolled Doug Schoenberger. Joe lent him the money to buy the Desert Inn.

We ran some computer checks. Joe Candy and Barmaid #1 came up dead. We found Barmaid #2. She worked at The Place—not the Desert Inn. She knew zilch about late-'50s El Monte.

We talked to El Monte police chief Wayne Clayton. He showed us a 1960 snapshot of Bert Beria. He didn't look like the Swarthy Man. He was too old and too bald. Clayton said he'd assigned two detectives to check old Bert out. He introduced us to Sergeant Tom Armstrong and Agent John Eckler. We ran our case by them and gave them a Xerox copy of the Blue Book. They checked their in-station files. They thought they might find a separate Jean Ellroy file built up by El Monte PD.

They found a file number. They found out the file was destroyed 20 years ago.

Armstrong and Eckler interviewed Bert Beria's widow and brother. They pegged Bert as a misanthrope and an all-purpose shit. They didn't think he killed Jean Ellroy.

We found Margie Trawick's daughter. She remembered the case. She was 14. We asked her for names. She didn't have any.

We found a deputy who knew computers backwards. His home system featured a 50-state reverse book. He ran Ruth Schienle through it. He got a long printout. Bill and I called 19 Ruth Schienles. None of them were our Ruth Schienle. None of them knew our Ruth Schienle. Women were hard to find. They got married and divorced. They got lost behind name changes.

We went back to the Ellroy Blue Book. We extracted four names. We wrote down "Tom Baker," "Tom Downey" and "Salvador Quiroz Serena." They were all exonerated. Serena worked at Airtek. He said he "could have had" my mother. We found the name "Grant Surface." He took polygraph tests on 6/25 and 7/1/59. The results were "inconclusive." "Psychological difficulties" fucked up the tests. We ran Baker, Downey, Serena and Surface through the 50-state reverse book and the state DMV and DOJ computers. We got no hits on Surface and Serena. We got a shitload for Baker and Downey. We called all the Bakers and Downeys. We did not find our Baker and Downey.

Bill called Rick Jackson at LAPD Homicide. Jackson checked rape-and-choke and bludgeon-choke murders from the Ellroy/Long time span. He found two LAPD cases. They were solved and successfully adjudicated.

Victim #1 was named Edith Lucille O'Brien. She was snuffed on 2/18/59. She was 43 years old. She was bludgeoned and dumped on a hilltop in Tujunga. Her slacks were turned inside out. Her bra was pushed up. It looked like a sex frenzy job.

Edith O'Brien prowled bars in Burbank and Glendale. She picked up men for sex. She was last seen at the Bamboo Hut on San Fernando Road. She left with a man. The man had a '53 Olds. The man came back to the Bamboo Hut alone. The man talked to another man. He said Edith was out in his car. She spilled spaghetti on the front seat. The men put their heads together and whispered. The car man stayed at the bar. The other man walked out.

The coroner said the killer lashed the victim's wrists tight. He probably wailed on her with a lug wrench. The LAPD popped a guy named Walter Edward Briley. He was tried and convicted. He was 21. He was tall and heavyset. He was sentenced to life in prison. He was paroled in 1978.

A man named Donald Kinman raped and strangled two women. The victims were named Ferne Wessel and Mary Louise Tardy. The DODs were 4/6/58 and 11/22/59. Kinman met Victim #1 in a bar. He rented a hotel room and killed her there. He met Victim #2 in a bar. He killed her in a trailer at his father's trailer park. He left fingerprints at both scenes. He turned himself in and confessed. Kinman was stocky and curly-haired. Kinman fell behind two counts of murder. Kinman went to prison for 21 years.

Kinman jazzed me. He played like a two-time-only killer. He was more volatile than the Swarthy Man. He was purely self-destructive. I saw alcohol as his trigger. The perfect booze intake and the perfect woman came his way twice. He said, "I don't know what came over me, but it just felt like something I had to do."

Bill and I debated the Swarthy Man as serial killer. Bill was pro. I was con. We kicked the ball back and forth a hundred dozen times. Bill said we should contact a psychological profiler.

Carlos Avila worked for the State DOJ. He taught profile procedures. He gave seminars. He worked Sheriff's Homicide for nine years and knew our geographical backdrop. We should commission a profile on the Ellroy and Long cases.

Bill called Carlos Avila. We lent him our files. He studied them and wrote up an opinion.

UNKNOWN SUBJECT;
GENEVA "JEAN" HILLIKER ELLROY; VICTIM (DECEASED);
AKA JEAN ELLROY;
JUNE 22, 1958;
ELSPETH "BOBBIE" LONG; VICTIM (DECEASED);
JANUARY 23, 1959;
LOS ANGELES COUNTY SHERIFF'S DEPARTMENT;
LOS ANGELES, CALIFORNIA;
HOMICIDE (CRIMINAL INVESTIGATIVE ANALYSIS).

The following Criminal Investigative Analysis was prepared by Criminal Investigative Profiler Carlos

Avila, Private Consultant in conjunction with Special
Agent Sharon Pagaling, California Department of
Justice, Bureau of Investigation. This analysis is based
upon a thorough review of the case materials submitted by Retired Los Angeles County Sheriff's
Sergeant William Stoner and James Ellroy, son of
victim Jean Ellroy. The conclusions are the results of
the knowledge drawn from the personal investigative
experience, educational background and research
conducted by these crime analysts.

It is not a substitute for a thorough, well planned
investigation, and should not be considered all
inclusive. The information provided is based upon
reviewing, analyzing, and researching criminal cases
similar to the cases submitted by Sergeant Stoner, Los
Angeles County Sheriff's Department (Retired).

Two separate offenses were reviewed for this
analysis. Due to analysis of submitted data and
discussion of the two cases reported, this analysis will
reflect a description of a singular personality type
believed responsible for the deaths of victims Ellroy
and Long.

*VICTIMOLOGY*

Examination of the victim's background is a
significant aspect of the analysis process. Their
vulnerability of becoming victims of a violent crime
was examined in conjunction with a review of their
lifestyles, behaviors, personal histories, and social/
sexual habits. Specifically, at what risk were they to
becoming victims of a violent crime.

Victim Jean Ellroy was a forty-three year old white
female, five feet five and one-half inches in height;
weighed approximately one hundred thirty-one pounds
and had red hair. She was divorced and had moved
with her minor son to a well kept rental home in El
Monte, California in 1958. She had been employed as

an industrial nurse in Los Angeles since 1956. Victim Ellroy was physically attractive and enjoyed frequenting nearby nightclubs during the weekends while her son visited his father. Ellroy's landlords described her as a quiet tenant who seemed to enjoy being alone with her son. She was described as being closed mouthed about her personal life and as having few close friends. After her death her landlords reported finding empty liquor bottles in the shrubbery near the victim's home and in the trash container.

Ellroy's landlords reported seeing her drive away from her residence at approximately 2000 hours on Saturday, June 21, 1958. Witnesses reported seeing Ellroy later that evening in the company of an unidentified adult male at a drive-in restaurant at approximately 2200 hours; at a nightclub dancing at approximately 2245 hours; and lastly, back at the drive-in restaurant at approximately 0215 hours the following morning. Her body was discovered at a nearby high school on June 22, 1958, at approximately 1000 hours. The area where the victim was last seen was described as having a "low crime rate" with no previous abductions, sexual assaults or similar crimes reported.

Ellroy's risk level of becoming a victim of a violent crime was elevated by her habit of frequenting nightclubs, socializing with persons she did not know well, and drinking alcoholic beverages. On the date of her death her risk level was further elevated by her personal circumstances: a woman alone in a car with a man.

Victim Bobbie Elspeth Long was a fifty-two year old white female, five feet five inches tall, weighed approximately one hundred thirty-two pounds and had dishwater blond hair. She was divorced and lived alone in a well kept two-room apartment in Los Angeles, which she had rented for the preceding four years. Long was employed as a waitress at a nearby restaurant where she worked the evening shift.

Various persons familiar with Long said she enjoyed gambling at the race tracks and was in debt to a bookmaker. She was described as secretive regarding her personal life and family history. Long routinely lied about her age and after her death was determined to be eight years older than she had often claimed. Long reportedly enjoyed being escorted socially by various men, but was described as unlikely to become sexually involved unless she had believed the contact would somehow be financially lucrative for her. A search of Long's apartment after her death revealed hidden liquor bottles. Long was described as having an outgoing assertive personality.

Long's body was discovered at approximately 0230 hours on Friday, January 23, 1959, lying near the side of a road in the city of La Puente. The previous day Long had taken a bus to the Santa Anita Race Track where witnesses reported seeing her betting on various races throughout the day. Persons familiar with Long believed it quite possible she would have accepted an offer of a ride home from a stranger she met at the race track if she found him acceptable.

The area in which Long was last seen was described as having a "low crime rate" with no previous abductions, sexual assaults, or similar crimes reported.

Long's risk level of becoming a victim of a violent crime was elevated by her assertive personality, involvement with gambling and subsequent indebtedness, and willingness to accept rides from strangers.

Overall, based upon the above circumstances in both cases, we believe the offender was socially acquainted with the victims to some degree, and that for some undefined initial period of time, the victims were willing to be in his company.


*MEDICAL EXAMINER'S REPORT*

The Medical Examiner's Reports provided an

evaluation of the injuries sustained by the victims and there is no need to reiterate those findings. However, a few points will be addressed and should be considered in the overall analysis of these crimes.

The pathologist listed victim Ellroy's death as asphyxia due to ligature strangulation. She also had deep lacerations to the scalp, a minor abrasion to the upper lid of her right eye and her vaginal smear was positive for spermatozoa. The victim was noted to be in a late menstrual phase. The toxicological tests performed showed she had a blood alcohol level of .08 percent.

Victim Long's cause of death was also asphyxia due to ligature strangulation. However, victim Long had a skull fracture with cerebral contusions as a result of distinct incision lacerations caused by blunt force trauma. These lacerations had a somewhat crescent shape with fairly incised like borders. The victim also had a fracture separation of the 6th cervical intervertebrate space.

Both victims were strangled with nylon stockings. In addition to the nylon stocking, victim Ellroy had a "clothes line" type cord tied tightly around her neck. Victim Long's vagina also contained spermatozoa. Her blood alcohol content was zero percent.


*CRIME SCENE ANALYSIS*

Although no attempts will be made to construct precise chronological scenarios of these crimes, certain observations about the crime scenes and their significance as they relate to the offender will be described. When examined individually, the two crime scenes do not provide an abundance of forensic evidence. However, when analyzed, the behavior exhibited by the offender at the crime scenes becomes more significant.

Victim Ellroy was last seen alive at approximately

0215–0230 hours on June 22, 1958, in the company of a male she had been with earlier in the evening.

She was later discovered at 1000 hours the same day lying on the ivy covered parkway of a high school in the city of El Monte. The victim was dressed, however her underpants were missing and her brassiere was unfastened and pulled up around her neck. The stocking on her left leg was pulled down around her ankle and the other was tied around her neck along with a length of cord. The victim's coat had been placed over the lower portion of her body.

It appears that the victim had engaged in consensual intercourse even though she was menstruating. A tampon was found in the victim's vagina at the time of the autopsy.

Shortly after intercourse was completed the offender struck the victim with a blunt force object, which was readily accessible, after which he applied the cord and finally the victim's stocking. Due to an obvious lack of defense wounds, it is unlikely that any struggle occurred initially. From witness reports the victim appeared at ease with the offender and she most likely never perceived the offender as posing a physical threat.

After leaving Stan's Drive-In the offender most likely drove directly to the location where the victim was found. The offender was familiar with the location and selected it for its isolation from public view and because it had been used as a "lovers lane" and his vehicle would not necessarily stand out.

The sex act would have occurred inside the offender's vehicle, hence the victim's underpants remained in the vehicle because the victim never had the opportunity to put them back on. Whatever circumstances triggered the offender's anger occurred after the victim had reinserted the tampon.

After the victim was strangled, the offender removed her from the vehicle and dumped her body on the ivy. In the process, the victim's pearl necklace broke and fell in the street. The offender's last act was to place the victim's coat over the lower portion of her body.

In respect to the death of victim Bobbie Long, and in the absence of any witness information, the specific chronology of events leading to the death of this victim cannot be recounted with any degree of specificity and/or detail; therefore, no attempt will be made to reconstruct the crime. There are however certain factors that are relative to the crime scene that suggest specific activities.

A return bus ticket found in the victim's purse supports witnesses' statements that the victim had planned to attend the horse races at Santa Anita Race Track on January 22, 1959.

Assuming the victim went to the horse races, she may have met the offender at the races that day or even been previously acquainted with him and accepted a ride. Since the victim had accepted rides from men she did not know well in the past, she did not apparently worry about her personal safety.

The victim was secretive about her personal life, but what little was known about her indicates that she was willing to take whatever a man had to offer.

The victim appeared to have consumed a Mexican dinner sometime in the early evening as evidenced by the autopsy report. The victim appeared to have participated in consensual sex with the offender. She was fully dressed, with the exception of her stockings, and her clothing was intact and not torn.

The victim was found lying on the grass shoulder of a dirt access road one-tenth of a mile off of a main road in the city of La Puente. She was lying on her back and the lower portion of her body was covered with her coat (similar to victim Ellroy). It appears she too was dumped on the ground after her death had occurred.

Victim Long's death occurred in very much the same manner as victim Ellroy's. After consensual sex, which may have also taken place in the offender's vehicle, she was unexpectedly struck with a blunt force object to the head numerous times, with an object the offender had readily accessible. After sustaining the blows, the offender applied what may have been one of the victim's stockings, placed it around her neck, and strangled the victim.

The offender then removed the victim from his vehicle and dumped her on the grass shoulder along with her purse. Again, the offender's last act was to place the victim's coat over the lower portion of her body, very similar to what had occurred to victim Ellroy.

The distance between the location of where victim Ellroy's body was found to that of victim Long's is approximately four and one-half miles. Victim Ellroy's body was found approximately one and one-half miles from the area where she was seen dancing and eating prior to her death. This area was less than a mile away from where victim Long's body was discovered.

In both deaths robbery did not appear to be the motive. We believe that in victim Ellroy's case, the offender simply forgot to discard the victim's purse prior to leaving. The sex acts, blunt force trauma followed by strangulation with the victims' nylons, and the covering of their lower bodies, appear to be the offender's signature or calling card.

## OFFENDER CHARACTERISTICS AND TRAITS

Statistically, crimes of violence are intraracial in nature, white on white, black on black. Therefore, without any physical evidence to the contrary, we would expect this offender to be a white male.

In consideration of the offender's age, a number of facts pertinent to the crime are examined. The victim's age, amount of control or lack of control exhibited by the offender, the degree of trauma inflicted, evidence taken or left behind, as well as sexual interaction, if any, with the victim, all become important factors. Based upon these factors we would anticipate this offender to have been in his late thirties. Age, however, is one of the most difficult categories to evaluate, as chronological and emotional age are frequently quite different. As we are evaluating age on the basis of behavior, which is a direct result of emotional and mental maturity, no suspect should be eliminated based upon age alone.

The offender in all probability is capable of having relationships with women. We would expect him to be single, however, and if he was married it was a troubled relationship and possibly marred by outbursts which may have included domestic violence. The offender could have been living with a woman in a common-law type relationship, but he would have continued to have sexual encounters with other women.

We would expect the offender to be of average to above average intelligence, to have completed high school, and been capable of college level work. He is more than likely employed and his employment history will be consistent with his academic background.

The offender in all likelihood is sufficiently familiar with the area where the victims' bodies were found to know they would be "reasonably safe" places to dispose of the bodies. It has been our experience in analyzing similar cases that offenders such as these dispose of bodies where they have some degree of association and/or knowledge. Therefore, the offender lived, worked or frequently visited the area where the victims were found. If seen, he would be able to provide a reasonable explanation for being in the area.

The offender will be conscious of his appearance and clothing and be in good physical condition. Since crime scenes generally reflect the offender's personality and life-style, we would expect the offender to be methodical and neat in his appearance. He has few close friends, but numerous acquaintances. He is frequently impulsive and seeks immediate self-gratification. He is a "lone wolf" rather than a loner.

The offender will appear to be confident but not overly "macho" to his peers. In his dealings with women, he will seek dominance and appear to be a very controlling individual. The offender might attempt to portray himself as being passive. He would avoid the appearance of having an explosive temper or being assaultive in nature. Episodes of explosive temper are intermingled with an indifference towards others. He will have shown aggressiveness in his dealings with people.

The offender will drink alcoholic beverages and may use drugs, but not to the point of total impairment. There is no indication of excessive use of alcohol or drugs at the time of the crimes, although he may have used one or both of these substances to lower his inhibitions.

The offender probably has a well-maintained vehicle which is consistent with the economic status of the individuals the victims previously dated. The offender enjoys driving and would be willing to travel outside the immediate area in which he resides to seek entertainment.

We don't believe the offender has an extensive criminal history. However, he may have been arrested for domestic disturbances or assault.

The offender's weapons of choice are believed to be items already on hand: a crescent shaped tool he most likely stored in his automobile; a piece of rope; and the victims' nylon hosiery. This, considered along with the fact that the offender struck each victim repeatedly in the head as a means of control, shows that the murders were probably not planned for a significant period of time before they were actually committed.

*POST OFFENSE BEHAVIOR*

In view of the time lapse since the commission of these crimes, post offense behavior, which is often the most enlightening aspect of the analysis, will take on a lesser significance in this case. The specifics of this section will be to analyze that behavior which would have occurred immediately following the commission of these crimes.

The offender would have gone directly home or to some other safe place following these crimes. He most likely soiled his clothing and vehicle from the blunt force trauma delivered to both victims and the menstrual blood of victim Ellroy.

Having committed what he considered to be an unwitnessed murder on each occasion, the offender would not have been overly concerned or stressed for any length of time. He may have briefly feigned illness in an attempt to isolate himself and he may have called in sick the following day if he was scheduled to work. Other than this initial withdrawal, your offender's daily routine would not have been altered significantly.

He would have avoided places he had been seen with either victim just prior to their death. These places include the Desert Inn, Stan's Drive-In and the Mexican restaurant he and victim Long may have gone to the night of her death.

He may have exhibited interest in television news accounts of the killings but would not have interjected himself into the police investigations. It is unlikely that he would volunteer theories about what happened. He would claim to have only vicarious knowledge of the crimes, gained through friends or the media.

Once the investigations began to wane, the offender would have been reassured that he was not seen with the victims and that he was not a suspect. He would not have felt any guilt or remorse for what he had done. These women were seen as "throw aways" and

he had justified it in his mind that they were somehow
to blame for making him do it. His only concern would
be for himself and what effect the crimes could have
on his life. By this time, he had probably forgotten
most of the details of these incidents.

Unless the offender was arrested and incarcerated
for some extended period of time, we would expect the
offender to have continued killing, if not in this state,
in others.

Carlos Avila
Criminal Investigative Profiler/Consultant


Avila thought we had a serial killer. He thought my mother
fucked the Swarthy Man willingly. He hedged to a slight
degree:

"*It appears* that the victim had engaged in consensual
intercourse."

"Whatever circumstances triggered the offender's anger
occurred after the victim had reinserted the tampon."

Bill and I discussed the profile in general and the
consensual-sex-versus-rape point in specific. We agreed with
Avila's take on the killer's psychology. Bill went along with his
serial killer conclusion. I disputed it. I conceded one point
only. My mother might have been the first victim in a serial
killer chain. Carlos Avila was an established criminological
expert. I wasn't. I distrusted his conclusion because it was
based on an aggregate knowledge of similar criminal cases and
their common pathological underpinnings. I distrusted the
logical strictures and the encapsulated knowledge that
prompted him to the conclusion. The conclusion undermined
my basic law of murder: Criminal passion derived from long-
suppressed fears brought to momentary consciousness by the
unique alchemy of killer and victim. Two unconscious states
dovetail and create an explicative flashpoint. The killer knows.
The killer goes ahead—"It just felt like something I had to do."
The victim feeds the killer the knowledge. Female victims tap
out signals in sex semaphore. Look at that chipped nail polish.

Look at how sordid lovemaking is two seconds after you come. Sex semaphore is all misogynist subtext. All men hate all women for tried-and-true reasons they share in jokes and banter every day. Now you know. You know that half the world will condone what you are just about to do. Look at the bags under the redhead's eyes. Look at her stretch marks. She's putting that cunt rag back in. She's getting blood all over your seat covers—

He killed *her* that night. He could not have killed any other woman. He did not seek out a woman to kill that night. She could not have prompted any other man to that explicative flashpoint. Their alchemy was binding and mutually exclusive.

Bill thought it was rape. I thought it was rape. Bill said we had to keep an open mind. I embraced the serial killer theory momentarily. I asked Bill if we could run a statewide or nationwide records check and catalog choke murders back to our time frame. He said most of the records weren't computerized. A lot of hand-filed records had already been destroyed. There was no systematic way to access the information. The big FBI computer did not store data that old. Publicity was still our best shot. The *L.A. Weekly* piece was coming out in mid-February. *Day One* was set to air in April. Some old cops might read the piece or see the program. They might call us and say, "I had a case like that. . . ."

We put the profile aside. We chased more names.

We found an old doctor. He had an office near the Desert Inn. He gave us the name Harry Bullard. Harry owned the Coconino. He mentioned the Pitkin brothers. They owned a couple of gas stations near Five Points.

We found the Pitkin brothers. They didn't give us any names. They told us Harry Bullard was dead.

We wanted to spark a name landslide. We were name-deprived and intractably determined to grab more names. The investigation was now three and a half months old.

Helen came out for Christmas. We spent Christmas Eve with Bill and Ann Stoner. Bill and I discussed the case by the Christmas tree. I ignored all the holiday chitchat. Helen knew the case inside out. We'd talked every night for three-plus months. She sent me out to chase a redheaded ghost. She didn't treat the ghost as a rival or a threat. She monitored her evolution through my thoughts and talked murder theory as precisely as Bill and I did. Helen was Geneva's deconstructor. She warned me not to judge her or glamorize her. Helen satirized Geneva's appetites. Helen fixed Geneva up with skeevy politicians and got some righteous laughs. Bill Clinton left Hillary for Geneva and blew the '96 election. Hillary moved to El Monte and started fucking Jim Boss Bennett. The Swarthy Man was big in the Right to Life movement. The Blonde had Newt Gingrich's love child.

Bill spent a week with his family. I spent a week with Helen. We put the case on temporary hold. I went into murder withdrawal. I talked to the boss at Sheriff's Homicide and went out on some active calls.

I carried a beeper. I got beeped and directed out to two crime scenes. I caught two gang killings. I saw bloodstains and bullet holes and grieving families. I wanted to write a magazine essay. I wanted to slam this new mechanistic horror up against my old sex horror. My thoughts didn't jell. I caught two male victims. I looked at spattered brain fluids and saw my mother on King's Row. I looked at a dead gangbanger's brother and saw my father poised and pleased at the El Monte Station. The old Sheriff's Homicide squad fielded 14 men. The current squad was a full-fledged division. L.A. County had 43 homicides in 1958. L.A. County had 500 this year. Sheriff's Homicide was a class-A unit. They called themselves the Bulldogs. The Sheriff's Homicide squad room was a fucking Bulldog pen. Bulldog regalia reigned. The place was sub-merged in desk clutter marked with Bulldog emblems. A plaque covered the front wall. It listed every detective who ever worked the unit.

The new Bulldogs were multiracial and bi-gender. They were up against high-tech murder and public accountability and racial polarization and overpopulation and a jurisdiction in gradual decline. The old Bulldogs were white men with bottles in their desks. The odds were stacked in their favor. They were up against low-tech murder in a stratified and segregated society. Everybody respected them or feared them. They could employ coercive methods with impunity. They could work a dual-world scheme without the fear of dual-world overlap. They could work murders in Niggertown or wetback El Monte and go home to the safe world where they stashed their families. They were bright men and driven men and men susceptible to the fleshpot temptations of their on-duty world. They were bright men. They weren't prescient thinkers or dystopian futurists. They couldn't predict that their on-duty world would swallow their safe world one day. There were 14 Bulldogs in 1958. There were 140 today. The increased number said there was no place to hide. The increased number contextualized my old horror. It implied that my old horror still packed some clout. My old horror lived in pre-tech memories. The Blonde told people. Barstool talk was still floating around. Memories meant names.

The holidays ended. Helen went home. Bill and I went back to work.

Chief Clayton gave us some names. The El Monte Museum director gave us some names. We checked them out. They went nowhere. We hit the two El Monte bars still in operation since 1958. They were redneck joints then. They were Latin joints now. They'd changed hands a dozen times. We tried to trace the ownerships back to '58. We ran into missing records. We ran into missing names.

We chased names around the San Gabriel Valley. People moved to the San Gabriel Valley and rarely moved out. Sometimes they moved to skunk towns like Colton and Fontana. Bill made me drive every day. Freeway driving made him retire. I made him unretire. This meant I had to play chauffeur. This meant I had to stand abuse for my poor driving skills.

We drove. We talked. We spun off our case and encapsulated the whole criminal world. We drove freeways and surface streets. Bill pointed out body dump locales and riffed on his old cases. I described my pathetic crime exploits. Bill described his patrol years with picaresque zeal. We both worshipped testosterone overload. We both reveled in tales of male energy displaced. We both saw through it. We both knew it killed my mother. Bill saw my mother's death in full-blown context. I loved him for it.

It rained like a motherfucker all through January. We sat out rush-hour traffic and freeway floods. We hit the Pacific Dining Car and ate big steak dinners. We talked. I started to see how much we both hated sloth and disorder. I lived it for 20 years solid. Bill lived it once-removed as a cop. Sloth and disorder could be sensual and seductive. We both knew it. We both understood the rush. It came back to testosterone. You had to control. You had to assert. It got crazy and forced you to capitulate and surrender. Cheap pleasure was a damnable temptation. Booze and dope and random sex gave you back a cheap version of the power you set out to relinquish. They destroyed your will to live a decent life. They sparked crime. They destroyed social contracts. The time-lost/time-regained dynamic taught me that. Pundits blamed crime on poverty and racism. They were right. I saw crime as a concurrent moral plague with entirely empathetic origins. Crime was male energy displaced. Crime was a mass yearning for ecstatic surrender. Crime was romantic yearning gone bad. Crime was the sloth and disorder of individual default on an epidemic scale. Free will existed. Human beings were better than lab rats reacting to stimuli. The world was a fucked-up place. We were all accountable anyway.

I knew it. Bill knew it. He tempered his knowledge with a greater sense of charity than I did. I judged myself harshly and passed the standards of my self-judgment on to other people. Bill believed in mitigation more than I did. He wanted me to extend a sense of mitigation to my mother.

He thought I was too hard on her. He liked my partner-to-partner candor and disliked my lack of son-to-mother sentimentality. I said I was trying to contain her presence. I was running a dialogue on her. It was mostly internal. My external mode was all critique and mock-objective appraisal. She took full flight inside me. She vexed me and vamped me. I put on a white smock and addressed her publicly as a clinician. I voiced blunt comments to provoke blunt responses. We had a two-faced relationship. We were like illicit lovers living in two worlds.

I knew Bill was falling for her. It wasn't a hard spill like the one he took for Phyllis "Bunny" Krauch. It wasn't a resurrection fantasy. It didn't play like his longing to see Tracy Stewart and Karen Reilly exhumed beyond victimhood. He was falling into the redhead's blank spaces. He wanted to solve the riddle of her character as much as he wanted to find her killer.

We drove. We talked. We chased names. We went off on anthropological tangents. We hit the car lot across the street from the Desert Inn site. We took some names and traced the ownership back to '58. The old owner's son owned a Toyota franchise. He gave us four names. We traced two to the morgue and two to car lots in Azusa and Covina. Bill had a hunch that the Swarthy Man was a car salesman. We worked that hunch for ten days straight. We talked to a shitload of old car salesmen. They were all fossilized locals.

None of them remembered our case. None of them remembered the rockin' Desert Inn. None of them ever noshed at Stan's Drive-in. They did not look like clean-living men. Most of them looked downright sodden. They all denied knowledge of the freewheeling El Monte bar scene.

We drove. We talked. We chased names. We rarely strayed out of the San Gabriel Valley. Every new lead and tangent brought us straight back. I learned all the freeway routes from Duarte to Rosemead to Covina and up to Glendora. I learned surface street routes in and out of El Monte. We always passed through El Monte. It was the shortest route to the 10 freeway east and the 605 freeway south. El Monte became dead familiar. The Desert Inn became Valenzuela's. The food was bad. The service was indifferent. It was a slop chute with a mariachi band. Repetition killed the joint for me. It lost its shock value and charm. It did not exist to chaperone me on mental dates with my mother. There was only one magnetic force field left in El Monte. It was King's Row by night.

They shut me out sometimes. I'd drive up around midnight and find the gate locked. King's Row was a high-school access road. It did not exist to reinject me with horror.

I'd find the gate open sometimes. I'd drive in and park with my lights out. I'd sit there. I'd get scared. I'd imagine all sorts of 1995 horror and sit still waiting for it. I wanted to put myself at physical risk in her name. I wanted to feel her fear in this place. I wanted her fear to meld with mine and transmogrify. I wanted to scare myself into a heightened awareness and come away with lucid new perceptions.

My fear always peaked and diminished. I never quite scared myself all the way back to that night.


The *L.A. Weekly* came out. The Ellroy-Stoner piece was beautifully executed. It laid out the Ellroy and Long cases in significant detail. It emphasized the Blonde. It omitted the fact that my mother was strangled with two ligatures. It stated that she was strangled with a silk stocking only. The omission was crucial. It would help us eliminate false confessions and confirm legitimate ones. The true facts were already published in *GQ* and in old newspaper accounts. The *L.A. Weekly* omission was a stopgap measure.

They printed our tip-line number in bold black type.

Calls came in. I kept my answering machine on 24 hours a day. I played my messages periodically and logged in the precise time that each call hit the line. Bill said 1-800 phone bills identified all incoming phone numbers. We could log in the time suspicious calls arrived and trace the callers through our monthly bills.

Forty-two people called and hung up the first day. Two psychics called and solicited business. A man called and said he could throw a seance and summon up my mother's spirit for a nominal fee. A movie-biz fuckhead called and said he saw my life as a big-budget feature. A woman called and said her father killed my mother. Four people called and said O. J. Simpson did it. An old buddy called and hit me up for a loan.

Twenty-nine people called and hung up the next day. Four psychics called. Two people called and snitched off O.J. Nine people called and wished me good luck. A woman called and said my books were sexy and let's get together. A man called and said my books were racist and homophobic. Three women called and said their fathers might have killed my mother. Two of them said their fathers molested them.

The calls continued.

We got more hang-ups and more O.J. calls. We got more psychic calls and more good-luck calls. We got two calls from women with repressed memory syndrome. They said their fathers abused them. They said their fathers might have killed my mother. We got three calls from one woman. She said her father killed my mother *and* the Black Dahlia.

Nobody called and said they knew the Blonde. Nobody called and said they knew my mother. No old cops called and said, I popped that swarthy motherfucker.

The call count dropped day by day. I cut down our callback list. I crossed off the nuts and the psychics and the Black Dahlia lady. Bill called the other women who snitched off their fathers and asked them some make-or-break questions.

Their answers cleared their fathers. Their fathers were too young. Their fathers were in prison in 1958. Their fathers did not look like the Swarthy Man.

The women wanted to talk. Bill said he'd listen. Six women told the same story. Their fathers beat up their mothers. Their fathers molested them. Their fathers blew the rent money. Their fathers skeeved on underaged females. Their fathers were dead or atrociously booze-impaired.

The fathers ran to a type. The women ran to a type. They were middle-aged and in therapy. They defined themselves in therapeutic terms. They lived therapy and talked therapy and used therapeutic jargon to express their sincere belief that their fathers really could have killed my mother. Bill taped three interviews. I listened to them. I believed every specific sex-abuse indictment. The women were betrayed and abused. They knew their fathers were rapists and killers at heart. They thought that therapy gave them preternatural insights. They were victims. They saw the world in victim-predator terms. They saw me as a victim. They wanted to create victim-predator families. They wanted to claim me as a brother and anoint my mother and their fathers as our dysfunctional parents. They thought the traumatic force that shaped their insights superseded plain logic. It didn't matter that their fathers did not look like the Swarthy Man. The Swarthy Man could have dropped my mother off at the Desert Inn. Their fathers could have snatched her in the parking lot. Their grief was all-inclusive. They wanted to take it public. They were writing the oral history of ravaged kids in our time. They wanted to include my story. They were evangelical recruiters.

They moved me and scared me. I replayed the tapes and nailed the source of my fear. The women sounded smug. They were entrenched and content in their victimhood.

The tip-line calls died out. The *Day One* producer called me. He said they couldn't run our 1-800 number. It violated their Standards and Practices Code. The on-camera host would drop a few words at the end of our segment. He'd tell potential tipsters to call Sheriff's Homicide. He would not include the Sheriff's Homicide phone number.

I was pissed. Bill was pissed. The code restriction fucked up our access to nationwide information. Sheriff's Homicide was not a toll-free number. Hinky people would call a 1-800 line. Hinky people would not call the fuzz. Poor people and cheap people would call a 1-800 line. Poor people and cheap people would not call long-distance.

Bill predicted 500 tip-line calls. He predicted 10 calls to Sheriff's Homicide.

I spent a week alone with the Jean Ellroy file. I read all the reports and note slips 14 dozen times. I zeroed in on one little detail.

Airtek Dynamics belonged to the Pachmyer Group. Pachmyer and Packard-Bell were phonetically similar. I thought my mother worked at Packard-Bell up to June '58. The Blue Book said no. I might have dreamed up Packard-Bell 40 years ago. It might be a dyslexic memory glitch.

Bill and I discussed the point. He said we should contact my relatives in Wisconsin. Uncle Ed and Aunt Leoda might still be alive. They could settle the Packard-Bell point. They might have some names. They might have my mother's funeral book. It might have some names in it. I said I talked to the Wagners in '78. I called Leoda and apologized for all the times I scammed her. We argued. She said my cousins Jeannie and

Janet were married and why wasn't I? She patronized me. She said caddy work didn't sound very challenging.

I blew the Wagners off right then. I blew them off permanently. I told Bill I didn't want to contact them now. He said, You're scared. You don't want to revive Lee Ellroy for even two seconds. I said, You're right.

We chased names. We found a 90-year-old woman. She was spry and lucid. She knew El Monte. She gave us some names. We traced them back to the morgue.

I spent two weeks alone with the Ellroy and Long files. I inventoried every note on every slip of paper. My inventory ran 61 pages. I Xeroxed a copy and gave it to Bill.

I found another crumpled note we both overlooked. It was a canvassing note. I recognized Bill Vickers' handwriting. Vickers talked to a waitress at the Mama Mia Restaurant. She saw my mother at the restaurant "about 8:00 p.m." Saturday night. She was alone. She stood in the doorway and checked the place out "like she was looking for someone."

I went over my inventory. I found a companion note. It said that Vickers called the Mama Mia waitress. She mentioned a redheaded woman. Vickers said he'd bring a photo of the victim in. The note I just found was the follow-up note. The waitress looked at the photo. She said the redheaded woman was my mother.

It was a major reconstructive lead.

My mother was "looking for someone." Bill and I extrapolated that "someone." She was looking for the Blonde and/or the Swarthy Man. At least one relationship existed prior to that night.

The *Day One* show aired. The Ellroy-Stoner segment was punchy and straight to the point. The director squeezed the story into ten minutes' screen time. He got the Blonde in. He showed the Identi-Kit portraits of the Swarthy Man. Diane Sawyer told potential tipsters to call Sheriff's Homicide.

The Black Dahlia lady called. Four more women called and said their fathers could have killed my mother. A man called and snitched off his father. A man called and snitched off his father-in-law. We called the callers. Their information played out 100% bogus.

I spent another week with the Ellroy and Long files. I forged no new connections. Bill cleared out his desk at the Bureau. He found an envelope marked Z-483-362.

It contained:

A name-and-address calling card for John Howell of Van Nuys, California.

Jean Ellroy's car payment book. She sent her last payment in on 6/5/58. Her payments ran $85.58 a month.

A canceled check for $15. The check was dated 4/15/58. Jean Ellroy signed the check on her 43rd birthday. A man named Charles Bellavia endorsed it.

A sheet of paper with a gummed scratch-pad border and a note on one side. The note read: "Nikola Zaha. Vic's boyfriend? Whittier."

We ran the new names through the DMV and DOJ computers. We got no DOJ hits. We got no DMV hit on Zaha. We got DMV hits on John Howell and Charles Bellavia. They were old men now. Bellavia lived in West L.A. Howell lived in Van Nuys. Bellavia was a rare name. We figured we had the right guy. We knew we had the right John Howell. His current address was a few digits off his calling card address.

We checked the reverse book for Zahas. We found two in Whittier. Zaha was a rare name. Whittier adjoined the San Gabriel Valley. The two Zahas were probably related to our Zaha.

I remembered my mother's old boyfriend Hank Hart. I found them in bed together. Hank Hart had one thumb. I found my mother in bed with another man. I didn't know his name. I didn't know the name Nikola Zaha.

Nikola Zaha might be a crucial witness. He might explain my mother's precipitous move to El Monte.

Bill and I drove out to Van Nuys. We found John Howell's house. The door was wide open. We found Howell and his wife in the kitchen. A nurse was preparing their lunch.

Mr. Howell was hooked up to a respirator. Mrs. Howell was sitting in a wheelchair. They were old and frail. They looked like they wouldn't live much longer.

We talked to them gently. The nurse ignored us. We explained our situation and asked them to think back a ways.

Mrs. Howell made the first connection. She said her mother was my old babysitter. Her mother died fifteen years ago. She was 88. I fought for the woman's name and snagged it.

Ethel Ings. Married to Tom Ings. Welsh immigrants. Ethel worshipped my mother. Ethel and Tom were in Europe in June '58. My mother drove them to the *Queen Mary*. My father called Ethel and told her my mother was dead. Ethel was distraught.

Mr. Howell said he remembered me. My name was Lee—not James. The cops found his calling card at my mother's house. They questioned him. They got pretty raw.

The nurse pointed to her wristwatch and held up two fingers. Bill leaned toward me. He said, "Names."

I saw an address book on the kitchen table. I asked Mr. Howell if I could look through it. He nodded yes. I looked through the book. I recognized one name.

Eula Lee Lloyd. Our next-door neighbor—circa '54. Eula Lee was married to a man named Harry Lloyd. She lived in North Hollywood now. I memorized her address and phone number.

The nurse tapped her watch. Mrs. Howell was shaking. Mr. Howell was gasping for breath. Bill and I said goodbye. The nurse showed us out and slammed the door behind us.


I got a glimpse of my own flawed memory. I didn't remember Eula Lee Lloyd. I didn't remember Ethel and Tom Ings. The investigation was nine months old. My memory gaps might be impeding our progress. I retrieved a memory. I went to the boat with Ethel and Tom and my mother. It was late May or early June '58. I thought I had that time microscopically framed. I thought I had every detail culled for analysis. The Howells taught me otherwise. My mother could have said things. My mother could have done things. She could have mentioned people. The cops questioned me and requestioned me. They wanted to trap my recent memories. I had to trap my old memories. I had to split myself in two. The 47-year-old man had to interrogate the 10-year-old boy. She lived in my purview. I had to live with her again. I had to exert extreme mental pressure and go at our shared past. I had to place my mother in fictional settings and try to mine real memories through symbolic expression. I had to relive my incestuous fantasies and contextualize them and embellish them past the shame and the sense of boundary that always restricted them. I had to shack up with my mother. I had to lie down in the dark with her and go—

I wasn't ready yet. I had to clear a block of time first. I had to track down Lloyd, Bellavia and Zaha and see where they took me. I wanted to go at my mother with a full load of recollective ammo. The Beckett trial was coming up. Bill would be at the prosecution table all day every day. I wanted to see the trial. I wanted to look at Daddy Beckett and put a hex on his worthless soul. I wanted to see Tracy Stewart get her altogether too late and unsatisfactory vengeance. Bill said the trial would probably last two weeks. It would probably conclude in late July or August. I could shack with the redhead then.

We had three hot names. We chased them full-time.

We called Eula Lee Lloyd and got no answer. We knocked on her door and got no answer. We called her and knocked on her door for three days straight and got no answers. We talked to the landlady. She said Eula Lee was holed up with a sick sister somewhere. We explained our situation. She said she'd talk to Eula Lee sooner or later. She'd tell her we wanted to chat. Bill gave her his home number. She said she'd be in touch.

We knocked on Charles Bellavia's door. His wife answered. She said Charles went to the store. Charles had a heart condition. He took a little walk every day. Bill showed her the canceled check. He said the woman who wrote the check was murdered two months later. He asked her why Charles Bellavia endorsed the check. She said it wasn't Charles' signature. I didn't believe her. Bill didn't believe her.

She told us to go away. We tried to sweet-talk her. She didn't buy our act. Bill touched my arm to say back-off-now.

We backed off. Bill said he'd shoot the check to the El Monte PD. Tom Armstrong and John Eckler could brace Old Man Bellavia.

We chased Nikola Zaha.

We drove out to Whittier and hit our first Zaha address. A teenaged girl was home alone. She said Nikola was her grandfather. He died a long time ago. The other local Zaha was her uncle's divorced wife.

We drove to the other Zaha address and knocked on the door. Nobody answered. We drove to the El Monte Station and dropped the check off with Armstrong and Eckler.

We drove back to Orange County and broke it off for the day. I drove to a Home Depot store and bought another corkboard. I mounted it on my bedroom wall.

I drew a Saturday night/Sunday morning time graph. It started at 756 Maple at 8:00 p.m. It ended at Arroyo High at 10:10 a.m. I placed my mother around Five Points hour by hour. I drew question marks to note her blocks of unaccountable time. I set her death at 3:15 a.m. I pinned the graph to the board. I tacked up a graphic crime scene shot at 3:20 a.m.

I stared at the graph for a good two hours. Bill called. He said he'd talked to Nikola Zaha's son and ex-daughter-in-law. They said Zaha died in '63. He was in his early 40s. He had a heart attack. He was a big drunk and a big pussy hound. He was an engineer. He worked at a bunch of manufacturing plants near downtown L.A. He might have worked at Airtek Dynamics. The son and his ex did not know the name Jean Ellroy. The son said his dad was a discreet pussy hound. Bill got two descriptions of Zaha. He looked antithetical to the Swarthy Man.

Bill said goodnight. I hung up and stared at my graph.


Armstrong and Eckler reported. They said they talked to Charles Bellavia. He said the signature on the check was not his signature. He was not convincing. He said he owned a lunch truck biz back in '58. His trucks serviced factories in downtown L.A. Armstrong had a theory. He figured Jean Ellroy bought some chow. She gave the lunch truck man a check and got ten or twelve bucks back in cash. Bellavia said he did not know Jean Ellroy. He was convincing. The lunch truck man gave Bellavia the check. He endorsed it and deposited it in his business account.

Eula Lee Lloyd's landlady reported. She said she'd talked to Eula Lee. Eula Lee remembered Jean Ellroy and her murder. She said she had nothing to tell us. Her sister was sick. She had to care for her. She had no time to talk about old homicides.

Bill began pretrial work with the Beckett prosecutor. I holed up with the Jean Ellroy file. The 1-800 line buzzed sporadically. I got O.J. calls and psychic calls. Four journalists called within a two-week period. They wanted to write up the Ellroy-Stoner quest. They all promised to include our 1-800 number. I scheduled time with reporters from the *L.A. Times*, the *San Gabriel Valley Tribune*, *Orange Coast* magazine and *La Opinión*.

We got a hot tip. A woman read the *L.A. Weekly* belatedly and called us. Her name was Peggy Forrest. She moved to El Monte in 1956. She wasn't a psychic. She didn't think her father killed my mother. She lived a mile from Bryant and Maple—then and now.

She left a provocative message. Bill called her and set up an interview. We drove out to her house. She lived on Embree Drive off Peck Road. It was due north of my old house.

Peggy Forrest was rangy and in her late 60s. She sat us down in her backyard and told us her story.

They found the nurse on a Sunday morning. It was on the radio. Willie Stopplemoor knocked on her door. She wanted to talk about it. "Willie" was short for "Wilma." Willie was married to Ernie Stopplemoor. They had two sons named Gailard and Jerry. Gailard went to Arroyo High. Ernie and Wilma were 35 to 40. They came from Iowa. They lived on Elrovia. Elrovia was near Peck Road.

Willie was agitated. She said the cops were looking for Clyde "Stubby" Green. They found Stubby's overcoat on the nurse's body. The nurse was selling Stubby dope.

Stubby Green lived across the street from Peggy Forrest. He worked at a machine shop with Ernie Stopplemoor. Stubby was 5'11" and stocky. He had a butch haircut. He was about 30 then. Stubby was married to Rita Green. They came from Vermont or New Hampshire. Rita was blond. She wore a ponytail. Stubby and Rita were barhoppers. Stubby was an "El Monte legend" and a "well-known bad boy." Stubby and Rita had a son named Gary and a daughter named Candy. They went to Cherrylee Elementary School. They were about six or seven years old in 1958. Peggy saw Stubby sneak home one morning. He was carrying some suits and sports jackets. It just didn't look right. Willie Stopplemoor did not mention Stubby or the nurse again. Peggy forgot about the whole thing. The kicker to the whole thing was this:

The Greens split for parts unknown a few weeks after the murder. They pulled their kids out of school. They blew off their mortgage and their house. They never returned to El Monte. The Stopplemoors did the same thing. They split unexpectedly. They did not tell a soul that they intended to move. They just up and vanished.

I asked Peggy to describe Ernie Stopplemoor. She said he was very tall and gangly. Willie Stopplemoor was chunky and plain-featured. Bill mentioned the machine shop. Peggy said she didn't know the name. It was somewhere in the San Gabriel Valley.

I asked her for names. I asked her to link some names to the Green incident. She said her father told her something. He said Bill Young and Margaret McGaughey knew the dead nurse.

Bill ran Peggy Forrest through her story again. She told it in the same precise manner. I wrote down all the names and ages and physical descriptions. I wrote out a priority list and underlined four things:

El Monte Museum—check '58 directories.

Check '59s—see if Greens & Stopplemoors really left El Monte.

Check school records—Green & Stopplemoor kids.

Run Greens & Stopplemoors nationwide and attempt to locate.

It felt like something. I liked the tight local vibe.

*

I showed Bill my list. He said it was good. We discussed the Green/Stopplemoor story. I said the coat bit was bullshit. The cops found my mother's coat on her body. Bill said the dope bit was bullshit. Jean probably had no access to salable narcotics. I said I dug the geographical angle. Elrovia was one block from Maple. I started to theorize. Bill told me to stop. We had to get more facts first.

We hit the El Monte Museum. We checked the directories. We found a Clyde Greene on Embree in 1958. His wife was listed as Lorraine, not Rita. We checked the '59, '60 and '61 books. There were no Clyde or Lorraine Greenes listed. We found the Stopplemoors on Elrovia for all four years.

Bill called Tom Armstrong. He ran the story by him and gave him the names and approximate ages of the four Greene and Stopplemoor kids. The Stopplemoors probably stuck around El Monte. The Greenes might have booked out quicksville. Armstrong said he'd check the appropriate school records. He'd try to determine if the Greenes and Stopplemoors yanked their kids.

Bill called Chief Clayton and Dave Wire. He dropped the names Ernie Stopplemoor and Clyde "Stubby" Greene—the "El Monte legend." The names didn't ring any bells. Clayton and Wire promised to call some old cops and report back.

They called some old cops. They reported back. Nobody recalled Ernie Stopplemoor or Clyde "Stubby" Greene.

We ran the Greenes, the Stopplemoors and their kids through the state DMV and DOJ computers and the 50-state reverse book. We ran the name Rita Greene and the name Lorraine Greene. We got precious few Greenes altogether. We called all of them. None of them acted suspicious. None of them said they used to live in El Monte. None of the Clydes copped to the nickname "Stubby." None of the Garys and Candys copped to daddies named Clyde or mamas named Lorraine or Rita.

We tagged three Stopplemoors in Iowa. They were blood kin to old Ernie. They said Ernie and Wilma were dead. Their son Jerry was dead. Their son Gailard was living in Northern California.

Bill got Gailard's number and called him. Gailard did not

recall the Greene family or the Jean Ellroy snuff or anything but hot rods and chicks in El Monte. He did not come off suspicious. He came off somnambulant.

Armstrong got us the school records. They proved that the Stopplemoors stayed in El Monte. They proved that the Greenes pulled their kids out of school in October '58. Stubby did not rabbit in July. Peggy Forrest had that wrong.

We tried to find Bill Young and Margaret McGaughey. We failed. We kissed the whole tangent off.

We met the *L.A. Times* reporter. We showed her the file. We showed her El Monte. We took her to Valenzuela's and Arroyo High and 756 Maple. She said she was backlogged. She might not get her piece out before Labor Day.

Bill resumed his trial preparations. I went back to the file. The file was an access road to my mother. I was going into hiding with her soon. The file was preparing me. I wanted to meet her with established facts and rumors synced to my imagination. The file smelled like old paper. I could turn that smell to spilled perfume and sex and her.

I holed up with the file. My apartment was un-air-conditioned and summertime hot. I stared at my corkboard displays. I had my meals delivered. I talked to Helen and Bill on the phone every night and nobody else. I kept the answering machine on. A string of psychics and soul channelers called and said they could help me. I erased the messages. I cooked up some crazy-ass measures and called them in to Bill. I said we could take out a big newspaper ad and request information on the Blonde and Swarthy Man. Bill said it would just attract more freaks and geeks and mystics. I said we could offer a big reward for the same information. It would galvanize the barflies who heard the Blonde's story. Bill said it would galvanize every greedy cocksucker in Los Angeles County. I said we could go through all the '58 phone books. We could check the El Monte, Baldwin Park, Rosemead, Duarte, La Puente, Arcadia, Temple City and San Gabriel books and write down every Greek and Italian and Latin-Caucasian sounding male name and run DOJ and DMV checks and take it from there. Bill said it was a screwy idea. It would take a year and result in nothing but bullshit and catastrophic aggravation.

He said I should read the file. He said I should think about my mother. I said I was doing it. I didn't say some part of me was running like she used to run. I didn't say my crazy suggestions were some kind of last-ditch effort to avoid her.

The Jean Ellroy reinvestigation was ten months old.

25

Daddy Beckett looked like Santa Claus. He was a hard-charging bad-ass in 1981. He was your white-bearded granddad now. He had a heart condition. He was a born-again Christian.

He went to trial at Division 107, L.A. County Superior Court. Judge Michael Cowles presided. Deputy DA Dale Davidson represented the county. A lawyer named Dale Rubin represented Daddy. The courtroom was wood-paneled and nicely air-conditioned. The acoustics were good. The spectator benches were hard and uncomfortable.

O. J. Simpson was on trial four doors down. The hallway was packed from 8:00 a.m. to closing time every day. We were ten floors up. Every elevator ride ran full capacity. The Criminal Courts Building was a multiplex entertainment center. It featured one hot attraction and some courtroom lounge acts. Media crews, picketers and T-shirt vendors circled the building. The pro-O.J. pickets were black. The anti-O.J. pickets were white. The T-shirt guys were biracial. The parking lot was full of camera trucks and sun-deflecting photo orbs on stilts. School was out. A lot of people brought their kids.

The Beckett trial was a box-office dud. Fuck Daddy Beckett. Daddy was low-rent. He was a schmuck with an accordion and a bad rug. The Main Room was four doors down. O. J. Simpson was the whole Rat Pack in their prime. Fuck Tracy Stewart. Nicole Simpson had bigger tits.

Daddy Beckett sat with Dale Rubin. Bill Stoner sat with Dale

Davidson. The jury sat along the right-hand wall and viewed the action sideways. The judge sat on a high perch and viewed the action directly. I sat up against the back wall.

I sat there every day. Tracy Stewart's parents sat in front of me. We never spoke.

Charlie Guenther flew down for the trial. Gary White flew in from Aspen. Bill stuck close to the Stewarts. He wanted to walk them through the trial and help them retrieve their daughter's remains. Daddy Beckett said he remembered the dump site. He told the Fort Lauderdale cops that he'd send the Stewarts an anonymous note and reveal the location. He hadn't done it yet. There was no percentage in it. The act could legally backfire. The Stewarts wanted to bury their daughter. They probably knew the whole concept of "closure" was bullshit. Their daughter vanished one day. They probably wanted to stage a reunion and mark her life with a piece of dirt and a stone.

Bill thought they'd never find the body. His ray of hope was a sham. Robbie Beckett said they drove Tracy south and dumped her near a fence. Nobody found her body. The body should have been found. The body might have been found and misidentified. The body might be buried under some other name. Daddy told Robbie to gut the inside of his van a few days after the murder. The act was irrational. The act implicitly contradicted Robbie's account of the murder. They hit Tracy with a sap. Daddy strangled her. They made a minimal mess.

The body should have been found.

They might have cut Tracy up in the van. They might have dumped her body parts in different locations.

Bill thought they'd never know. Robbie would stick to his story. Daddy would not send that note. Closure was bullshit. They'd convict Daddy. The judge would not impose the death penalty. They needed a body. They needed to prove that Daddy raped Tracy. Robbie said Daddy raped Tracy. It wasn't sufficient proof. Robbie said that he did not rape Tracy. Bill did not believe him.

Charlie Guenther testified. He described the Tracy Stewart missing-persons case. He described Gary White's work for the

Aspen PD. He consulted a pocket notebook and listed his dates and locations precisely. Daddy Beckett watched him. Dale Rubin challenged a few dates and locations. Guenther checked his notes and corroborated them. Daddy watched. Daddy wore a long-sleeved sport shirt and slacks. His threads complemented his white hair and glasses. His cellmates probably called him "Pops."

Gloria Stewart testified. She described Tracy's life and the events preceding her disappearance. Tracy was a shy and fearful girl. Tracy had trouble in high school and dropped out prematurely. Tracy rarely had dates. Tracy ran errands and answered the phone for her parents. Tracy stayed home a lot.

Dale Davidson was gentle. He phrased his questions deferentially. Dale Rubin questioned the witness. He implied that Tracy's home life was cloistered and extremely neurotic. He came off skittish and unconvinced of his own argument. I watched the jury. I burrowed into their heads. I knew they found the implications unconscionable. Tracy was murdered. Her home life was irrelevant.

Davidson was gentle. Rubin was almost polite. Gloria Stewart was fierce.

She trembled. She cried. She looked at Daddy Beckett. She sobbed and coughed and stumbled over her words. Her testimony said, There is no closure. Her hatred filled the room. She saw Robbie's trial. She saw him convicted. It was just a passing moment in her hatred. This was one more moment. It was nothing compared to the aggregate force of the hate she sustained every day. She left the witness stand. She veered by the defense table and looked at Daddy Beckett close up. She trembled. She walked to her bench and sat down. Her husband put an arm around her.

I never felt her kind of hatred. I never had a flesh-and-blood target.

The Beckett trial continued. The Simpson trial continued four doors down. I saw Johnnie Cochran every day. He was a perfectly groomed and tailored little man. He dressed better than Dale Davidson and Dale Rubin.

Sharon Hatch testified. She was Daddy Beckett's squeeze in '81. She said she dumped Daddy. Daddy flipped out. He threatened her and her kids. Sharon Hatch looked at Dale Davidson. Daddy looked at Sharon Hatch. She said Daddy never hit her. He never threatened her before she dumped him. I followed Davidson's logic. He was establishing Daddy's psyche pre- and post-breakup. Daddy was calm before. Daddy wigged out after. I distrusted the before-and-after line. It was a coded cause-and-effect indictment aimed at an innocent woman. The line might hit the men on the jury square in the gonads. They might commiserate with Daddy. The poor guy got fucked by a cold-hearted cunt. I looked at Sharon Hatch. I tried to read her. She seemed passably smart. She probably knew that Daddy was wigged out well in advance of their breakup. He was a strongarm loan collector. He was an armor fetishist. His chivalry to women was a symptom of his hatred for women. He was a sex psycho hibernating. He knew that he wanted to rape and kill women. The breakup gave him a justification. It was based on one part rage and two parts self-pity. You could not date his gender-wide hatred to the moment Sharon Hatch said, "Walk, sweetie." Daddy Beckett was working toward his explicative flashpoint already. He was like the Swarthy Man in the spring of '58. I felt a little jolt of empathy for the Swarthy Man. I felt a big jolt of hate for Daddy Beckett. My mother was 43 years old. She was caustic. She could put weak men in their place. Tracy Stewart was utterly helpless. Daddy Beckett trapped her in his bedroom. She was a lamb in his slaughterhouse.

Dale Davidson and Sharon Hatch worked well together. They set Daddy up as a frayed fuse about to unravel. Dale Rubin raised some objections. Judge Cowles overruled some and sustained some. The objections pertained to points of law and flew right over my head. I was back in the South Bay in 1981. I was a half-step from that night 23 years before.

The judge called a recess. Daddy walked to his holding booth outside the courtroom. Two plainclothes cops brought Robbie in. He was handcuffed and shackled. He was wearing jail denims. The cops sat him down in the witness box and uncuffed and unshackled him. He saw Bill Stoner and Dale Davidson and waved. They walked up to him. Everybody started smiling and talking.

Robbie was rough trade. He was tall and broad. His body fat ran about .05%. He had long brown hair and a long, droopy mustache. He looked like he benched 350 and ran a hundred yards in 9.6 seconds.

Court reconvened. The plainclothes cops sat near the jury box. A bailiff waltzed Daddy in. He sat down beside Dale Rubin.

Robbie looked at Daddy. Daddy looked at Robbie. They checked each other out and looked away.

The clerk swore Robbie in. Dale Davidson approached the witness stand. He asked Robbie some preliminary questions.

Robbie talked with a swagger. He was here to vent a patricidal grudge. He emphasized words like "ain't" and phrases like "He didn't have no." He was saying, I know better and I don't give a fuck. The implication was, I'm me and my father made me who I am.

Daddy watched Robbie. The Stewarts watched Robbie. Davidson led Robbie back to Redondo Beach and Tracy's house and Daddy's apartment. Dale Rubin raised several objections. The judge overruled or sustained them. Rubin looked bewildered. He couldn't divert Robbie's momentum. Robbie started looking straight at Daddy.

Davidson worked slowly and deliberately. He took Robbie right up to *the* moment. Robbie started stuttering and crying. He walked Tracy into the bedroom. He gave her to Daddy. Daddy started touching her—

Robbie lost it. He faltered and tripped over his words. Dale Davidson paused. He suspended his questions for a superbly calculated little pocket of time. He asked Robbie if he could talk now. Robbie wiped his face and nodded. Davidson fed him some water and told him to continue. Robbie plugged away at his story like a trouper.

He got drunk. Daddy raped Tracy. Daddy said, We've got to kill her. They walked her downstairs. He hit her with the sap—

Robbie faltered again. He faltered on cue. Nobody fed him

the cue. He pulled an internal boo-hoo number and choked himself up. He wept for his own misspent life. He didn't intend to kill a girl that night. His father made him do it. He wasn't weeping for the girl he killed. He was weeping for his own forfeiture.

Robbie was good. Robbie understood dramatic displacement. He reached for the old self-pity and pulled out some tears and hit the old redemption seeker chord molto bravissimo. He was bad—but not as bad as his father. His wretched character and beautifully feigned remorse gave him instant charisma and credibility. I time-traveled back to 8/9/81. A man had to kill a woman. A boy had to please his father. Daddy only killed women with other males present. Daddy needed Robbie. Daddy couldn't kill Tracy without him. Robbie knew what Daddy wanted. Did you rape her, too? Did you rape her because Daddy raped her and you hated him and you couldn't stand to see him have more fun than you? Did you rape her because you knew Daddy would kill her and what's one more rape then? Did you lay out some garbage bags and dismember her in the back of the van?

Davidson led Robbie through the rest of the night and his initial mop-up procedures. Robbie stuck to his often-told and formally recorded story. Davidson thanked him and turned him over to Dale Rubin. Robbie got real then. This was Robbie versus Daddy—with no expendable piece of ass to distort the goddamn issue.

Rubin tried to discredit Robbie. He said, Didn't you bring Tracy home for yourself? Robbie denied it. Rubin rephrased the question repeatedly. Robbie denied it repeatedly. Robbie raised his voice with each denial. Robbie was all pride now. He strutted from a sitting position. He said "No" with exaggerated inflections and bobbed his head up and down like he was talking to a fucking retard. Rubin asked Robbie if he got in fights back then. Robbie said he was a red-blooded guy. He liked to kick ass. He learned it from his father. He learned all the bad things he knew from his father. Rubin asked Robbie if he beat up on his girlfriends. Robbie said no. Rubin expressed disbelief. Robbie told Rubin he could think what the hell he liked. Robbie bobbed his head harder and harder each time he said "No." Rubin persisted. Robbie persisted with much greater flair. He had at least ten stock readings for the word "No." He stared at Daddy Beckett. He smiled at Dale Rubin. The smiles said, You can't win because I've got nothing to lose.

Daddy Beckett stared at his hands. He looked up and locked eyeballs with Robbie a few provocative times. He always looked down first. He didn't look down from fear or shame. He looked down because he was tired. He had a bad heart. He was too old to play mind games with young buck convicts.

Robbie spent a day and a half in the box. He was questioned and cross-questioned and coddled and badgered. He endured. He never wavered. He never appeared to dissemble. It was patricidal performance art. Robbie was bravura. Robbie sang grand opera. Robbie probably overestimated the effect on his father. Daddy Beckett was yawning a lot.

Davidson brought up the Sue Hamway case. Robbie told the court what he knew. Davidson brought up Paul Serio. Robbie portrayed him as a quiff and Daddy Beckett's stooge. Rubin brought up Serio. Robbie satirized the quiff's body language and worked it into his head-bob routine. Rubin could not shake Robbie. His hate filled the room. It was generically infantile hatred reasoned out over time. Robbie was starring in his own life story. Tracy Stewart was the ingenue lead. Robbie felt nothing for her. She was just a bitch who sideswiped two men and made things go blooey.

Robbie finished his testimony. The judge called a recess. I almost applauded.


Daddy's first ex-wife testified. She said Daddy was an awful daddy. He was brutal with Robbie, David and Debbie. David Beckett testified. He pointed to Daddy in open court and called him a "piece of shit." Dale Rubin cross-examined David. He said, Aren't you a convicted child molester? David said he was. He pointed to Daddy and said he learned it from him. He didn't elaborate. Debbie Beckett could not testify. She was dead of AIDS attributed to intravenous drug use.

Paul Serio testified. He described his part in the Susan Hamway murder. He laid all the blame on Daddy. He didn't know it was a hit. He thought it was a debt shakedown. Daddy iced Sue Hamway solo. Daddy whipped out a dildo and said, Let's make it look like a sex snuff.

Serio pitched some regret for Sue Hamway's baby. The baby starved to death while Sue Hamway decomposed.

Bill Stoner testified. He described the Beckett investigation from day one on. He was calm and authoritative. He counterbalanced Robbie's histrionics. He was an independent auditor called in to itemize and total up the cost. Dale Rubin tried to ruffle him. Dale Rubin failed.

The defense called three witnesses. Two of Robbie's old pals testified. They said Robbie used to pound on total strangers for no reason. Rubin controlled his witnesses. They sketched a nice picture. The pre-Tracy Robbie was impetuous and unpredictably violent. The revelation lacked punch. Robbie's pre-emptive strike nullified it. Robbie drew the same picture. He drew it more dramatically and in the first person.

Rubin called his last witness. Another old pal testified. He said Robbie said he raped Tracy Stewart. I believed him. I couldn't read the jury. I figured their response was, So what? Robbie's in prison already. You can't discredit Robbie. He upstaged you with his self-immolation. We're tired. We want to go home. Thanks for the ride. We've got jury box whiplash. It was fun. It was groovier and less protracted than the Simpson mess. We got sex and family discord. We bypassed the scientific shit and the specious rants on race. The lounge act blitzed the Main Room show.

The trial was almost over. Bill predicted a fast guilty verdict. Gloria Stewart could stand up in court and confront Daddy Beckett. She could abuse him. She could beg for Tracy's body. The Victim Confrontation was new legal stuff. It promoted victim's rights and psychological cleansing. I told Bill I didn't want to see the closing arguments and the Stewart confrontation. Daddy would yawn. Gloria would say her piece and go on grieving. The confrontation law was passed by morons hooked on daytime TV. I didn't want to see Gloria's audition. I didn't want to see her as a professional victim. Bill never introduced us. He never told her who I was or who I lost in June '58. He knew we'd have nothing to say to each other. He knew I never hurt like she did.

The Beckett trial lasted two weeks. Bill and I drove up in separate cars every day. Bill went out with Dale Davidson and Charlie Guenther most nights. They'd hook up with Phil Vanatter sometimes. Vanatter was famous now. He worked the murder case of the century. The Beckett crew went out to celebrate the end of the trial. Vanatter went with them. Bill invited me. I took a pass. I wasn't a cop or a deputy district attorney. I didn't want to talk shop with pros. I didn't want to commiserate or discuss the farcical aspects of the Simpson case. I was running low on white man's outrage. The LAPD kicked indiscriminate black ass for fifty-plus years. Mark Fuhrman was Jack Webb with fangs. DNA was unassailably precise and confusing. Racist conspiracies carried more dramatic weight. Bill knew it. He was too gracious to rub it in Phil Vanatter's face. Marcia Clark needed a black Robbie Beckett. A black Robbie could indict O.J. with home-grown soul. Justice was politics and theater. O. J. Simpson wasn't Emmett Till or the Scottsboro Boys. Victimhood was exploitable. I wasn't Gloria Stewart.

I drove out to West L.A. I wanted to find a private pay phone and call Helen. I wanted to talk about Tracy and Geneva.

I remembered the phone bank at the Mondrian Hotel. It was rush hour. Sunset Boulevard was probably jammed. I turned north on Sweetzer. I crossed Santa Monica Boulevard and saw where I was.

I was driving through a murder zone.

Karyn Kupcinet died at 830-something North Sweetzer. It was late 11/63. Jack Kennedy was four or five days dead. Somebody strangled Karyn in her apartment. She was nude. Her living room was a mess. She was facedown on the sofa. Sheriff's Homicide handled the case. Ward Hallinen worked it. They looked at Karyn's actor boyfriend and one of Karyn's freaky neighbors. Karyn's father was Irv Kupcinet. He was a big talk-show host and columnist in Chicago. Karyn moved to L.A. to score as an actress. Her dad was floating her. She wasn't making it. Her boyfriend and his friends were. Karyn ran a few pounds over svelte. She took diet pills to control her weight and fly. Charlie Guenther thought she died accidentally. They found a book on the coffee table near her body. It was all about nude dancing. You could dance like a wood nymph and free your inhibitions. Guenther figured she was bombed. She was dancing stark nude. She fell down and broke her hyoid bone on the coffee table. She crawled up on the couch and died. Bill thought she was murdered. It could have been the boyfriend or the freaky neighbor or some geek she picked up at a bar. They got a lot of tips in '63. They still got tips. An FBI guy called in a tip recently. He said he got it off a wiretap recording. A mob guy said he had the real goods. Karyn was giving a guy some skull and choked to death on his dick.

I turned west at Sweetzer and Fountain. I saw the El Mirador building. Judy Dull lived there. She was 19. She had an estranged husband and a kid already. She posed for cheesecake pix. Harvey Glatman found her. Glatman was a Jean Ellroy suspect. Jack Lawton cleared him on Ellroy and nailed him on Dull.

I turned north on La Cienega. Georgette Bauerdorf's apartment house stood right there. Georgette Bauerdorf was murdered on 10/12/44. A man broke into her pad. He stuffed a bandage roll in her mouth and raped her. She choked to death on the roll. They never found the killer. Ray Hopkinson worked the case. Georgette was 19—like Judy Dull. Georgette had money—like Karyn Kupcinet. Georgette volunteered at the USO Canteen. Her family was back in New York. Her friends said she was nervous and smoked too much. She lived all by herself. She drove around L.A. impulsively.

Karyn was running on dope and hiding out behind her father's money. Judy was running from too much life too fast. Georgette got cabin fever and ran to the boys at the USO Canteen. Tracy hid out at home. Robbie picked her up there. Jean picked the wrong town to hide in.

I saw their faces. I formed them into a group shot. I made

my mother their mother. I placed her in the middle of the frame.

Tell me why.

Tell me why it was you and not somebody else.

Take me back and show me how you got there.

# 26

My mother said she saw the Feds gun down John Dillinger. She was a nursing school student in Chicago. Dillinger was killed on 7/22/34. Geneva Hilliker was 19 then. My father said he was Babe Ruth's trainer. He had a display case full of medals he didn't really win. Her stories were always more plausible. He was more desperate and anxious to impress. She lied to get what she wanted. She understood the limits of verisimilitude. She could have been three blocks away from the Biograph Theater. She could have heard gunshots. She could have made the jump from sound to sight through pure imagination. She could have filled in the details over bourbon highballs and convinced herself that they were true. She could have told me the story in good faith. She was 19 then. She could have been saying, Look how bright and hopeful I was.

My father was a liar. My mother was a fabricator. I knew them for six years together and four years apart. I spent seven more years with my father. He brought my mother up and shot her down. His stories were self-inflated and spiteful. His stories were suspect. He defamed my mother at leisurely whim for the last seven years of his life.

I stayed in touch with my aunt Leoda. She told me things about Geneva. She praised Geneva. She lauded her. I couldn't remember a thing she said. I hated Leoda. I was the con man and she was the mark with the cash.

I had lies to build from. I couldn't discount them. I wanted to build perception from contradictory viewpoints. I had my own memory. It was in sound working order. I test-fired it after the Beckett trial. I remembered the names of old classmates. I remembered every park and jail I ever crashed out in. I had my chronological life with my mother mapped out year by year. I remembered the names of old dope connections and all my junior-high teachers. My mind was sharp. My memory was strong. I could counter synaptic failures with fantasy riffs. I could run alternative scenes in my head. What if she did this. Maybe she did that. She might have reacted thusly. The literal truth was crucial. It might come in limited quantities. My memory wasn't repressed. My memory might lack resiliency.

I had no family photographs. I had no pictures of her at 10, 20 and 30. I had pictures of her at 42 and on her way down and pictures of her dead. I didn't know much about our ancestry. She never mentioned her parents or her favorite aunts and uncles.

I had a strong mental will. I remembered my thoughts from light years ago. I could strip-mine my brain and replay my old thoughts about her. My imagination might help me. It might hinder me. It might shut down at lustful junctures. I had to get explicit. I owed her that. I had to take her further.

Bill was up in L.A. He was waiting out the Beckett verdict. I told him I wanted to get lost for a while. He said he understood. He had Tracy Stewart on the brain bad.

I was test-fired and ready. I unplugged the phone and turned the lights off. I stretched out on the bed and closed my eyes.


She came from Tunnel City, Wisconsin. Tunnel City was a railroad stop and not much else. She moved to Chicago. She moved to San Diego. My father said he met her at the Del Coronado Hotel. He said it was 1939. He said they heard the second Louis-Schmeling fight together. The fight occurred in '38. She was 23 then. He was 40. He dressed to the nines. He wore prewar suits all the time I knew him. They looked incongruous in 1960. They got more and more raggedy as our living standard declined. They were au courant in '38. He looked good. She fell hard. He had a hot girl-woman he thought he could control forever. He probably took her to the bullfights down in T.J. He spoke fluent Spanish. He ordered all her food in Spanish. He took her to Mexico to woo her and control her. They drove down to Ensenada. She took me to Ensenada in 1956. She wore a white off-the-shoulder dress. I watched her shave her underarms. I wanted to kiss her there. He got her torched on margaritas. She wasn't a drunk yet. He poured salt and squeezed lime juice on her hand and licked it off. He was desperately attentive. She didn't have his number yet. She got it over time. I worked on a time-lost/time-regained dynamic. She viewed her lost time as unregainable. She pinned her loss on my father. She lowered her sights. Bourbon highballs made machine-shop studs controllable and alluring. She never asked herself why she craved weak and cheap men.

She had superb carriage. She seemed taller than the recorded height on her autopsy report. She had big hands and feet. She had delicate shoulders. I wanted to kiss her neck and smell her perfume and cup her breasts from behind. She wore Tweed perfume. She kept a bottle on her nightstand in El Monte. I poured some on a handkerchief once and took it to school with me.

She had long legs. She had stretch marks across her stomach. The autopsy pictures were shocking and instructive. Her breasts were smaller than I remembered. She was slender throughout her upper body and thick from the hips down. I memorized her body early on. I reworked her dimensions. I altered her contours to match my taste for lustily built women. I grew up with that nude vision and accepted it as fact. My real mother was a much different flesh-and-bones woman.

My parents got married. They moved to L.A. He said they had a pad at 8th and New Hampshire. She got a nurse gig. He went Hollywood. They moved to 459 North Doheny Drive. It was Beverly Hills. The address was ritzier than the pad. My mother said it was just a small apartment. My father snagged a job with Rita Hayworth. I was born in March '48. My father handled Rita's marriage to Aly Khan. The Hayworth stuff was true. I saw my father's name in two Hayworth biographies.

We moved to 9031 Alden Drive. It was over the West

Hollywood line. We lived in a Spanish-style building. Eula Lee Lloyd and her husband lived there. A spinster lady lived there. She idolized my mother. My father said she was a dyke. He had dykes on the brain. He said there was a dyke bounty out on Rita Hayworth. I allegedly met Rita Hayworth at a hot dog stand. It was '50 or '51. I allegedly spilled a grape drink all over her. Rita was allegedly a nympho. My father had nymphos on the brain. He said all the big actors were fags. He had fags on the brain. Rita fired my father. He started sleeping all day. He slept on the couch like Dagwood Bumstead. My mother told him to get a job. He said he had pull. He was waiting for the right opportunity. My mother hailed from rural Wisconsin. She didn't know from pull. She pulled the plug on her marriage.

My memories were running in a straight chronological line. My fantasies were running as adjuncts and outtakes. I thought I'd be criss-crossing the memory map. I thought I'd be stumbling over real-life minutiae. I was on the road to recollection. I'd conjured up Tweed perfume and some period snapshots. I was running a linear flowchart I already knew.

I downshifted. The redhead stripped. She had her real-life body and her 42-year-old face. I couldn't take it any further.

I wasn't afraid to. I just didn't want to. It seemed unnecessary.

I let my mind wander. I thought of Tracy Stewart. I'd seen Daddy Beckett's old apartment. I went out with Bill and Dale Davidson. I saw the key Beckett locations. I saw the living room and the bedroom and the steps down to the van. I walked Robbie and Tracy up those steps. I went from my mother nude to Robbie and Tracy within six heartbeats. Robbie walked Tracy into the bedroom. Robbie gave her to Daddy.

I stopped there. I wasn't afraid. I knew I could make it horrifying. I didn't think I could learn anything from it.

I let my mind wander. I went back to '55. I had a time line going. I decided to let it ride.

My father was gone. It was her and me and nobody else. I saw her in white seersucker. I saw her in a navy blue robe. I put her in bed with some assembly line studs. I gave the guys pompadours and knife scars. They looked like Steve Cochran

in *Private Hell 36*. I was working for hyperbole. I thought ugly
details might resurrect ugly memories. I wanted to chart the
redhead's sex roll from my father to the Swarthy Man. My
father was weak. He had a tough guy's body and a candy-ass
soul. My mother kicked him out of her life and went
minimalistic. All men were weak and some men were weak and
attractive. You could not control their weakness. You could
limit your awareness of it and euphemize it past recognition.
You could let men into your life in limited dosages. I did not
see a male stampede to my mother's door. I caught her in
flagrante twice. My father said she was a whore. I believed him.
I sensed her sexual bent. I filtered my awareness through my
own lust for her. She lived with my father for 15 years. She
succumbed to an image. She wised up. Disillusionment was
enlightenment. She went at men from a disillusioned and
wholly male perspective. Men were containable. Sex and
liquor was the way to contain them. She flushed 15 years down
the toilet. She knew she was passively complicit. She despised
her own stupidity and weakness. She saw cheap men as her
consolation prize. She saw me as her redemption. She sent me
to church and made me study. She preached diligence and
discipline. She didn't want me to turn into my father. She
didn't smother me with love and turn me into a '50s textbook
faggot. She lived in two worlds. I marked the dividing line. She
thought her dual-world scheme was sustainable. She miscalculated. She didn't know that suppression never works. She had
liquor and men over here. She had her little boy over there.
She spread herself thin. She saw her worlds blur together. My
father rubbed her honky-tonk world in my face. He out-
propagandized her. He taught me to hate her every weekend.
She scorned him every weekday. She fed me scorn with less
virulence than he fed me hatred. She preached hard work and
determination. She was a drunk and a whore and thus a
hypocrite. The world she built around me did not exist. I had
x-ray-eye access to her hidden world.

I caught her in bed with a man. She pulled a sheet up over
her breasts. I caught her in bed with Hank Hart. They were
naked. I saw a bottle and an ashtray on the nightstand. She
moved us to El Monte. I saw a whore in flight. She might have

fled to create a space between her two worlds. She said we were moving for my sake. I wrote it off as a lie. Say I was wrong. Say she ran for both of us. She ran too fast and misread El Monte. She saw it as a buffer zone. It looked like a good place for weekend revelry. It looked like a good place to raise a little boy.

She tried to teach me things. I learned them belatedly. I became more disciplined and meticulous and diligent and determined than she ever could have hoped for. I surpassed all her dreams for my success. I couldn't buy her a house and a Cadillac and express my gratitude in true nouveau riche fashion.

We time-traveled. We covered our ten years together. We made irregular jumps back and forth. Old memories played out contrapuntally. Every Jean-the-profligate-redhead blip sparked a counterpoint image. There's Jean drunk. There's Jean with her ungrateful son. He fell out of a tree. She's pulling splinters from his arms. She's swabbing him with witch hazel. She's holding a pair of tweezers under a magnifying glass.

We time-traveled. I lost track of real time in the dark. That counterweighted balance held. I ran out of memories and opened my eyes.

I saw my wall graph. I felt the sweat on my pillow.

I turned off my time machine. I didn't want to take her anywhere else. I didn't want to place her in fictional settings or wrap my revelations up and call them her life summarized. I didn't want to write her off as complex and ambiguous. I didn't want to shortchange her.

I was hungry and restless. I wanted to breathe fresh air and look at live people.


I drove to a mall. I walked to a food court and got a sandwich. The place was jammed. I watched people. I watched men and women together. I looked for seductions. Robbie courted Tracy in public. The Swarthy Man took Jean to Stan's Drive-In. Harvey knocked on Judy's door and made her feel safe.

I didn't see anything suspicious.

I quit surveilling. I sat still. People crossed my line of sight.

I felt buoyant. I was on some kind of oxygen high.

It hit me softly.

The Swarthy Man was irrelevant. He was dead or he wasn't. We'd find him or we wouldn't. We'd never stop looking. He was only a directional sign. He forced me to extend myself and give my mother her full due.

She was no less than my salvation.

# 27

The jury delivered. Daddy Beckett fell for Tracy Stewart. Bill said he'd get life without. Gloria Stewart confronted him. She pled for her daughter's body and called Daddy terrible names. I said there was no body and no closure. Daddy got life. Gloria got life with Daddy and Robbie.

Bill threw a backyard party. He called it a pre-Labor Day bash. It was really a goodbye party aimed at Daddy Beckett.

I attended. Dale Davidson and his wife attended. Vivian Davidson was a deputy DA. She knew the Beckett case intimately. Some other DAs came down. Gary White and his girlfriend came down. Bill's father showed up. Bill's neighbors walked over. Everybody ate hot dogs and burgers and talked murder. The cops and DAs were relieved that the Beckett mess was over. The non-cops and non-DAs thought that meant closure. I wanted to find the fool who invented closure and shove a big closure plaque up his ass. Everybody talked about O.J. Everybody riffed on the potential verdict and its potential ramifications. I didn't talk much. I was at my own party with the redhead. She was playful. She was snagging potato chips off my plate. We were sharing our own private jokes.

I watched Bill toss burgers and talk to his friends. I knew he was relieved. I knew his relief dated back to Daddy Beckett's arrest. He circumvented Daddy's shot at killing other women. That was a hypothetically sound resolution. The guilty verdict was more ambiguous. Daddy was old and infirm. His rape-and-kill days were gone. Robbie was still in his rape-and-kill and beat-up-women prime. He just turned in a stunning perform-ance. It facilitated justice in the matter *of L.A. County vs. Robert Wayne Beckett Sr.* It made him friends in law enforcement. He committed patricide in their name. It looked good on his prison record. It might serve to influence a premature parole.

Bill was still on the Drop Zone Expressway. He was serving out his own life sentence. He chose murder. Murder chose me. He came to murder as a moral duty. I came to murder as a voyeur. He became a voyeur. He had to look. He had to know. He succumbed to repeated seductions. My seductions started and stopped with my mother. Bill and I were indictable co-defendants. We were on trial in the Court of Murder Victim Preference. We favored female victims. Why sublimate your lust when you can use it as a tool of perception? Most women were killed for sex. That was our voyeuristic justification. Bill was a professional detective. He knew how to look and sift and stand back from his findings and retain his professional composure. I could eschew those restraints. I did not have to build courtroom evidence. I did not have to establish coherent and explainable motives. I could wallow in my mother's sex and the sex of other dead women. I could categorize them and revere them as sisters in horror. I could look and sift and compare and analyze and build my own set of sexual and nonsexual links. I could call them valid on a gender-wide basis and attribute a broad range of detail to my mother's life and death. I wasn't chasing active suspects. I wasn't chasing facts to conform to any prestructured thesis. I was chasing knowledge. I was chasing my mother as truth. She taught me some truths in a dark bedroom. I wanted to reciprocate. I wanted to honor murdered women in her name. It sounded wholly grandiose and egotistical. It said I was looking at life on the Drop Zone Expressway. It brought that moment at the food court back in perfect reprise. It pointed me one way right now.

I had to know her life the way I knew her death.


I held the notion. I harbored it privately. We went back to work.

We met the reporters from *La Opinión, Orange Coast* and

the *San Gabriel Valley Tribune*. We showed them around El Monte. The *L.A. Times* came out. We got 60 calls total. We got hang-ups and psychic calls and O.J. gag calls and good-luck calls. Two women called and said their fathers could have killed my mother. We answered those calls. We heard more child-abuse stories. We cleared the two fathers.

A young woman called. She snitched off an old woman. She said the old woman lived in El Monte. The old woman worked at Packard-Bell circa 1950. She was blond. She wore a ponytail.

We found the old woman. She did not act suspicious. She did not remember my mother. She could not place my mother at Packard-Bell Electronics.

*La Opinión* came out. We got zero calls. *La Opinión* was printed in Spanish. *La Opinión* was a longshot.

The *San Gabriel Valley Tribune* came out. We got 41 calls total. We got hang-ups and psychic calls. We got O.J. gag calls. A man called. He said he was an old El Monte cat. He knew a swarthy cat back in the late '50s. The swarthy cat hung out at a gas station on Peck Road. He didn't remember the swarthy cat's name. The gas station was long gone. He knew lots of cats from '58 El Monte.

We met the cat. He gave us some names. We ran them by Dave Wire and Chief Clayton. They remembered a few of the cats. They did not look like *the* Swarthy Cat. We ran the cats through our three computers. We got no statewide or nationwide hits.

An Associated Press reporter called me. He wanted to write a piece on the Ellroy-Stoner quest. It would run nationwide. He'd include our 1-800 number. I said, Let's do it.

We took him to El Monte. He wrote his piece. It appeared in numerous newspapers. Editors butchered it. Most of them cut the 1-800 number. We got very few calls.

Three psychics called. The Black Dahlia lady called. Nobody called and said they knew the Blonde. Nobody called and said they knew my mother.

We ran our key names again. We wanted to cover our bets. We thought we might hit some new data-bank listings. We didn't. Ruth Schienle and Stubby Greene were dead or effectively elusive. Salvador Quiroz Serena might be back in

Mexico. We couldn't find Grant Surface. He took two lie detector tests in 1959. He didn't pass them or fail them. We wanted to challenge the inconclusive results.

Bill played a hunch and called Duane Rasure. Rasure found his Will Lenard Miller notes and FedExed them down. We read the notes. We found six Airtek names. We found two of the people alive. They remembered my mother. They said she worked at Packard-Bell before she came to Airtek. They didn't know the name Nikola Zaha. They couldn't ID my mother's old boyfriends. They gave us more Airtek names. They said Ruth Schienle divorced her husband and married a man named Rolf Wire. Rolf Wire was allegedly dead. We ran Rolf and Ruth Wire through our three computers and got no hits. We ran the new Airtek names. We got no hits. We drove out to the Pachmyer Group's corporate office. Bill said they wouldn't let us see their personnel files. I said, Let's ask. I wasn't chasing leads on the Swarthy Man. I was chasing leads on my mother.

The Pachmyer people were gracious. They said the Airtek division bellied up in '59 or '60. All the Airtek files were destroyed.

I took the loss unprofessionally hard. My mother worked at Airtek from 9/56 on. I wanted to know her then.

The Jean Ellroy reinvestigation was 13 months old.


O. J. Simpson was acquitted. L.A. waxed apocalyptic. The media went nuts behind the words "potential ramifications." All murders ramified. Ask Gloria Stewart or Irv Kupcinet. The Simpson case would cripple the immediate survivors. L.A. would get over it. A more celebrated man would snuff a more beautiful woman sooner or later. The case would micro-cosmically expose an even sexier and more ludicrous lifestyle. The media would build off O.J. and make the case an even bigger event.

I wanted to go home. I wanted to see Helen. I wanted to write this memoir. Dead women were holding me back. They died in L.A. and told me to stick around for a while. I was burned out on detective work. I was fried to the eyeballs on negative computer runs and misinformation. I had the redhead inside me. I could carry her away. Bill could chase leads and stalk the facts of her life in my absence. I stuck around for a shot at some brand-new ghosts.

I made four solo trips to the Bureau. I pulled old Blue Books. I read adjudicated cases cover to cover. I had no crime scene photos. I brain-cammed my own. I read dead body reports and autopsy reports and background reports and brain-screened my own history of vivisected women. I looked. I sifted. I wallowed. I didn't compare and analyze the way I thought I would. The women stood out as individuals. They didn't bring me back to my mother. They didn't teach me. I couldn't protect them. I couldn't avenge their deaths. I couldn't honor them in my mother's name because I didn't really know who they were. I didn't know who she was. I had inklings and a big fucking hunger to know more.

I started to feel like a grave robber. I knew I was burned out on death altogether. I wanted to score some leads on the redhead. I wanted to snag more information and hoard it and take it home with me. I thought up some last-ditch measures to keep me in L.A. I thought up newspaper ads and infomercials and on-line computer broadsides. Bill said it was all crazy shit. He said we should brace the Wagners in Wisconsin. He said I was scared. He didn't elaborate. He didn't have to. He knew my mother made me unique. He knew I embraced her selfishly. The Wagners had their own claim. They might dispute mine. They might welcome me back and try to turn me into a docile stiff with an extended family. They had a claim on my mother. I didn't want to share my claim. I didn't want to break the spell of her and me and what she made me.

Bill was right. I knew it was time to go home.

I packed up my corkboards and graphs and shipped them east. Bill transferred our tip-line number to an answering service. I took the file home with me.

Bill stayed on the case. He lost a partner and gained one back. Joe Walker was a crime analyst. He was on the L.A. Sheriff's Department. He knew the law enforcement computer network intimately. He was hopped up on the Karen Reilly case. He thought a black serial killer snuffed Karen Reilly. He wanted to work the Jean Ellroy case. Bill told him he could.

I missed Bill. He'd become my closest friend. He chaperoned me for 14 months. He cut me loose at the perfect moment of impasse. He sent me away with my mother and my unresolved claim.

I didn't nail up my corkboards at home. I didn't need to. She was always there with me.

*Orange Coast* came out. *Orange Coast* was an Orange County rag. The piece was good. They ran our 1-800 number. We got five calls. Two psychics called. Three people called and wished us good luck.

The holidays ended. A TV producer called me. She worked for the *Unsolved Mysteries* show. She knew all about the Ellroy-Stoner quest. She wanted to do a segment on the Jean Ellroy case. They would dramatize that Saturday night and include a plea for specific information. The show solved crimes. Old people watched the show. Old cops watched the show. They had their own tip-line number and operators on duty 24 hours a day. They reran their episodes in the summer. They FedExed all their tips to the victim's next-of-kin and the lead investigating detective.

I said yes. The producer said they wanted to shoot the actual locations. I said I'd fly out. I called Bill and told him the news. He said it was a fabulous break. I said we had to densify our segment. We had to saturate it with details on my mother's life. I wanted people to call in and say, "I knew that woman."

The Wagners might see the show. They might assail the portrait of my mother. She sent her son to church. Her son cashed in on her death. He turned her into a cheap femme fatale. He was a boyhood con artist. He was a character assassin now. He defamed his mother. He totaled up the balance sheet of her life incorrectly and gave the world a faulty accounting. He staked his claim of ownership on skewed memories and his worthless father's lies. He egregiously misrepresented his mother for all fucking time.

I went back to that dark bedroom and the food court

epiphany. The new memory balance. Bill's implication. The exclusive bond that I would not sever. The Wagners might see the show. They never saw or never reacted to the book I dedicated to my mother. They were midwestern stiffs. They weren't media hip. They might have sailed past me in newspapers and magazines. Leoda underestimated me. I hated her for it. I wanted to rub my real-life mother in her face and say, See how she was and see how I revere her anyway. She could cut me down with a few stern words. She could say, You didn't talk to us. You didn't trace your mother back to Tunnel City, Wisconsin. You based your portrait on insufficient data.

I didn't want to go back yet. I didn't want to break the bond. I did not want to disturb the core of sex that still defined it. Dead people belong to the live people who claim them most obsessively. She was all mine.


They filmed our segment in four days. They shot Bill and me at the El Monte Station. I re-enacted the moment at the evidence vault. I opened a plastic bag and pulled out a silk stocking.

It wasn't *the* stocking. Somebody twisted up an old stocking and knotted it. I didn't pick up a simulated sash cord. We omitted the two-ligature detail.

The director praised my performance. We shot the scene fast.

The crew was great. They were up for some laughs. The shoot played like a party in Jean Ellroy's honor.

I met the actor who portrayed the Swarthy Man. He called me Little Jimmy. I called him Shitbird. He was lean and mean. He looked like the Identi-Kit portraits. I met the actress who portrayed my mother. I called her Mom. She called me Son. She had red hair. She looked more Hollywood than rural Wisconsin. I kidded her. I said, "Don't go out chasing men while I'm gone this weekend." She said, "Buzz off, Jimmy—I need some action!" Mom and Swarthy came to laugh. We got some good shtick going. Bill showed up every day. He had a total blast.

They shot the Desert Inn sequence at a sleazy cocktail lounge in Downey. The set looked anachronistic. I met the actress who portrayed the Blonde. She was skanky bar bait personified. The Swarthy Man was dressed to kill. He wore a nubby silk-jacket-and-slacks combo. My mother wore a mock-up of the dress they found her in.

They filmed the three-way dynamic. The Swarthy Man looked evil. My mother looked too healthy. The Blonde hit the right skank chord. I wanted a noir vignette. They shot a faithful expository scene.

We moved down the street to Harvey's Broiler. I saw 20 vintage cars lined up. Harvey's Broiler was Stan's Drive-In. A bit actress was set to sling trays and portray Lavonne Chambers.

The Swarthy Man and my mother got in a '55 Olds. Lavonne brought them menus. They were miked up and ready to act. The producer gave me headphones. I listened to their dialogue and some random chitchat. Swarthy made a real-life play for my mom.

They shot the murder at the real location. The crew commandeered Arroyo High School. They brought in camera trucks, sound trucks, a catering truck and a wardrobe van. Some locals strolled by. I counted 32 people at one point.

They set up arc lights. King's Row went hallucinogenic. The '55 Olds pulled up. A chaste murder prelude and a simulated murder occurred. I watched the prelude and the murder and the body dump 25 times. It wasn't painful. I was a murder pro now. I was more than a victim's son and less than a homicide detective.

They shot two scenes at my old house. They paid Geno Guevara a site fee. I met the actor who played me as a kid. He looked like me at age ten. He wore clothes like I wore on 6/22/58.

The El Monte PD blocked off Bryant and Maple. The crew dressed the street with three vintage cars. Chief Clayton showed up. Spectators gathered. A 1950s cab materialized. The director rehearsed the Ellroy kid and the cop who gave him the news.

They blocked out the arrival scene. The cab pulled up. The

boy got out. The cop told him his mother was dead. Thirty or forty people watched.

They shot and reshot the scene. The word went around. I was the kid in the cab half a lifetime ago. People pointed to me. People waved.

They shot a domestic scene in my old kitchen. The kitchen was dressed up '50s style. My mother wore a white uniform. I wore my arrival outfit. My mother called me into the kitchen and told me to eat my dinner. I crashed into a chair and ignored my food. It was wholesome TV fare. Bill said they should have shot me looking down my mother's dress.

We broke for lunch. A catering truck arrived. A grip set up service for 20 on Geno Guevara's front lawn. The buffet line stretched out to the street. Some local yokels grabbed plates and crashed the party.

I sat down beside a total stranger. I sent a prayer out to the redhead. I said, This is for you.

**28**

The party ended. I went home. Our segment was scheduled for 3/22/96.

Bill and I top-loaded our interviews. We stressed Airtek. We stressed my mother's maiden name and "Jean" as short for "Geneva." We were pros now. We talked in sound bites. We had a shot at a huge audience. We wanted to stimulate and provoke them with perfectly precise and simply stated details.

She was out there. I felt her. I spent a month in calm anticipation. I bypassed the Blonde and the Swarthy Man. She was out there. People would call and say they knew her.

Bill was back in Orange County. He was working with Joe Walker. They were gearing up for names. The show would give us an unprecedented shitload of names. Local names. Names nationwide. Informants' names and potential Blonde and Swarthy Man names. Names to verify and run for criminal records. Names to contact and discard and scrutinize and compare to other names and dismiss from the standpoint of pure lunacy.

Names.

Her ex-lovers. Her ex-colleagues. Her ex-confidants. The people who glimpsed her flight pattern.

Names.

Bill was ready for them. He gave Joe Walker a backup mandate.

Check official records. Follow paper trails and raid data banks. Take us from Tunnel City to El Monte.

Joe said he'd check marriage and divorce records. Bill said he'd check directory listings. He said we should go to Wisconsin. I said, Not yet. He wanted to jump my claim. I wanted to plunder our new names and reinforce it.

I watched the show at home. Bill watched it at the studio phone center. Louie Danoff joined him. They hung out with some cops from other segments.

The setup was space age. A dozen operators worked the phones and typed their tips on computer screens simultaneously. The cops could read the screens and listen to hot calls on headsets. Tipsters called fast. They saw the show. They recognized suspects. They recognized lost loved ones or old acquaintances. They called because a segment tugged their heartstrings. They called because a segment fucked with their heads.

I watched the show with Helen. The Jean Ellroy segment was boffo. It was the best show since Robbie Beckett Live. Robert Stack narrated. I saw him and laughed out loud. I caddied for him a few times at Bel-Air Country Club. The dramatic scenes were vivid. The director hit a nice balance. He understood viewer demographics. The murder was spooky and no more. It would not offend old people or shock potential tipsters unduly. I was good. Bill was good. Robert Stack stressed the Airtek connection. The proper information went out. The proper pictures of my mother and the Swarthy Man went out. The story was simply and properly told.

The phones rang.

A man from Oklahoma City, Oklahoma, called. He said the Swarthy Man looked like a guy named Bob Sones. Bob murdered his wife, Sherry, and committed suicide. It was late '58. The crime occurred in North Hollywood. A man from Centralia, Washington, called. He said his father was the Swarthy Man. His father was 6'6" and weighed 240 pounds. His father carried a gun and lots of ammunition. A man from Savage, Minnesota, called. He said the Swarthy Man looked like his father. His father lived in El Monte back then. His father was abusive. His father served prison time. His father was a gambler and a skirt chaser. A man from Dallas, Texas, called. He said the Swarthy Man looked familiar. He looked like his neighbor a long time ago. The guy had a blond wife. He drove a blue-and-white Buick. A man from Rochester, New York, called. He said his grandfather was the Swarthy Man. Gramps lived in a nursing home. The man supplied the address and phone number. A woman from Sacramento, California, called. She said the Swarthy Man looked like a local doctor. The doctor lived with his mother. The doctor hated women. The doctor was a vegetarian. A woman from Lakeport, California, called. She said the Swarthy Man looked like her ex-husband. Her ex chased women. She didn't know where he was now. A woman from Fort Lauderdale, Florida, called. She said her sister was murdered. She said she read a lot of crime novels. A woman from Covina, California, called. She said her sister was raped and strangled in El Monte. It happened in 1992. A man from Huntington Beach, California, called. He said he wanted to talk to Bill Stoner. Bill came on the line. The man hung up. A woman from Paso Robles, California, called. She said the Swarthy Man looked familiar. She met a man like that in 1957. He wanted sex. She said no. He said he wanted to kill her. He lived in Alhambra then. A man from Los Angeles, California, called. He said his grandmother knew Jean Ellroy. They were friends. His grandmother lived in Orange County.

The operator waved Bill over. Bill checked her computer screen. The operator told the man to hold please. The man hung up.

The Black Dahlia lady called. She said her father killed Jean Ellroy and the Black Dahlia. A woman from Los Angeles, California, called. She said the Swarthy Man looked like her father. Her father died in August '58. A woman from Los Angeles, California, called. She said the Blonde looked familiar. She knew a couple in the late '50s. The husband was Italian. The wife was blond. He worked at a missile range. She worked at a dance studio. His name was Wally. Her name was Nita. A woman from Phoenix, Arizona, called. She said the Swarthy Man looked like her dead uncle. He lived in L.A. in 1958. A woman from Pinetop, Arizona, called. She said the Swarthy Man looked like a swarthy boy that she knew. The Swarthy

Boy was 16 in 1958. A woman from Saginaw, Michigan, called. She said the Swarthy Man looked like her ex-husband. Her ex vanished. She didn't know where he was. A woman from Tucson, Arizona, called. She said she was a psychologist. She said James Ellroy was very angry. He relived his mother's death to punish himself. He wasn't there for her. He felt guilty. He needed treatment. A woman from Cartwright, Oklahoma, called. She said the Swarthy Man looked like her mother's ex-husband. He raped her and tried to kill her mother. He was a devil. He was a truck driver. He drove Buicks. He picked up women and taunted her mother. She didn't know if he was still alive. A woman from Benwood, West Virginia, called. She said a man stalked her and her brother in Los Angeles. She was six years old. The man had dark hair and good teeth. He drove a truck. He took off her clothes, fondled her and kissed her. She saw him on a TV game show several years later. It might have been the Groucho Marx show. A woman from Westminster, Maryland, called. She said the Swarthy Man looked like a man named Larry. Larry was 40 now. The Swarthy Man might be his father. A man from New Boston, Texas, called. He said his wife's uncle moved to Texas in 1958. He looked like the Swarthy Man. He was a child molester. He died ten years ago. He was buried in Comway, Arkansas.

We tanked. We logged in jive and innuendo. The show was a family show. We logged in some family trauma. No Airtek people called. No ex-cops called. No ex-lovers, ex-colleagues or ex-confidants called. The Wagners didn't call. The one hot caller hung up. I felt like a pussy-whipped chump. I was stood up, cuckolded and jilted. I'm waiting by the phone. I'm waiting for a special woman or any woman to call.

The producer said we'd get more calls. Bill had all the tip sheets and callback numbers. He checked out the Bob and Sherry Sones tip. He couldn't find a case listing. He called the woman in Paso Robles. They discussed the Swarthy Dude from Alhambra. The Swarthy Dude was too young. He couldn't be the Swarthy Man. The tip was a dud. All our tips were duds.

More tips came in. Bill and I got tip sheets via FedEx.

A man from Alexandria, Virginia, called. He said the Swarthy Man looked like his brother. His brother was 6'2" and rangy. He did time at Chino State Prison. A man from Española, New Mexico, called. He said he lived in El Monte in 1961. The Swarthy Man looked very familiar. A woman from Jackson, Mississippi, called. She said her father killed a person in 1958. He did time at Alcatraz. He had tattoos on his right forearm and no right index finger. He tried to kill her mother. He drove a blue Chevy. The Black Dahlia lady called. She said her father killed my mother and the Black Dahlia. A woman from Virginia Beach, Virginia, called. She said she knew the Swarthy Man. He worked at the Lynn Haven Mall in Lynn Haven, Virginia.

A woman from La Puente called. Her name was Barbara Grover. She said she was Ellis Outlaw's ex-sister-in-law. Ellis was married to Alberta Low Outlaw. Ellis and Alberta were dead. Barbara Grover was married to Alberta's brother Reuben. He looked like the Swarthy Man. He was a drunk and a pervert. He hung out at the Desert Inn. He was murdered in L.A. in 1974.

Bill called Barbara Grover. She said Reuben hung out at Stan's Drive-in. He had mastoid surgery once. He developed a thin jaw line like that swarthy guy.

Bill met Barbara Grover in person. She said she met Reuben Low in 1951. He was 24. She was 16. He was dating her mother. He dropped her mother. He took up with her. They got married on 5/10/53. Her mother lived with them. Reuben had sex with her mother. Reuben abused them. Reuben bought cars and blew off the payments. Reuben was brutal. He tried to kill her with a beer bottle once. He liked guns and cars. He chased women. He had strange sexual tastes. He came home with scratches on his face all the time. He hated to work. He serviced vending machines sometimes. He lost the tip of his right index finger in a shop accident. She left Reuben in the early '60s. He got killed 10 or 12 years later. He was living in South L.A. He was walking home from a liquor store. Two black kids robbed him and shanked him.

Reuben never said he killed a woman. The Outlaws never told her he did. Maybe he killed Jean Ellroy. Maybe the Outlaws knew it. Maybe they protected him.

Barbara Grover showed Bill a picture. The young Reuben Low looked like a young Swarthy Man. He looked hillbilly. He didn't look Latin. His missing fingertip stood out.

Bill called LAPD Homicide. A friend pulled the Reuben Low file. The DOD was 1/27/74. The killers were captured and convicted.

Bill and I discussed Reuben Low. I said Margie Trawick would have known him. He was a Desert Inn habitué. He had a deformity. Bill said Hallinen and Lawton would have nailed him. They probably leaned on him and exonerated him.

We crossed him off our suspect list. He was the only motherfucker on our suspect list.

We got another tip via FedEx. A man from Somerset, California, called. His name was Dan Jones. He said he worked at Airtek in 1957. He knew my mother. He liked her. He had a picture of her.

Bill called Dan Jones. He said Jean went by "Hilliker" at Airtek. He said he left Airtek in early '58. He never talked to the cops. He didn't know who Jean was dating.

He gave Bill some Airtek names. Bill ran them statewide. He found eleven Airtek people in Southern California.

Dan Jones sent me four color snapshots. I time-traveled back to Christmas '57.

The Airtek Christmas party.

Everybody was drinking. Everybody was smoking. Everybody was having a blast. My mother appeared in one photograph.

She was standing by the bar. She was wearing a white uniform and a hip-length windbreaker. I couldn't see her face. I recognized her legs and hands. She was holding a drink and a cigarette. A man was leaning in to kiss her. His left hand was poised near her right breast.

Bill interviewed the Airtek people. Most of them remembered my mother. Bill wrote up the interviews and sent them to me. The details sent me airborne.

Airtek was Romance City. Airtek people worked hard and partied twice as hard. People came to Airtek. They caught the Airtek virus and ditched their wives and husbands. The Airtek virus was hot. It was the boogie-woogie flu. Airtek had a wife-swapping coven. Jean split Packard-Bell and came to Airtek. Ruth Schienle and Margie Stipp came too. Margie was dead now. Ruth disappeared. Jean was a beautiful lady. She drank too much. She knew it. She drank too much by Airtek standards. Airtek standards were very permissive. She drank at Julie's Restaurant near the Coliseum. She dawdled over lunchtime drinks. Nick Zaha worked at Airtek. He had a thing going with Jean. Airtek men drank hard. Jean gave them B-1 shots for their hangovers. The Airtek kids staged a wake for Jean. They played the Johnny Mathis tune "Chances Are" over and over. Jean got drunk at an Airtek party and rode a forklift platform up to the top of the main warehouse ceiling. Jean told a guy that another guy was giving her grief. She didn't mention his name. She got killed a week later. Will Miller worked at Airtek. He was some nice guy. An Airtek guy went to Europe two weeks before the murder. Jean asked him to send her a bottle of Chanel No. 5. Jean was nice. Jean worked hard. Jean's red hair sparkled behind three bourbon highballs.

She was sparkling now. I wanted more. We were in a parked car together. She was there under duress. I couldn't wheedle or arouse her for more. Other people had to give it to me.

I didn't know how to get more. Bill acted independently and showed me.

Joe Walker ran all the Hillikers in Wisconsin. He got a Leigh Hilliker in Tomah. Tomah was near Tunnel City. Bill called Leigh Hilliker. He was 84 years old. He was my mother's first cousin. He said Leoda Wagner was dead. Ed Wagner was hospitalized in Cross Plains, Wisconsin. Jeannie Wagner was now Jeannie Wagner Beck. She lived in Avalanche, Wisconsin. She had a husband and three kids. Janet Wagner was now Janet Wagner Klock. She lived in Cross Plains. She had a husband and four kids. Leigh Hilliker knew the Ellroy-Stoner story. He saw the *Day One* show last year. Bill asked him if the Wagners knew. He said he didn't know. He had their addresses and phone numbers. He didn't stay in touch. He didn't call them and mention the show.

Bill got Janet Klock's number and Ed Wagner's hospital number. He called them. He told them what we were doing.

They were flabbergasted and altogether delighted. They figured I died in some L.A. gutter 15 years ago.

Uncle Ed was 80. He had congestive heart disease. Leoda died seven years back. She had cancer. Janet was 42. She was the town administrator of Cross Plains, Wisconsin. She said she had some lovely photographs. Her mother gave them to her. Aunt Jean was beautiful. She said the pictures went back to her childhood.

She said Aunt Jean was married once before. It was a very brief marriage. She was married to a young man named Spalding. He was an heir to the Spalding sporting goods fortune.

Bill called me and broke the news. I was more than stunned. Bill said we should go to Wisconsin. He stressed the family angle. I agreed to go. The family bit did not factor in to my decision. The photographs and the Spalding rumor convinced me.

It was more. It was her.

# 29

Ed Wagner died. We postponed our trip to Wisconsin.

Ed was old and sick. He wasn't terminal. He died unexpectedly. The Wagner sisters buried him beside Leoda. The cemetery was a hundred yards from Janet's back door.

I didn't know him. I saw him a dozen times total. I took my father's hard line against him. He was a kraut and a draft dodger. It was a shaky indictment. Ed always treated me well. He was pleased to learn that I was alive and successful. I never called him. I wanted to see him. I owed him apologies. I wanted to extend them face-to-face.

I called the Wagner sisters. We made travel plans before their father died. We started out nervous. We unclenched. Janet said Leoda would have been so proud of me. I disagreed. I wanted to destroy Leoda's take on her sister. Janet said Leoda would not tolerate slurs on Geneva. Ed was more open-minded. He had a balanced view. Jean drank too much. She was troubled. She never shared her troubles.

I spoke frankly. My cousins reciprocated. I described my mother's life and death in blunt terms. They said I broke Leoda's heart. I said I tried to patch things up with her 18 years ago. I critiqued my mother tactlessly. Leoda was shocked. I blew my shot at reconciliation.

Jeannie was 49. She managed a local greenhouse. Her husband was a college professor. They had two sons and a daughter. Janet married a carpenter. They had three sons and a daughter. The last time I saw them was Christmas '66. Leoda flew me to Wisconsin. The mark wasn't hip to the con man.

Leoda got hip. She hipped her daughters. Leoda packed a mean grudge. Her daughters didn't. They welcomed me back. Jeannie was reserved. Janet was enthusiastic. She said she didn't know much about the Spalding marriage. She knew the marriage bellied up fast. She didn't know the wedding site or the circumstances surrounding the annulment or divorce. She didn't know Spalding's first name. Janet was four years old in June '58. Jeannie was almost twelve. Leoda said Aunt Jean went to the store and got kidnapped. The police found her body the next morning. Leoda abridged my mother's death the same way she expurgated her life.

Janet sent me a copy of the Hilliker family tree. It surprised me. I thought my grandparents were German immigrants. I don't know where I got the idea. My ancestors had English names. My grandmother's name was Jessie Woodard Hilliker. She had a twin sister named Geneva. The tree listed Hillikers, Woodards, Smiths, Pierces and Linscotts. They went back 150 years in America.

Ed and Leoda were dead. They couldn't dispute my claim. I would have fought Leoda's claim tactfully. My cousins barely knew my mother. I could let them in. I could share my mother superficially. I could hoard her dark heart for myself.


Cross Plains was a Madison suburb. Bill and I flew in to the Madison Airport.

Janet met us. She brought her husband, her youngest son and her daughter. I didn't recognize her. She was 12 years old in '66. I didn't see any Hilliker resemblance.

Brian Klock was 47. We shared the same birthday. Janet said Leoda prayed for me on Brian's birthday. It was my birthday. She never forgot it. Brian was short and stocky. All the Klocks were short and stocky. Mindy Klock was 16. She played classical piano. She said she'd play some Beethoven for me. Casey Klock was 12. He looked like a rambunctious kid. The male Klocks had great hair. I expressed envy. Brian and

Casey laughed. Bill eased right into the flow. He was the most deft social creature I'd ever known.

The Klocks drove us to a Holiday Inn. We took them to dinner downstairs. Talk flowed evenly. Bill described our investigation. Mindy asked me if I knew any movie stars. She mentioned her current flames. I said they were homosexual. She didn't believe me. I ran down some Hollywood gossip. Janet and Brian laughed. Bill laughed and said I was full of shit. Casey picked his nose and played with his food.

We had a good time. Janet laid out the plan for tomorrow. We'd drive to Tunnel City and Tomah. We'd pick up Jeannie en route. I mentioned the pictures. She said she had them at home. We could see them first thing tomorrow.

We lingered over dinner. The food was strange. Every dish came with an order of melted cheese and sausage. I figured it was a regional aberration. The Klocks had regional accents. All their words were upwardly inflected. Ed and Leoda talked that way. Their voices came out of thin air. I couldn't recall my mother's voice.

We talked about her. Janet and Brian were reverent. I told them to loosen up a little.


The pictures were old. They were pasted into scrapbooks and pulled out of envelopes. I examined them at Janet's kitchen table. The kitchen window overlooked the Wagner gravesite.

Most of the pictures were black & white and sepia-tinted. A few were late-'40s color. I looked at my ancestors first. I got a glimpse of Tunnel City, Wisconsin. I saw railroad tracks in every outdoor shot.

My great-grandparents. A stern Victorian couple. They posed sternly. Candid snapshots didn't exist then. I saw the Hilliker-Woodard wedding portrait. Earle looked like a gritty young man. Jessie was frail and lovely. She had a version of my face and my mother's face and some features we didn't inherit. She wore glasses. She had our small eyes. She gave my mother delicate shoulders and soft white skin.

I saw my mother. I followed her from infanthood to ten

years old. I saw her with Leoda. Leoda stared at her big sister. Every picture framed her adulation. Geneva wore glasses. She had light red hair. She smiled. She looked happy. Her interior backdrops were spare. She was raised in a no-frills house. Her exterior backdrops were beautiful and raw. Western Wisconsin was dark green in bloom or snowy and dead-tree barren.

I jumped ahead. I had to. There were no pictures of my mother as an adolescent. I jumped ten years. I saw Geneva at 20. Her hair was darker. She possessed a severe and breath-takingly implacable beauty.

She wore her hair in a bun. She parted it down the middle. It was a frumpy hairdo. She wore it with imperious confidence. She knew how she should look. She knew how to control her image.

She looked proud. She looked determined. She looked like she was thinking about something.

I jumped ahead. I saw three color snaps from August '47. My mother was two months pregnant. She was standing with Leoda. One of the pictures was cropped. Leoda probably x'd out my father. My mother was 32. Her features had settled in resolutely. She still wore that bun. Why get frivolous and mess with your trademark? She was smiling. She wasn't abstracted. She wasn't so fiercely proud.

I saw a black & white shot. My father wrote the date on the back. I recognized his printing. He wrote a little note below the date:

"Perfection. And who am I to gild the lily?"

It was August '46. It was Beverly Hills. It couldn't be any place else. A swimming pool. Some French-chateau cabanas. A scene from a movie-biz party. My mother was sitting in a deck chair. She was wearing a summer dress. She was smiling. She looked delightedly content.

She was with my father then. He was on Rita Hayworth's payroll.

I saw some more black & white shots. They were mid-'40s vintage. I recognized the common exterior. It was 459 North Doheny. My mother was wearing a light-colored dress and spectator pumps. The dress was perfect for her. It looked like high fashion on a low budget. She was poised. She wore a different hairstyle. Her bun was braided and pinned on the sides. I couldn't read her face.

I came to the most stunning pictures. They were posed photographs blown up to portrait size.

My mother was sitting on and standing by a split-rail fence. She was 24 or 25 years old. She was wearing a plaid shirt, a windbreaker, jodhpurs and boots that laced up to the knees. She was wearing a wedding ring. The pictures looked like honeymoon shots sans husband. My father or the Spalding guy were somewhere off-camera. This was Geneva Hilliker. This was my mother with no male surname. She was too proud to pander. Men came to her. She pinned her hair up and made competence and rectitude beauty. She was there with a man. She was standing alone. She was defying all claims past and present.

Tunnel City and Tomah were three hours northwest. We drove there in Brian Klock's van. Brian and Janet sat up front. Bill and I sat in the back.

We took back roads. Wisconsin shot by in five basic colors. The hills were green. The sky was blue. The barns and silos were red, white and silver.

The landscape was nice. I ignored it. I balanced a stack of pictures on my lap. I looked at them. I held them out at different angles. I held them up to odd shafts of light. Bill asked me if I was okay. I said, I don't know.

We picked up Jeannie. I recognized her. She had my beady brown eyes. We got the beads from Jessie Hilliker and the brown from our respective fathers.

Jeannie found this Ellroy thing disruptive. Her father died three weeks ago. Bill and I were drama that she did not need. She was distant. She wasn't rude or inhospitable. Bill asked her about the murder. She retold Leoda's story verbatim. Her parents never talked about the murder. Leoda stonewalled it. She lied about her sister's death and revised her sister's life accordingly.

We drove through boondock Wisconsin. I talked to Jeannie

and looked at the pictures. Jeannie thawed out a bit. She got into the road trip spirit. I held some pictures up to my window and did some juxtapositions.

We passed an army base. I saw a sign for Tunnel City. Janet said the graveyard was just off the highway. She drove out here once before. She knew the key Hilliker sites.

We stopped at the graveyard. It was 30 yards square and unkempt. I looked at the headstones. I matched names to my family tree. I saw Hillikers, Woodards, Linscotts, Smiths and Pierces. Their birthdates ran back to 1840. Earle and Jessie were buried together. He died at 49. She died at 59. They died young. Their graves were badly neglected.

We drove into Tunnel City. I saw the railroad tracks and the railroad tunnel. Tunnel City was four streets wide and a third of a mile long. It was built along one hillside. The houses were brick and old clapboard. Some were nicely maintained. Some were not. Some people mowed their lawns. Some people dumped junk cars and speedboats on their lawns. There was no town center. There was a post office and a Methodist church. My mother went to that church. It was boarded up now. The railroad station was padlocked. Janet showed us the old Hilliker house. It looked like a raised bomb shelter. It was red brick and 25 feet square.

I looked at the town. I looked at the pictures.

We drove to Tomah. We passed a sign for Hilliker's Tree Farm. Janet said Leigh's kids owned it. We pulled into Tomah. Janet said the sisters moved here in '30. Tomah was a time-warp town. It was a prewar movie set. The Pizza Hut and Kinko's signs gave away the era. The main drag was called Superior Avenue. Residential streets cut across it. The lots were big. The houses were all white clapboard. The Hilliker house was two blocks off the avenue. It was adorned and refurbished and rendered anachronistic. My mother lived in that house. She grew into her stern beauty in this pretty little town.

We parked and looked at the house. I looked at the pictures. Bill looked at them. He said Geneva was the best-looking girl in Tomah, Wisconsin. I said she couldn't wait to get out forever.

*

We drove back to Avalanche. We had dinner at Jeannie's house. I met Jeannie's husband, Terry, and her two sons. Her daughter was away at college.

Terry had long hair and a beard. He looked like the Unabomber. The boys were 17 and 12. They wanted to hear some cop stories. Bill riffed and riffed and took the social heat off me. I lapsed into a spectator mode. The pictures were back in the van. I resisted an urge to blow off the party and hole up with them.

Jeannie thawed out some more. Bill and I crashed her life. We distracted her. We jelled with her husband and kids. We gained credibility.

The party broke up at 11:00. I was dead-ass tired and speeding. Bill was fried. I knew he was running at a high RPM.

The Klocks drove us back to the Holiday Inn. We drank some late-night coffee and flew. I said we had to hit Chicago and Wisconsin again. We had to hit Geneva's nursing school and Tomah. We had to find old classmates and old friends and surviving Hillikers. Bill agreed. He said he should make the trip solo. People might freeze up around Geneva's son. He wanted them to talk with total candor.

I agreed. Bill said he'd set things up and fly east again.

I knew I wouldn't sleep. I had the pictures upstairs. My mind wandered. Bill asked me what I was thinking.

I said, I hate the Swarthy Man now.


I went home. Bill went home. He set up interviews in Tomah and Chicago. Joe Walker found my parents' divorce file. He found their marriage license and some old directory listings. He came up with some big surprises. Bill flew east. He checked newspaper files. He talked to Leigh Hilliker and his wife and three 80-year-old women. He talked to the superintendent of the West Suburban College of Nursing. He took rigorous notes. He flew home. He found Geneva's nursing school roommate. He sent me his paperwork. Joe Walker sent me his. I read it. I read it with the pictures in front of me. Janet found more pictures. I saw Geneva in sunglasses and a shirt-and-slacks ensemble. I saw her in boots and jodhpurs again. The investigation cohered. The paperwork and the pictures formed a life in ellipsis.

**30**

Gibb Hilliker was a farmer and a stone mason. He married Ida Linscott and had four sons and two daughters. They named their sons Vernon, Earle, Hugh and Belden. They named their daughters Blanche and Norma. Ida bore children from 1888 to 1905.

They lived in Tunnel City. Two railroad lines ran through the town. It was in Monroe County. The main industries were logging and fur trapping. Dove shooting was big. It was a sport and an occupation. Bird meat was popular then. Monroe County was full of edible game birds. Monroe County was full of rowdy Indians. They loved to drink and raise hell.

Earle Hilliker loved to drink and raise hell. Earle was stubborn. Earle was short-tempered. He went to Minnesota and got a job on a farm. He met a girl named Jessie Woodard. He married her. They might have been blood-related. The rumor persisted. Earle brought Jessie back to Tunnel City. They had a daughter in 1915. They named her Geneva Odelia Hilliker.

Earle was appointed State Conservation Warden for Monroe County, Wisconsin. It was 1917. He was a forest ranger. He caught poachers and roughed them up. He hired Indians to put out forest fires. They took his money and bought liquor. They started more fires to make more money. Earle liked to fight. He'd take on any two white men. He didn't fuck with the Indians. They fought dirty. They stuck together. They held grudges and jumped you from behind.

Earle and Jessie had another daughter. Leoda Hilliker was born in 1919.

Jessie raised the girls. She was gentle and soft-spoken. Geneva was a bright child. She became a bright and pensive adolescent. She was quiet and self-assured. She had this small-town je ne sais quoi.

She did well in school. She excelled at sports. She was more mature than other kids her age.

It was 1930. The Hillikers moved to Tomah.

Earle was drinking hard. He squandered his money and paid his bills late. The Depression was on. Vernon Hilliker went broke and lost his dairy farm. Earle hired him. He made him a forest ranger and let him run the Monroe County Office. Vernon did all the work. Earle drank and played cards all day. Vernon told Earle to watch out. Earle ignored him. The State Conservation boss visited Tomah. He found Earle drunk. He demoted him and transferred him to the Bowler Ranger Station. He gave Vernon Earle's job. Earle took it hard. He broke off all contact with Vernon and Vernon's family. Earle moved to Bowler. Jessie refused to go with him. She stayed in Tomah. Her daughters stayed with her. Geneva grew close to Earle's sister Norma.

Norma was nine years older than Geneva. She was the most beautiful woman in Tomah. Geneva was the most beautiful girl. Norma was married to "Pete" Pedersen. Pete owned the Tomah drugstore. He was 15 years older than Norma. He built her a beauty salon. Norma ran it as a lark. Norma and Pete had money. They gave Earle and Jessie handouts. Norma was a local cause célèbre. She allegedly had an affair with a Methodist minister. He allegedly left Tomah and committed suicide. Norma and Geneva acted like sisters or best friends. They didn't act like aunt and niece. They were thick as thieves.

Geneva was a poised young woman now. She went to town dances. Earle came down from Bowler and played chaperone. He did not like other men snouting around his daughter.

Geneva graduated high school in June '34. She wanted to be a registered nurse. She picked out a nursing school near Chicago. Norma said she'd pay her tuition and all her expenses. Geneva applied at West Suburban College. She was accepted. She left her mother and kid sister in Tomah. She left her drunken father in Bowler. She came back for brief visits only.

She moved to Oak Park, Illinois. She shortened her name to Jean. She got a room at the West Suburban dorm. She bunked with a girl named Mary Evans. They shared a room for six months. They moved to adjoining rooms and shared a bathroom for two years. They became close friends. Mary had a doctor lover. Jean liked Mary's wild side. Mary liked Jean's wild side. Jean dated boys and stayed out after curfew. It was like she blew off small-town life and went a little crazy. Mary and Jean worked a curfew dodge. They messed with the lock on their fire escape ladder. They could ditch the dorm and sneak back unseen. Mary could see her doctor. Jean could meet men and cut loose. Jean was quiet and reserved most of the time. She liked to read. She liked to sit around and daydream. Jean had a different side. Mary watched it develop. It was Jean with her blinders off. Jean started to drink quite a bit. Jean was *always* drinking. Jean went out drinking and came back after curfew. She sat on the toilet and peed for a dog's age. She came back one night and commandeered the toilet. She lit a cigarette and dropped the match in. A wad of toilet paper ignited and singed her behind. Jean laughed and laughed.

Jean liked to brood. Jean held her own counsel. She never mentioned her parents. Her aunt Norma visited her. Her parents never did. Mary thought it was strange. Jean liked older people. She liked older men. She liked older women as friends. Jean became close friends with a nurse named Jean Atchison. Jean Atchison was ten years older than Jean. Jean Atchison did not date men. Jean Atchison was completely absorbed in Jean Hilliker. She followed her around. Everybody talked about it. Everybody thought they were lesbian lovers. Mary thought Jean Atchison was a lesbo. Jean Hilliker liked men too much to be lez.

Jean fell in love with a man named Dan Coffey. Dan was 25. Jean was 20. Dan was a diabetic and a far-gone drunk. Jean worried about him. She drank with him most nights. She saw him every night for a solid year and a half. Jean confided to Mary. Jean said she drank too much.

Jean knew how to balance things. She was a good nursing student. She learned quickly. She was dutiful and kind to her patients. She could stay out late and perform the next day. Jean was competent and capable and deliberate.

Dan Coffey left her. Jean took it bad. She brooded and chased men. She liked rough boys. Some of them looked like gangsters or hoodlum riffraff.

Jean graduated in May '37. She was now a registered nurse. She got a full-time job at West Suburban. She moved out of the dorm. Jean Atchison found an apartment in Oak Park. She asked Jean and Mary Evans to move in with her. Mary had her own bedroom. Jean shared a bedroom with Jean Atchison. They slept in the same bed.

Mary's boyfriend got Jean a watchdog gig. She had to drive two elderly drunks to New York City. The wife was dying of cancer. Her husband wanted to take her to Europe before she checked out. Jean was supposed to keep them sober and transport them to the boat.

The job was a pain in the ass. The drunks wandered off at rest stops. Jean found bottles in their luggage and emptied them. The drunks scrounged up more liquor. Jean capitulated. She encouraged them to pass out and let her drive in peace. She reached Manhattan. She dumped the drunks at the dock. The husband said he had a hotel suite booked in his name. She could rest up there before she drove back to Chicago.

Jean found the hotel and checked in. She met an artist there. He drew a charcoal sketch of Jean in the nude. They had a few wild days together. Jean called Jean Atchison and Mary Evans and told them to come to the Apple. They could stay in her suite until somebody kicked them out. Jean Atchison and Mary rounded up another nurse named Nancy Kirkland. Nancy had a car. They drove to New York and raised hell with Jean. They partied for four or five days.

The girls went back to Chicago. Mary moved out of the apartment. Her boyfriend set her up in her own place. Jean Atchison saw an ad for a glamour contest. It was sponsored by Elmo Beauty Products. They wanted to find four women. They wanted to crown them the "Most Charming" Blonde, Brunette, Grayhead and Redhead. They wanted to fête them and send them to Hollywood. Jean Atchison sent in an application and a picture of Jean Hilliker. She didn't tell Jean. She knew Jean wouldn't approve.

Jean won the contest. She was now America's Most Charming Redhead. She got mad at Jean Atchison. Her anger subsided. She flew to L.A. on 12/12/38. She met the other Most Charming ladies. They spent a week in L.A. They stayed at the Ambassador Hotel. They got $1,000 apiece. They saw the sights. Talent scouts perused them. Jean took a screen test. The Tomah paper ran a piece on the Most Charming Redhead. She was "a quiet, unassuming and very attractive young lady."

Jean returned to Chicago. The trip was fun. She made some money. She liked California. The screen test was fun and no more. She didn't want to be a movie star.

It was 1939. Jean turned 24 in April. Aunt Norma ditched her husband. She took up with another local pastor. They left Tomah forever. Norma lost track of Jean. They never saw each other again. Jean lost track of Mary Evans. They never saw each other again. Leoda Hilliker married Ed Wagner on 6/7/39. Jean attended the wedding in Madison, Wisconsin. Jean had a lover or lovers then. She got pregnant. She called Mary's boyfriend and asked him to abort her. He refused. Jean aborted herself. She killed the fetus and hemorrhaged. She called Mary's boyfriend. He treated her. He did not report the abortion.

Jean moved to Los Angeles. She might have met the Spalding man there. They were married somewhere. It wasn't Chicago. It wasn't in L.A. County, Orange County, San Diego County, Ventura County, Las Vegas or Reno. Bill Stoner checked marriage records in all those locations. Janet Klock found some old notes. They pertained to the split-rail-fence portraits. My mother wrote the notes. She said the pictures were taken near Mount Charleston, Nevada. My mother alluded to "we." She wore a wedding ring. They looked like honeymoon photos. The Hilliker-Spalding marriage could not be verified. Leoda never met the Spalding man. Jean's friends never met the Spalding man. Nobody knew his first name. Two men qualified as heirs to the Spalding sporting goods fortune. One man died in World War I. The surviving son was named

Keith Spalding. Bill Stoner could not link him to my mother. She might have married him. She might have married a Spalding with no blood ties to *the* Spaldings. The marriage was brief. Five witnesses confirmed that fact or rumor. Bill found a Geneva Spalding in the '39 L.A. directory. Her occupation was listed as "Maid." Her address was 852 Bedford in West Los Angeles. The '39 directories came out in '40. She had time to marry and divorce Mr. Spalding. She had time to find work and an apartment of her own.

Earle Hilliker died in 1940. He checked out behind pneumonia. Jean Hilliker was listed in the '41 L.A. book. She was a stenographer. She lived at 854 South Harvard. She'd moved east to the Wilshire District. She was probably working toward her nurse's certification.

And a rendezvous with my father.

My father moved to San Diego after World War I. He told me that. He was a liar. All his statements were suspect. Bill Stoner checked old San Diego directories. He found my father in the '26 book. He was listed as a deputy county auditor. He held the job through 1929. He was a salesman in '30. He managed a hotel in '31. He worked at the U.S. Grant Hotel for the next four years. He was a house detective and an assistant auditor. He changed jobs in '35. He became a salesman. He worked for A.M. Fidelity. He wasn't listed in the '36 or '37 book. He was listed in the '37 L.A. directory. His occupation was not listed. He lived at 2819 Leeward. He was listed at the same address in '38 and '39. 2819 Leeward was Central L.A. It was four miles east of Geneva Spalding's '39 address. The '40 book listed my father at 2845 West 27th. The '41 book listed him at 408 South Burlington. The address was a mile and a half from Jean Hilliker's '41 address.

My father married a woman in San Diego. The date was 12/22/34. Her name was Mildred Jean Feese. She came from Nebraska. My father "willfully deserted" her on 6/5/41. She filed for divorce on 9/11/44. She said my father treated her in a "cruel and inhuman manner, which caused this plaintiff grievous mental suffering and distress, resulting in her becoming extremely nervous, suffering physical anguish, and becoming physically ill."

My father received a court summons. He did not appear in court. A default decree was filed on 11/20/44. The divorce was finalized on 11/27/45. The marriage produced no children. The final decree did not mention alimony payments.

My father was listed in the '41 book. He deserted his wife on 6/5/41. Mildred Jean Ellroy was listed in the '42 book. She lived at 690½ South Catalina. Jean Hilliker was listed in the '42 book. She was listed as a nurse. She lived at 548¼ South New Hampshire. It was three blocks from 690½ South Catalina. My father said he lived with my mother at 8th and New Hampshire. He said they lived there when Pearl Harbor was bombed. His memory was spotty. They lived three blocks north at 5th and New Hampshire.

Bill and I reconstructed the probable events.

My father met the redhead in 1941. He met her in L.A. He deserted his wife. He moved in with Jean Hilliker. He ran from a woman. He ran to a woman. The jilted woman gave up the pad she shared with him. She moved to a pad three blocks away from her husband's love nest. The move was coincidental or spitefully planned.

Maybe she stalked my father.

Maybe she moved three blocks away to punish herself.

Maybe she moved there to see the redhead and gloat. She knew what my father was. She knew what the redhead had coming.

There were no L.A. directories issued for the rest of the war. The '46 and '47 books were missing. The Beverly Hills books were missing. We couldn't nail the move to 459 North Doheny.

They shacked up somewhere. The Spalding divorce was finalized in '39 or '40. My father's divorce was finalized in late '45. They were free to marry then.

They were married in Ventura County. The date was 8/29/47. My mother was 32. She was two and a half months pregnant. The marriage license listed a common address. It was 459 North Doheny. The license stated that this was the second marriage for both parties.

I was born in March '48. Jessie Hilliker died in '50. She had a stroke and keeled over. My parents moved to 9031 Alden Drive. The marriage went bad. My mother filed for divorce on 1/3/55.

She cited "extreme cruelty." She listed her joint property as furniture and a car. She stated her desire to be my full-time parent.

My father accepted her terms. He signed a property settlement on 2/3/55. She got the car and the furniture. She got me for my school months and part of the summer. He got two weekly visits and some summer time with me. He had to pay her lawyer's bill and $50 a month child support.

A hearing was held on 2/28/55. My father was summoned. He did not appear. My mother's lawyer filed a default motion. My father told me she was fucking her lawyer.

The default decree was granted on 3/30/55. It was interlocutory. The divorce would be finalized a year later. My mother filed a nuisance claim against my father. The claim summoned him to court on 1/11/56. The claim laid out her specific charges.

She said my father brought me home Thanksgiving night. He stood outside the front door. He eavesdropped. He broke into the apartment on 11/27/55. He went through her clothes and her bureau drawers. He cornered her at the Ralph's Market at 3rd and San Vicente. He yelled insults at her as she shopped. The incident occurred in late November '55.

My father got a lawyer. He wrote up a brief and countered my mother's claim. He said my mother's mode of life was inimical to my moral and social development. My father feared for my health and safety.

My parents saw a judge. He appointed a court assistant. He told her to investigate the charges.

She interviewed my father. He said Jean was a good mother five days a week. She drank two-thirds of a bottle of wine every night and "went berserk" on the weekends. He said she was a sex maniac. Her drinking went along with her sex mania. He said he didn't eavesdrop that night. He brought his son back at 5:15. Jean answered the door. Her hair was mussed up. She had liquor on her breath. This Hank Hart guy was sitting at the kitchen table. He was in his undershirt. A bottle of champagne, three cans of beer, a bottle of wine and a fifth of whisky were out in plain sight.

He left the apartment. He decided to visit some friends in the neighborhood. He walked past the apartment again. He heard his son yelling. He heard some "other confusion." He walked to the kitchen window and peered in. He saw his son walk into the bathroom and take a bath. He saw Jean and Hank Hart lie down on the living room sofa. They started necking. Hart stuck his hand under Jean's dress. His son walked into the living room. He was wearing pajamas. He watched TV. Hank Hart teased him. The boy went to bed. Hank Hart took off his trousers. Jean lifted her skirt. They had intercourse on the sofa.

My father said he went home. He called my mother. He asked her if she had no shame. Jean said she would do as she pleased. He didn't browbeat Jean at Ralph's Market. He brought his son home a few days after Thanksgiving. Jean wasn't there. His son showed him how to enter the apartment. He opened some French windows. He entered the apartment. He did not look through Jean's clothes or open her bureau drawers. He never called Jean filthy names. She phoned him and called him filthy names.

The investigator talked to Ethel Ings. She said Jean was an excellent mother. Jean paid her 75 cents an hour. She looked after Jean's son. Jean never left her son home alone. He went to a Lutheran church every Sunday. Jean never raised her voice to him. She never used foul language.

The investigator talked to the principal of Children's Paradise School. She said Jean was an excellent mother. The father pampered the boy and did not make him study. The father used the boy. He used him to get back at his mother. He called him every night and asked him questions about his mother. He told him to answer "yes" or "no" when his mother was nearby.

The investigator talked to Eula Lee Lloyd. She said Jean was an excellent mother. Mr. Ellroy was not a good father. She saw Mr. Ellroy several times recently. He was crouched outside Jean's apartment. He was looking in the windows.

The investigator talked to my mother. She contradicted my

father's account of her actions. She denied his charges of sex mania and dipsomaniacal behavior. She said her ex-husband lied to her son repeatedly. He told him he owned a retail store in Norwalk. He told him he was buying a house with a swimming pool. He wanted to possess the boy entirely. Her ex-husband called her vile names. He did it in front of her son. Her ex-husband was a latent homosexual. She had medical proof.

The investigator sided with my mother. She cited my mother's salutary work record. She said my mother seemed to possess a sound character. She did not act like a drunk or a slattern. The judge sided with my mother. He issued a formal decree. He told the plaintiff and the defendant not to annoy or harass each other. He told my father not to break into my mother's apartment. He told him not to lurk and loiter outside it. He told him to pick me up and drop me off and stay the fuck away.

The decree was dated 2/29/56. My mother was two years and four months away from Saturday Night. The notes and records catalogued her life in misalliance. I could label the investigation successful. I knew one thing past all doubt. I did not know who killed my mother. I knew how she came to King's Row.

**31**

I t wasn't enough. It was a momentary pause and a spark point. I had to know more. I had to honor my debt and pursue my claim. My will to look and learn was still strong and still perversely attuned. I was my father crouched outside my mother's bedroom window.

I didn't want it to end. I wouldn't let it end. I didn't want to lose her again.

King's Row was just a window facing backward. The Swarthy Man was just a witness with a few memories. I was a detective with no official sanction and no evidential rules to restrict me. I could take implication and rumor and hold them as fact. I could travel her life at my own mental speed. I could linger at Tunnel City and El Monte and all points in between. I could grow old in my search. I could fear my own death. I could relive her Sundays at that church by the railroad tracks. They preached heavenly reunions there. I could learn to believe. I could write off my search with a godly dispensation and await the time we lock eyes on a cloud.

It won't happen. She walked away from that church. She went to that church at gunpoint. She sat in her pew and dreamed. I know her well enough to state that as fact. I know myself well enough to state that I will never stop looking.

I will not let this end. I will not betray her or abandon her again.

*I'm with you now. You ran and hid and I found you. Your secrets were not safe with me. You earned my devotion. You paid for it in public disclosure.*

*I robbed your grave. I revealed you. I showed you in shameful moments. I learned things about you. Everything I learned made me love you more dearly.*

*I'll learn more. I'll follow your tracks and invade your hidden time. I'll uncover your lies. I'll rewrite your history and revise my judgment as your old secrets explode. I will justify it all in the name of the obsessive life you gave me.*

*I can't hear your voice. I can smell you and taste your breath. I can feel you. You're brushing against me. You're gone and I want more of you.*

James Ellroy's devastating new memoir

# The
# Hilliker Curse

My Pursuit of Women

**Read on for an exclusive extract . . .**

The lectern was raised, the room was packed, I had a slay-the-audience view. She sat at the left rear. I caught her gray-streaked hair first. She expanded and filled my frame. Two hundred people receded.

I read from *My Dark Places*. I brain-spoke to the woman at pause points. I described the wish-named Joan and stated the resemblance. The woman was skeptical—college prof up for a fight.

May 28, '04. Sacramento in a spring heat wave. The six thousandth public performance of my dead-mother act.

I was boffo. I read from pitch-perfect memory and laid down even eye contact. I had a pulpit and an eons-deep Protestant bloodline. I was the predatory preacher prowling for prey. The woman was my pivot point. I eyeball-tracked the audience and clicked back to her. She had deep brown eyes. Her features were the wish-named Joan's, aged and age-askewed. I pondered a family resemblance. The woman laughed. It made me toss the thought.

A Q&A session followed. Two hundred sociologists—a dead-mom-tour first. A man asked me how I stage-managed grief.

I cited repetition. I cited faith and a buoyant will that sometimes swerved to obsessiveness. The man called me glib. I brusquely rebuked him. I said she was my mother—not his. I said I'd paid the price—and he hadn't.

The exchange sparked a rumble. I eyeball-drilled the man. He shrugged and shut up. I looked directly at the woman. She looked directly back. She asked me what different forms my mother assumed.

I swooned a little. In that moment, I *knew*.

I pointed to heaven and back down to earth. I said, She's there and I'm here. I said other women had been known to intercede and fuck with my head.

The woman laughed. A few chuckles drifted out. I ended the gig with an elegiac quote. The folks clapped and lined up to get their books signed.

The woman stood behind them and moved toward me in small steps. She got closer and eclipsed the prophecy. Her features became hers alone. She distorted then and now and blitzed iconography. I thanked her for her question and asked her her name.

She said, Joan, and stated her surname. My legs shook. I asked her if she'd like to have a drink later. She said, Assuredly, yes.


Sacramento was the first Joan Zone. It was three hours northeast of Carmel and always swamp hot. It was full of pols and lobbyists sucking the state-government tit. There were hayseed and rock-and-roll contingents. Sacramento always vexed me. That first night was a ghoul show. I got to the lobby bar early. People booze-effused and walked through with cocktails. They were dog-den crashers. I was tensed up to fight or run. First-date portent: I must contain Joan within a public place.

·   ·   ·

She showed on time. She'd changed clothes: summer dress to skirt/boots ensemble. Her arms were bare. She had a tattoo on her right bicep. First-date apostasy: I fucking *dug* it.

We arranged chairs beside a table. It was semi-private. I guzzled coffee as Joan sipped scotch. She left lipstick prints on her tumbler. It should have instilled a preacher's kid fury. It didn't. First-date apostasy #2.

She'd read my books and knew some of my story. I supplanted it and laid in a first-date rationale. My wife and I were headed for Splitsville. Divorce was a fait accompli. It was set for an indeterminate date. Helen and I had our deal in the meantime.

I was disingenuous, verging on mendacious. My relationship with Helen was tortuous and open-ended. My life was a daily process of atonement. I could not conceive of a life without Helen Knode. I started double-dealing Joan at the outset. I wanted Helen for companionship and the long shot of sex resurrected. I wanted Joan for her flaming expression of selfhood.

We talked. I got Joan a second scotch. She barely touched it. Not a juicehead—good.

Monologues followed. Joan went first. She was from New York City. Her bloodline was left-wing/Jewish. Mom and dad were divorced. Dad was a college professor and mom was a shrink. She'd been partially raised in a commune. She had a brother in San Francisco. She'd matriculated at Cornell—Helen's alma mater. She had two master's degrees. She was teaching at Cal Davis and was earning her doctorate.

She'd knocked around a lot. She'd pitched some left-wing woo-woo. She'd spent time in the radical women's movement and the punk-rock scene.

I asked her what *punk rock* meant—that shit had slid by

me. Joan called it a rebuttal to Ronald Reagan. I said that I disliked rock and roll and greatly admired Reagan.

It was a test. Joan more than passed it. She smiled and said, That's okay. She picked up my left hand and dropped it in her lap. She laced up our fingers and contained *me*.

I wondered how we looked together. The age/style gap scorched me. I was bald and a foot taller. I felt awkward. I wore a pink polo shirt and wheat jeans.

My monologue followed. I mentioned the crack-up and fresh sobriety. Joan bluntly stated that open-union deals don't work—she'd been through it.

*Her jaw was wide. Her mouth connoted harshness and determination. Her smile undermined a seething grievance. A raucous-kid aspect simmered. She knew when to deploy it. She inhabited moments intensely and performed and observed them in concurrence. She was the most stunning woman I had ever seen.*

I moved my hand to her knee. I floated someplace. We exchanged phone numbers and addresses. We had some silent spells.

I thanked God for bringing Joan to me. I counted the runs in her black stockings.


The ride home was swervy. I drove too fast and played Beethoven in murmurs and crescendos. I sent Joan flowers and a note en route.

Boomerang car: I zoomed south and whooshed north with equal force.

Helen was out. Margaret growled and retreated to Helen's bedroom. I checked my office phone machine. Joan's name was on the display.

Her message began, "Hey, it's Joan." She continued and thanked me for the flowers. Her voice was softer than it had been the night before. I caught some Brooklyn in her vowels. A few upward tones implied gratitude. She invited me to call her.

I played the message 30-odd times. I memorized every word and every inflection. I don't know how long I cried. It was bright daylight when I started and full night when I stopped.

The Joan Zone, the Knode Abode, three hours between sites. The civil contract that made it okay.

It began with phone calls and letters. The house was large and permitted privacy. I snagged the mail every day. My office was sealed off. Helen rarely walked through. Margaret *stormed* through and barked her outrage. I conducted the courtship sans disruption and overt lies.

It felt exhilarating and wrong. It was a second-to-second Joan-to-Helen parlay. I wanted to regain Helen's respect. I wanted to know who Joan was and what she portended. Joan was new and I was a seasoned opportunist. Opportunists ruthlessly cling to emergent imagery and people. Joan was urgently vivid. My loyalty tipped *toward* her. It made me queasy, despite the deal. I fawned around the dream house in redress. Helen acknowledged my efforts with an offhandedness shaped by her justified grudge. *I wasn't who I said I was.* I sensed that I could never regain my stature.

*Opportunists move on.* My task was to create credibility with Joan. Written words and phone calls were my métier once more. Joan became the ultimate female spirit in possession of my time alone in the dark.

Her letters were brief. They expressed her attraction to me and ridiculed the Knode-Ellroy contract. My letters described the forthcoming dissolution of the marriage. It was preposterous. I had spent a total of two hours in Joan's presence. I was having it both ways. I was mending fences I intended to jump. Two women got the Ellroy troika: seduce, apologize and explain.

My letters were romantic and oozed sweet intent. I FedExed them to goose the process. I was hard-selling a potential lover. I came on too strong. Joan scolded me and prompted epistolary retreat. I plumbed Joan's character and besieged her with perceptions. I never mentioned her wish-named antecedent. Joan praised my ardor and conceded my acuity. She kept postponing rendezvous in Sacramento and Frisco. I was a dipshit bubblegummer scaling The Mountain of *Looooove*.

It was a tough climb. Joan was a tough woman. I struggled for handholds as she pried at my grip. It was exhilarating. Joan made me work. Written praise sent me summit-bound. Written rebuke kicked me back to earth. I *lived* for her voice in the dark.

Helen and Margaret retired early. My nerves were still shot. Sleep came late, if at all. Panic attacks *still* zapped me daily. Joan and I talked most nights. Her implied rule was, I'll call when I call. I was breathless with the forfeit of male control and mindful of it as a means of seduction. I doused the lights at 9:00 p.m. I played the Chopin nocturnes and killed the sound at 9:45. Darkness held me. I heard crickets and the waves on Carmel beach. The phone rang when it rang—and almost always at 10:30.

She always said, "Hey, it's Joan." Her voice carried a husk and registered as mid-range contralto. I'd ask her if her hair was up or down and whether or not she was wearing her glasses. She'd say "Up" or "Down" and "Yes" or "No" with a swoopy inflection. It always pulled tears out of me. I never told her this. I was grateful for every small kindness she showed me. My gratitude was there at the start. My gratitude remains in Joan's long-standing absence.

Our talks were affectionate and often contentious. Joan's university status bewildered me. I didn't quite get what she did. She provided brisk word portraits of her many friends and colleagues. My interest waned then. I wanted to milk our sex vibe and set up a face-to-face meet. Academic code deterred me. I believed that anecdotes should ping-pong between people. Joan questioned my interlocutory style. I was supposed to respond along set lines and not talk about myself so much. Academians deployed this method and balked when interlocutors ignored it. This constrained me. I wanted to wow Joan with my story. She wanted to establish parity with a storytelling pro. I came up short most times. I was bucking a woman from a different world and another generation. Our talks always got around to *us* at the phone-call finale. The road ran circuitous. Joan challenged me. I found a way to stay in the fight. I knew that I had to change. My old woman ways had decimated my marriage. Joan astounded me. I had to think and act from her perspective. It felt like film noir. The amnesiac assumes that the black-clad woman has the answers. The price was a certain submission. It rankled me. I respected Joan for her fight. I wanted to get her to an enclosed space. I wanted to tussle with her and get past words. I believed that mutual surrender would lead us someplace very *soft*.

She was left-wing, I was right-wing. She was Jewish, I was Gentile. She was an atheist, I was a believer. Her cultural influences bored me. Her punk-rock shit was jejune. Our conversations fractured and rebuilt around desire. We flabbergasted each other. She possessed a surpassing personal power. I told her this. Joan told me that my power leveled her. She hinted at a roundelay of role reversals. We always got there as we said good night. I always put the phone down, trembling.

.   .   .

I won a book prize in Italy. It entailed an a.m. flight from Frisco. I decided to spend the preceding night there. Joan agreed to meet me.

I got a suite at the Ritz-Carlton. Joan rang the bell right on time. I held her in the doorway. She found the suite constraining and suggested a stroll. Her local travelogue delighted me. The Coit Tower kiss kept me attentive. I let her walk ahead of me. She saw it as packed-street etiquette and my means to study her. She let me take charge then. I took her hand and spieled a run of kid-crime tales. She laughed and let me lead her to a restaurant. I didn't want to eat and blitz my adrenaline rush. She understood. She studied me and reported her findings.

She nailed my beady eyes. They were ruthless. My body language was jerky *and* deferential. That showed my desire and my instinct not to crowd her. I riffed on her performing sense and her tripartite inhabiting of all moments. She said I was the first man who ever got that.

We walked uphill to the Ritz. Our legs fluttered. We kissed until 3:00 a.m. and kept our clothes on. I pre-imagined one thing correctly. The clash was strenuous. Our bodies ached from the meld.

Milan was a portable Joan Zone. Our transatlantic calls featured a softened rapport and frequent sex sighs. Carmel was Joan and Helen coiled contrapuntal. My moral sanction impeded, rather than liberated, me. I felt loyal to both women. I had to regain Helen's trust and gain Joan's trust. The deal was "Don't ask/Don't tell." Helen did not say "Don't pray" and "Don't brood." The Hilliker Curse required me to protect *all* the women I loved. There were two of them now. Prayer pushed me toward either/or dictums. I was, and am, decisive by nature. That native trait failed me here. Extra brood sessions compensated. I assessed Helen and Joan sans a decision-making process. I came to this: they were the only two women who had ever astonished me.

They emboldened me and made me fear my heedless maleness. They encompassed differing strains of strongly held belief and made me ponder meaning. Helen's swami shtick imbued my Christian view with a lighter secular touch. Joan's strident leftism gave me the passion of the red flag aswirl and contextualized her personal grievance as historical and therefore empirically valid. They were big women suffused with big ideas. Helen and I had 13 years together. She still had the power to move me, jazz me, fuel me. I had squandered sex with her. It felt irretrievable. Joan was the prospect of sex as endless ride. Joan represented dialogue to spark enormous change. Her sporadic softness engendered my full-time softness. All my praying and brooding buttressed my love for both women. My addiction to woman imagery and the force of The Curse pushed me toward Joan.

Summer courtship, '04. The prelude extends.

Joan invited me to Sacto for Independence Day. It's a long weekend. Get a room at the Sheraton—it's near my place.

A film-director colleague lived close by. That provided my alibi. I drove up in an ever-present heat wave. The Delta Valley was always hot. This was the blast oven–Everglades combo. I checked in at the hotel and walked to Joan's pad with flowers.

She wore a white blouse and jeans. Her hair was down and she wore her glasses. I smiled at that. Joan said "Down" and "Yes" and kissed my cheek. She put the flowers in a vase. I checked out her bookshelves. The only shit I recognized were three of my own novels. The other tomes: labor history, Commie tracts, gender polemics.

Window units barely kept the heat out. Sweat seeped through my shirt. My pulse raced and produced more wetness. Joan served a roast chicken and salad dinner. It was simple and tasty. I hardly touched it. Talk was difficult. I wanted to tell her everything I'd never revealed to a woman. Helen trumped Joan here. She already knew *all* my stories. Joan chatted up her teaching load and a bar-b-q the next day. Some friends were throwing a bash. I was invited.

All I had were expressions of love and alone-in-the-dark perceptions. They seemed precipitous and untimely. Declarations of chivalry bubbled up and almost choked out. Joan mentioned her atheism. My chivalry pitch cited God as a primary resource. I kept my mouth shut. I got tensed up to fight or run.

We washed the dishes and sat down on the couch. Joan smiled. Some lipstick was stuck to her teeth. I wiped it off with my shirttail. Joan asked me what I was afraid of. I said, "You." I asked her what she was afraid of. She pointed to me.

We kissed. We fell into the meld and stayed there. Joan held my face. I kissed her gray streaks. Joan pushed the coffee table back to make room for my legs.

I started to lay out my declarations. Joan touched my lips and shushed me. My heart rate went haywire. Joan sensed something wrong and held me. My shirt was halfway off. Joan removed it. I unbuttoned her blouse. I saw her breasts and started sobbing.

She let it be for a while. She said things like "Hey, now." She saw that it wasn't about to stop. She eased me up and got me to the door and told me she'd see me tomorrow.

· · · ·

Sleep was impossible. The air conditioner rattled and tossed ice chips. Drunks careened down the outside hallway all night.

I kept the lights off. I saw Joan's face and fought half-nude imagery. I conjured Helen and told her we could work things out. I never completed my spiels. Joan appeared, Joan smiled, I dabbed traces of red off her teeth.

The bar-b-q was above Sacramento, near the UC campus. Joan had a VW stamped with pro-labor stickers. We crossed a drawbridge and hit a greenbelt. Joan said, Last night was all right, you know. I touched her hand on the steering wheel. She curled a finger around my wrist.

*We drove in silence. It marked fifty rides we took in a similar quiet. I never knew what Joan was thinking. I would have given anything to know then. I would give anything to know now.*

The shindig was outdoors. The crowd was thirtyish academics. Joan introduced me around. She kept a hand on my arm to indicate that we were a couple. It was stunningly decorous. She said "James" and left off the Ellroy. I felt weightless without my hot-shit surname. Joan caught it and touched me that much more.

Sunstroke heat, burgers and guacamole. Weightlessness and sleeplessness. The vertigo that Joan always inspired.

A young couple recognized me. That gave me a task beyond yearn and obsess. I regaled them with outtakes from my perved-out past. I eyeball-trolled for Joan about once per minute. I caught her looking my way at the same rate. She winked on one occasion.

· · · ·

My hotel was near the statehouse. We watched a fireworks display from my room.

Joan sat on the window ledge. I sat on the bed. We imbibed room-service libations. The show produced a sputtery sound track. Joan's silence was a roar. I started to tell a trademark story. Joan said, "I've read your books, you know."

The fireworks crescendoed and died. I smelled gunpowder through the AC vents. Joan walked to the door. I got up and followed her. She touched my cheek and told me not to worry.

Sleep was impossible. I was terrified. She walked out the door and took my body with her. I checked my mouth for malignant bumps and my arms for seeping melanomas. I went from the bed to the bathroom mirror, all night. I conjured Joan's face. The process tore at my fear. Every Joan image invoked Helen. Every Helen image returned me to Joan.

Dawn came up. I forced myself to shave and shower. I bolted half a bagel and coffee. I was tensed up to fight or run. There was no one to fight. I had no body to fight with—so I ran.

I drove to Joan's place and rang the bell. Joan opened up and saw me. She sat me down and let me find some breath. I got light-headed words out. "I love you," "I'm scared," and "I've got to go home" are all I remember.

The dream house was empty. Margaret was kenneled up. Helen was back in K.C. with her mother. I gobbled food out of the refrigerator and fell down on the couch. I woke up at midnight. I ran to my phone machine. The number 0 glowed.

Four days went by. I called Helen in K.C. and reveled in her family minutiae. I worked on a TV pilot and played raging Beethoven and soft Rachmaninoff. I wondered when I'd get my body back. I saw her face every few seconds. It wasn't a conjuring. She was omniscient.

The doorbell rang. Friday, midafternoon, FedEx for sure.

*Take note of what you are seeking, for it is—*

She looked grave and sweet, all bollixed some new way. She said, "Hi," with her swoopy inflection.

I folded her up and kissed her gray streaks. I said, "I'll never run away again."

# JAMES ELLROY

# The Hilliker Curse

## My Pursuit of Women

America's greatest living crime writer gives us a raw, brutally candid memoir – as high intensity and as riveting as any of his novels – about his obsessive search for 'atonement in women'.

The year was 1958. Jean Hilliker had divorced her fast-buck hustler husband and resurrected her maiden name. Her son, James, was ten years old. He hated and lusted for his mother and 'summoned her dead'. She was murdered three months later.

The Hilliker Curse is a predator's confession, a treatise on guilt and the power of malediction, and above all a *cri de cœur*. Ellroy unsparingly describes his shattered childhood, his delinquent teens, his writing life, his love affairs and marriages, his nervous breakdown and the beginning of a relationship with an extraordinary woman who may just be the long-sought *Her*.

A layered narrative of time and place, emotion and insight, sexuality and spiritual quest, The Hilliker Curse is a brilliant, soul-baring revelation of self. It is unlike any memoir you have ever read.

WILLIAM HEINEMANN: LONDON